A

HISTORICAL VINDICATION

OF THE

ABROGATION OF THE PLAN OF UNION

BY THE

Presbyterian Church

IN THE UNITED STATES OF AMERICA.

BY THE

Rev. ISAAC V. BROWN, A. M.

Am I therefore become your enemy, because I tell you the truth?—Gal. iv. 16.

PHILADELPHIA:
WM. S. & ALFRED MARTIEN,
144 Chestnut Street,
1855.

PREFACE.

This volume aims to vindicate the reform system adopted in the Presbyterian church, May, 1837, from the disingenuous statements and inferences by which its opposers have endeavored, and still strive, to screen themselves from just censure, and to injure the good name of those who stood foremost in the decisive hour, to save the church by dispossessing her adversaries.

No true church can exist which has not the uncorrupted word of God for her basis, and the cardinal doctrines of grace for her chief corner stones, her pedestals, her porches, her columns, and her imperishable wall of defence.

It cannot be denied, that the palpable perversions of religious truth and moral obligation, the distorted views of man's native powers and responsibilities, which pervade the whole mass of New School speculation and romance, if not speedily checked and effectually remedied must prove the programme to an age of infidelity, and introduce upon the American stage the shocking theological panorama of universal derangement and confusion in the elements of the moral world; as a parallel to which we may point only to the reign of terror and triumph of ungodliness in the *French Revolution*, at the close of the last century. Considering the excitability and elasticity of the American mind, its love of novelty and the readiness with which it catches at theories most untried and extravagant, this is a fearful idea. Cases of wild fanaticism, sufficient to warrant these unwelcome anticipations, may be gleaned, not only from the history of New School innovations within the last thirty years, but from the recollections and records of kindred associations of visionary and dangerous errorists.

If the infatuated men who led the New School defection, in their attempt to subjugate the vast and growing numbers of the Presbyterian community to their power and influence, had succeeded in their efforts, none can tell what would have been the direful result. It is justly said, that "truth is powerful and will prevail." But it is equally true, that error is powerful, and if furnished with loose rein among the masses, like a wild war-horse, will exhibit tremendous power and havoc. The contest with this unbroken and gigantic foe is difficult and eventful. Let us candidly record the steps by which he achieved his somewhat successful campaign, and trace the movements observed by the friends of truth in checking his disastrous march.

Considering cotemporary documents published by individuals, by ecclesiastical bodies, religious conventions, associations, and periodicals, better adapted than any thing that could be written, *de novo*, to furnish reliable data, to explain and confirm every thing which it is important to know and to preserve upon this agitating subject, the writer does not purpose to introduce more new matter than appears requisite to keep up the chain of evidence and illustration, and to sustain a due degree of connexion and unity throughout the work. From the great mass of documentary publications which the friends of truth and order, at that period, had time and zeal enough to oppose to the rushing tide of error and distraction which was flooding the church, we shall select a few specimens of such as appeared best calculated to save her from the triumphant usurpation of her invaders, by exposing the iniquity of their strides and the desolation of their successes. These documents, it may be fairly presumed, will, if any thing can, exhibit the tempers, motives, and aims of the actors in this great ecclesiastical drama, much better than the capricious assumptions, special pleadings, or unwarrantable surmises of any writers of the present day. It is a consideration of importance, too, in this connexion, that although most of these documents were widely dispersed at the time of their first publication, probably at least four-fifths of those now living and who are to judge of these papers, never had an opportunity to give them a deliberate reading, if they ever saw or heard of them at all.

The grand motive which governed the Presbyterian body, in the *abrogation act*, was their love of the church. This love may be resolved into their love for her doctrines and a love for her order. Much as Presbyterian Christians love gospel truth and cherish its inspiring hopes, it is probable that their decisive action in the final hour was in no small degree prompted by their heart-felt devotion to the order and discipline of God's house. Here their early prepossessions, their fixed habits, their pious sympathies, enlivened and invigorated by constant exercise, seemed to cluster around these forms of devotion, always visible and precious, now become venerable by time, by usage, by associations, and by imminent perils from rude assailants, seemed to combine their influence, to invest the order of the church with a magnitude of interest and a sacredness of attraction subordinate only to that which encircled the charter of their immortal hopes

But when this two-fold force of attachment to Presbyterianism, as it is, became concentrated in one confluent, sweeping stream of devotion to our beloved Zion, the mind of the great congregation was harmonized, spirits flowed together like kindred drops, and moved with irresistible efficiency in redeeming the jeopardised Ark of the Lord.

Since a considerable portion of every community cherish the impression that it is wrong to expose the errors and censure the characters of clergymen, as it tends to diminish their influence by lowering their standing in society, a question has been raised by some whether it is right to execute such a sketch or volume as necessarily involves these results. Is not the cause of religion, they ask, injured by such criticisms and exposures? It must be admitted that it has a chilling influence upon the faith and manners of the people at large, and upon the church herself, to see those very men who are set as patterns and defenders of truth, purity, and fidelity to trust; foremost in daring and prominence to propagate errors, violate pledges, rend peaceful communities, and shamelessly deny or pervert those great truths of the Christian religion, which they are bound by most solemn sanctions to cherish and protect. Truths and obligations which their leaders sport with, the people will lightly esteem. This dissatisfaction with strict scrutiny into the principles and conduct of clergymen, is founded, in part, upon indifference to pure, consistent religion; and still more, upon the false assumption that it is no matter what a man, or even a minister believes, provided he is tolerably correct in his opinions and actions. But sound theologians and moralists believe that *truth* is in order to *godliness*, and that the life cannot be right where the head, if not the heart is wrong.

It is true, that great tenderness is to be manifested for the reputation of aggressors of this class against public truth and order, and we should exercise due caution against taking up an evil impression or belief against them on insufficient grounds; but where the offence is public, notorious, repeated, and long continued, nay, publicly confirmed and sealed by their signature and irrevocable attestation, the offences, complained of, become not only undoubted as to their reality, but aggravatedly criminal and pernicious. In such cases we cannot but think that it is rather an honour, than an injury, to religion, that some can be found diligent and laborious enough to detect, bold enough to reprove, and faithful enough to withstand, if possible, the error and iniquity with which the church is flooded and the world threatened. What other resort against error and evil has the church, the cause of truth, the testimony of God, in this evil world? Is it a course more salutary in itself and conformed to the actions of prudent men, in other matters of importance, to permit the insidious errors complained of to lie in concealment, gradually but incessantly, like the deadly cancer, striking its roots deeper and deeper, shooting its fatal ramifications more diffusively and mortally in every direction, and working out the work of death in a stealthful and malignant progress, which timely attention and appropriate remedies might have arrested? On the whole, if offences, in certain ministers of the gospel, are detected and exposed, to the *scandal* of religion, it is the crime which creates the *scandal;* its exposure is only the remedy.

ISAAC V. BROWN.

TRENTON, June, 1854.

INTRODUCTION.

CHAPTER I.

New School charge of intolerance refuted—Rev. F. Mackemie, the founder of Presbyterian Church, about 1680, Calvinistic—Immigrants numerous—Creeds and subscriptions tc them—Reasons for it—Adopting act, 1729—Object to exclude heresy—Its character explained—Confession of Faith and Westminster Catechisms adopted as standards—New England orthodox early—The first Presbytery formed 1704, in Philadelphia—The Synod of Philadelphia 1716—Both sound in the faith—Whole Presbyterian body orthodox—Never intolerant—English, Dutch, Scotch, Irish and French settlers multiplied—The schism which existed in the old Synod healed, 1758—General Assembly formed, 1789—The work of missions immediately commenced.

The work of bringing together into one condensed view, the scattered fragments which must form and exhibit the true origin and character of the great Presbyterian family of Christians in the United States of America, was long since pronounced by the General Assembly, on many accounts, very difficult, while very desirable. From the youthfulness of the country; the wide and thin dispersion of the people over an extensive area; the imperfect organization and frequent changes occurring in our infant ecclesiastical communities; the negligence and inaccuracy which marked most of the early records to be found; the confusion and destruction of documents occasioned by the Revolutionary war: the whole subject was invested with the character of peculiar complexness and difficulty, so as to present to any writer an uninviting field of labor. About the commencement of the present century, the General Assembly being overtured to take measures to supply this *desideratum,* expressed an importunate request that a suitable writer to perform this task would undertake it. The request proved unsuccessful, and the work, after a short interim, was respectfully committed to E. Hazard, Esq., of Philadelphia, and all available documents and facilities were placed at his disposal. Mr. Hazard spent much time and labor in collecting from Presbyterial records, from congregations and their pastors, in the form of extracts and letters, materials for the work to a considerable amount. But failing to accomplish the task, and complaining of its burdensome nature, it was transferred to Dr. Ashbel Green, who had been some time his voluntary associate in this labor, and was for a long period his bosom friend. Dr. Green, after some trial, not finding it practicable to prosecute the task with as much success as he desired, in consequence of the multiplicity of his pastoral duties and the feebleness of his health, the trust was, by his request, tendered to Dr. Samuel Miller, Professor of the Theological Seminary, at Princeton, in the hope that he might find time to fulfill what his predecessors in this charge had failed to accomplish, especially as it fell within the sphere of his official labors as historian of that institution; which relation brought him into close alliance with the Presbyterian Church. But providential circumstances finally placed the materials, so far as collected for this work, in hands adapted to secure its prompt and faithful performance.*

While attempting, in this preliminary sketch, to bring to light, to some extent, the primary features of early and progressive Presbyterianism, in her forming period, it is not our object or intention to attempt a general history of the church; but rather to repel the slanderous imputations cast by New School men and books upon the founders of our church, and false constructions applied to their theological principles and ecclesiastical measures.

The charges and perversions here referred to have had a wide circulation, through the channels frequented by New School writers in general; but recently they have been comprised within narrower limits, and in more specific form, by a small and very feeble volume, executed by "A Committee of the Synod of New York and New Jersey, (as they call themselves,) published by M. W. Dodd, New York, 1852." Of this volume, denominated "A history of the division of the Presbyterian Church in the United States of America," G. N. Judd appears to own the copyright, and is understood to have been the writer, under the control and supervision of the Synodical Committee.

In regard to the title, "Division of the Church," it ought to be observed, that it conveys a mistaken idea of the great ecclesiastical measure of 1837. An amicable division of the church was proposed by the majority at that meeting of the General Assem-

* Dr. Charles Hodge, of the same Seminary, has from the scant materials furnished him, and others gleaned by great industry from many sources, as his references show, elaborated a valuable historical compend of the origin, progress and establishment of the Presbyterian Church, in two volumes, 8vo, entitled "Constitutional History of the Presbyterian Church in the United States of America." Published, 1839, by Wm. S. Martien, Philadelphia.

bly, but it was never accepted or ratified. After the abrogation and excision she was precisely the same as before, only diminished in numbers. Indeed, she lived unimpaired and unchanged through that afflicting crisis; came out of that fiery trial and now exists and rejoices in a condition of perfect identity with her former state, in every feature and lineament; more pure, more consolidated, more harmonious, more prosperous than ever before. The only change in the sacred edifice consisted in knocking away a rotten and baseless lean-to, which our fathers had unwisely erected to sustain the building before completed, but which was discovered to be working out its downfall every day.

With regard to the kindred term, "Constitutional Church," absurdly assumed by the New School, after the fall of their decayed cabin, it is in the highest degree inappropriate and deceptive. Their whole course of action in the Presbyterian body, while nominally connected with it, exhibited strong outlines of disorder, and most of their closing movements presented traits of outrageous disregard to all law and decency. The sequel will confirm these statements.

The New School brethren have not only assumed to themselves most undeserved names and distinctions, but they have profusely heaped upon the Old School most unwarrantable and offensive appellations, going far back; upon the church of Scotland vulgar names—"sour orthodoxy, stiff Scotch Presbyterianism, narrow prejudices, antiquated notions, foreign elements," &c. And upon the orthodox of more modern times, "relaxation from *tolerant principles*, departure from a *liberal* spirit," &c. And Dr. Judd, in the same kind temper, attempts to brand those of the present day with opprobrious epithets—"ambition, bigotry, desire of power, ultraism, unconstitutionality, high churchism, wholesale slander," and other similar distinctions, which indicate quite a genius, taste and relish for calling hard names. The charge of *intolerance*,* which is as comprehensive, significant and odious as any that could be selected, he makes quite threadbare.

Indeed the charge of *intolerance* is repeated so often, with a degree of bitterness and positiveness, that may induce some unwary readers to believe there is some truth in it. Hence we shall feel obligated to take some pains to show the utter falseness of this injurious insinuation.

When facts are examined and the character of our theological fathers is placed in its true light, according to evidence, their defamers will be disappointed in their hopes of finding a sanction for their laxness in church discipline and unsoundness in Chris-

* Division of the Church, pp. 88, 90, 91 92, &c.

tian doctrine, in the false allegation or pretence that the founders of our church were compromising men, satisfied with agreement in a few doctrinal "heads," or thoughts.

The allegation is two-fold, *viz:* That the original stock or founders of the church were latitudinarians, or indifferentists, with regard to creeds and principles; and, that the present generation of orthodox Presbyterians are bigoted and intolerant, having departed from "the liberal and accommodating principles" adopted and observed by their early ecclesiastical predecessors and fathers. The first class they set up as a model for themselves, in accommodating *laxness* of theological principle; and the latter they charge with rancorous and *intolerant* hostility to all who differ from themselves. Both charges are unfounded.

The assertion, so arrogantly employed, that the founders of the church were lax, compromising, or accommodating, in regard to theological creeds and tenets, is so serious as to demand scrutiny. A fair exhibition of the sound orthodoxy of the Presbyterian Church from the beginning, will refute both branches of this New School slander—disgusting *laxness*, sanctioning *error*, on the one side, and excessive *rigor*, constituting *intolerance*, on the other. Now, the fact is, that neither *indifferentism* nor *intolerance* was ever a prevalent feature of the Presbyterian Church.

As our principal object, at this point, is to refute the spurious charge of Dr. Judd against the founders of the Presbyterian Church, we shall go no farther back than to his place of beginning.* "It will be found upon reference to the history of bygone days, that on the 6th of April, 1691, the Presbyterian and Congregational denominations of Christians, in Great Britain, met at Stepney, and there, by the blessing of Almighty God, after talking over their differences and their agreements, consummated a union of the two denominations, by adopting what was then called 'Heads of Agreement,' embracing a *few cardinal* principles, which were to govern them in their fraternal intercourse." No book on this subject, accessible to us, defines these "heads" of agreement. Certain it is, from living records, that multitudes of Presbyterians, eminent for talents and piety, of both the puritan and independent denominations, existed previous to 1691, in various parts of England. Dr. Judd, without assigning any satisfactory authority, or furnishing any explanation, sets up that agreement of 1691 as the standard of all religious opinions every where, and endeavors to make the *impression* that the Stepney Assembly, by their influence, impressed the stamp of their theological views upon the infant settlements of Presbyterians in these United States, so as to establish their religious character, even at

* Division of the Church, p. 84.

the present time. Indeed, he claims some of the first Presbyteries formed in America as the offspring of the London Association of 1691, and then institutes the charge, that the orthodox of this country have "rashly departed from the liberal and fraternal principles" of 1691, in which they were organized. He adds afterwards, in the same connexion, (p. 84,) that the first Presbytery in America was formed in 1704, by the name of the Presbytery of Philadelphia, upon the "liberal principles which governed the London Association." On the following page he speaks of the same company as "establishing a modified Presbyterianism in America." The inference which he evidently aims to have drawn from these statements, is, that these remote transatlantic movements exerted a controlling and directing influence in the introduction of Presbyterianism into these United States.

Now, the truth is, *that* London Association had nothing to do with the founding or forming of our American Presbyterianism; it may, and not improbably had some influence, at a later day, in corrupting it. The Rev. *Francis Mackemie*, the true founder of our church, was here on the ground, engaged in this noble Christian enterprise, about eight years before the London Association met.

Dr. Judd, and all who sympathize with him on this point, unconsciously admit their own degeneracy and departure from sound standards, by setting up the more lax compromise scheme of London as the grand predominating model for our religious principles at that early period. He advocates and eulogises that plan because he thinks it was much more flexible and accommodating than Calvinistic standards; lower than our American platform in doctrinal soundness.

The evidence in favor of Mr. Mackemie as the "founder of Presbyterianism in these United States," is so decisive that honest New School men admit it. But then, to nullify the force of that admission against themselves, they attempt to impair his high character by branding him, "as a loose Presbyterian." If this suggestion were true, they could claim him as a shield for their own defaults and obliquities. But this is out of the question. First in the field among us, he was first in rank, first in zeal, first in action, unquestioned in theological soundness; by his influence he formed the first Presbytery in Philadelphia. He was the principal instrument in bringing Presbyterianism into New York, and history tells us he was imprisoned there on account of it.

The fact has recently been ascertained that "a gentleman in Maryland, beside Virginia," wrote to the Presbytery of Lagan, in Ireland, 1680, requesting them to send a minister or missionary to the district where he resided. That gentleman was Col. Stevens, whose grave and sepulchral inscription have been discovered. In consequence of that invitation, Mr. Mackemie visited

Accomac, Virginia, and was prominently engaged in settling that county, about the year 1690. And yet the London Association had never met. Still the New School writers of the present day are ignorant, or preposterous enough, to insist that this very *Mackemie* was an agent or missionary of that Union to plant the gospel in America.*

The arguments which New School men have used to prove his mission to this country by the club which met in London, 1691, have all proved to be fallacious; and the charge brought against his strict orthodoxy, or adherence to Calvinistic doctrines, equally unfounded. His views of religious experience are untinctured with any unsound admixtures or suspicious elements. His publications on the cardinal doctrines of the gospel prove his agreement with the Westminster Confession. This he openly avowed when interrogated on the subject in high places, with menace and peril. This decided and fearless Presbyterianism is such as was to be expected from a minister of the gospel, who had been born, educated and ordained amidst scrutinies and trials. The Presbytery of Lagan, in Ireland, which inducted him into the ministry, encountered suffering among their members from the government for their rigid adherence to unadulterated orthodoxy, and corresponding forms of devotion. The whole religious texture and constitution of Mr. Mackemie were such as to fortify him against prelatic persecutions and popish terrors; to make him a shining light in propagating religious principle, and pre-eminent in every field of evangelic effort; a bold and fearless vindicator of his sacred creed before hostile judges and governors; a dying witness, if not martyr, to the excellence and glory of the Old School system, in which he had been nurtured from the cradle, and in propagating which he had spent his life.

That Mr. Mackemie was instrumental in organizing the first Presbytery of Philadelphia, is too plain to be questioned; and that he brought out two† members of that body from the North of Ireland about 1705, is positively asserted on good evidence.

* For several of the facts here recited, see Presbyterian Magazine, Philadelphia, vol. III., No. 6, pp., 90—94. By C. Van Rensselaer, D. D.

From an article in the Presbyterian, May 20th ultimo, we perceive that Dr. Spotswood, in a statement made at the dedication of a new church at Newcastle, Delaware, claims the old church recently taken down as the oldest Presbyterian church erected on this continent. But it appears afterwards that the old church was built at first, 1684, by Swedes; the Dutch some time afterwards succeeded in occupying that church. Neither the time nor manner of transferring the church to the Presbyterians is at all stated. Dr. Spotswood at the same time alleges that the first church in Philadelphia was built about 1701. Its erection has been generally dated at 1704.

† Jno. Hampton and George McNish.

The famous Jedediah Andrews, pastor of the First Church in Philadelphia, was a member of the first Presbytery. Mr. Judd claims him and says, "the first Presbytery in America was formed in 1704, by the name of the Presbytery of Philadelphia, upon the *liberal principles which* governed the London Association, and was composed partly of Presbyterian and partly of Congregational ministers and churches. The Rev. Jedediah Andrews, the first pastor of the first Presbyterian church in Philadelphia, was one of the original members of this Presbytery, and decidedly favorable to Congregational church government."* This Presbytery, at its first erection, was composed of seven members, and Mr. Hazard in his MS. history says, "It is probable that all, except Mr. Andrews, were foreigners by birth, and that they were ordained to the Gospel ministry in Scotland and Ireland." Dr. Van Rensselaer and Dr. Hodge agree in stating that Mr. Andrews was from Massachusetts—a man of great labor and influence in the Presbytery—orthodox in doctrine—and in every season of difficulty he was found on the Old side. Hence, Mr. Judd's statement that the first Presbytery was, in part, constituted of Congregational materials, proves contrary to facts.

We are warranted, then, in recording it as an established truth, in this compilation of our church's early history, that its first Presbytery, and the founders of it, were Calvinistic in principle; and we now state what is equally clear, that the Synod of Philadelphia, organized about the year 1716, was undoubtedly of the same character—because, if for no other reason, she was substantially of the same materials. It contained, at first, seventeen members, among whom "Old School Presbyterianism and orthodoxy" maintained their strength and influence in full proportion.

While these transactions and many others akin to them, were occurring in the city and vicinity of Philadelphia, immigration to the New England States, and to parts of New York and New Jersey, was rapidly progressing. This newly-discovered country was considered in Europe as the asylum of the persecuted and refuge of the oppressed, both for religious and political freedom. Hence, large companies of English puritans—of Dutch settlers—of Scotch and Irish emigrants—and, after the revocation of the edict of Nantes, large companies of French Protestants, gladly flocked hither, to secure to themselves and their children that religious liberty and those rights of conscience which were denied them in their native lands.

These emigrants of every nation, were, for the greater part, a population of decidedly religious character—of much intelligence—of property and honour—of moderation and order. They

* See Presbyterian, p. 94. Judd, p. 84.

fixed their homes, many in New England, some at New Paltz and New Rochelle, some on Long Island, others on *Staten Island*,* and in eastern and central New Jersey. The descendants from these colonists are numerous and distinguishable still. These having felt the sting of persecution and yoke of oppression in their father-lands, cannot rationally be supposed, either speedily to have forgotten their wrongs and their sufferings, or to have been very ready to attempt, by violence, to impose upon the consciences of others, the fetters and the tortures they had so recently escaped. And Dr. Hodge says of those who early joined the Synod, in addition to those constituting the Presbytery of Philadelphia—"Some were among the strictest of the whole body, and not one of them was a Congregationalist, or inclined to Congregationalism." p. 97, Vol. 1.

Men of such character, faith and morals, arriving, in succession, in increasing numbers, became the component parts of the Presbyterian body, wherever they went. And they sustain this character to the present day. The faith of the Church of Scotland was thoroughly understood and highly appreciated in all Protestant lands, and not less so in these United States. Calvinism was the polar star of these colonists—the cardinal feature of the faith they insisted on.

* To the colony of that name, which settled, soon after the revocation, around where the city of Richmond now stands, on Staten Island, the writer traces his genealogical extraction—the ancestors of both his paternal great grand parents, having been fully embraced, under appropriate names, in that company of Huguenots.

An interesting account of this colony is furnished by Mr. Charles Weiss, Historian of the "French Protestant Refugees": Vol. I., pp. 314–20. While many successive groups located themselves in New Paltz, New Rochelle, and New York, "Staten Island, that enchanting spot, in the beautiful bay of New York, became a favorite asylum for the French Protestants. It should be called the Huguenot Island. As far as we can ascertain, they reached this region in considerable numbers about the year 1675, with a pastor, and erected a church near Richmond village. Few regions are blessed with more churches. Most of the official and zealous members of these churches were lineal branches of the French Protestants. *Channing More*, former Bishop of Virginia, was connected with this colony. 'Dr. Bedell, father of the gentleman of that name now in New York, was of the same origin on the maternal side.'"

The following Huguenot names occur in the records of Staten Island—Fontaine, *Rezeau*, La Tourette, Bedell, Poulon, Mercereau, La Conte, Perrin. Those who sympathize with the late Rev. A. *Rezeau* Brown, of Lawrenceville, son of the writer, who fell an early victim of pulmonary disease, a Biographical Notice of whom was written and published by Rev. James W. Alexander, A. D. 1833, in the Biblical Repertory, will detect among the Huguenots above recited, the *patronymic* of his baptismal name, which was given to him in reference to the ancestral family of *Rezeau*, which is still prominent among the descendants, in that consecrated island.

It is true, there was some difficulty in ascertaining the religious opinions of the immigrants. It was, at first, not considered of great importance whether this was attempted—when the work became necessary—by personal *examination*, by individual *subscription*, or by authentic *papers*. The mode of scrutiny probably varied some time to suit circumstances. But some definite form of ascertainment was in a few years pronounced indispensable—especially as it had become clear, that some emigrants from the North of Ireland, seeking admission into our church, had imported with them theological sentiments manifestly differing from our standards, and showing the necessity of an efficient guard against insidious error.

Several instances of written declaration or actual subscription to formularies of doctrine are on record, which shed light on this subject. The Rev. Wm. Tennent, who had been Episcopally inducted in Ireland, on arriving in this country applied for admission to the Synod of Philadelphia.* That body requested him to give a written statement of his reasons for leaving the Episcopal Church. The most prominent reason he assigned was, that the Church of Ireland connived at Arminian doctrines. It is a natural inference that he would not desire admission to a church less sound than the one he was leaving. In 1724, William McMillan subscribed this brief avowal; Archibald Cook and Hugh Stevenson in 1726: "I do own the Westminster Confession of Faith as the confession of my faith." John Tennent, September 18, 1729, subscribed the following formulary: "I do own the Westminster Confession of Faith, before God and these witnesses, together with the *Larger and Shorter Catechisms*, with the Directory thereto annexed, to be the confession of my faith and rule of faith and manners, according to the word of God." p. 103. These subsubscriptions took place in the Presbytery of Newcastle, who were among the first to disavow confidence in written testimonials, particularly those brought from the North of Ireland, which furnished a large proportion of the applicants for admission to their body. Hence, they were among the first to change the form of entrânce into the church, and to demand the adoption of the Westminster Confession of Faith. For this timely and decided act, the lax religionists of that day, and the more decidedly heretical of succeeding days, have not ceased to pursue them with "railing accusations," endeavoring to make appear as their SHAME what is really their *glory*. That act of the Newcastle Presbytery was the dawn of a brighter day; unmixed light began to shine with more splendour from other quarters, and darkness and doubt to flee away. The fact that the Newcastle Presby-

* Dr. Hodge, vol. I., p. 101.

tery and the Synod of Philadelphia, about this time, had found it necessary to reject several applicants for admission on account of their unsoundness in the faith, hastened on these decisive measures which soon followed and increased their strictness. It is evident that the process of *forming* the church had proceeded so far as to require some prominent measure to test and confirm all additions to her body; to certify and establish ministerial soundness and communion on a stable and satisfactory foundation.

The *Adopting Act*, as it is called, arose out of this crisis in our ecclesiastical affairs. Dr. Judd represents this act as if intended to get clear of the difficulty by dispensing with a strict compliance with the Calvinistic standards of the church, which he denominates "arbitrary principles," and then declares the object of the Act to have been "to re-affirm some liberal principles;" to which he refers as "establishing a modified Presbyterianism in America." Then to open a hidden yet capacious channel for the free admission of errors and errorists, Dr. Judd seems to combine his little strength with that of Dr. L. Halsey, of Pittsburgh, in his letter, published in the Cincinnati Journal, 1836, representing the Act of 1729 as an indefinitely lax and compromising measure, "requiring in the visible union of Christians what was essential, and treating accordingly what was not essential;" that is, affording to men of unsound and discordant opinions, on entering the Presbyterian Church, most complete shelter and safety. This Dr. Judd calls union—beautiful harmony!

Now the truth is, that construction is positively and directly opposed to the avowed design, the letter, and the whole spirit of the Act. Its sole and manifest object was to enforce strict union in the truth, as exhibited in the standards the Assembly professed to regard—not to make the church Calvinistic, as a new thing, but to show that such had always been her character, and to exhibit her fixed determination so to continue; thus to elevate and refine public sentiment, and to exclude all spurious forms of opinion in religious matters. To this act they were prompted by the detection of dangerous errors, such as Arminianism, Pelagianism, Arianism, and others among the emigrants, who had thronged and annoyed them considerably, from the North of Ireland.

The preceding pages have illustrated the theological character of the infant Presbyterian Church, from the beginning. The Synodical Acts which will be specially presented, will afford irresistible proof that their authors intended rigorously to protect the opinions they had hitherto maintained, by adopting most vigilant precautionary rules and guards to exclude forever every phase of false doctrine.

The memorial presented to the Synod, praying for this Act, and headed "An overture, (Dr. Hodge, 162,) humbly offered to the consideration of the Rev. Synod, wherein is *proposed an expedient for preventing the ingress and spreading of dangerous errors* among either *ourselves* or the *flocks* committed to our care," *viz:*

"Although the Synod do not claim or pretend to any authority* of *imposing our faith upon other men's consciences*, but do profess our just dissatisfaction with, and abhorrence of, such *impositions*, and do utterly disclaim all legislative power and authority in the church, being willing to receive one another as Christ has received us, to the Glory of God, and admit to fellowship in sacred ordinances all such as we have grounds to believe Christ will at last admit to the kingdom of heaven, yet we are undoubtedly obliged to take care that the faith once delivered to the saints be kept pure and uncorrupt *among us* and so *handed down to posterity;* and do therefore agree that all the ministers of this Synod, or that shall hereafter be admitted into this Synod. shall declare their agreement in, and approbation of, the Confession of Faith, with the Larger and Shorter Catechisms of the assembly of Divines at Westminster, as being in all respects the essential and necessary articles, good forms of sound words and systems of Christian doctrine; and do also adopt the said Confession and Catechism as the confession of our faith. And we do also agree, that all the Presbyteries within our bounds shall always take care not to admit any candidate of the ministry into the exercise of the sacred function, but what declares his agreement in opinion with all the essential and necessary articles of said Confession, either by subscribing the said Confession of Faith and Catechisms, or by a verbal declaration of their consent thereto, as such minister or candidate shall think best. And in case any minister of this Synod, or any candidate for the ministry, shall have scruple with regard to any article or articles of said Confession or Catechisms, he shall, *at the time of making said declaration*, declare his sentiments to the Presbytery or Synod, who shall, notwithstanding, admit him to the exercise of the ministry within our bounds, and to ministerial communion, *if* the Synod or Presbytery shall *judge* his *scruple* or *mistake* to be only about articles *not essential* and necessary in doctrine, worship or government. But if the Synod or Presbytery *shall judge* such ministers or candidates erroneous in essential and necessary articles of faith, the Synod or Presbytery shall declare them incapable of communion with them."

As great importance has been attached to this act of the Synod of Philadelphia of 1729, and some doubts were expressed at the time of its passage, and have been expressed in modern times,

* The very essence of intolerance is distinctly disavowed.

by the opposers of orthodox opinions, some vindication, as well as explanation of it, may be permitted.

1. First, we think any sensible and liberal man will infallibly perceive that its professed object was to *suppress* error and to maintain sound doctrines in the church.

The preamble to an act often declares its nature and character as fully as its bodily substance. The introduction to this memorial declares it to be "an expedient for preventing the ingress and spreading of dangerous errors among either ourselves or the flocks committed to our care."

2. The act or declaration of the Synod is as specifically adapted to the object contemplated in the caption, as could be conceived or expressed. The following terms of the memorial will sufficiently particularize the character of the act.* "Now the expedient which I would humbly propose you may take, is as follows: first, that our Synod, as an ecclesiastical judicatory of Christ, clothed with ministerial authority to act in concert in behalf of truth, and in opposition to error, would do something of this kind at such a juncture, when error seems to grow so fast that unless we be well fortified it is likely to *swallow us up*. Secondly, that in pursuance hereof, the Synod would, by an act of its own, publicly and authoritatively adopt the Westminster Confession of Faith, Catechisms, &c., for the public confession of our faith, as we are a particular organized church." In continuation, the whole object contemplated, and the form of process designated in the memorial, and the character of the measure cannot be doubted. It is not denied that there was some opposition to the measure, even in anticipation of it; but this opposition was founded much more upon the predilection of Independents, who had been trained and habituated to that form of church government, than to any doctrines or opinions embraced in the Confession of Faith, and could be much more easily removed. On account of this obstacle to perfect agreement, and an indifference. for a time prevalent in the minds of some principal men engaged in this important matter, some objections were made, even in the committee to whom the memorial was referred, and who reported the act to the Synod.†

On examining the act in detail, it cannot fail to be perceived, that in every lineament it corresponds with the object designated

* These are the words of Mr. Thompson, who wrote the memorial. Dr. Hodge, p. 166, Vol. I.

† Among these was to be found even President Dickinson, who being opposed to all creeds, did not at first concur in the measure; but all these difficulties with him and others were speedily overcome, and the act passed by a unanimous vote.

in the caption, and the specifications particularized in the body of the memorial.

A few passages in the act of 1729 will give a perfectly clear exposition of its object and meaning. The first clause disavows that the Synod had any thought of exercising arbitrary power or *intolerance* in the least degree. "Although the Synod do not claim or pretend to any authority of imposing our faith upon other men's consciences, yet are we undoubtedly obliged to take care that the faith once delivered to the saints be kept pure and uncorrupt among us." It was certainly right and necessary that the truth, the foundation of the church, should be well ascertained and secured. Then follows, prospectively, the bearing which their action should have upon following generations, "*and so handed down to posterity.*" This is continuing the same precautionary spirit for the safety of following ages, for us and ours in this day of REBUKE. Then succeeds, in most explicit terms, the manner of accomplishing these great ends. "We do therefore agree that all the ministers of this Synod, or that shall hereafter be admitted into this Synod, shall declare their agreement in and approbation of the *Confession of Faith*, with the Longer and Shorter Catechisms of the assembly of Divines at Westminster, as being, in all the essential and necessary articles, good forms of sound words and systems of Christian doctrine." All ministers, for the present or future, are first to declare their agreement in and approbation of the Westminster Confession and Catechisms; but this declaration they did not think sacred and strong enough; they are "also to adopt the said Confession and Catechisms as the confession of their faith." All Presbyteries are required to exact the same declaration of agreement and approbation from all ministers and candidates for the sacred function, "either by subscribing the said Confession of Faith and Catechisms, or by a verbal declaration of his assent thereto." Can any thing be more clear and less equivocal? More perfectly intelligible and binding? And yet all are at liberty to agree or decline.

But the Synod proceed to provide for every conceivable difficulty in the case. "In case any minister of this Synod, or candidate for the ministry, shall have any scruple with respect to any article or articles of said Confession or Catechisms, he shall, *at the time* of his making the said declaration, declare his sentiments to the Presbytery or Synod." Take notice! These cavils are to be stated openly at the time of making or signing the declaration; not uttered and proclaimed afterwards through the church; no license of this kind is allowed forever afterwards. But the scruple being stated, what then? "The Synod or Presbytery shall admit him to the exercise of the ministry within our bounds, and to ministerial communion." Under what conditions? "If the Synod or Presbytery shall judge his scruple, or *mistake*, to be only about articles not essential and necessary in doctrine, worship or government." After the scruple, or *mistake*, has been stated, the Synod or Presbytery before which it occurs, proceed immediately and settle the question of admission or rejection. "And if the Synod or Presbytery shall judge such minister or candidate erroneous in essential or necessary articles of faith, the Synod or Presbytery shall declare them incapable of communion with them." Here the process rests; it is conclusive; the import of the act is as clear as light; it is effectual for the purpose; it contains nothing arbitrary or *intolerant;* it leaves every minister and candidate to his own sovereign discretion to comply with the rule and enter the church, under the favorable decision of the judicatory, or cherish his *mistakes* and withdraw.

The Adopting Act having reference only to the *Confession of Faith* and *Catechisms*, the same year "the Synod, on motion, gave their judgment that the *Directory* for worship, discipline and government, commonly annexed to the Westminster Confession, is agreeable to the word of God and founded thereupon, and therefore unanimously recommend the same to all their members, to be by them observed, as near as circumstances will allow and Christian prudence direct."

Although this act is as perfectly clear and specific as any human composition can be made, yet there were a few individuals who disapproved of it, on the ground of alleged obscurity, principally in regard to the import of the terms, "essential and necessary articles; good forms of sound words and systems of Christian doctrine." But from a candid and just inspection of these words, we do not see how it can be rationally doubted that they refer to the matter and substance contained in the preceding terms, "the Confession of Faith, with the Longer and Shorter Catechisms of the assembly of Divines at Westminster." To remove all ambiguity and doubt, the Synod of 1730, the year following the act, make the following record, *viz:* "Whereas some persons have been dissatisfied with the manner of wording our last year's agreement about the Confession, &c., supposing some expressions not sufficiently obligatory upon *intrants;* overtured that the Synod do now declare that they understand those clauses that respect the admission of intrants in such a sense as to oblige them to receive and adopt the *Confession and Catechisms*, at their admission, in the same manner and as fully as the members of the Synod that were then present. Which overture was *unanimously* agreed to by the Synod." Their meaning is, that they allow objections to be made only to parts of the twentieth and twenty-third chapters, giving privilege and power to civil magistrates to interfere with religious matters. The Synod certainly had power, and none can question their right, to explain and confirm their own transactions. It was substantially the same body or company of individuals, and they declare what their mind was, and that it remains unchanged.

Some discontent still remaining, from want of full and prompt explanations accompanying the act, a fresh avowal of its meaning was made by the Synod in the year 1736. The records for that year show, that "an overture of the committee, upon the supplication of the people of Paxton and Derry, was brought in, and is as follows: That the Synod do declare, that inasmuch as we understand that many persons of our persuasion, both more lately and formerly, have been offended with some expressions, or distinctions, in the first or preliminary act of our Synod for adopting the Westminster Confession and Catechisms, &c.; that in order to remove said offence, and all jealousies that have arisen, or may arise, in any of our people's minds, on occasion of said distinctions and expressions, the Synod doth declare, that the Synod have adopted and still do adhere to the *Westminster Confession, Catechisms and Directory*, without the *least variation* or alteration, and without any regard to said distinctions. And we do further declare this was our meaning and true intent in our first adopting the said confession, as may particularly appear by our Adopting Act, which is as followeth: 'All the ministers of Synod which are now present, (eighteen in number,) except one who declared himself not prepared, after proposing all the scruples that any of them had to make against any articles and expressions in the Confession of Faith and Larger and Shorter Catechisms of the assembly of Divines at Westminster, have unanimously agreed in the solution of those scruples, and in declaring the said Confession and Catechisms to be the confession of their faith, except only some clauses in the twentieth and twenty-third chapters, concerning which clauses the Synod do unanimously declare, that they do not receive those articles in any such sense as to suppose the civil magistrate has a controlling power over Synod, with respect to the exercise of their ministerial authority, or power to persecute any for their religion, or in any sense contrary to the protestant succession to the throne of Great Britain. And we do hope and desire, that this our Synodical declaration and explanation, may satisfy all our people as to our firm attachment to our 'good old received doctrines' contained in the said Confession, without the *least variation* or *alteration*, and that they will lay aside their jealousies that have been entertained through occasion of the above hinted expressions and declarations, as groundless.'" This overture was approved without dissent. This great and important public measure, so solemnly introduced in the caption and memorial; so deliberately scanned and adopted by the Synod in 1729; so anxiously and honestly reviewed and re-affirmed with amplifications in 1730; so solemnly re-examined and still farther elucidated and absolutely confirmed in 1736, stands as a monument of the original faith and purity and fidelity of our early predecessors in the Presbyterian Church. Here, in the Adopting Act, is a splendid light-house, or luminary, seen from afar; it beams upon Presbyterians from another world, and irradiates their foot-way every step they take in the path of true and sound orthodox Christianity.

The orthodox and fair men of that day, and of this day, so understand the document of 1729. We are the followers of the adopters of that act—we honor their names and their deeds here recorded—we construed, apply, and commend their act, just as they did. But this feeling in the orthodox body, of favor towards "a rigid adherence to the Confession of Faith, Catechisms, and Directory," strikes the New School brethren with horror. They prouounce it,* "a rash departure from the tolerant and fraternal principles of 1691 in England, and 1729 in America." This act of 1729, they pronounce, "a return to, or re-affirmation of, the liberal principles of 1691, upon which the Presbyterian Church in America was based," and construing it thus, they claim it as the model and the screen for all their false theology, which will be exhibited in the sequel of this work. On the contrary, the Presbyterian Church required this orthodox protection and security against error, in her infant and exposed state, and the surrounding church and country strongly sympathized with this act, tallying, as it does, so strikingly with our Confession of Faith and Catechisms. Even the Puritans, and Independents or Congregationalists of New England, notwithstanding their peculiar forms of church government, were, by far the greater part, devoted to orthodox evangelic religion, and the act of 1729 gave them no uneasiness or offence. The Westminster Confession had been adopted in New England long before, and the Westminster Catechisms were taught there, as carefully as in Scotland. So that New School men would gain very little, if they could establish the untenable assumption that the Presbyterian system is based upon Congregationalism. The truth is, the New Englandism of that day differed *toto celo* from its present phases, and the errorists who now attempt to shelter themselves, and lower the character of the Presbyterian Church by casting this unjust imputation upon the Puritan and Pilgrim fathers, would have fared little better there in that day, than they do here at present. The deteriorating and deceptive terms, "heads of agreement," "for sub-

* Division, p. 88.

stance of doctrine," "essentials and non-essentials," &c., were not in use, because uncalled for at that time.*

The reader can now judge how far the system adopted in 1729, ratified and confirmed in 1730 and 1736, to purify and guard the church, then and ever afterwards, furnishes a *grant* or *concession* to New School speculators, to violate their vows, to maintain the Confession of our Church, and maintain its purity and peace, by introducing and circulating at pleasure, their novel, ever-varying, conflicting, and injurious errors, upon every cardinal doctrine of our sacred standards. This is what the New School claim as their right and their privilege; and the orthodox body are denounced as *intolerant* because they adhere to their standards and vows.

It is reasonable to suppose that the first settlers in New England, from their proximity to the Presbyterian districts and constant intercourse with them, should exert considerable influence upon the Presbyterian population, and their religious character, in its early days. This admitted, New School men, in endeavouring to give the early Presbyterians an unsound character—to awaken jealousies and suspicions against them—do great injustice, in some instances, to the early character of New England herself. From her mixed population, they infer the impurity of the Presbyterian people, with whom they associated so freely. Because some of this multitude were Puritans, some Quakers, some Congregationalists, some Independents, they would infer that all were unsound, or at best, lax in principle—indefinite, fluctuating, and unreliable—and of course, (this is their argument,) so were the so-called Presbyterian mass. This is doing great injustice to

* (Saml. Blair.) "There never was any scruple, that I heard of, made by any member of the Synod, about any part of the *Confession of Faith*, but only about some particular clauses in the twentieth and twenty-third chapters, (about the civil magistrate) and those clauses were excepted against in the Synod's act receiving the Confession of Faith, only in *such sense*, which, for my part, I believe the reverend composers never intended in them, but which might notwithstanding be readily impressed upon them." The cordial approbation of that act, and the method of subscription to it which it proposes, as generally prevalent, is here placed beyond controversy. Any person desiring still further evidence of the universal popularity and acceptance of the synodical acts and ratifications, are referred to the Presbyterian Magazine, Vol. III., No. 3, p. 141. They will find there, that the Synod of Philadelphia, the Presbytery of New Brunswick, the Synod of New York, and the two Synods united, in 1758, all agree with the act, to profess the same principles of faith, the same form of worship, government, and discipline. At the time of organizing the General Assembly in 1789, the same sentiments, the same confidence and harmony, pervaded the whole Presbyterian mass. No schism or disagreement that ever occurred in the church, impaired materially this unanimity in the church, in regard to Catechisms, forms of devotion, government and discipline, till New Schoolism, like Pandora's box, made its appearance.

New England, as well as to our own church. Without being partial to her, we must be just to all. Now the truth is, there is no lack of evidence to vindicate the first adventurers from the Plymouth rock into the rude and uncultivated hills of Massachusetts and Connecticut, from this implied aspersion. The early Presbyterians derived no contamination from their intermixture with such a noble company, or partial extraction from such a source. Most of her learned and excellent men were strenuous defenders of those very articles of scriptural faith, for which we ourselves earnestly contend. "Cotton Mather," in his Magnalia, Vol. I., p. 266, informs us that a gentleman of New England having published a book, in which he attempted to prove "that Christ bore not our sins, by God's imputation, and therefore did not bear the curse of the law for them, the General Court of Massachusetts," (the highest authority in the state,) concerned that the glorious truths of the gospel might be rescued from the confusion whereinto the essay of this gentleman had thrown them, and afraid lest the Church of God abroad should suspect that New England allowed such exorbitant aberrations, appointed Mr. Norton to draw up an answer to that erroneous treatise. This work he performed with a most elaborate and judicious pen, in a book afterwards published under the title: "A discussion of that great point in divinity, the sufferings of Christ, and the question about his active and passive obedience, and the imputation thereof." The great assertion explained and maintained, is, according to the words of the reverend author, "that the Lord Jesus Christ, as God-man and mediator according to the will of the Father, and his own voluntary consent, fully obeyed the law, doing the command in the way of works, and suffering the essential punishment of the curse, in the way of satisfaction unto divine justice, thereby exactly fulfilling the first covenant; which active and passive obedience of his, together with his original righteousness as a surety, God, of his rich grace, actually imputeth unto believers; whom, by the receipt thereof, by the grace of faith, he declareth and accepteth as perfectly righteous, and acknowledgeth them to have a right unto eternal life." At the close of this volume, to prove that it spoke the sense and meaning of the churches generally through the country, there is an attestation signed by five distinguished names, Cotton, Wilson, Mather, Symmes, and Thompson, who declare, "as they believe, they also profess, that the obedience of Christ to the whole law, which is the law of righteousness, is the matter of our justification; and the imputation of our sins to Christ, and thereupon his suffering the sense of the wrath of God upon him for our sins, and the imputation of his obedience to us, are the formal cause of our justification, which is the life of our souls, and of our religion, and therefore called the justification unto life."

Even Dr. Beecher follows up this eulogy, justly deserved, by an important attestation, in regard to a kindred doctrine. "Our Puritan fathers," says he, "adhered to the doctrine of original sin, as consisting in the imputation of Adam's sin, and in a hereditary depravity; and this continued to be the received doctrine of the churches of New England, until after the time of Edwards. He adopted the views of the Reformers on the subject of original sin, as consisting in the imputation of Adam's sin, and depraved nature, transmitted by descent.* 'Tis not to New England, in her pristine days, that we are authorized to look for theological discrepancies, but to her more modern period of novelties and changes. She has been becoming, for many years past, in morals, in politics, in divinity, biblical criticism, in almost every feature, progressively degenerate. This we record, with pain and without prejudice, from a close and constant observation of facts and tendencies, during the last forty years. The attempt, therefore, of Dr. Judd, or any other writer, inferentially to prove the laxness, the compromising and vascillating spirit and character of early Presbyterianism, from its supposed sympathy for, and association with the early settlers of New England, and thus indirectly to establish the charge of sternness and despotism, or intolerance against the Presbyterian Church of the present day, on account of her energetic and decisive efforts to purify herself from a mass of corruption and contagion, is unsupported by fact, is opposed by authentic and incontestible history.

Previous to the Adopting Act of 1729, and for many years after it, the attention of the church, of her judicatories, her ministers and her people, was engrossed chiefly with the question of orthodoxy and order in the church, the influx of religionists of various grades from abroad being so great, and of such mixed character, as to awaken their fears and inspire their constant vigilance and zeal. That portion of the excellent and venerable ministers and elders, who had manifested pre-eminent devotion and firmness, in raising and sustaining to the utmost an effectual standard against unsound and disorderly principles and forms, brought upon themselves, from brethren in the same church, not so tenacious on these points as they were, the charge of comparitive indifference and even laxness, in regard to the religious knowledge, experience, and piety of professing members—candidates for the ministry—and preachers from abroad applying for admission to the church.† This want of confidence, at first feebly

* Spirit of the Pilgrims, Vol. I., p. 158.

† They were charged with exhibiting more rigor and zeal for maintaining inviolate their Creeds and Confessions, than for preserving a rigid tone and

whispered, waxed stronger and stronger, till it broke out in a positive and violent charge, so exciting and inflammatory, as to become mainly instrumental in producing the great ecclesiastical schism of 1741.*

As our object, in this introductory chapter, is merely to refute the groundless charges of the New School against the purity of our early church, and true import of her acts, and various developments of theological opinion; believing that this object is sufficiently established, we shall here suspend the historic detail, with a few additional statements connected with the subject in prospect.

The Synods of New York and Philadelphia, which had been some time divided, were re-united in 1758, and immediately recognized their obligations to perform missionary service, and commenced the work by sending laborers to the South. In 1766, they began to create a missionary fund, by asking contributions from the Presbyteries. In 1770, they took measures to send the gospel to Georgia, to the Alleghanies; and to the Northern frontiers in New York, to the west of Albany, about 1776.

The General Assembly was organized in 1789, and entered at once upon the missionary work, as far as circumstances would admit. Their first missionaries to northern Pennsylvania and western New York, were commissioned in the years 1791–92. In 1800, the Rev. Jedediah Chapman was appointed "a stated missionary on the frontiers." The Connecticut Missionary Society was organized a little earlier, and commenced its work about 1798. In 1803, Rev. Gideon Blackbourne was appointed a missionary to the Cherokee Indians, living in the southern part of Tennessee, and northern part of Mississippi.

strict form of practical piety through the church generally, and more particularly among those appointed as leaders, or selected as candidates.

* For numerous interesting details connected with our church at this important period, from 1741 to 1789, her feuds, her revivals, her re-union of discordant branches, the erection of the Synod of New York, and the General Assembly of the Presbyterian Church, see Presbyterian, Vol. III., No. 4. Also, Dr. Hodge's History, Vol. I., in extenso.

CHAPTER II.

The state of the Church and country at 1800—Effects of the Revolutionary War—Indifference of the people to religious enterprise—Efforts to improve—To promote missions in New Jersey, and elsewhere.

THE nineteenth century found the Presbyterian Church in a condition of at least lamentable repose. To this many influences unhappily conduced. Even the powerful revivals experienced, many years preceding, in New England, in the central and more Southern colonies, lent efficient aid in producing a strong and deplorable reaction in the churches generally. The preaching of Edwards, at Northampton and in the surrounding country; and of Whitfield and Tennent every where, especially in the Northern and Eastern States, though astonishingly impressive and awakening in multitudes of instances, seemed, in the midst of their signally gracious triumphs, and immediately thereafter, to open a way and give an impulse favorable to Arminian errors, and kindred heresies of a grosser kind. The extravagant excitements and fanatical zeal and action attending these revivals speedily exhausted themselves, and were succeeded by a spirit of slumber, in the American churches, which lasted for a long period. Other causes aggravated these results, and raised up formidable obstacles in the way of reform or of progress.

The freedom of the people, and the Constitution of the United States, had been recently established, by a protracted and exhausting war. The lively sympathies of the people had been turned off from their altars of devotion to the standard of liberty and the firesides of home. The country, disorganized and confused by the tumult of war and the disaster of battles, required all the wisdom of its councils to restore order; and being not less dilapidated and impoverished by the galling burdens they had sustained, as the price of their liberty, all their remaining energies and resources were taxed to the utmost to repair the wasted strength and productiveness of their farms, their counting-houses, and their workshops.

Most of the country, west of Pittsburgh, was the red man's home and hunting ground; a vast wilderness. The territory of New York, west and north of Albany, was but little removed from a state of nature, excepting a few favoured spots on the banks and the flats which skirted the Mohawk river, where towns and churches began early to rise in quick succession. The thirteen states, the most cultivated and improved portion of the country, after enduring the heat and burden of the Revolutionary conflict, were poor and powerless. The most populous states themselves were very imperfectly supplied with institutions of learning, and still more destitute of the means of grace. Around and before them lay a wild and vast desolation, which presented itself to them as an almost boundless missionary field, little, if at all explored. A comparatively small number of gospel ministers, eminent for talents and venerable for piety and services, were scattered through the land, occupying the more conspicuous and responsible posts in the large cities and growing villages of the country. The noble and animating Christian zeal with which many of the churches in the Southern, Central and Northeastern districts of the land had been inspired some years before by the preaching of Whitfield, the Tennents, the Blairs, the Brainards, the Rogerses, the Finleys, the Davises, the Witherspoons, the Masons, McKnights, Nesbits, Sproats, Dickinsons, Smiths, Burrs, Edwards, the Woodhulls, and other apostolic men, in connexion with the influence of the extensive revivals of 1741, had not only in great measure lost their power and effect, but were succeeded by a spirit of indifference to all religion, tinctured with a proneness, imported from the mother country, in very many instances, to skepticism and downright hostility to revealed truth.

Several formidable obstacles combined their influence to obstruct the plans formed, by the wise and excellent men of that day, to restore the impaired energies of the people; to direct and concentrate their efforts in striving to increase the number of evangelical ministers; to build up literary institutions; to erect churches in destitute places, and to inspire the congregations with just views and corresponding zeal in the cause of missions. With great numbers, not only their poverty disabled and discouraged them from participating in any movement of this kind, but an anti-evangelic impression prevailed extensively, that the whole heathen world were situated beyond the reach of divine mercy, and that the Indian tribes were so deeply sunk in ignorance and hardened in barbarity and vice, as to be utterly incorrigible in their habits, and irredeemable even by gospel grace.

At this incipient stage of gospel enterprise, the Church of Scotland, the *alma mater*, as well as origin of American Presbyterianism, and the great pioneer in diffusing knowledge and spreading the gospel far and wide, had lifted her standard and uttered her watchword. The rays of light, from the society in Scotland for propagating religious knowledge, had already reached these recently emancipated States with their cheering radiance. Simultaneously, however, an eloquent and popular sermon, preached by Doctor Hardy, of Edinburgh, before that society in Scotland, presented the objection, above stated, to missions among the Indians and other savage tribes, in a manner so plausible and so forcible, especially so well adapted to their parsimony, their ignorance and unbelief, and to their cold indifference or fixed opposition to every work of benevolence, that yielding to its specious pretext, "that civilization must precede the gospel and prepare men for the reception of Christianity," no small portion of the people, wherever it circulated, beguiled by its sophistry, were paralyzed by its power and plunged into an unfortunate and criminal slumber, from which it was found no easy matter to rouse them.* Reason and scripture and fact, with rational men, might correct the grand mistake, "that you must make Indians and savages civilized and cultivated men before you can make them Christians," but reason and scripture, and even fact, proved too feeble to awaken multitudes out of a profound delusion which they seemed to court and cherish.

Notwithstanding the apathy which depressed the public mind in general, and paralyzed all action in connexion with ecclesiastical enterprise, the excellent men who then controlled the interests of the church, impelled by a determined zeal for her enlargement and prosperity, and to extend relief to the destitute and suffering around on every side, united their counsels, their prayers, and importunate appeals, to the slumbering pastors and people, to inspire them with an enlightened and liberal energy in this great work. This was especially true as applied to the Presbytery of New Brunswick, which embraced within its limits nearly the whole state of New Jersey. The opposition to collections and taxations, for religious use, and especially for missionary purposes, was so decisive in the congregations generally, that to procure the assent of the people to a very moderate and equitable assessment for the missionary cause, the Presbytery appointed one† of their most aged, venerable, and influential members, to visit the churches, to enlighten them on the subject of missions, to explain their duty, and by direct and impressive appeals, to induce them to admit the principle of taxation, and to observe the assess-

* It may be a fact of some interest with the reader to know, that the subject of these cavils against missionary labor, was gravely recited and discussed by the illustrious Dr. John M. Mason, pastor of the Scots Presbyterian Church in the city of New York, in a sermon preached before the New York Missionary Society, Nov. 7, 1797, published the same year by T. & J. Swords, of that city. Could those cold, callous objectors now return to earth and cast their eyes over the missionary field, survey the mountains of India, the islands of the Southern Sea, and the vast Christianized regions of the North and West, with what indescribable emotions of astonishment and remorse would their bosoms heave!

† That member was the Rev. Joseph Clark, pastor of the Church in New Brunswick, a man and a minister of decided talents, piety, and Christian zeal, known and beloved in all the churches. For an extended sketch, see Appendix of the Memoir of Rev. Robert Finley, published by Terhune & Letson, New Brunswick, 1819, by I. V. Brown.

ment of the Presbytery. This agency was promptly performed with great fidelity and success. The amount realized annually from that measure was small indeed, but sufficient to meet their limited plans and outlays. Its most important benefit lay in the effect it produced upon the minds and habits of the people. The salutary influence of this apportionment was distinctly visible in the congregations for many years. The principle was clearly stated and powerfully commended, that providing for the support of the gospel at home, and not less for the sending of it to the destitute abroad, involves the highest and most sacred responsibility of the Christian *name*, or in other words that the church of Christ is a missionary society. This being once settled, the way is open immediately for the introduction of that large and liberal policy in sustaining and enlarging the interests of Zion, which characterizes the Presbyterian Church in these United States, and in exemplifying which the congregations in New Jersey have maintained an honorable grade.

CHAPTER III.

Plan of Union founded in the uncongeniality of Presbyterianism and Congregationalism on the Mohawk and vicinity—Westward—The Plan of Union was proposed first by the General Association of Connecticut—Particulars stated—Plan of Union introduced.

The beautiful and fertile regions on both sides of the Mohawk and extending far westward, began early to attract to that interesting district, a crowd of settlers from the more populous parts of New York, from East Jersey, and from the New England states, principally of the Presbyterian and Congregational denominations. The people thus emigrating and the religious teachers accompanying, differed very much among themselves in education, in sectional feelings, in ecclesiastical forms, and in theological opinions. The principles, in particular, of Presbyterian and Congregational Church government, were soon found to be so uncongenial, as to present great difficulties to those of this mixed character, who attempted as one body to build churches and conduct ecclesiastical affairs. Their infant efforts at missionary enterprise were met by the same obstacles and speedily produced unhappy results.

On this arena in western New York, whose settlements were new and heterogeneous, the difficulty originated which agitated the Presbyterian Church most painfully for some years, till it produced the convulsive disruption of 1837. This afflicting process, in all its stages, was introduced and coerced by the abuse of a compromise measure, agreed upon between the Congregational and Presbyterian denominations, A. D. 1801, and usually called the *Plan of Union, in the new settlements.** Dr. Judd has mistaken one fact in regard to the origin of this plan. His words are, "Here let it be borne in mind, that this plan originated with Presbyterians, and was by their General Assembly proposed to the General Association of Connecticut, and by both bodies unanimously adopted." Probably, this error has proceeded from the fact, that the authority relied upon for the history of this transaction, is the Assembly's Digest, which does not contain the whole record. By referring to the minutes of the Assembly for 1800–1801, it will be perceived that the Plan was first proposed by the General Association of Connecticut. "In the minutes for 1800 is the following: the Rev. Dr. Jonathan Edwards, the Rev. Asa Hyllier, and Jonathan Freeman, were appointed delegates from this Assembly to the General Association of Connecticut," &c. In the minutes of 1801, we find their report, as follows: "The delegates from the General Assembly to the General Association of Connecticut, report, that they have attended according to appointment, through the whole course of the sessions of the General Association. That besides the business peculiar to the churches of Connecticut, the General Association appointed a committee to confer with a committee *that may* be appointed by the General Assembly, on measures which may promote union among the inhabitants of the new settlements, and the missionaries to those settlements, as appears by the enclosed paper." Immediately after the committee had reported, the paper referred to above was read, the minute concerning which is as follows: "A communication was read from the General Association of the state of Connecticut, appointing a committee to confer with a committee of the Presbyterian Church, to consider the measures proper to be adopted by the General Association and the General Assembly, for establishing a uniform system of church government between the inhabitants of the new settlements, who are attached to the Presbyterian form of government, and those who prefer the Congregational form."

"Ordered that the said communication lie on the table." Succeeding this, on the same page, is the following: The Rev. Drs. Edwards, McKnight, and Woodhull, the Rev. Mr. Blatchford and Mr. Hutton, were appointed a committee to consider and digest a plan of government for the churches in the new settlements, *agreeably to the proposal of the General Association of Con-*

* Division of the Church, p. 11.

necticut, and report the same as soon as convenient. Then follows the report of the committee, as contained in the Digest, page 297, as follows:

"The report of the committee appointed to consider and digest a plan of government for the churches in the new settlements, was taken up and considered, and after mature deliberation on the same, approved, as follows:

"*Regulations adopted by the General Assembly of the Presbyterian Church in America, and by the General Association of the state of Connecticut, (provided said Association agrees to them,) with a view to prevent alienation and promote union and harmony in those new settlements which are composed of inhabitants from these bodies:*

"I. It is strictly enjoined on all their missionaries to the new settlements, to endeavor by all means to promote mutual forbearance and accomodation between those inhabitants of the new settlements who hold the Presbyterian and those who hold the Congregational form of church government.

"II. If in the new settlements any church of the Congregational order shall settle a minister of the Presbyterian order, that church may, if they choose, still conduct their discipline according to Congregational principles, settling their difficulties among themselves, or by a council mutually agreed upon for that purpose. But if any difficulty shall exist between the minister and the church, or any member of it, it shall be referred to the Presbytery to which the minister shall belong, provided both parties agree to it; if not, to a council, consisting of an equal number of Presbyterians and Congregationalists, agreed upon by both parties.

"III. If a Presbyterian church shall settle a minister of Congregational principles, that church may still continue their discipline according to Presbyterian principles; except that if a difficulty arise between him and his church, or any member of it, the cause shall be tried by the association to which the said minister shall belong, provided both parties agree to it; otherwise by a council, one half Congregationalists and the other half Presbyterians, mutually agreed on by the parties.

"IV. If any congregation consist partly of those who hold the Congregational form of discipline, and partly of those who hold the Presbyterian form, we *recommend* to both parties that this be no obstruction to their uniting in one church and settling a minister; and that in this case the church choose a *standing committee* from the communicants of said church, whose business it shall be to call to account every member of the church who shall conduct himself inconsistently with the laws of Christianity, and to give judgment on such conduct; and if the person condemned by their judgment be a Presbyterian, he shall have liberty to appeal to the Presbytery; if a Congregationalist, he shall have liberty to appeal to the body of the male communicants of the church; in the former case, the determination of the Presbytery shall be final, unless the church consent to a further appeal to the Synod or to the General Assembly; and in the latter case, if the party condemned shall wish for a trial by a mutual council, the cause shall be referred to said council; and provided the said standing committee of any church shall depute one of themselves to attend the Presbytery, he may have the same right *to sit and act in the Presbytery*, as a ruling elder of the Presbyterian Church.

"Unanimously adopted by the Association."

CHAPTER IV.

General character of the Plan of Union—Objects of the parties to it—Their character, probable feelings, and aims—Temporary and transient import of the title, "Plan of Union for the New Settlements."

In the following detail, the matters which relate to church government and theological opinion, will be considered separate and apart, as far as found practicable. At this point in the illustration, we shall confine ourselves to the subject of ecclesiastical government, as most intimately connected with the Plan of Union. As a preliminary remark, we observe that in surveying the compromise scheme, it cannot be doubted, that it was intended primarily and principally to accommodate the good people of the mixed character referred to, who were living on the frontiers, principally of Western New York, or in the new settlements. Nor will any who candidly estimate the terms, the circumstances, and the time of the Plan, deny that this friendly arrangement was intended to be temporary, and to pass away with the period and the exigencies which gave it birth. Surely, nobody expected that those settlements and locations were always to continue *new*, or that the people of each distinct and opposite religious class were forever to remain untaught, inexperienced, and unmitigatedly hostile towards every form of ecclesiastical administration but their own. Now the Presbyterian fathers, who were active then, in yielding to this innovation, many of them from the beginning considering it of doubtful expediency, unquestionably contemplated, as a second and weighty motive in favor of the *Plan*, the enlargement of their own church; they had a right to do so; this was to them a legitimate result; the ground was universally considered as Presbyterian; it was no part of New England: their preponderance in numbers on the ground was very great. Hence their confident belief was, that the Congregational brethren living already within the bosom of the Presbyterian family, after becoming practically familiar with their name, their principles, and forms, would gradually amalgamate with the great Presbyterian body, and render the existence of this incongruous plan of intercourse in a short time no longer requisite.

As the genius of New England had scarcely begun to develop itself, it was quite easy and natural for the unsuspecting fathers of the Presbyterian family, who unfortunately became, in some sort, a party to the platform of 1801, to make an erroneous estimate of the people with whom they were treating, and of the result they fondly anticipated. Indeed, the talent and enterprise of the New England people, as since displayed in every field, in every clime, in every art, in all forms of business, at home and abroad, upon the land and the sea, have not failed to excite the surprise and the admiration of mankind. In the arts of invention, performance, and endurance, in the school room, the laboratory, the forum, the council chamber or cathedral, in the legislative hall or judicial tribunal, they are always at home and at ease. Whether tasked to manufacture a pin or a comb, to make a silk reel, a cotton gin, a steam engine, or a telescope, they have a tact, a versatility, a plenitude of skill and resort, always adequate and ever at command.

What folly then to attempt to limit or bind such minds—such a generation of men—by a loosely and absurdly constituted *bond of union* or of *intercourse*, like that of 1801! It was certainly a measure of daring and doubtful adventure, to admit at all, into so near and intimate ecclesiastic alliance, a company of men so inspired with restless activity and enterprise, so eminently fond of change, as well as of progress. As monumental evidence of their theological deflections at home from the right standard, we may recite from observation made about thirty years ago, that a traveller passing through their towns and villages, would see, in most of them, in shocking juxtaposition and contrast, the *Unitarian* and so called *Orthodox* church, visible from the same position. It is not wonderful that the same people, emigrating to other lands and neighborhoods, should carry with them, and scatter profusely, similar aberrations.

The New England party who had proposed this negotiation, no doubt looked on with great interest. With the penetration and intelligence belonging naturally to their craggy hills, they could not fail to perceive the picturesque and beautiful features which marked even the wilderness and solitary place, and they could easily anticipate the order, fertility, and comeliness, which talent and industry, taste and refinement, would soon intermingle with the wild simplicity and rude magnificence of nature, in that new and romantic region. How strong, then, must have been the attractions of that field of promise, much more than of fiction, when, in the glowing ardor of their warm imaginations, enlightened and enlivened by their Christian zeal, the first New England adventurers surveyed those extended hills and vales, as radiated, adorned, and sanctified by gospel grace! The secret stimulating and thrilling hope, that this land would soon be theirs, that their Christian enterprise and earnestness would leave the slow and plodding footsteps of tardy Presbyterians, though first in the field, far behind, and secure to Congregational schools and churches, religious doctrines and forms of devotion, a decided pre-eminence and acknowledged triumph. With these feelings in the breasts of many of New England's Levitical sons, the competition commenced, on the platform of 1801, *in the new settlements.* The results are to be presented in these pages.

Thus our honest, kind, and excellent ecclesiastical fathers committed a great mistake. They never dreamed that a large portion of the mixed population from the Eastern States were making calculations on the subject of church extension, of the same kind with themselves, Little did the majority at all apprehend the sad inroads upon their system, by the new settlers, which their successors have found it imperiously necessary to remedy by a decisive act of amputation, which it is the object of these pages to explain and to vindicate.

Certainly, no reasonable man, who knew the organization of these distinct branches of the church and regarded the interests of true religion, could expect that two religious bodies, under a fictitious, not a real union, each retaining its own peculiar and irreconcilable features, should continue long to act harmoniously together, or that the profoundly sagacious and politic actors, on the Presbyterian part, should, notwithstanding their zeal for harmony, deliberately devise and adopt a plan for perpetual observance, in which elements so uncongenial hold so prominent and governing a place; bringing incessantly into juxtaposition, or unavoidable conflict, the essential features of the scheme; the end of which collision must necessarily be discord and strife.

By this apparently conciliatory devise of 1801, the Presbyterian church threw down their walls of defence; they opened their bosom to the ingress of strangers; they invited the active leaven of discord and confusion to enter; they entailed, undesignedly, upon their sons and their successors, a task, the necessity of which they will never cease to deplore, but the firm and righteous performance of which they will as soon cease to justify.

Were those new settlements still *new* after a lapse of thirty-five years? Had not those frontiers long before been lost and overwhelmed by the vast tide of emigration and improvement going west; put off their infant character in the midst of a dense population, of full maturity and large resources? Were they to be kept forever under the same system of tutelage and temporary yoke of bondage as those who have always need to be taught which be the first principles of the oracles of faith and order in the Christian church? If then the plan adapted to the new settlements, in their new and infant state, was temporary, how long should it last? Certainly no longer than to prove itself extensively successful or entirely abortive. Certainly not after it had plainly become mischievous; not after the mischief springing from it had multiplied to such an enormous extent as to threaten speedy extermination and complete revolution to the whole church.

CHAPTER V.

Chief grounds of the Vindication stated—Unconstitutionality of the Plan of Union considered and exposed.

The writer bases his vindication of the measures pursued by the Old School in the Presbyterian Church, to correct the grand mistake of 1801, and to terminate its evil results, mainly upon the four following grounds, *viz:*

I. The unconstitutionality of the *Plan of Union.*

II. The disorders which proceeded from it in the Presbyterian Church.

III. The false and dangerous theological opinions to which that plan gave rise, within the limits of the Presbyterian body.

IV. The fact that a combination was detected among the New School party in the church, whose object was to demolish the whole fabric of the Presbyterian organization, in every essential feature, and to substitute another, differently constructed; indeed, founded and to be conducted upon principles totally irreconcilable with the organization and administration of the Presbyterian Church.

We shall not very particularly labor to observe this division of the subject, especially in the order stated, and yet we hope not to fail of producing an abundance of material to illustrate and support each and every one of the particulars above presented.

I. The unconstitutionality of the *Plan of Union* is here presented as a ground upon which to justify its abrogation.

As there has been much exhibited on this subject, which is now in print, in the form of speeches, discussions, and criticisms, all couched in well arranged thought and language, we shall select freely, in the sequel, from the materials before us, what appears best adapted to our purpose, without particularity of reference.

Unconstitutionality may relate to the powers of the parties engaged in framing the plan, or to the matter involved in it. A few references from articles in the constitution of the Presbyterian Church, will enable any one to see at once the utter incompatibility of the *Plan of Union* with that instrument. "Before any overtures or regulations, proposed by the Assembly to be established as constitutional rules shall be obligatory on the churches, it shall be necessary to transmit them to all the Presbyteries, and to receive the returns of at least a majority of them, in writing, approving thereof." See Constitution, chapter XII., section 6. Here the General Assembly are positively prohibited from adopting any principle, regulation, or agreement, on any subject, with any party, under any circumstances, tending to enlarge or abridge, infringe, or change, any part of the constitution of the Church. Having no power in themselves to make any change in our ecclesiastical system, without authority derived from the Presbyteries, all their attempts at it are necessarily null and void. This being most manifestly true, the people, the great body of the church, cannot be bound by their unauthorized act. It is not material which party proposed the *Plan of Union*—whether the General Association of Connecticut, which is the fact, or the General Assembly of the Presbyterian Church—neither had power to make it binding. The former of these bodies does not exist and act in such character and manner as to give validity to such a transaction, and the latter is restricted by a positive prohibition. Now the interests, the rights, the forms invested, as is said, or secured in this plan of action of 1801, will show at once that it repudiates and defies all constitutional provisions and arrangements. Let us analyze the plan, and examine it in a few particulars. This new mode of action authorizes "a Presbyterian preacher to become the pastor of a Congregational Church, (see Plan of Union, sections 1 and 2, this vol. p. 32,) and the church may still, if they choose, conduct their discipline according to Congregational principles, settling their difficulties among themselves, or by a council mutually agreed upon for that purpose;" "but if any difficulty should arise between the minister and the church, or any member of it, it shall be referred to the Presbytery to which the minister shall belong, provided both parties agree to it; if not, to a council composed of an equal number of Presbyterians and Congregationalists, agreed upon by both parties."

Again, the Plan provides that when a Presbyterian Church has a Congregational pastor, the discipline must be exercised on the Presbyterian plan. If difficulty arises between such a pastor and his church, the matter in dispute must be referred to his association, or to a mutual council.

Again, the Plan provides, that when a congregation is composed partly of Presbyterians and partly of Congregationalists, the Plan recommends that they should unite and form one congregation, settle a minister, choose a standing committee to administer discipline; that a Congregationalist may appeal from the judgments of this committee to the male members of the church; a Presbyterian may appeal to his own Presbytery, whose decision shall settle the difficulty, unless the church consent to a further appeal to the Synod or General Assembly.

Again, observe a concluding provision of much importance, which has been greatly abused. "If a standing committee, while this case of discipline is in process, shall depute one of themselves to attend Presbytery, he may have the same right to sit and act *in Presbytery as a ruling elder* of the *Presbyterian* Church."

Now, after this brief recital of the outlines of this anomalous plan, may we not ask, what part of the plain, consistent, and well ordered constitution of the Presbyterian Church is not violated and set aside by this incongruous engrafture? No wit of man could more effectually supersede Presbyterianism, or devise a scheme better adapted to create difficulty and confusion. The leading features of our ecclesiastical system, are placed in a character of entire subversion or perpetual vacillations, and a compound fabric of immisceable elements is substituted for it. Surely it must be admitted, that under the Presbyterian organization, every rule enjoined is intended for pure Presbyterian congregations and Presbyterian pastors, to be received as such, retained as such, and observed as such. The Plan of Union, pursuing an object entirely different, provides for bringing into this connexion, Congregational churches and ministers, and making them an integral component part of our body, members of the Presbyterian Church. Besides, the Plan allows these Congregationalists, unchanged in their principles and sympathies, to continue in the Presbyterian body *ad libitum;* to enjoy the rights and privileges of pure Presbyterians; to exercise the powers of Presbyterians in the church, in administering its discipline, governing its members, and wielding its power; thus assisting to make and enforce rules and decisions over others to which they themselves are not in the slightest degree amenable; for be it remembered, they are permitted, in any emergency, to take refuge under the provisions of the Congregational Church.

For example, in those mixed congregations, the constitutional rule requiring the church to be organized with a pastor and bench of elders, is set aside; and for the elders is substituted a standing committee, who are to exercise the same powers as elders, without any responsibility to the Presbyterian Church. On this plan, the whole theory and process of church discipline is converted into a fluctuating caprice or scene of confusion. Trials for offences, among church members, on Presbyterian principles, are plain and easy. By the Plan of Union, offenders are sometimes tried by the male members of the church, sometimes by a standing committee, and the remedy of appeal, it may be, from their ignorant and erring decisions, to higher courts, can be obtained only by getting the consent of masses who are not Presbyterians themselves, thus completely closing the avenues to justice, and frustrating one of the cardinal and most precious features to be found in this or any other judicial code, *the right of appeal, to courts of higher order, or of the last resort.*

The ministers of the gospel, by the Presbyterian system, have a right to be tried by their own Presbytery, but the Plan of Union provides that pastors shall be tried by men who have adopted a different system of faith, different rules of evidence, and different forms of discipline. The constitution of the Presbyterian Church requires that every candidate for the sacred office, before his installation to a church, must adopt our Confession of Faith and form of government. But this Plan comes in upon our church with a tremendous avalanche; it permits a Congregationalist to assume the pastoral office, with all its sacred responsibilities, in a manner most perfectly free from all restriction or ceremony. The candidate enters, to preside in church sessions, to sit in Presbytery, to occupy a place in Synod and General Assembly,* and to preach the gospel, entirely disregarding the constitutional claims of the church upon every intrant, for suitable qualifications and pledges. Is this total exemption from rule, or elevation above it, ever permitted in the induction of a regular Presbyterian candidate? In no case whatever. Who, then, can be so blind, or so prejudiced, as not to see that the Plan of Union is a thing entirely different, in every important point, from the constitution of the Presbyterian Church? It is precisely such a device as enemies of the church ought to desire for the purpose of breaking down its old landmarks, introducing novelties, enabling Christians of another character, spirit, and form, to bring in, mix up, diffuse piecemeal, and establish uncongenial peculiarities of another organization, gradually, but incessantly asserting its corrupting influence, and confirming its power, till, like leaven, it leavens the whole lump.

* This is the construction New School men have put upon the last clause of Section 4. See Plan of Union, p. 32.

The facilities are fully afforded in this New England plan of amalgamation, for accomplishing a complete change in the Presbyterian Church. Only set such a company of men to work, under privileges and auxiliaries so well adapted, with such talent, industry, unscrupulousness, and perseverance, and revolution in the church will as certainly follow, as water continue to run down hill, or attraction and gravitation to prevail in matter. The facts to be presented in this history will confirm the truth of these statements.

It is true, this scheme was gravely *headed, a Plan of Union!* It is, in reality, a plan of division; a plan of undermining the Presbyterian Church; a plan of substituting a heterogeneous monster in its place; a plan for making a huge mass of guano, out of which almost spontaneously shall vegetate enormous excresences; a Upas tree, which, let alone, would speedily generate poison enough to infect the whole body of Christ's Church in this western world. We may well ask, who has a right to supplant the constitution of the Presbyterian Church, and place in its stead a device so opposite and hostile to it at every point? The fact is conceded on all sides that the General Assembly had not this power. It is equally clear and certain that the General Association of Connecticut had no power. The document, therefore, which was executed by these two ecclesiastical bodies, for the purpose of becoming an instrument of binding force, was just as susceptible of it as would have been a sheet of blank paper. The whole transaction bears the aspect of a legislative or advisory act, for the benefit of the churches in the new settlements. To this declaration, the Association merely grant their assent, without giving or receiving any pledge. The Assembly then assume the exclusive agency, and are the only party in the case. It becomes a domestic, a home concern, with them, to promote the best interests of their feeble and scattered flocks, and to be continued or cease at their discretion.

CHAPTER VI.

Lathrop's Case stated—Encroachments of New School men—First Principles, extract from a sermon delivered, Princeton, 1820—Opinions of Vattel.

II. An irresistible argument in favor of repealing this Plan is drawn from the irregularities and disorders deforming and disturbing the church, which have been for many years flowing in at this unlawful inlet. It is true that many years before the abrogation, the remark was frequently made, that there was no objection to the *Plan of Union*. This, however, was a great mistake. For a number of years, probably eight or ten, it made but little impression on the public mind. And when dissatisfaction began to speak out, to its feeble whispers of apprehension, which began to be uttered about 1810 or 1812, it was responded by the careless and the cunning, why trouble ourselves about the Plan of Union; it is an inoperative, harmless thing, and if let alone, it will die of itself. In this manner the spirit of vigilance and resistance was partially put to rest at the time. Soon afterwards, when farther developments of its mischeivous tendency had produced deeper impressions of disgust, and louder remonstrance, criticism and censure were objected to on an opposite ground. Oh! say the friends of this incipient New School wedge, the Plan has existed so long that it has received the sanction of the church; the silence and acquiescence of the Presbyterian body have given to it their sanction, and confirmed it as a valid, integral part of their great system. The attempt, however, to gain some advantages for Congregationalism, from usage and from apparently tacit indulgence, while it seemed to encourage the bold advances of the intruders, inspired the greater alarm among the possessors.

A striking instance of this kind occurred in the General Assembly of 1820, of which the writer happened to be a member. At the organization, a young man, in appearance about twenty-five years of age, by name Daniel W. Lathrop, delegated by Hartford Presbytery, New Connecticut, presented himself under the character of a committee man, and demanded a seat in the House. The minutes for that year record nothing peculiar in the case, but the facts are perfectly well recollected, and are here presented as a specimen of what occurred frequently soon after in the Assembly, and yet the minutes make very little record of the serious struggles which occurred on these occasions. Mr. Lathrop boldly avowed himself as a committee man in a congregation of the Presbytery of Hartford. His admission was opposed by many members, from different districts of the church, on constitutional grounds. It was urged very temperately, that Congregationalism was always out of place, and then becoming increasingly dangerous within the Presbyterian Church; that encroachments were multiplying in various ways, and our church and her institutions, already suffering injury, and liable every year to aggravated harm from those influences; that unless a prompt and efficient check were put upon these infractions of our elementary principles and safeguards, no man could tell when and where they would end. Some of the opposers, after examining the charter of the church and the Plan of Union, declared without fear or reservation, that the claimant had not the slightest shade of a right to a seat in the Assembly. On more particular inquiry, it was ascertained that the church which sent him did not possess a feature of Presbyterianism at all. A warm debate ensued. The principal advocates for his admission were from the vicinity of Albany, and the neighborhood of the Western Reserve, Ohio. Rev. Arthur I. Stansbury, from the city of Albany, was prominent in advocating the admission of Mr. Lathrop. Old fashioned Presbyterians, who lifted their voice, had but little influence. The mild and paternal counsel of the Rev. Dr. John Woodhull, of New Brunswick Presbytery, one of the committee who reported the Plan of Union, in the Assembly of 1801, but was never satisfied with the Plan, amidst the noisy vociferation of several young speakers, which pervaded the house, in favor of the motion to admit, scarcely obtained a deliberate hearing. The advocates appealed *exquisitely* to the sympathies of the members, and protested against the rudeness and discourtesy of sending Mr. Lathrop back under a frown, after so long a travel over the mountains to secure what they called *his rights*.

After a short interim in the business of the Assembly, and a conference had been held in a corner of the house, on the left hand of the Moderator's chair, a committee from Mr. Lathrop's advocates was gravely sent to the writer of these sheets, with an importunate request that he would withdraw his opposition, and acquiesce in the application, as a matter of personal favor. Of this committee, two individuals are distinctly recollected, Rev. Arthur I. Stansbury, of Albany, and Rev. Matthew G. Wallace, of Miami Presbytery, Synod of Ohio. At this critical moment, the illustrious Jos. Caldwell, D. D., of Chapel Hill, North Carolina, reputed a philosopher, a mathematician, and a theologian, made a labored speech in favor of Mr. Lathrop. It was called the one idea speech, yet it was so magically important in the absence of every thing like argument, that it really seemed to decide the question. The argument, if it may be so called, of Dr. Caldwell, with its one idea, was so profound and convincing, while extremely simple, that the power of resistance seemed, in great measure, annihilated in the house. This was the orator's magical plea: "Mr. Moderator—It is true that our system recognizes in this Assembly, from the *churches*, only *ruling elders*, as members. But Mr. Lathrop was appointed to do the work of an elder in this house, and he comes *in the place* of an elder, and, therefore, *he is an elder*, and ought to be received." Such absurd language, coming from a man of supposed sense and reason, impressed the house with the idea that resistance at that time was useless. The New School were so elated with this victory, that it was currently reported, that they had placed the successful adventurer on trials for the ministry, without even allowing him time to visit home. In a few months, he came out of their mill, accomplished, according to their incipient system, as a laborer in the field. The success of this enterprise, in forcing Lathrop upon the General Assembly, exerted a powerful influence upon the party, in augmenting their confidence, their zeal, and the sphere of their action. The predictions of several prominent men, at this period, soon became matter of general remark.

These minutiæ are introduced to show how unfounded the assertion was, so often made about that period, that the Presbyterian Church, as a body, by tacit consent, approved and confirmed the Plan of Union. The event above recorded took place in the General Assembly, seventeen years before the Abrogation, and cases analogous to it occurred soon after. It is particularly to be regretted, that the judge and counsellors concerned in adjudicating this case, in *Nisi Prius*, should have given opinions and made statements so conflicting with one another, and contrary to fact. For example, Judge Rogers, in his charge, in *Nisi Prius*, (see Judd, p. 232,) says, "all parties acquiesced in it for *thirty-six years*." Into this grand mistake, Chancellor Kent had fallen some time before. In his opinion, (Judd 264,) he says, "the Plan of Union was carried into operation with great success, and with the continued approbation of the Presbyteries and General Assemblies of the Presbyterian Church, down to its final abrogation in 1837." Again, page 232, Rogers says, "the court is also of opinion, that after an acquiescence of nearly forty years," &c., &c. This is entirely irreconcilable with true history, as the Assembly's minutes will show.

From what the writer observed in the General Assembly of 1820, he returned home deeply convinced that decided Congregationalists, and ministers unduly influenced by Congregational sympathies, were more thickly scattered through the church, and much more actively and pertinaciously engaged in propagating their own views, than was generally supposed. It was still asserted by some,—"the church is quiet and safe—there is no danger."

To call public attention to the subject, the writer, being appointed by Presbytery to deliver a discourse at the installation of the Rev. George S. Woodhull, Princeton, N. J., July 5th, 1820, preached a sermon, which was printed, with the title, "First Principles: or, Hints to suit the times, and calculated to promote ecclesiastical union," from the text, Romans x. 2: "For I bear them record, that they have a zeal of God, but not according to knowledge." The following extracts from that discourse are inserted here to exhibit the feelings and views prevalent, at that period, in regard to the *Plan of Union* and the New School faction, in the Presbyterian Church, among the members of this respectable Presbytery. It is true, there were a few individuals in that body who lifted the syren voice—*Peace! Peace!!* This voice it was that destroyed confidence and aggravated alarm.

A portion of this discourse is addressed "To those within the body of our own church, who entertain sentiments not conformed to our established standards." We extract, p.

"That a considerable number of individuals of this description exist in the Presbyterian Church, is now well known. I shall not attempt to specify the points respecting which they differ, nor to estimate their importance. That this difference exists, is the fact assumed, as the basis of my remarks, under this head.

"The question has been forced upon the church, what course ought she to pursue in regard to her dissenting members? It would be presumption in me to attempt definitely to prescribe her duty. But in the exercise of that privilege, and under the constraints of that responsibility, which are common to all, it is conceived not to be foreign from the business of this day to suggest some considerations which will assist in forming an opinion on this subject, and which ought to have influence in all future proceedings relative to this unhappy dissention.

"The following principles I shall lay down on this subject, conceiving them to be incontrovertibly sanctioned by reason, common sense, and the usages of mankind.

"'I. The first principle is, that all people have a right to associate together for religious purposes, in any manner suited to their views, under the direction of the word of God, to determine the articles of their faith, their plan of worship, their form of government, and their terms of membership.'

"'II. * * * * * *

"'III. The third principle affirmed is, that all persons becoming members of a community distinctly organized, are bound to comply with the spirit and letter of the terms of admission.'

"The principles of common candour and honour require conformity in civil society, and above all, conscience and consistency should enforce it in a religious community. The idea that any member, however voluntarily and sincerely he may have avowed at first, is not bound afterwards to regard his obligations; that he is at liberty, with any alteration of views that may occur, to change his faith and his practice, still continuing in the bosom of the society he has chosen, is subversive of all uniformity, good faith, and established order, in the world; it tends to loosen the ties of every compact; it represents the most sacred engagements as a mere empty form of momentary convenience, but possessing no practical influence or binding force. What can be more shocking than the avowal of such a sentiment in the Christian church! The articles adopted may not be agreeable to the views of every individual; the *Plan of Union* may be defective; the compliance required may be attended with some difficulties; but until the constitution is regularly altered, it must be observed in all its distinguishing features, according to the pledge originally given."

* * * * * * *

"The obligations imposed upon ministers of the gospel, upon ruling elders, and implicitly upon all professors of religion, in the Presbyterian Church, are of the most strong, unequivocal and sacred nature. They 'declare that they sincerely receive and adopt the confession of faith of this church, as containing the systems of doctrines taught in the Holy Scriptures;' and 'that they approve of the government and discipline of the Presbyterian Church, as prescribed in the form.'* The obligations required, though comprised in seven distinct questions, are to be considered as united in one in their object and spirit. Every question proposed, and every idea suggested, must be viewed as inseparably connected with all that precedes and follows.

"'IV. The fourth principle is this, when an individual belonging to a community, whose standards he has engaged to observe, avows sentiments opposed to those standards, and pursues a course calculated to contravene the established principles and or-

* The form of obligation observed in the Presbyterian Church is in substance the same as that which has been used in the Church of Scotland. As the custom there was to subscribe the formula, it was reduced to one concise declaration. For the gratification of the reader, we insert the following formula, enacted by the Assembly of the Church of Scotland, A. D. 1711, to be subscribed by all such as shall pass trials in order to be licensed, and that shall be ordained ministers, or admitted to parishes.

"I, ———, do hereby declare, that I do sincerely own and believe the whole doctrine contained in the Confession of Faith, approved by the General Assembly of this National Church, and ratified by law, in the year 1690, and frequently confirmed by divers acts of Parliament since that time, to be the truths of God, and I do own the same as the confession of my faith. As likewise I do own the purity of the worship presently authorised and practiced in this church, and also the Presbyterian government and discipline now so happily established therein: which doctrine, worship and church government I am persuaded are founded upon the word of God and are agreeable thereto: and I promise, that through the grace of God, I shall firmly and constantly adhere to the same, and to the utmost of my power shall, in my place and station, assert, maintain and defend the said doctrine, worship, discipline and government of this church, by Kirk Sessions, Presbyteries, Provincial Synods, and General Assemblies; and that I shall in my practice conform myself to the said worship and submit to the said discipline and government, and never endeavour, directly nor indirectly, the prejudice or subversion of the same."

See preface to a collection of the Confessions of Faith in the Church of Scotland. See also Form of Government, ch. xiv. sec. 10.

der of the system, he violates his engagements, he is a disorganizer in that society, and a disturber of its peace.'

"A foreign emigrant, who obtains citizenship in an adopted country by subscribing the oath of allegiance to its sovereign and obedience to its laws, and is found afterwards to entertain sentiments hostile to the grand charter of state; to diffuse a spirit of insubordination to law, and of rebellion against legitimate authority, is accounted a seditious, treacherous subject.* He is justly charged with all the guilt and evil attached to such conduct. He is an aggressor against a peaceful and well ordered society. These principles will apply with increased force to dissenting members of a religious community, in which there is reasonably expected a more scrupulous regard to moral obligation, and where there can be extended comparatively but little indulgence to aggressors. Whatever painful jealousies, interruptions of harmony, and alienations of affection exist, in connexion with the matters in controversy, must necessarily be ascribed to the influence of their dissention!

"'V. Fifth principle. That every community is privileged and obligated to preserve and perfect itself, as far as practicable, agreeably to the plan of its organization, by guarding its institutions, enacting and enforcing laws, and pursuing such a system of measures as it may esteem calculated to improve its character and promote the great end of its being.'

"These are rights and duties which unquestionably pertain to societies in general. Man, as an individual endowed with various faculties and susceptible of indefinite improvement, is obligated to preserve himself from harm, to cultivate his powers, and so to pursue the end of his existence in that manner which appears to him most conducive to it. And groups of men, associated for purposes of improvement and benevolence, possess corresponding rights and are under similar obligations. 'In the act of association, in virtue of which a number of men form a state or nation, each individual has entered into an engagement with all, and all have entered into engagements with each individual, to prosecute the common welfare.' Again, 'If a nation is obliged to preserve itself, it is not less obliged to preserve all its members. The nation owes this to itself, since the loss of even one of its members weakens it, and is injurious to its own preserva-

* The works of Vattel, as applied to political communities, are exceedingly strong. "If every man is obligated to entertain a sincere love for his country, and to procure it all the happiness in his power, it is a shameful and detestable crime to injure that very country. He who becomes guilty of it, violates his most sacred engagements and sinks into base ingratitude; he dishonors himself by the blackest perfidy, since he abuses the confidence of his fellow-citizens, and treats as enemies those who had a right to expect his assistance and services."—*Laws of Nations.*

tion.' Again, 'Since a nation has a right to preserve itself, it has a right to every thing necessary to its preservation, for the law of nature gives us a right to every thing without which we could not fulfil our obligation. A nation has a right to every thing that can secure it from threatening danger, and keep at a distance whatever is capable of causing its ruin.'*

"These general principles will apply to religious as well as to civil societies. The fundamental rule of duty for every moral being towards itself, is to live in a manner conformable to its own nature; '*naturæ convenienter vivere.*' The Presbyterian Church is a confederation of a great number of presbyteries, churches, and individuals, for the purpose of glorifying God, and promoting the best interests of all her parts, by giving the greatest practical effect to her doctrines, laws, and ordinances, as exhibited in the Confession of Faith. It is her faith that constitutes the character, the life, and the glory of the church. This is indeed her all; for it, then, she ought earnestly to contend. Her morals, her devotion, her happiness, her reputation and prosperity, are all essentially dependent upon her faith. This is the test by which she is tried and estimated, on earth and in heaven. The political laws and institutions of a state may be defective and badly administered, and the state notwithstanding be opulent, orderly, and powerful. But if the sacred creed of the church be mutilated, her glory is departed.

"VI. The sixth and last principle here stated is, that when the highest authority in a regularly organized community, connives at the introduction of opinions opposed to the essential articles of its constitution, and attended by insubordinate conduct, it opens a way for greater and greater deviations from good order, encroachments on its stability and peace, and so becomes accessory to its own ruin.

"Let the church admit the idea that deviations from her confession may be tolerated, and a door is opened immediately for the introduction of all kinds of spurious sentiments. If there is any thing amiss in our standards, let it be corrected. If any points now embraced in our summary are of so little importance that individuals may modify them at pleasure, let those points be distinctly designated by competent authority. But nothing can be more dangerous than to countenance indefinite deviations from public standards. This is placing the whole faith of the church in the hands, it may be, of the least discreet individuals, to be altered or superseded at pleasure, according to all the varieties of perception and feeling that may exist through the whole Presbyterian body. If one person may be permitted to expunge or alter an indefinite part of the Confession, which has become offensive

* Vattel. Book I.

to him, the same indulgence must be extended to a second, a third, a fourth, and so on till you exhaust the whole number of the Presbyterian Church. If the principle of indefinite deviation be yielded, it is a large and unbounded grant. Numberless schemes and amendments may be at once set up, and the utmost confusion be created through the whole church. Indeed, the church may be brought in this way to exhibit the anomalous spectacle of a religious community without a creed, or as possessing a creed which nobody believes; or what is still more absurd, as maintaining a creed and no creed, at the same time.

"That pernicious errors often grow out of small departures from sound system of faith and order, the protestant world can abundantly attest. This often happens contrary to the designs and expectations of those who attempt to improve upon established forms. Good men, frequently, through their fondness for novelty and distinction, proceed much farther* in the business of reforming and overturning than they at first contemplated. The mind becomes pleased with its own imaginary success, and pursues its course, vainly supposing it is adding triumph to triumph, till it accomplishes a mighty desolation!"

CHAPTER VII.

Second general reason for the Abrogation—Disorders in theChurch—In the exscinded Synods—Testimony of Dr. James Wood—His character—Encroachments of Congregationalists—Cases recited, and facts to illustrate—Congregational and Presbyterial statistics—Synod of Utica—Of Geneva—Of Genesee—Of Western Reserve—Comparative numbers of both parties.

In continuing the history of Congregational encroachments upon the Presbyterian Church, we shall closely observe the narrative published by the Rev. James Wood, in a pamphlet headed,

*"To attack the Constitution of the state, and to violate its laws, is a capital crime against society; and if those guilty of it are vested with authority, they add to their crime a perfidious abuse of the power with which they are entrusted. The nation ought constantly to suppress these abuses with its utmost vigor and vigilance, as the importance of the case requires. It is very uncommon to see the constitution and laws of a state openly and boldly opposed; it it against *silent* and *slow attacks* that a nation ought to be particularly on its guard. Sudden revolutions strike the imaginations of men; we write histories of them and unfold their causes. But we neglect the changes that insensibly happen, by a long train of steps, that are but

"Facts and observations concerning the organization and state of the Churches in the three Synods of Western New York, and the Synod of Western Reserve, printed Saratoga Springs, 1837." In the correctness of Mr. Wood's statements, the fullest confidence may be placed. He was a native of the settlements in question; he witnessed himself a great portion of what he records; he is a man of great moderation, and of incorruptible truth and integrity. With toil and sacrifice, he explored the region lying west to the lakes and far beyond, to collect the appropriate and convincing facts embodied in his pamphlet of about forty-eight pages. On the thirty-sixth page of this pamphlet, we find the following remark: "The Plan was originally intended, not as the medium through which Congregationalism would be perpetuated in the Presbyterian Church, but to give opportunity for Congregationalists (if, after learning the character of our system, they approved of it,) to become Presbyterians. This remark applies to both parties in the arrangement. The ministers of Connecticut were favorable to the Presbyterian form of government; one feature of it was already in existence in their churches, and they felt willing, not to say desirous, to have their people who should emigrate to other states, become Presbyterian. Dr. McAuley, in a speech on this subject, 1826, had said, 'As to the union, they had said, that it had not been gone into for their accommodation, but for ours; that they had agreed to it for two reasons; first, because it was a help to many New England people, in the infant settlements, towards obtaining gospel ordinances; and secondly, because it assisted the Assembly in spreading Presbyterianism through that region.'" But, instead of spreading Presbyterianism, Dr. Wood goes on to say, "it has, in a large number of cases, spread Congregationalism under the Presbyterian name. Presbyteries have not only been formed of Congregational materials, but with an express stipulation that they might always remain so, and yet continue in the Presbyterian Church. And then, by such a *construction* of the *Plan of Union* as was never intended by the original framers, they claimed the right of sending commissioners, who were not ruling elders, to the General Assembly. Accordingly," Dr. Wood continues, "in 1826, a commissioner who was not a ruling elder, from Rochester Presbytery, was received by the Assembly, but a protest was immediately entered against it,

little observed. It would be doing an important service to nations, to show from history, how states have entirely changed their nature, and lost their original constitution. This would awaken the attention of the people, and from thence-forward, filled with the excellent maxim, no less essential in politics than in morals, '*principiis obsta*,' they would no longer shut their eyes against innovations, which, though inconsiderable in themselves, may serve as steps to mount to higher and more pernicious enterprises." Vattel, Book 1., chapter III.

signed by forty-two members. In 1831, a committee-man was received by the Assembly, as a commissioner from Grand River Presbytery, against which a protest was entered, signed by sixty-seven members." A part of this protest we shall transcribe. "The articles of agreement alluded to in the beginning of this paper," referring to the Plan of Union of 1801, "are supposed to give this individual, and all others similarly situated, a seat in this Assembly. That agreement is altogether anomalous to our form of government, and so far as it does extend, is in derogation of it. Those articles can never cover this case."

Although the Assembly received the commissioner above referred to, they adopted a resolution that the appointment, by some Presbyteries, as has occurred in a few cases, of members of standing committees, to be members of General Assembly, is inexpedient and of questionable constitutionality, and therefore, ought not, in future, to be made; yet the very next year, the *same Presbytery* delegated *two committee-men* as commissioners to the Assembly; but their commissions, after being placed in the hands of a committee, were withdrawn.

At the same meeting, there was a commissioner from a Presbytery in Western New York, who was neither an elder nor a committee-man; nobody present being acquainted with the circumstance, he was received. The next year a committee-man appeared from the Presbytery of Oswego, and would have been received, as his commission did not specify his true character; but one of the members, who had incidentally become acquainted with the fact, made it known to the house, when leave was given him to withdraw his commission. "These facts," observes Dr. Wood, most justly, "are introduced to show with what tenacity those Presbyteries which were formed in pursuance of the Plan of Union, adhered to the practice of sending up commissioners, even after the Assembly had adopted a resolution against it. In connexion with these facts, let it be remembered, that the churches formed on the Plan of Union, had become very numerous; that their feelings and policy were at variance with strict Presbyterial order; that, in many instances, doctrines were held which are inconsistent with our standards; and that, claiming a right from the provisions of the plan, to be represented in the General Assembly, they had well nigh obtained an ascendancy in that body, and were rapidly bringing about a revolution in the church."

DISORDER.

The following record will exhibit the manner in which the three ejected Synods, Utica, Geneva, and Genesee, were originally constituted, and the materials out of which they were made. A minute detail of this process, however interesting, would be tedious and exceed our limits, as it would require a transcript of nearly the whole of Dr. Wood's pamphlet, the Western Memorial and other documents. We shall restrict ourselves to a few particular instances of disorder, and a statistical summary of the whole.

Synod of Utica.

The Synod of Utica was constituted in 1829, by a division of the Synod of Albany, and contains five Presbyteries, Oneida, Watertown, Otsego, St. Lawrence, and Oswego. Some of these have changed names since the Synodical organization. That we may form some idea of the rapid and incessant changes occurring in these new settlements, take a brief sketch of the Presbytery of Oneida, formed by the General Assembly of 1802, out of the Presbytery of Albany, and consisting then of six ministers. In 1803, they reported seventeen churches, eight of which were probably Presbyterian. In 1805, they reported twenty churches, two of which were Congregational, received on the Plan of 1801. The next year, they reported only eight churches, the others having been detached to form the Presbytery of Geneva. One of the eight is Congregational. From this time, there was a gradual increase till 1816, when the Presbytery was again divided, and a new one formed by the name of St. Lawrence (now Watertown.) But their loss here was much more than made up in 1819, by the reception of twelve ministers and nine congregations, all Congregational, and from Congregational associations.

The same year (1819,) this Presbytery was again divided, and a new one constituted, by the name of Otsego. During the three years following, they received nine Congregational Churches, which restored their number at the expense of their purity. In the year 1822, another division took place, and a new Presbytery arose out of the confusion, by the name of Oswego. In this proportion, and subject to similar fluctuations, they have gone on to the present time. This is a faint sample of the Presbyterianism, in organization and in operation, which prevails in the Synod of Utica. We suppose the reader will be sufficiently instructed, after inspecting the statistical table, to dismiss this district from farther review.

Presbyteries.	Churches.	Presbyterian.	Congregational.
Oneida,	40	27	13
Watertown,	23		
Otsego,	16	8	8
St. Lawrence,	11		
Oswego,	25	8	17
Total as far as known,	115	43	38

(See Dr. Wood's pamphlet.)

Synod of Geneva.

The Synod of Geneva was constituted by a division of the Synod of Albany, in 1812. It then consisted of three Presbyteries, Geneva, Cayuga, and Onondaga, to which the following have since been added: Bath, Cortland, Chenango, Tioga, Delaware and Chemung. The Presbytery of Geneva was formed from a part of the Presbytery of Oneida, in 1805, and consisted of four ministers. After many changes and much increase, in 1814 they reported thirty-one churches, five of which, at least, were Congregational. A report of 1811 shows that the Presbytery of Cayuga had fifteen congregations, and the Presbytery of Onondaga thirteen. Within the eight following years, these Presbyteries, taken together, had more than doubled. Cayuga reported, in 1819, twenty-eight congregations; Onondaga twenty-nine. Their increase in number was owing to the dissolution of the Onondaga Association, the ministers and churches belonging to which joined these two Presbyteries. But while it augmented their numbers, it increased their unsoundness in full proportion, for they were all Congregational. The Presbytery of Cortland was organized from the Presbytery of Onondaga, in 1825. In their first report, 1827, they had fourteen churches, seven Congregational, and a large portion of the others most probably of the same character. See minutes of the Assembly for 1814–1818–1825, from which it will appear that nearly all these churches had their origin in the Middle Association, or bear other marks of Congregationalism. The Presbytery of Tioga was formed from the Presbytery of Cayuga, in 1829. In the following year they reported fourteen churches, five of which were Congregational; and it may be inferred from the character of the Presbytery out of which it was formed, that the remaining number were of this description.

The Presbytery of Delaware was formed from Chenango in 1831, and consisted, according to their first report, of fourteen churches, nearly all of which were undoubtedly Congregational.

The character of the Synod of Geneva may be fairly presented in the following tabular view:

Presbyteries.	Churches.	Presbyterian.	Congregational.
Geneva,	39	38	1
Cayuga,	31		
Onondaga,	24		
Bath,	19	17	2
Cortland,	15	8	7
Chenango,	19	5	14
Tioga,	18	9	9
Delaware,	19	10	9
Chemung,	22	22	
Total as far as known,	206	109	42

Synod of Genesee.

This Synod was constituted in 1821, by a division of the Synod of Geneva, and consisted of four Presbyteries, Niagara, Genesee, Rochester, and Ontario, to which Buffalo and Angelica have since been added. In this Synod, as in all the others, great changes have taken place; new Presbyteries have been formed, divisions and detachments ordered.

The Presbytery of Buffalo was constituted from the Presbytery of Niagara, in 1822-3, and was composed principally of Congregational Churches. In 1831, they reported thirty-four churches, at which time there were not more than six or eight Presbyterian Churches in the Presbytery. At present (1837,) there are about twelve Presbyterian and eight Congregational. If the ratio of these should prove the same as that of the others, there are seventeen Presbyterian and twenty-six Congregational. The following is a summary of the whole:

Presbyteries.	Churches.	Presbyterian.	Congregational.
Niagara,	16	12	4
Genesee,	26	20	6
Rochester,	29	24	5
Ontario,	24	18	6
Buffalo,	43	17	26
Angelica,	18	12	6
	156	103	53

This preponderance of Presbyterial numbers over Congregational, Dr. Wood writes, is rather nominal than real. In Niagara, Rochester, and Genesee Presbyteries, there exist many dissatisfactions among the people, with regard to their ecclesiastical connexion, which threaten, with speed and certainty, to increase Congregational extension and influence.

Synod of the Western Reserve.

The origin of that Synod, as published in the Ohio Observer, is as follows: The Presbytery of Grand River, agreeably to the order of the Synod of Pittsburgh, was organized in the autumn of 1814. This Presbytery, and the Presbyteries of Portage and Huron, which were organized soon after, drew up articles adapted to their circumstances, and to carry out the *Plan of Union* of 1801. These Congregationalists, for so they were without exception, having been early taught the Westminster Assembly's Shorter Catechism, which was prevalent in New England among their fathers, were inclined to the Calvinistic system, and found but little difficulty in agreeing to approve the Confession of Faith and discipline of the Presbyterian Church, in the United States of America; but in their constitution, they incorporate particulars designed to carry out the Plan of Union, to which allusion is here so often made. The leading and fatal feature of their plan was, that their ministers and churches may adopt either the Congregational or Presbyterian mode of government and discipline, and that this article or provision shall be of perpetual obligation. The ministers and people really seemed to believe that they were not only permitted, but bound to establish this point, and pledge themselves mutually to each other to maintain and observe it. The Synod of Pittsburgh, at the period of receiving records, as a matter of courtesy and expediency, in dealing with those new settlements, not only connived at this unconstitutional excrescence, but actually approved it. Thus did the Synod of Pittsburgh, in 1815, ratify the mischievous Plan adopted by the General Assembly in 1801. In 1819, the records of the Presbytery of Portage, and 1824, the records of the Presbytery of Huron, each containing the same features, passed through the same process, and received the same sanction. By the Assembly of 1825, a new Synod was formed out of the Synod of Pittsburgh, to consist of the three Presbyteries situated chiefly in New Connecticut, Grand River, Portage, and Huron, which was to be called the Synod of Western Reserve. It was accordingly organized at Hudson, September 27, 1825.

There are at present in this Synod, according to statements made at the Auburn Convention, thirty-one Presbyterian Churches. At the same time, a member of the Presbytery of Grand River expressed a doubt whether there is a single Presbyterian Church in that Presbytery. It was stated, on the floor of the last General Assembly, by members of that Synod, that Trumbull Presbytery and Medina, each contained but one Presbyterian Church. The feelings of the people are decidedly in favor of Congregationalism. They avow it, and manifest it without reserve. After the meeting of the General Assembly of 1835, a plan was drawn up by several ministers, to change the order of the church, and a convention was called to execute the plan, but, through the *influence of Dr. Beecher* and others, this was deferred. In the fall of 1836, another convention was called for the same purpose, and an association was formed. This measure was opposed by several ministers present. One of them, to justify his opposition, alleged, that if *they would put it off another year, the New School would have the majority in the General Assembly*, in which case the Old School would probably secede, and then they would have the ground. This minister was a member of the Auburn Convention, and advocated sending up commissioners to the General Assembly, "to fight every inch of ground." This is not the first indication of their revolutionary designs.

It is too prolix to attempt a full development of Congregationalism in this manner. Before we present the tabular statement of this Synod, the reader will permit us to insert one of the deceptive artifices employed by the advocates of the Congregationalists, to forward their secret and hostile plans against the Presbyterian Church. After the Assembly had passed a resolution refusing to receive committee-men as commissioners, the Presbytery of Grand River, in order to obtain place in the Assembly for a layman whose seat would not be disputed, appointed a man who had been a ruling elder in the state of New York, though he was then at the time of his appointment, a member of a Congregational Church in Ohio. Thus the New School party, operating by all manner of means, encouraged themselves in their unrighteous work, and were frequently heard to say, "that they are reforming the Presbyterian Church, working out the old leaven, &c., and that in a few years more they will succeed."

Presbyteries.	Churches.	Presbyterian.	Congregational.
Grand River,	35	2	33
Portage,	24	3	21
Huron,	25	15	10
Maumee,	8	2	6
Trumbull,	18	2	16
Lorain,	12	2	10
Cleveland,	10	4	6
Medina,	13	2	11
Total,	145	32	113

It has been said that the modification of the Plan of 1801, by the Synod of Albany, in her act of 1808, warranted the Northern Association to claim a connexion with the Presbyterian Church. But in reply to this assertion, nothing more is necessary, than to say that the act of the Synod of Albany, 1808, was as unconstitutional and irregular as the Assembly's act of 1801.

To give a bird's-eye glance at the irregular additions and encroachments here recited, as prevalent in the four exscinded Synods, let us exhibit a summary of their statistics:

Presbyterian Congregations, 287; Congregational, 246.

Here it appears that the two contending parties are very nearly equally balanced. The intruders into the church under the alienating influence of Congregational sympathy, exerting all their skill and power to acquire complete ascendancy in the four Synods, and even in the General Assembly. The uncontaminated portion of these Synods make a reasonable but vain resistance to these anti-Presbyterian schemes and measures.

The facts here presented prove that a large proportion of those reported as Presbyterian, are chiefly Congregational. They have just left the Church of their fathers; some are anxious to return to it; others are actively engaged in laying schemes to get back; some are held in their Presbyterian connexion by the hope of making larger conquests among them, if they remain; others hang on, determined, as they say, "to fight every inch of ground," in the anticipation of a complete triumph. This is the fruit of the *Plan of Union* of 1801. This picture drawn from real life, reflects somewhat the real character of this great and extensive district of Christ's earthly kingdom. At this stage, who can tell what is to be the result of this mixed, morbid, semi-revolutionary ecclesiastical exhibition? Behold the changes daily occurring. With what facility and despatch do they emigrate, they march, they countermarch, they change name, church relations and ties fly asunder, pastors and people are ever on the wing. Violations (see p. 42,) of church order, infractions, or perfect disregard of principles and rules most plain, most positive, most essential, most solemnly assumed, are unscrupulously set at nought. What a beautiful picture this scene presents! What delightful Christian harmony, purity, and comfort! Such is the result of attempting to make Congregational and Presbyterian men live together in one church, under such a Plan of Union as that of 1801.

CHAPTER VIII.

Doctrinal errors stated as existing in the exscinded Synods—The facts here presented, from Dr. Wood's pamphlet—Synod of Utica—Synod of Geneva—Synod of Genesee—Of Western Reserve.

THESE errors are introduced as specimens of the false theology actually in circulation through the congregations of the exscinded Synods.

For the truth of these statements we shall appeal again to the faithful witness, the pamphlet of Dr. James Wood, freely used upon another topic preceding.

We begin with the Synod of *Utica*, observing simply that the facts here presented refer to the third ground of our vindication.

In the words of Dr. Wood, "As we do not wish to incur the charge of circulating vague reports, we shall specify some particulars. There is probably a majority, in all these bodies, who are opposed to those extreme views in doctrine. But their existence among them shows that there is cause for alarm; and the length of time during which they have prevailed affords proof of culpable lenity, on the part of those who disapprove of them, in not bringing their abettors (except in a few instances,) under ecclesiastical censure."

"During my excursion I had an interview with a layman of some intelligence and standing in society, who, until a short time past, has been a member for ten or twelve years of one of the churches in Oneida Presbytery, but is now connected with a church in the Presbytery of Oswego. He said he believed Adam sinned because God could not prevent him without altering his plan of government. I replied, if God could not prevent Adam from falling, can he prevent Christians from falling? He answered, no; if they resolve not to be influenced by the motives which he presents to encourage them to persevere, I believe Christians may all fall away. He said, he did not believe in the imputation of Adam's sin, or that we were born sinners, but that when we are born we are destitute of moral character. In regard to conversion, he said, there are some things which God cannot do for the sinner; they are the sinner's own acts and not God's. He commands the sinner to repent and make to himself a new heart, and he can do it if he *will*. He was told he can do it by the assistance of God's spirit. He replied, I will not say this, though I admit the Holy Spirit has an agency in the conversion of the sinner. He was asked, what kind of agency? Just such agency, said he, as I should exert over you in persuading you to go to Rome. I observed to him, you might fail in persuading me to go to Rome. So may God fail, said he, of the conversion of the sinner. God is as dependent upon the sinner in his conversion, as the sinner is upon God. The moment in which a sinner is converted, he said, the sinner is holy; he is right; he is just as God requires him to be; he loves God with all the heart, and soul, and strength, and mind, and he might continue in this state if he would, but he yields to temptation and so falls into sin. I asked him if the church, to which he formerly belonged, held as he did. He answered, yes. And does the minister of that church believe and preach so? He replied, yes. I have had long conversations with him, and have met with nobody that so nearly accords with my sentiments as he does, except brother ———.

"Perfectionism exists to some extent in several churches in the Oswego Presbytery. In one of them it prevails to such a degree that their pastor, after endeavoring in vain for several months to resist the current, has given up in discouragement, and removed to another congregation. It is not countenanced by the ministers, but is regarded with some favor by a considerable number of the people. Some of the ministers, however, though opposed to perfectionism, embrace the New Haven theology. In several of them, we could specify individuals who are known to be favorable to that system. And in regard to others, we have authority for saying, that the views of Dr. Taylor are more or less prevalent.

"In the spring of 1833, I became acquainted with a licentiate of a Congregational Association, who was desirous of entering the Presbyterian Church. After conversing with him for an hour, I told him frankly, but kindly, that I hoped he never would seek admission into our church; that, in my opinion, a man entertaining his views, could not, with propriety, subscribe our standards. Shortly after, he was ordained by an association, and settled over a church connected with us, on the accommodation plan, in the Presbytery of Watertown. He is now a member of the Presbytery of Oneida. Some time after, he wrote a letter to a friend, in part as follows: 'For my part, I am awfully prejudiced against the Old School divinity. I cannot invite a man to preach for me whose doctrines are so utterly repugnant to the word of God. I do not here speak of Mr. Wood at all, but of a certain class of men, such as for instance, the individuals near me. Dr. Sprague of Albany, I mean, and old Dr. Green, of Philadelphia, and Dr. Griffin, and Miller, and Alexander, &c., &c. Have you seen Dr. Sprague's Book on Revivals? O! I am afraid that man will ruin souls in hell by that pernicious book. I want you candidly to answer the following questions. Do you believe infants have a moral character? Are we to be accountable for the moral acts of our first parents? What do you think of the New Haven theology? Do you acquiesce in Dr. Taylor's notions? Do you consider agreeable with the scriptures? His divinity is spreading very widely.' In Oneida Presbytery, a majority of ministers are disposed to do all they can to correct the errors of the past." *Dr. Wood's Pamphlet*, pp. 12, 13, 14.

Synod of Geneva.

Writing in regard to some of the Presbyteries, Dr. Wood remarks: "To show the jealousy which they feel towards Presbyterianism," he said, "the pastor of one of the churches proposed, as the first article of a Confession of Faith for that church, that they adopt the *Confession of Faith* of the *Presbyterian Church, as containing the system of doctrines* taught in the *sacred scriptures;* but it was rejected, not because the church did not approve of our Confession of Faith, but because they regarded it as the first step towards endeavoring to make them Presbyterians. A letter which was first published in the Hartford Christian Watchman, soon after the meeting of the last Assembly, and which is understood to have been written by a member of the Cortland Presbytery, contains the following: 'I declared more than once before the Assembly, that the errors against which the

Convention (1837) testified, do exist. In my views of the existence of those errors, and of the *duty of condemning* them, I presume at least one half of the delegation from the interior of New York, coincide.' 'In a few churches, in several of the Presbyteries, perfectionism has prevailed to a greater or less extent. In 1833, a very laudable zeal was manifested in endeavouring to prevent the errors and extravagancies of Mr. Myrick, and they also entered a complaint against him to the Oneida Presbytery. The Presbyteries of Cayuga and Onondaga issued a circular warning the churches against him.' Here follow some things concerning this Mr. Myrick, worthy of notice. 1st. His entering other congregations, and holding protracted meetings, without the consent of either pastor or church. 2d. Irreverent praying, such as 'God smite the devil,' 'God smite the whited sepulchres,' 'Jesus Christ come down here and attend to these hard cases,' accompanied by loud groaning, leaping, stamping, smiting hands and fists, pounding on the floor, &c. 3d. Profane language, such as 'you are black as hell,' 'wicked as hell,' 'proud as hell,' 'damned devils,' 'the devil is in you,' 'hell hardened.' 4th. Abusive treatment of professed christians and ministers, who did not unite with him. He called them 'the children of the devil,' 'drone bees in God's hive,' 'too cursed lazy to work,' 'fattening on the blood of damned souls.' 5th. Erroneous doctrines. He says, 'the Holy Ghost never operates on impenitent sinners; that the sinner does not need the spirit in order to repent; that all such professors as have any remaining sin are not born of God, but are going to hell; that real Christians do fall into this impenitent state and go to hell,' &c., and many more similar delusions. 6th. He denounces in strong terms, all creeds, confessions of faith, commentaries on the Bible, and systems of divinity. Is it not astonishing and lamentable that such blasphemous stuff as this, should be tolerated within its bounds by any Presbytery? This heretical monster, in 1837, was the editor of a paper, and by that means, as well as by his impious babbling, was propagating his corrupt opinions. With what degree of success, it is considered very difficult to form any correct opinion." *Wood's Pamphlet*, pp. 20, 22, 23.

Synod of Genesee.

"There have been material departures among many in this Synod, from the old orthodox times, and this has been accompanied, in some instances, by measures of a very doubtful character, and in others by such as were wild and extravagant." A member of the Buffalo Presbytery writes thus: "Ministers and churches in this Presbytery have become so much disposed to favor Arminian doctrines, and are so fond of new things, that it is *difficult to preach the doctrines of our Confession*, or even to use our endeavours to correct abuses and extravagances in measures, without hearing the cry of, Old School, opposed to revivals, &c. That Presbytery, some time ago, adopted a set of articles of faith, for the use of their churches, from which almost everything distinguishing is excluded. Among other points is that of infant baptism; and hence, in practice, it is left optional with parents to have their children baptized or not, just as they please. This last article has been erased from the Confession of several of the churches in Genesee Presbytery; not by the sanction of the Presbytery, so much as through the influence of one of their members." "An intelligent and pious man told me, concerning a minister in Niagara Presbytery, under whose preaching he sat for several months, that he heard him say he did not believe in the imputation of Adam's sin; and on one occasion, he almost ridiculed the idea of the special influences of the Holy Spirit." One of the ministers in Genesee Presbytery, and a part of his church, are perfectionists. He believes it essential to a man's being a Christian, to be perfect. When a Christian sins, he *un*-Christians himself, and consequently a Christian remaining such cannot commit sin. A spice of perfectionism is found in several of the churches, which, though small, is enough to embitter the comfort of their Christian brethren.

In relation to irregularities, a member of the Rochester Presbytery affirmed publicly at their meeting, some time last summer, that there was but one thing mentioned of this kind on the floor of the last Assembly, but what can be proved to have occurred, within a short period of time, in the bounds of the Genesee Synod. Another member of the same Presbytery, in private conversation, corroborated his statement, and went still farther, by saying that *worse* things had occurred there than any which had been alluded to on the floor of the Assembly. In some Presbyteries, the people are sounder than the ministers, of which I had in two or three cases ample proof. Though ministers are set for the defence of the gospel, the people form *the sacramental host* and will often stand firm, even though the *standard bearer fainteth*. They are the pillars of the church, which will remain unshaken, though the priest at the altar should *be spoiled through philosophy and vain deceit*." pp. 26, 7, 8.

Synod of Western Reserve.

"A few years ago, Congregational ministers were frequently received into their Presbyteries, at least into some of them, without answering the constitutional questions; but of late, since the practice was censured by the General Assembly, the constitutional questions have generally, and perhaps always, been propounded." "A majority of the ministers and of the members, in most of the churches, accord in doctrine and measures with Mr. Finney. This is inferred, concerning the ministers, from the fact that about two years ago, a paper was signed by fifty ministers, or more, inviting Mr. Finney to become professor of theology in the Western Reserve College; and concerning ministers and people both, it may be inferred from the fact that Mr. Lucius Foote has attended protracted meetings pretty extensively on the Reserve, and was generally approved by the ministers and churches. Mr. Foote, it is said, agrees substantially with Mr. Finney, but goes farther than the latter, in some points, from what is called Old School Theology."

The result of this examination is, that at least one half, probably a greater proportion, of the four disowned Synods, are in church government, Congregational; and in theological opinion, far removed from the standards of the Presbyterian Church.

Additional intelligence confirming the preceding statements may be derived from the following article, No. 4, of a series published in the Presbyterian, A. D. 1834, "On the state and prospects of the Presbyterian Church," viz:

"That heresy exists in the Presbyterian Church, is manifest. But since it is questioned by some, we shall adduce additional evidence. We consider it somewhat unaccountable that real doubts on this subject should remain in the minds of any who have observed, with common penetration and candour, the condition of the church for years past, conversed with ministers and candidates, attended the judicatories of the church, looked into the histories of their transactions, read the periodicals, printed sermons, and religious journals of the present day, studied the characters of various Theological Seminaries, their Professors, and the opinions expressed, and correspondence conducted by them. These have been before the public eye in diversified forms, furnishing evidence of error so irresistable, that we had supposed not even the most obtuse and slow of heart to believe, could hesitate.

"In the history and detection of heresy, denial, concealment, and evasion, have always been popular and perplexing resorts. These artifices were practised, not only by the arch-heretics Arius, Pelagius, Arminius, and Socinus, but by all their ephemeral cotemporaries, and successors in error. We are aware, that the plea 'not guilty,' from the mouth of the adversary of truth, when brought to the bar, has had its effect with the American public, and the church. It has damped the ardour, and palsied the action of some who profess to be truth-men, and produced temporary suspense in the work of honest inquiry. It is painful to think unfavorably of men professing religion, and placed as lights in the world, but the honest hour has come, the season of reaction has arrived, the mask must be stripped off, whatever deformities and horrors may be exposed. Careful investigation and calm reflection, have proved decisively that there is no mistake in this matter. Let the church and the world judge of the fact, from the incidental and direct evidence produced.

"The first class of errors mentioned in the 'Act and Testimony,' respects our relation to Adam, and asserts, 'That we have no more to do with the first sin of Adam, than with the sins of any other parent.' Barnes' sermon, page 5—7. Duffield on Regeneration, 287—393. With this, compare Confession of Faith. chapter vi., section 3. 'They (our first parents,) being the root of all mankind, the guilt of this sin (i. e. eating the forbidden fruit,) was imputed, and the same death in sin, and corrupted nature, conveyed to all their posterity.'

"The second error recited, is the following: 'That there is no such thing as original sin; that infants come into the world as perfectly free from corruption of nature, as Adam was when he was created; that, by original sin, nothing more is meant, than the fact that all the posterity of Adam, though born entirely free from moral defilement, will always begin to sin when they begin to exercise moral agency, and that this fact is somehow connected with the fall of Adam.' Barnes' sermon, 5—7. Duffield on Regeneration, 283—394. Dr. Beecher's sermon, National Preacher, Vol. II., p. 12. See Confession of Faith, chap. vi , sec. 3, above, also chap. vi., sec. 2. 'By this sin, (eating the forbidden fruit,) they (our first parents,) fell from their original righteousness and communion with God, and so became dead in sin, and wholly defiled in all the faculties and parts of soul and body.'

"3. 'That the doctrine of imputed sin and imputed righteousness, is a novelty, and is nonsense.' Barnes' sermon, 5—6. Duffield on Regeneration. Compare Confession of Faith, chap. vi., sec. 2, 3, above; also chap. xi., sec. 1. 'Those whom God effectually calleth, he also freely justifieth, not for any thing wrought in them, or done by them, but for Christ's sake alone; not by imputing faith itself, the act of believing, or any other evangelical obedience to them, as their righteousness, but by imputing the obedience and satisfaction of Christ unto them.'

"4. 'That the impenitent sinner is by nature, and independently of the aid of the Holy Spirit, in full possession of all the powers necessary to a compliance with the commands of God, and that, if he labored under any kind of inability, natural or moral, which he could not remove himself, he would be excusable for not complying with God's will.' Barnes' sermon, p. 14. Beman's fourth sermon, p. 119—120. Duffield on Regeneration. Dr. Coxe's sermon. Beecher's sermon on Dependance and Free Agency, p. 9—37. See Confession of Faith, chap. vi., sec. 4. 'From this original corruption, whereby we are utterly indisposed, disabled, and made opposite to all good, and wholly inclined to all evil, do proceed all actual transgressions.' Also chap. ix., sec. 3. 'Man by his fall into a state of sin, hath wholly lost all ability of will to any spiritual good accompanying salvation, so as a natural man being altogether averse to that which is good, and dead in sin, is not able, by his own strength, to convert himself, or to prepare himself thereunto.'

"5. 'That man's regeneration is his own act; that it consists merely in the change of our governing purpose, which change, we must of ourselves produce.' Duffield on Regeneration, 200—231. See Confession of Faith, chap. x., sec. 1. 'Taking away their heart of stone, and giving unto them a heart of flesh, by his Almighty power, determining them unto that which is good.' Also, sec. 2. 'Not from anything at all forseen in man; *who is altogether passive therein*, until being quickened and renewed by the Holy Spirit, he is thereby enabled to answer this call.'

"6. 'That God cannot exert such an influence on the minds of men, as to make it certain that they will choose and act in a particular manner, without destroying their moral agency; and that in a moral system, God could not prevent the existence of sin, however much he might desire it.'

"This doctrine is extensively circulated through the Christian Spectator, a work emanating from the Theological School at New Haven; a school in which a number of young men have been educated, who are now ministers in our church, and who, as there is every reason to believe, maintain the doctrines of their teachers. The speculation in itself is rash, unauthorized and presumptuous, and as related to the system of which it forms a part, is dangerous. It decides upon the extent of the Divine power, without any warrant from the word of God, and is thus opposed to the spirit of our standards.

"7. 'That Christ's sufferings were not truly and properly vicarious.'—Beman's sermons, &c. Confession of Faith, chap. viii., sec. 5. 'The Lord Jesus by his perfect obedience and sacrifice of himself, which he, through the Eternal Spirit, once offered up unto God, hath fully satisfied the justice of his Father, and purchased not only reconciliation, but an everlasting inheritance in the kingdom of heaven, for all those whom the Father hath given unto him.' Sec. 8. 'Making intercession for them.' Chap. xi., sec. 3. 'Christ by his obedience and death, did fully discharge the debt of all those that are thus justified, and did make a proper, real and full satisfaction to his Father's justice, in their behalf.' Sec. 4. 'Christ did in the fullness of time die for their sins.'

"A careful consideration of this statement will satisfy any unprejudiced man, that the opinions referred to in the 'Act and Testimony,' are held by ministers in the Presbyterian church, and that they are contrary to the Confession of Faith. It would be a useless expenditure of time, to show that they are as palpably at war with the Bible. The extent to which they are held, is to be learned more from the acknowledgments and pulpit instructions of those who maintain them, than from their published writings, as few comparatively commit their thoughts to the press. To ascertain the extent to which they have spread, is the ultimate object proposed by the Act and Testimony. However novel these errors may appear to many in the present day, to those acquainted with the history of the Christian church, they are not new. On examination, they will be found to be only ancient forms of error, revived and new moddelled. There is probably no surer method of impressing the public mind with a sense of the reality and pernicious tendency of these opinions, than that of showing their identity, with glaring and destructive heresies, which at various periods have invaded the church.

"Early in the fifth century, the Pelagians held the following sentiments: 'That there is no such thing as original sin—That Adam's guilt did not descend to his posterity—That all mankind are born in the same state of perfection with their great primogenitor—That man may, by the native exertion of his own faculties, be inclined to what is good, and able to perform it, without the direct assistance of divine grace, and that men may arrive to such a pitch of holines, as to be no more subject to the dominion of sin.'—Nesbit's Church History, Edinburg, 8vo. p. 80. In confirmation of this, for the satisfaction of those who may not find it convenient to refer to original authorities, we add the testimony of Mosheim, Church History, 2 vol. 8vo. p. 84. 'These monks, (Pelagius and his disciple Cœlestius,) looked upon the doctrines which were commonly received, concerning the original corruption of human nature, and the necessity of divine grace, to enlighten the understanding and purify the heart, as prejudicial to the progress of holiness and virtue, and tending to lull mankind into a presumptuous and fatal security. They maintained, that these doctrines were as false as they were pernicious, that the sins of our first parents were imputed to *them alone*, and not to their posterity; that we derive no corruption from their fall, but are born as pure and unspotted as Adam came out of the forming hand of his Creator; that mankind, therefore, are capable of repentance and amendment, and of arriving to the highest degrees of piety and virtue, by the use of their natural faculties and powers. That indeed external grace is necessary to excite their endeavours, but that they have no need of internal succours of the Divine Spirit.' These anti-scriptural motives were propagated in Rome, in Sicily, in Africa, and Palestine, deeply afflicting the church wherever they went. At last they were arrested in their course, by the counsel of Ephesus, repressed by several successive councils, and denounced by the authority of Imperial edicts.

"The most prominent of these errors were presented afresh by the Arminians in the sixteenth century, under a very imposing garb. And now our hitherto pure and peaceful church, is writhing under a similar calamitous visitation. How striking the coincidence between New School divinity, and the ancient heresies, which we see Christian orators and philosophers, evangelic councils and emperors, conspiring with holy zeal to detect and suppress! And are these errors less appalling now than then? Is the church less precious? Have the souls of men dwindled into cyphers? Heaven and hell become a chimera, that they may be so lightly sported with?—that the stupendous scheme of salvation which God revealed—which Christ achieved—which angels sang—which millions of sanctified ones have gone to inherit, should be so sedulously, so tranquilly, almost without observation, metamorphosed into an ignoble, dark, and wretched device of human caprice, and passion, and power!

"What the learned and pious historian Joseph Milner declares of Pelagianism in the fifth century, we affirm of it in the nineteenth; 'That it seems little more than a revival of deism, or what is commonly called natural religion!' Eccl. Hist. vol. 2, p. 361. And shall the church still slumber—the watchmen on the walls of Zion fold their arms and say peace, peace! Let the intelligent and serious carefully examine the nature and bearing of these tenets, and they cannot fail to pronounce them diametrically opposed both to the letter and spirit of the gospel. If there are any doctrines truly fundamental and absolutely indispensable in our system of faith, they are the very opposite to those denounced in the 'Act and Testimony.'

"The sufficiency of human reason, in matters of religion, is, evidently, the stale and untenable basis upon which this antichristian scheme is built. This was the foundation selected by ancient heathen philosophers, by primitive heretics, and modern rationalists. In these delusive vagaries they all agree. That man is not inherently depraved—that his powers of mind and body are adequate to all his wants and duties—that the idea of dependence upon the merit of another for justification, or the enlightening and renovating influence of God himself, for sanctification, is repugnant to human reason, inconsistent with human liberty and moral obligation. Thus the whole plan of the gospel, is inverted and outraged. The ruined, wretched creature man, is depicted as harmless and all-sufficient, buoyed up with delusive ideas of safety, while reposing on himself, and inflated with pride and self-trust. Thus the eternal God of wisdom, sovereignty and grace, is called to the bar of the presumptuous, vain-glorious speculator, robbed of his honour, and 'Christ is made light of.'

"These heretical notions, not only affect the soundness of our doctrinal views, but the moral purity, the vital godliness of the great body of the people. They are demoralizing in their influence on the human mind. The gospel will ever be lightly esteemed by those who are taught to believe, that they are not deeply depraved creatures, 'exceeding sinful,' altogether helpless and in need of divine succour. 'The whole need not a physician, but they that are sick.' The thought, that human faculties and powers are of themselves sufficient to arrest the progress of sinful desire and action—to turn the heart to God—and produce the important change from sin to holiness, must necessarily tend to inspire indifference to the gospel, awaken a feeling of independence on God, and such an inflating self-confidence, as will deeply impair the force of the sacred, transforming, and endearing ties of moral obligation, and for ever exclude evangelic humiliation, love and truth. Indeed, the whole scheme seems admirably contrived to counteract the heavenly design and saving influence of the gospel of Christ.

"We ask, in the spirit of honest anxiety, are we prepared to receive these noxious speculations as a substitute for the beloved gospel and our excellent summary—to teach them to our children—to introduce them into our Sabbath schools—to incorporate them in our tracts—to send them to the destitute? Is the Presbyterian Church prepared to give entrance to such principles into her Theological Seminaries—to place men who hold them, in her Theological Professorships—to have her hundreds of intelligent, pious candidates for the ministry, the beneficiaries of the church, and the hope of the world, poisoned with such infidel dogmas, and all her pious funds applied to their propagation and support? Are these the soul-enlightening and renovating truths on which to carry forward our glorious system of revivals and of missions? Are these the doctrines which our Saviour inculcated, which apostles preached, for which martyrs bled? Shall those ministers of our ecclesiastical communion, who, in the glowing spirit of *Reformation*, have the religious integrity and the moral courage to resist these stale heresies, by bearing testimony against them, be accounted uncharitable and persecuting? If this be persecution, I plead guilty of the charge, and glory in it.

"But the plea urged for toleration, that the propagators of these anti-christian notions, are for the most part men of age, of popular talents, and of reputed piety, is deceptive and inadmissible. That they have, to some extent, talent and character, constitutes the greatest aggravation of their guilt. The heretical opinions of Pelagius did not appear till he was far advanced in life; and Augustin, his chief antagonist, acknowledges that his previous reputation for piety was great in the Christian world.* His followers, in our church, in some cases, we admit, prostitute distinguished powers, work with a strong arm, employ, sometimes, as did Pelagius, the eloquence of *gray hairs* (*eloquar an sileam*) to enforce their ensnaring sophisms, and secure their victims. But shall they, because distinguished and even honoured in the church, well furnished and located to corrupt and destroy, be permitted to go on without a check? Did Augustin so judge and so act, in the period of the arch deceiver, Pelagius? What? the criminal arraigned to plead in mitigation of his offence, his standing and influence? This very power is chiefly to be feared, and most of all should it arouse the church. Left to itself, it spreads its fatal influence with a greater and greater degree of expansiveness, through a thousand channels, over the young, the ignorant, the credulous, and the wavering multitude. To avoid suspicion and detection, glosses and evasions may be expected, the arts of philosophy and 'the oppositions of science, falsely so called,' and all 'the deceivableness of unrighteousness,' will be tried, not only to beguile the unwary, but, 'if it were possible, to deceive the very elect.' Mat. xxiv., 24.

"A MEMBER OF NEW BRUNSWICK PRESBYTERY."

The recent introduction of Rev. Albert Barnes, with his glaring heresies, into Philadelphia, and the unhappy means employed by the New School men belonging to the ecclesiastical judicatories about that city, with which he came into contact, their spurious measures and their occasional successes, in screening him and his false doctrines from merited condemnation, justly struck alarm through the whole church, and caused the meeting of the General Assembly for 1834, to be looked for with serious apprehension. To this impression, the rapid and wide diffusion of disorder and misrule through the churches, the extensive dissemination of New School errors in doctrine, the supineness of the church in general on the subject, the laxness and neglect of several preceding General Assemblies, through the wily influence of Congregational artifice, in regard to correcting abuses, a duty which had been cogently urged upon her attention to awaken her to timely vigilance and reform, all seemed strongly conducive. The few watchmen on the walls of Zion who were awake, saw the peril thickening and the crisis approaching.

* Mil. Ch. Hist., Vol. II., p. 358.

CHAPTER IX.

Case of Albert Barnes presented—As introductory to his character and appearance, extracts from *The Crisis* are inserted—Irregular action of the General Assembly of 1834—Character of that body—Western Memorials—The report of Committee—Resolutions of Assembly—Protest by minority—Its character.

THE case of Albert Barnes was the torch applied by the New School faction in Philadelphia, to the mass of combustibles which had been accumulating in that city and its vicinity for years. The troubles he occasioned in the church were protracted and complex. An accurate detail of them would necessarily cover much paper. As a connecting link in this chain of illustration, and as the best outline we can present of that imprudent and troublesome man, we can do nothing better than transfer to these pages, some extracts from a pamphlet called *The Crisis*, published by the writer, in March, 1836, two successive editions of which were issued by Robert Carter, Esq., New York, over the author's geneological signature, *A son of the Huguenots.* The facts for this pamphlet had been on hand some time, and the work in waiting for farther developments, till the publication seemed to be imperatively demanded.

In introducing the Crisis here, we observe rather the order in which it was prepared, than that of its original publication.

THE CRISIS.

"The evils threatened to our beloved church, and the designs of her adversaries, whether partially fulfilled or still prospective, are clearly concentrated in the case of the Rev. Albert Barnes. Although it is not the object of these pages to enter directly into the controversy between him and Dr. Junkin, we cannot withhold a few passing remarks upon the *Notes on the Romans*, and the character of their author.

"No undertaking requires so many peculiar, rare, and high qualifications, as that of a sacred commentator. To this work, Mr. Barnes' capacity is by no means adapted. He does not possess the precision and accuracy of mind, the nice discrimination, the comprehensiveness of view, the age, patience, distrust of self-exemption from prejudice, extensive, various, and well-digested knowledge necessary to execute this arduous task with success. Besides, suspected as he always has been, especially since he published his sermon on the *Way of Salvation*, by a large and respectable number of his brethren who had the best means of knowing, with holding erroneous opinions, doctrines offensive to the church because at variance with her standards, and satisfied of the fact, as he appears to have been, it was certainly a very rash measure so hastily to spread before the world his crude strictures on the Romans. What has occurred, under such circumstances, could not fail to occur. The performance is very imperfect; sufficient greatly to depress, if not destroy, his reputation as a theologian and scholar in the estimation of sound and accurate men. The Apostle's profound and comprehensive arguments, either from design to misrepresent them, or from want of clear and expanded views, are exhibited, in many places, in detached and broken parts, as incoherent fragments of thought, often destitute of meaning, force, or beauty. In some of the most difficult and important passages, there is much perversion, evasion, and concealment; and, in some instances, attempts to annihilate what the learned and pious have ever pronounced to be the very essence of the sacred text. The plainest principles of Greek grammar, which every schoolboy ought to be familiar with, are set at naught; and the best established rules of exegetical exposition outraged, to make the Apostle's language tally with his expositor's preconceived opinions.

"That Mr. Barnes holds unsound doctrines is now established by his own statements and concessions; and I do most honestly declare that I never was fully satisfied of his serious criminality till I received the conviction from a careful reading of his own attempt at vindication. The very effort he makes to pervert the nature and impair the force of our ordination vows, to resolve these most sacred engagements into mere matters of form, allowing numberless reserves and departures from their letter and spirit, abrogating, at once, their solemn sanctions and binding force, gives origin to most painful suspicions; and is an enormity never before, in our land, with so much effrontery, put forth to the light; an enormity deserving the solemn consideration and rebuke of the church.

"Our strictures will be confined chiefly to Mr. Barnes' preliminary remarks in his defence, which abound with positions of the most unwarrantable nature, inasmuch as their direct tendency is to destroy the purity and peace of our church.

"The leading object of these sheets is to show design, in Mr. Barnes and his adherents, to introduce into our church corruption of doctrine and order; to evade honest investigation and constitutional trial; to mislead the public mind by uncandid and inflammatory statements; to excite odium against the truth and its advocates; in a word, to defeat judicial proceedings, and paralyze all discipline in the church, with a design to open a wide door for the entrance of every 'unclean thing.'

"In his defence against the charges of Dr. Junkin, Mr. Barnes has so far implicated the Theological Seminary at Princeton, and the Presbytery of New Brunswick, as to render necessary some statement of the opinion entertained respecting him while on trials before that judicatory. So far as the writer recollects or can ascertain now, he was considered, by those who knew him best, as a young man of pretty good parts, hopeful piety, desirous of knowledge and addicted to study, but imprudently fond of Eastern theories and speculations, tenacious of novel and doubtful opinions, often occasioning among his fellow students unprofitable and perplexing disputations; on the whole, as to his theological course, rather creating painful apprehensions than inspiring confidence. In his trials before the Presbytery, his evasive and equivocal terms, and unusual statements on some cardinal points, excited dissatisfaction in the minds of some members. But supposing, as they did, that they might have been somewhat mistaken, that the candidate might have spoken unguardedly, that he would obtain more clear and satisfactory views by age and reflection, and inclining to great moderation and indulgence, there was no open objection made to Mr. Barnes' licensure. Soon after he was transferred, for ordination, to a sister Presbytery, upon whom devolved the chief responsibility of inducting him into the sacred office.

"Here it is to be observed, that a designing, artful candidate can deceive any Presbytery. Mr. Barnes now informs us, that while at Princeton, *his views were the same as now!* If this be true, it is a serious fact, as we shall discover, a dark and melancholy chapter in his history. In his assertion, that this was *fully known*, he commits a monstrous mistake! Had he honestly and fully disclosed his opinions, as they are now *fully known*, there cannot be a doubt—fidelity to the principles and character of that pure and respectable company of Christian ministers compels the declaration—that he would assuredly have been rebuked and rejected. It is evident, from his own words, that he entered the holy office as a probationer, by such an act as ought to affect any minister's public character. We regret Mr. Barnes' reference to this Presbytery, as it imposes, to some extent, the painful duty of explanation. Even if that body, in its Presbyterial capacity, choose passively to bear the reference, some individual members feel a desire to wipe off the stigma. It is always offensive to be duped. But how uncandid and unjust does it seem to make the Presbytery responsible for a licensure which, his own words roundly aver, was obtained by double-dealing; that is, by assenting to the standards in one form, and silently and secretly intending to interpret them in another! For, as we shall see from Mr. Barnes' own account of this transaction, such is its just import.

"The plan of making secret exceptions and mental reservations in forming contracts, has always been considered by honest men as culpable and disgraceful. Our Confession condemns it, chap. xxii., sec. 4: 'An oath is to be taken in the plain and common sense of the words, *without equivocation or mental reservation!*' This dishonest course was denounced in the Assembly of 1834, which did more to favour heresy than any preceding General Assembly, viz: 'Resolved, that in receiving and adopting the formularies of our church, every person ought to be supposed, without evidence to the contrary, to receive and adopt them according to the *obvious, known,* and *established meaning of the terms,* as *the confession of his faith;* and that if objections be made, the Presbytery, unless he withdraw such objections, should not license, or ordain, or admit him.' Ex. p. 26. The Presbytery of New Brunswick, in taking Mr. Barnes' solemn engagement, really believed he was receiving and adopting the Confession of Faith according to the obvious, known, and established meaning of its terms. But Mr. Barnes now discloses something widely different. 'The *system* of doctrines contained in the *standards,* I received *as a system.* I received it, *not indeed ever expressing my assent to every expression and form of expression,* but as *reserving* to myself *the right,* in common with *all others,* of *examining* the language, and *forming an opinion* of its meaning.' This is in direct violation of the above extracts from the Confession of Faith and the minutes of the Assembly. Mr. Barnes here takes a position, we think, far in advance of the main body of troublesome intruders into our church. They have practised this artifice, been suspected of it, been charged with it, but from fear of public opinion and the shame of detection, they have stoutly denied the charge! Mr. Barnes throws off all restraint, takes the very ground of Unitarians, Pelagians, Taylorites, of his Eastern theological fraternity, and openly asserts the right of signing the Confession as a whole, for doctrine, for substance, intending to interpret, mutilate, or distort the individual parts of the system, to suit any other system which latent scepticism, false philosophy, fanaticism, or folly may suggest. Is not this monstrous for a man laying claims to common sense and common honesty? He even asserts that he entered the sacred office exercising this right, these secret reserves and hidden intentions; thus imposing upon the pure and unsuspecting judicatories through which he passed; nay, he tells us, that on this right of secret reserves and exceptions he vindicates himself in holding the false doctrines of which he now stands convicted before the church. Now, what is this but setting up one crime to vindicate another—practising fraud to secure advantages for propagating heresy? Without preferring any charge, we would here recommend to Mr. Barnes, for serious consideration, the remarkable, and, as we conceive, not inappropriate language of Peter to Ananias, Acts v., 3: 'Why hath Satan filled thine heart to lie to the Holy Ghost, and to keep back part of the price (promise)? While it remained, was it not thine own? Why hast thou conceived this thing in thine heart? Thou hast not lied unto man, but unto God.'

"In examining Mr. Barnes' subsequent course, as devoloped by himself, we find similar exhibitions of unsound and disorderly views, with short interims, down to the present time; and a party striving by every means in their power to sustain him. In accordance with this, we find, in his sermon on *The Way of Salvation*, he unhesitatingly discards the public standards: 'Nor is he to be *cramped* by any *frame-work* of faith that has been reared around the Bible.' How decisive and contemptuous is such language, from a man who had bound himself, by the most impressive and awful sanctions, to regard that very frame-work honestly, according to its spirit and letter! for such is the interpretation put upon the oath by those who administered it. Seldom, indeed, have we been more astonished and grieved than at finding so many indications of this character. The sermon containing this renunciation of our standards exhibits principles and views opposed to some most important doctrines of our Confession. Hence the zeal and perseverance of his adherents to screen both himself and his discourse from deserved censure. The result is well known. Mr. Barnes' account of the transaction is quite remarkable: 'Charges similar to these had been alleged against me, not indeed in a formal and regular manner, but in an irregular manner, by the Presbytery of Philadelphia. Those accusations had been laid before the General Assembly, and the highest judicature of the Presbyterian Church had *fully acquitted me of them!*' Did that General Assembly, or any other, ever declare that Mr. Barnes did not hold the opinions charged as errors? Mr. Barnes knows to the contrary. This full acquittal was such as left more than two-fifths of that Assembly fully persuaded of his guilt in the matter of accusation. The decision, as was openly avowed by a large portion both of the majority and minority, turned much more on points of policy than upon the merits of the charges. The same controversy was continued, in different forms, till the Assembly of 1834 introduced and sanctioned the affinity system. This decisive step in favor of heresy, instead of acquitting Mr. Barnes, admitted his guilt, and was designed to provide for him a safe retreat in his heretical course. In all these complicate measures, from year to year, the same man in substance is indirectly under process. In the back ground we discover a conspiracy in progress to shelter these dangerous opinions and their author from merited condemnation; to provide inlets for large numbers of these spurious operators; and eventually to overturn the whole

Presbyterian system. Mr. Barnes never has been acquitted in the Presbyterian Church; and while *he* holds his heretical opinions, and *she* adheres to her standards, based upon the pure gospel of Jesus Christ, he never can be set free from the charges now alleged.

"Mr. Barnes' sermon before the Theological Seminary at Princeton, September, 1834, still farther discloses his rage for speculation on the truths of the Bible. 'Nor is it,' says he, referring to modern discoveries in science, 'nor is it demonstrated that the limit of advancement is yet reached; or that the human mind must pause here and hope to proceed no farther. These men (philosophers named) have just opened illimitable fields of thought before the mind. *And so it may be in Theology.* The *system* was as perfect *in the Scriptures as Astronomy was before Newton* lived; yet it is *possible that there are truths,* and relations of truths, which the *mind* has *not yet contemplated.*' We introduce this extract merely to exhibit Mr. Barnes' real character to the public, whom he has so elaborately and voluminously addressed, to show how completely he has thrown off all the restraints of our standards, and rejected the landmarks of reason and common sense. Concede to him that Theology, the meaning of the Bible, is to be altered, amended, or new-modelled, as Astronomy was by Newton, as a system of experimental philosophy; or like the progressive science of Botany or Chemistry, like a cotton gin or steam engine; and all religious truth may be sublimated, frittered away, and ejected from the world, by the insatiable spirit of innovation. Besides, what confidence can be placed in the public ministry of a man whose opinions rest upon so visionary and fluctuating a basis? How can he himself proclaim and urge any thing upon dying souls as the truth of God and able to save, when it may be an obsolete error, a total mistake, which the march of mind and increase of light may supersede; and then follow with some new vision, to be, in its turn, admired and abandoned?

"Mr. Barnes' defence is replete with painful indications of design to evade his ordination vows, and to depart from the confession of our faith. The following passage admits the charges and evinces fixed purpose, at least, under the present process, to cleave to his errors, and brave all consequences. 'I am not conscious of being so obstinately attached to the exposition which I have adopted, as to be unwilling to be convinced of error; and, if convinced, to abandon the sentiments which I have expressed. Whether the mode that will be most likely to secure a change of opinion is that of arraigning me for the high misdemeanor of heresy, is the most desirable to secure such a result, I shall not now inquire. In *this land* and in *these times,* a change of opinion is to be effected, not by the language of *authority*, not by an appeal to the *fathers*, not by calling on us simply to listen to the voice of other times; but by the sober and solid exposition of the oracles of God. *Men, even in error*, listen respectfully to those who attempt to reason with them, and to convince them that they are wrong; *they turn instinctively away* when denunciation takes the place of argument, and the cry of heresy is the substitute for a sober appeal to the understanding.' Mr. Barnes' reformation then is hopeless! He admits that he is in error. He quarrels dreadfully with Dr. Junkin's constitutional resort to set him right. He has proved incorrigible under a constant course of warning and admonition ever since he entered Philadelphia. The history of our church for the last five years, is an indelible record of that fact! If Dr. Junkin had approached him with bended knee and suppliant tone, if the church had come (not with *authority!*) humbly suing at his feet, he might have deigned to *listen*. But the name of heresy, accusations, charges, dreadful! *He turns instinctively away!* Yes, and hugs his false opinions closer than ever. Remember this is the profoundly meek and devout Mr. Barnes. Remember, too, when in error, his embracing or refusing reform depends not upon the nature, the evidence, the importance of truth; but upon the gentleness, the soft and timid reserve, the courtesy, with which it is commended to him. Admirable trait in a New School commentator!!

"But Mr. Barnes' course is very different. He openly declares that he commenced his Notes with *an intention not to be influenced by a regard to the Confession of Faith*. And now, after finishing the work, being convicted of heresy, and even acknowledging himself in error, he avows it as the *deliberate and settled purpose of his mind always to be governed by this principle;* and yet pertinaciously continues in the church whose purity he has marred, whose peace he has wounded, and whose authority he has contemned! After this, no man will do Mr. Barnes the injustice to charge him with being a Presbyterian; with belonging, in heart and spirit, to that or any other denomination; with having, indeed, any settled views of truth at all. If he should be found to agree with our constitutional forms in any instance, it will be by mere chance! Really, his declarations are so wild and extravagant, that they seem scarcely compatible with sanity of intellect, certainly at the farthest remove from all consistency with that integrity and candour of purpose and practice which constitute the very essence of fidelity to our holy ecclesiastical compact.

"It would appear from Mr. Barnes' statements, that our church has been very indulgent toward unsound members in former times. It is to be regretted that he has exposed himself so sadly to painful remark on this topic. We can scarcely conceive how he could be ignorant of the long line of facts opposed to his representations, or expect to escape detection in misstatements so notorious. The early history of the church records few cases of error, and consequently of discipline. Nothing is more certain than this, the farther you look back into our ecclesiastical character, the greater strictness and even rigor will you find continually in exercise to guard against the approach of every error. Even in 1810, the Rev. W. C. Davis, whose 'gospel plan' was under process for heresy, found not a man in the Assembly to advocate his cause. The vote to condemn his book, containing substantially the same false doctrine now revived by Mr. Barnes, was unanimous. The whole business occupied half a day. Times have greatly changed. Now, the promoters of corruption and discord have augmented their numbers, and clog the wheels of discipline; they even reprove the advocates of truth and order for attempting at all to obstruct their desolating course, and boldly denounce us as persecutors; a charge which might as justly be urged by a felon at the bar against the court and jury engaged in ferreting out his crimes.

"In maintaining his false and dangerous positions, Mr. Barnes calls to his aid the Biblical Repertory, Princeton, Vol. III., p. 521, &c., where he finds the following passage: 'The Confession, as framed by the Westminster Divines, was an acknowledged compromise between two classes of theologians. When adopted by the Presbyterian Church in this country, it was with the understanding that the *mode of subscription* did *not imply strict uniformity of views.*' The character of this journal is such as to require a consideration of what is here advanced. The passage quoted is the mere opinion of one man, or at most of a very few, superintending a periodical at a time calculated to lull vigilance. Instead of receiving the sanction of public opinion, it was met by general disapprobation, as opening a door for mischievous innovators to intrude themselves *unawares.* That the understanding, here gratuitously proclaimed as universal, might have existed in the minds of a few obstinate sticklers for opinion in that large conclave which formed the Confession, at Westminster, and adopted it in this country, may be supposed; but that such was the designed and approved import of the pledge and signature, to be required in all after-time, is really too romantic to be for a moment admitted. Who does not see that in this case our bond of union must immediately have proved a rope of sand—our beautiful system, a promiscuous heap of fragments—and the church, not a *glorious building, fitly framed and compacted together*, but a heterogeneous image of gold and silver, brass and iron! The sequel of this extract from the Repertory is still more revolting, as it really appears to concede every thing which the direst foes of our system are struggling for; the right of adopting her standards *for doctrine,* the very evasion practised by Mr. Barnes. 'The very terms, "system of doctrines," conveys a definite idea, the idea of a regular series of connected opinions having a natual relation, and constituting *one whole.* These doctrines are clearly expressed; such as the doctrine of the Trinity, the incarnation and supreme deity of Christ, the fall, and original sin, atonement, justification by faith. With respect to each of these several points there are, and *may safely be, various modes* of statement and *explanation, consistent with* their *sincere reception.*' In connexion with this, the writer asks, 'How is the subscription, or assent to our standards, to be interpreted? or with what degree of strictness is the phrase "system of doctrines," as it occurs in the ordination service, to be explained? who is to judge whether an explanation does, or does not, interfere with what is essential to a particular doctrine? We answer, in the first place, this is a question for every man to answer.' The writer's remarks too much favour the supposition that the main force of our ordination promise falls upon the words 'system of doctrines.' As this is deeply interesting, let us examine it. 'Do you sincerely receive and adopt the Confession of Faith of this church, as containing the system of doctrines taught in the Holy Scriptures?' Now according to the apparent meaning of the Repertory, the candidate primarily and principally *receives* and *adopts* '*the system of doctrine.*' We ask what is the particular form and character of these doctrines? The writer's answer is, 'This is a question for every man to answer' as he may please. If so, the terms 'Confession of Faith of this church,' might as well be expunged altogether. But we apprehend this to be an entirely erroneous construction of the whole article. Examine the question proposed: 'Do you sincerely receive and adopt'—what?—'the system of doctrines?' No, 'the Confession of Faith of this Church.' This is the very gist of the question, and here rests the main force of the obligation. Why receive 'the Confession of Faith?' because we believe it 'contains the system of doctrines taught in the Holy Scriptures.' Now, suppose any man should insist that this Confession does not contain the doctrines of the Sacred Scriptures; it is plain he cannot be an honest Presbyterian; for this point is settled by our form of induction into the church, and every sincere signer professes his confirmed belief in this principle. There were, doubtless, present to the minds of the framers of our *Confession* many systems of doctrine, and there exist still many forms of faith, at war with each other, all represented by their respective advocates to be embraced by the Holy Scriptures. *Our Confession* makes its selection and exhibits its choice, to the exclusion of every opposing form of words, in distinct and permanent traits; and every honest receiver yields and records his unqualified and unwavering assent *to it.* Does any man inquire what the doctrinal system of the Presbyterian Church is? We refer him—not to the evasive speculations or dubious *answers* of others—but directly to 'the Confession of Faith,' which the book describes as containing this system. We tell the inquirer the very object of the Confession was to prevent private and devious explanation; to distinguish our system from all opposing systems; to prevent any mistake or confusion among ourselves respecting the real character and import of our doctrines.

"Our meaning may be appositely illustrated in a few particulars from the case now pending. Mr. Barnes has subscribed to the doctrine of the '*fall and original sin.*' How does he explain it? '*All sin is voluntary!*' of course, there is no corruption of nature nor guilt till moral agency commences. 'Sinners have no federal relation to Adam, and are not answerable for his guilt.' 'The notion of imputation is an invention of modern times.' As this doctrine is explained by Mr. Barnes, men have no sin till they create it by actual transgression. 'It is a result secured by bad conduct, just as the drunkard becomes such and ruins his family by bad habits.' Now, is this explanation consistent with an honest reception of either the Bible or the Confession of Faith? We think far otherwise.

"Again: Mr. Barnes holds the doctrine of *Atonement.* Now for his explanation of this vital truth: 'The sin of Adam and his seed was not imputed to Christ, and he punished on account of it.' Of course, he asserts 'Christ did not endure the precise penalty of the law,' nor make certain the salvation of any one. What then did he do that resembles the work of atonement? Mr. Barnes does not inform us. As Christ *had no sin* himself, and was not charged with the sin of others, he must have suffered as an innocent person, to make an exhibition of some kind, and this is Mr. Barnes' view, to satisfy public justice, the ends of the divine government; but without real expiation or purchase at all! And yet he very gravely talks about the *atonement.*

"Once more: Mr. Barnes holds to *justification by faith.* His explanation, so far as it goes, completely removes the true doctrine on this fundamental point out of the world. Having discarded the principle of imputation, which runs through the whole Bible, and is so strikingly prominent in our Confession, of course neither the person, nor the work, or righteousness of Christ, has anything to do with the sinner's justification. The old doctrine, on which we have been accustomed to repose our eternal hopes of justification through Christ's righteousness imputed to the sinner and received by *faith of God,* is completely set aside as a stale error, or, more absurdly, as a modern invention; and its place is supplied, in Mr. Barnes' explanation, by an attempt to make this infinitely important matter, *justification before God,* depend upon a blind mystical faith itself, or to resolve it into simple pardon for sin. Thus the peculiar doctrines which form the basis of the glorious gospel may be explained away, and enveloped in impenetrable and cheerless clouds.

"Thus, it seems to us, Mr. Barnes' own testimony, candidly estimated, is sufficient to place him before the church in a predicament as little to be envied as any that can be conceived. And when the conduct of his advocates is viewed in connexion with his public *declarations* and *acts,* a fixed purpose is clearly developed by them to evade honest investigation and constitutional trial altogether. No matter who is the *accused,* who the *prosecutor,* or what the *charge;* they have combined to trample the constitution under their feet, and to nullify all its salutary provisions.

"We find much serious cause to be dissatisfied with Mr. Barnes' treatment of Dr. Junkin. His attempt to resolve his conduct into selfish, suspicious, and unhallowed motives, cannot fail to shock every impartial and honourable mind. 'To Dr. Junkin I had done no injury, I had made no allusion; his opinions I had not attacked; nor in the book on which the charges are based, have I made the remotest allusion to him or his doctrines.' Strange indeed! Has then Mr. Barnes the weakness to intimate, or suppose, that process can be properly instituted or reasonably expected against a minister extensively charged with heresy, only where personal offence has been given, where passion has been provoked and is in exercise? Can his *large liberality* and *abounding charity* conceive and admit of no higher, no holier motive, in this solemn and eventful measure? Is then the love of Christ, the love of his pure gospel, the love of his church, the love of souls, to him a strange passion? Or does it glow exclusively in his own breast? Judge ye! What shall we say of the effort he makes to hold up Dr. Junkin to ridicule and reproach as a self-constituted guardian of the orthodoxy and peace of the church? How unkind and unchristian are such insinuations! The public are not so obtuse as to mistake the meaning. The heretic must go free at all events, and the prosecutor become a victim of party combination and violence. Even the College of Lafayette, which belongs to the cause of science and truth, is not sacred if it come in the way of such party rancor. Not only the President, but the important and growing institution under his care, must be swept away by this proscriptive besom. And what has excited this exterminating spirit? Why, Dr. Junkin's simply proposing, in a manner which all pronounce necessary, and regular, and Christian, after the whole church had been *invited by act of the General Assembly* to this issue, proposing to show according to the book, that the Notes on the Romans contain doctrines opposed to our standards. If innocent and nothing to fear, why this asperity and rage? Mr. Barnes says, 'In my own Presbytery I was in good standing.' True, because the whole body, one minister only excepted, it is believed, embraced the same heresies. But had Mr. Barnes no wish to stand well in the church at large? Trial is the only method of removing suspicions. This, neither Mr. Barnes nor his associates are prepared for. Hence this outrageous attack upon a Christian minister, who undertakes an arduous public service, as we believe, from profound devotedness to duty, and exercising great self-denial, not courting distinction, not following the impulses of an irregular and excited mind, not cherishing a lofty pride or unhallowed ambition, as is cruelly insinuated in the defence, but at the often repeated challenge of the aggressing faction, and on the suggestion and with the approbation of many of the advocates of truth and purity in the Presbyterian body. In our Saviour's words, the plain inference is, 'Every one that doeth evil hateth the light, neither cometh to the light, lest his deeds should be reproved.'

"The exculpatory sentence of the second Presbytery of Philadelphia in Mr. Barnes' case, was such as the public anticipated, knowing it to be deeply tinctured with the same false doctrines. The only fact, therefore, established by the trial before them, is, that the court are in the same condemnation with their protege, with this additional enormity, that to previous individual corruption they have added the guilt of public official perfidy as guardians of the church.

"After openly and repeatedly announcing the fact, that he entered the ministry with reserves and exceptions—after a laborious and protracted argument to vindicate his heretical sentiments on the assumed right of construction: and after boldly declaring his *settled* purpose always to disregard every confession and formula, we are really surprised and grieved to find Mr. Barnes adding, to the egregious mass of inconsistencies elsewhere displayed, the gross absurdity of an attempt to reconcile his *Notes* with the *Confession of Faith*. His whole defence is conducted on the admission, that these discrepancies exist as stated. Hence the attempt to distort the nature and impair the force of the ordination *Vow*. Hence also the various excuses and pretexts offered to vindicate the errors alleged and their author. What is the import of the following extract from this defence? 'The question which this Presbytery is now called on to decide, is, whether the views which are expressed in these Notes are any longer to be tolerated in the Presbyterian Church in the United States; whether a man who *held* them at the *time* of his *licensure*, who has held and preached them for ten years, is to be allowed peaceably to hold them still; or whether he is to be pronounced heretical and unsound?' What opinions are these here referred to? Certainly not any doctrines of the Confession of Faith. There is no controversy about them. No: they are undoubtedly the heresies presented by Dr. Junkin. The whole charge is here, as in other places, substantially admitted. But, presently, Mr. Barnes' courage fails, and he turns short about, adding to the guilt of acknowledged error the criminality of uncandid subterfuge, and commences a jesuitical process to prove these very opinions to be the same with those of our standards. To such monstrous absurdities heresy never fails to reduce its deluded propagators. The impossibility of this reconciliation will appear from a comparison of Dr. Junkin's argument with the standards of the church.

"Let the public observe—Mr. Barnes has brought upon himself all the guilt—the charges—the censures—the mortification and disgrace—and the painful apprehensions he may suffer, by his rash and incorrigible course. He has nobody to blame but himself and his cruel advisers. His plea for suspension of process, or discharge from condemnation, amounts to the *simple, modest,* and *reasonable* request, that all the sworn friends of truth and order in our church, who feel sacredly 'bound, with zeal and fidelity, to maintain the truths of the gospel and the purity and peace of the church,' shall profanely violate their vows, and stand idly by, when the Ark of the law and testimony is rapaciously assailed by aliens from the commonwealth of Israel and *strangers* from our *covenant and promise.* What renders his case most desperate is, that his defence, now before the public, constituted as it is, contains from his own hand the elements of self-destruction. Unless the sentiments it contains are promptly and totally retracted, and the whole ground he there assumes for defence abandoned as untenable, that very defence will prove a bill of indictment and must seal his fate. If the principles which that defence avows are sanctioned in the General Assembly, the Presbyterian Church, as established by our wise and venerable forefathers, is that moment, and forever after, dissolved; on those principles no pure church ever existed, or can exist, beneath the sun. So that we have here presented a bold, insidious, and determined assault upon the vital existence of our sacred union—an attempt, at a stroke, to sever the tie that binds us in this great Christian fraternity—and then to plead the profane dissolution itself, as a defence for the enormities under process before our sacred tribunals.

"Our former remarks upon Mr. Barnes' statements respecting his views of the engagement made on first assuming the sacred office, were intended chiefly to correct his erroneous and dangerous construction of that sacred promise as a part of our church policy. We now proceed to consider the morality of Mr. Barnes' conduct in this solemn transaction, as developed by himself. The subject is truly momentous and impressive; and nothing but a lively view of its comprehensive bearing and influence, and a solemn sense of duty, awakened by Mr. Barnes' alarming disclosures, prompts us to enter upon this solemn discussion. We pity this deluded and unhappy man, whose friends, by foolish flattery and infatuated counsel, have brought him blindfold to the precipice. As the *question* with us now is *between* the *Church of Christ* and *Albert Barnes,* we have no alternative but to proceed with the exposition.

"From our view of this subject in its moral relations, the conclusion is, that Mr. Barnes' conduct involves an offence of the greatest magnitude and guilt. The office of a Christian minister is the most exalted and responsible office existing in this world. Ministers are representatives, 'sub-delegated messengers,' of the great God, in his dispensation of grace. 'We are ambassadors of Christ,' says the great Apostle; 'We pray you in Christ's stead,' &c. To this high vocation are they appointed, and the Presbytery is the divinely constituted instrument to clothe them with its sacred functions. Now, the whole transaction, in which candidates are received, and bound, and commissioned to this holy service, has ever been considered as partaking the nature and solemnity of a *formal oath.* The engagement being made primarily to God, from whom proceed the office—the call to it—and both the power and form of initiation, every candidate is justly conceived to make a solemn appeal to the searcher of hearts for the rectitude and sincerity of his professions. Hence a violation of this oath, in any of its particulars, according to their natural, obvious, customary, and established import, can justly be viewed no otherwise than as an act of perjury; especially must this construction be put upon the violation, if the candidate, by subsequent declarations and actions, refuse to correct his error, and obstinately persist in a course directly opposed to that clearly required by his solemn vow.

"Let us hear the opinion of a man, whose penetration, purity, and fidelity, as a witness for God, have been proclaimed through the world as pre-eminently deserving universal confidence. 'But, for men, at their entrance on the sacred office solemnly to subscribe to the truth of what, all their lives after, they strive to undermine and destroy, is at once so criminal and absurd, that no reproof given to it can possibly exceed in point of severity. This is so direct a violation of sincerity, that it is astonishing to think how men can set their minds at ease in the prospect, or keep them in peace after the deliberate commission of it. The very excuses and evasions that are offered in defence of it are a disgrace to reason as well as a scandal to religion. What success can be expected from that man's ministry who begins it with an act of so complicated guilt? How can he take upon him to reprove others for sin, or to train them up in virtue and true goodness, while himself is chargeable with direct, premeditated and perpetual perjury!'*

"Falsehood has been properly defined to consist in 'That which deceives and disappoints confidence.' Perjury is of the same general nature, but inconceivably aggravated in guilt by a direct appeal to God, which involves an imprecation of his judgments upon any thing deceptive in the engagement made, fraudulent or unfaithful in the execution of it. These characteristics will be found, on close inspection, applicable to the case before us. From his own testimony and attending circumstances, it cannot be doubted that Mr. Barnes deceived the Presbytery of New Brunswick at his licensure; and it is equally clear that he has disappointed their expectations. The points of greatest importance, in the obligations assumed, on entering the sacred office, are embraced in the following questions: 'Do you sincerely receive and *adopt the Confession of Faith* of this church, as containing the system of doctrines taught in the Holy Scriptures? Do you promise to study the peace, unity, and purity of the church?' In all sound Presbyteries these obligations have been uniformly understood to imply the utmost singleness and sincerity of purpose, required also by act of the General Assembly—'In receiving and adopting the formularies of the church, according to the obvious, known, and established meaning of the terms, *as the Confession of their Faith.*' Our Confession itself demands the engagement to be taken 'in the plain and common sense of the words, without equivocation or mental reservation.' The Presbytery of New Brunswick have always acted in conformity with these views; the students of the Seminary, who are generally witnesses of their transactions, and especially those on trial before them, could not fail to be impressed with this fact—that Presbytery never conceived the thought that any candidate had presumed to stand before them with any other view; in the act of licensing Mr. Barnes, as there was *no scruple stated*, they supposed him to be honestly receiving and adopting the *Book*, in its known and established import, as the *Confession of his Faith.* Reposing this confidence in his supposed sincerity, they committed to him the momentous trust of *preaching this faith* to dying men. With astonishment we now learn from Mr. Barnes himself, that he assumed the prescribed obligations and trust, cherishing, secretly, reserves, evasions, and designs, in direct conflict

* Witherspoon's works, Vol. III. p. 197.

with what the Presbytery and the church at large understood that solemn promise to import; indeed, entirely overlooking and renouncing the Confession of Faith, both in letter and in practical effect. 'The system of doctrines contained in the standards I received *as a system.* I received it, *not* indeed *ever* expressing my *assent* to every expression and form of expression; but as *reserving* to myself the *right* of examining the language, and forming an opinion of its meaning.' Language more explicit, testimony more unequivocal and irresistible, to prove the high immorality of Mr. Barnes' conduct in this sacred transaction, need not, could not, exist.

"The corrupt and dangerous practice of signing creeds and confessions, *for doctrine* and for *substance*, with reserved rights of construction and explanation, which the honest friends of truth regard with abhorrence, is here practically introduced, boldly avowed, audaciously held up as an example in the church, and pleaded as an apology for this unparalleled violation of moral honesty. A most pertinacious adherence to this deceptive course is here fully evinced. 'I have not changed my views materially since I was licensed to preach the gospel.' Again, he declares, that 'He held the views expressed in these Notes at the time of his *licensure* and *ordination*, that he has held and preached them *ten years.*' Again: he avows 'His intention not to be influenced by regard to any creed or Confession of Faith: because it is his *deliberate* and *settled purpose* of mind; the principle by which he expects *always* to be *governed.*' This dogmatical, reiterated, deliberate, and determined rejection of our Confession, in the very act in which he pledged his sacred truth and honour, before God, to adopt and maintain it, must produce through our church indescribable emotions.

"False speaking and false swearing are justly held up for public execration by all men. Perjury, even where money, office, or honour, is its object, and where its injurious effects are comparatively trivial, is exposed to punishment by fine or imprisonment. But what man or angel can calculate the guilt of treachery in an ambassador of Christ? It may be estimated in some small measure by considering the extent of a minister's obligations to God, to the Presbytery, to the church, and to the souls of men. As these obligations are manifold and weighty, a violation of them must incur complicate and awful guilt. It is a most aggravating circumstance in Mr. Barnes' course, that he is persisting, against the warnings and entreaties of *years* past, and pursuing an object of the greatest enormity, the perversion of the truth of God and the ruin of his church.

"If this dishonest system should be sustained, and become the law of the church, it is evident that every licensure and ordination in our land may become an inlet to some new form or grade of heresy, under the impenetrable and imposing guise of reserves and explanations. It surely needs no words to show how well adapted Mr. Barnes' model will be, to lead candidates of his non-committal and inventive cast, completely to evade every constitutional guard against error, and to import into the church every abomination. Hitherto it has been considered the duty of candidates, before admission, *after* or *during* a thorough course of theological reading, to inspect our Book of Faith, ponder its sacred contents, and decide upon their character; that they may act intelligently and sincerely, if at all, in assuming its obligations and avowing its principles; but a new method of procedure is now exhibited, to *swear* to the Book *first* as a *Confession of Faith*, and *examine* its language *afterwards* to form an opinion of its *meaning!*

"It is now a very serious inquiry in what light the advocates of Mr. Barnes are to be viewed. Possessing, we have no doubt, much more accurate knowledge on this point than we can claim, his assertion is not to be passed lightly over 'that he holds the opinions here in question, in common with no small part of the more than two thousand ministers in our connexion.' This appears to us unquestionable, that, if they entered our church with any other view than that of honest compliance with the spirit of their ordination vow and strict conformity to the letter of our church standards, they committed a profane and criminal violation of the most solemn oath ever administered to man; and if they continue in our church, as Mr. Barnes does, in open conflict with the pledge they gave and the standards they voluntarily assumed, their public ministry and their whole life is a constant repetition and aggravation of the most criminal act ever perpetrated in this world. And whatever may have been at first their principle of action and mode of introduction, their vindicating a man who not only holds heretical opinions, corrupting to the Church of Christ, but assumes and exercises rights directly subversive of that branch of his church which they have sworn to protect and advance, they are undoubtedly to be considered abettors of heresy, instigators and promoters of consummate mischief to Zion, and are justly held accountable to God and to his church for all the corruption and confusion produced by their unfaithful course.

"To the great body of candid and reflecting men of all denominations, the wonder constantly is, why Mr. Barnes and those of his class, most manifestly and radically differing from the standards of the Presbyterian Church, pertinaciously pursuing measures which produce incessant discord, which rend congregations, church judicatories, missionary societies, benevolent institutions, which subject large sections of our church and country to painful conflicts, keep the public mind unceasingly agitated with feuds and animosities; the wonder is, why they should wish to remain for an hour in connexion with this church. It is perfectly plain, that if their uncandid, inconsistent, and offensive action and influence were removed from the Presbyterian body, all would be peaceful, prosperous, and happy, within her bosom. No difficulty, no evils of any magnitude, have afflicted the church for many years not justly ascribable to the influence of New England men, New School principles, and sympathies for them. How preposterous and how criminal is it for men to insist on wearing the name of Presbyterians, when their hearts are opposed to Presbyterianism, at enmity with its peculiar and essential doctrines and forms! Why do they not retire from the Presbyterian Church and erect an *independent* standard, where they can enjoy, unmolested and without giving offence, the anomalies they so much covet, without cherishing wiles and creating conflicts, perpetual in their character, painful to all, wounding to the church, offensive to God, chilling to devotion, and paralyzing to the noblest energies and interests of Zion? If they have no regard for truth and consistency, no concern for the comfort of the great body of ministers, and elders, and people, whom they continually disturb and pain, for the sake of the Lord Jesus Christ, who loves, inculcates, and enjoins *peace*, let them and their adherents *withdraw*, that the land may have rest and Zion throw off her sackcloth. The land is wide enough for them and for us. They have congregations, schools, colleges, seminaries, societies of every name, sufficient to make them respectable in numbers and strength. Thus separated by a voluntary and amicable recession from a church into which they have dishonestly intruded and continued, only to weaken and destroy it; whose interests they never intended to promote; and whose honest and faithful members never can and never will unresistingly tolerate their wicked abuse of her institutions, and corruption of her faith and purity; thus separated, the fruits of the Spirit may again be hailed among us; and they may, with some appearance of consistency and honour, escape from the guilt and obloquy which in this connection, must for ever accumulate and rest upon them.

"If the hope of plunder keeps them back from separation—the only honourable escape from their present ignominious and self-condemned position—let me tell them that such a hope is desperate. No; let not this detain them. The adjudications of the highest tribunals, both of Europe and America, have recently confirmed the dictates of common sense and sound equity, by repeated declarations that the faith of a church constitutes her being, decides her character, establishes her rights, and secures her property. The apostacy of the New School from the Confession of Faith is now as clearly ascertained as it can be, both by their language and their actions. Their heresy has gone abroad, written as with sunbeams, to the ends of the earth. The stand taken and the course pursued by the minority in the Assembly of 1834, were designed to produce this result. Subsequent events have completed the development, a development which cannot fail to prove an impregnable panoply for the uncorrupted church against any and every assault of art or violence which the great King of Zion may permit. The prospect of additional 'loaves and fishes,' from the orthodox body, by any other process than insidious and meddlesome gleaning, is too dubious to recompense the sacrifice of public good, and of individual character, consequent upon a farther continuance in this uncongenial connexion, and prosecution of measures so productive of bitterness, so disgraceful to reason, and so scandalous to the Christian name.

"From such instances of insincerity and immorality in the ministers of religion, a withering effect must be expected to descend upon the pious affections of the great body of Christian people, who are themselves astonished and mourning spectators of this solemn mockery, this affecting insensibility to crime and guilt, in those who serve at the altar, and who should, by lives of *simplicity and Godly sincerity*, lead the way to heaven. Need we inquire why religion languishes and the ways of Zion mourn? Can we be at a loss to understand why the Most High has withdrawn his blessed spirit from his church below? Can we reasonably expect in general through the church, those seasons of genuine awakening and revival, which have happily distinguished former days, while the truth of God is corruptly preached; while Christ and his righteousness are *openly made light of;* and the essential principles of his gospel contravened; while there is visible, under so many symptoms of favour, a combined movement in the citadel of the church to screen the propagators of heresy, insulting to heaven and damning to souls? Indeed, should not the cold inaction of many true friends of gospel truth, the indecision of others, and the tardiness with which many advance to the help of the Lord, be considered deeply offensive in his holy sight; sufficient to bring down the rebuke of a frigid winter or a dreary night upon regions recently rejoicing in the sunshine of spiritual day? Besides, have not the intestine wars and confusions enkindled by the invaders of our peaceful church struck alarm through all our borders, and driven many faithful laborers from the direct care of souls and dissemination of truth, to the painful work of defence against troops of ambushed and open foes?

"It is an inquiry, also, of absorbing interest, what is to be the influence of this public profanation of oaths by the professed ministers of Jesus Christ, on the morals of society in general. We apprehend the most deleterious effects. That the continuance of this system of equivocation and subterfuge, in a matter so sacred, will operate with a paralyzing influence on the moral perceptions and sensibilities of the perpetrators themselves, is too clear to be doubted. Indeed, we are much mistaken, in a matter, too, where we would gladly find ourselves in error, if practical indications of a decisive and alarming character have not already been given, in many instances, of the deplorable truth of these apprehensions. The Argus eyes of the unholy multitude are ever placed with invidious scrutiny on the vestments of the holy order. A spot discovered in their lawn will produce a shout of unhallowed satisfaction through all the camp of the enemy. And though it is hard to induce any of their company to follow a step in the progress of holy virtue, yet the slightest signal will prompt a host to triumphant emulation in the career of profligacy and guilt. In vain shall we deplore the general relaxation of public morals, reprove the general violation of truth and profanation of oaths, and the light esteem of every thing sacred, among the common orders, while so large a number of the consecrated teachers and defenders of pure morality, by violating their most sacred engagements, and leagueing together to screen transgressors, enable the multitude, with just reproach and biting sarcasm, to retort, 'Thou that teachest another, teachest thou not thyself? Thou that abhorrest idols, dost thou commit *sacrilege?* Thou that makest thy *boast* of the law, through *breaking the law dishonorest* thou God?' Rom. xvi., 21, 23."

At the opening of the momentous Assembly, May 15th, 1834, in the city of Philadelphia, it was soon discovered that the church was in the hands of her adversary—the New School faction having a large majority. As the unscrupulous designs of the assailants became sufficiently developed, it could no longer be doubted, that every thing in the church, dear to sound Presbyterians, was in jeopardy. The numerical majority of the New School, in this Assembly, varied upon the test questions occurring daily, from fifteen to sixty votes. As several of the most important subjects, in connexion with which the unsoundness of this majority disclosed itself, will come under review in other parts of this work, we shall here restrict the reader's attention to this Assembly's action on the *Western Memorial*, to portions of which impressive document reference has already been made.

And here, as the best exposition of their insidious attempts to screen from deserved correction the defaults of church judicatories, which they had previously converted into machines to accomplish their purposes; to throw the mantle of concealment or protection over the busy infecters of our ecclesiastical body; to continue in operation the Plan of Union of 1801, as the prolific inlet of those vitiating influences which had long been coming in like a flood; and in fact to refuse, by evasions, denials and arts, all reasonable and salutary remedies for the mischiefs which were most manifestly shaking the Presbyterian Church to its centre, we shall transfer to these sheets their several resolutions on the Western Memorial, and other important subjects.

The first irregular and pernicious measure of this Assembly, was that of sustaining the complaint and appeal of the Assembly's Second Presbytery of Philadelphia against the Synod. The history of the case is in few words. In 1832, the General Assembly constituted the Second Presbytery of Philadelphia, within the bounds of the Synod of Philadelphia, and without her consent. The Synod, considering their constitutional rights invaded by that act, dissolved the Second Presbytery of Philadelphia. The Presbytery complained and appealed to the General Assembly of 1834, against the act of the Synod. The General Assembly sustained the complaint and appeal of the Second Presbytery. Against this act of the Assembly of 1834, a protest was entered and recorded on their minutes, page 32. We transfer to these pages only the second objection to the Assembly's action, contained in the protest, viz: "While we disapprove the act performed by the Assembly as being unconstitutional, we solemnly protest against the practice, whether by the Assembly or Synods, of forming Presbyteries on the principle of *elective affinity*, distinctly avowed and recognized as the basis of this act, being fully persuaded that the tendency of this principle will be to impair the standards of our church, to open a door to error, and to violate the purity, good order, and peace of the church."

Such deviations as are clearly discoverable in the acts of the Assembly, from constitutional law and sound discretion and usage in the church, unsettle all principle, disturb order, and destroy confidence. Whatever may be the object, these are the fruits. But in the formation of the Second Presbytery of Philadelphia, the New School majority in the Assembly of 1832 manifestly had a particular object in view. Their predominating motive was to provide a safe retreat for Albert Barnes, who was in difficulty on account of his heretical opinions, published in his sermon on the Way of Salvation. By placing together, in one Presbytery, a company of men embracing the same errors, and pursuing the same course of misrule in church government, they could employ their power, their prejudices, and corruptions, to propagate their false notions in theology, and screen their infecting and disorganizing policy from church censure. To designate this spurious mass, they gave to them the brief but expressive name of *elective affinity*, because they were selected and associated in one Presbytery, for the very reason that they were all alike unsound, and thus adapted to diffuse New School infection in any region or in any manner proposed. On this account, the orthodox protested against the *elective affinity* principle and organization altogether, as menacing the purity and peace of the church.

The Assembly of 1834 was not, as former Assemblies, a timid, temporising body; they were cunning, but not cautious. Confiding in their strength, and flushed with apparent success, as was visible on the roll and minutes of the House, and relying upon the sympathy of many who had been, or wished to be, counted leaders of the Old School, they played a lofty and decisive game. But their movements were precipitate and reckless; estimating the paucity of Old School representation in the House as evidence of apathy among the people, or incipient abandonment of old-fashioned, honest Presbyterianism, they passed acts substantially broaching false doctrines, tallying with the false books many of them had already for sale in the market. But they discovered in a few months, that their majority in the Assembly of 1834, was, in many instances, the result of neglect and thoughtless indifference on the part of sound Presbyterians, in selecting delegates to the Assembly. Their qualifications, in many cases, had not been carefully estimated in the choice. Some were preferred on their own solicitation. Many others had sought the delegation for purposes of business, of health, or of pleasure.

The Memorial from Western Presbyteries and elders, as soon as announced to the Assembly, was realized by all present as a very impressive document, and its influence upon the New School party was agitating and confounding. To break its force, if possible, required all their art. Their first effort, before it was read as is customary on such occasions, was to appoint as imposing a committee as they could raise, to mutilate and pervert the document, and piecemeal to paralyze its power. The individuals selected for this service were well adapted to the purpose, consisting of experienced leaders on the one hand, and, on the other, of raw recruits, sure to follow the dictates of their masters.

From this Memorial, showing the state of the Western Church, and furnishing a large amount of important intelligence on this subject, we present the following extracts, viz:

"MEMORIAL.

" *To the Moderator and Members of the General Assembly of the Presbyterian Church in the United States, to meet in the city of Philadelphia, May 15th,* 1834.

"Reverend Fathers and Brethren:—We, the subscribers, feel alarmed at the evidences which press upon us, of the prevalence of unsoundness in doctrine and laxity in discipline; and we view it as an aggravating consideration, that the General Assembly, the constitutional guardian of the church's purity, even when a knowledge of such evils has been brought before it in an orderly manner, has, within these few years past, either directly or indirectly, refused to apply the constitutional remedy. Appeals, references, complaints, and memorials, from individuals, Presbyteries, and Synods, have been dismissed on some slight grounds, perhaps not noticed at all, or merged in some compromise which aggravated the evils intended to be removed.

"That we may not be misunderstood, we premise here, our free admission that some of the measures about to be complained of, were adopted at the time, with the best intentions, and if the results could have been foreseen by the authors of those measures, they would never have been carried into effect.

"1. We believe this to have been particularly the case with regard to the 'Plan of Union' with Congregational Churches, adopted in 1801. A careful comparison of that plan (see Digest 297,) with the constitution of our church, will make it evident that the General Assembly of 1801, in adopting it, assumed power nowhere assigned to them in the constitution. They established an ecclesiastical tribunal for the government of a part of the Presbyterian Church, such as is not acknowledged by the constitution, and is plainly repugnant to it. We allude to the 'Mutual Council,' recognized in that Plan. In the same act, the Assembly also granted the powers and privileges to 'committee-men,' which was contrary both to the letter and spirit of the constitution, &c.

"Closely connected with the influence of Congregational principles and prepossessions, introduced gradually into our church through the Plan of Union of 1801, we regard the existence of a sentiment now avowed by numbers who bear the Presbyterian name, that every man, in professing to receive and adopt our ecclesiastical formularies, has a right to put thereon his *own construction*, without being responsible for the construction or the character of his explanations. They who hold this principle, practice accordingly, and thus an unnatural mixture of conflicting elements is brought into the bosom of the church, unfavourable alike to its purity and peace.

"We next notice another course of unconstitutional proceedings, which adds to the evils that now afflict us. We refer to the practice of Presbyteries, in ordaining men, *sine titulo*, to preach and administer the ordinances of the gospel in other parts of the Presbyterian Church, where Presbyteries already exist and are ready to perform their constitutional functions as the necessities of the churches under their care require. There is also just ground to suspect, that in many cases of such ordination, it is done to suit the convenience of men who are not prepared to pass through the constitutional ordeal, when applied by those Presbyteries within whose bounds they expect to labor, either on account of their lack of ministerial furniture, or because they do not cordially receive either our creed or form of government; hence they prefer to receive licensure and ordination in such Presbyteries as are known, or supposed to be, not particular on these points.

"Especially do we complain of, and testify against, what has more than once occurred during the last few years—the ordaining of six, eight, or ten young men at a time, most of them just licensed, who have been reared, up from infancy to manhood, in Congregational views, feelings, and habits, and who are thus suddenly, nominally and *geographically*, converted into Presbyterian ministers, before it was possible, in the nature of things, that they could have just and clear views of the nature of Presbyterianism. For where could they acquire them? Certainly not in the Congregational Churches, in which they were trained up; and not in Congregational Theological Schools; for in them, no provision is made for expounding the doctrines of the Presbyterian Confession of *Faith* and form of government. The fact is, that every year, numbers of these Congregationalists come directly into Presbyteries and Presbyterian Churches in the West, with certificates of their standing as ministers of the Presbyterian Church, while in many instances it is evident that they are almost entire strangers to that Confession of Faith, which, unless their certificates be an imposition, they must, in the most solemn manner, have 'received and adopted' as their *Confession of Faith*. Among the many references which might be made in illustration of the justice of our representations under this head, we point only to the instances afforded by the Newburyport Presbytery and the third Presbytery of New York; the former of which, a few years ago, ordained *nine* young men at one time, as evangelists for the A. Home Missionary Society, six or seven of whom, were, in a short time, located in Ohio, in which state there were, at that time, fourteen Presbyteries, exercising ecclesiastical jurisdiction. The latter Presbytery, in the fall of 1831, ordained *ten* young men at *one* time, for the A. Home Missionary Society, most of whom were sent directly into the bounds of Presbyteries in the West.

"The same Presbytery, (New York,) in 1832, received the Rev. L. Beecher, D. D., from a Congregational Association, and forthwith, at the same meeting, dismissed him to join the Presbytery of Cincinnati, to which place he was journeying, to take charge of Lane Seminary, upon condition that he should be acknowledged as a minister of the Presbyterian Church. The third Presbytery of New York did this, without his personally appearing before them, and upon his written request simply, although they knew, at the time they received him in this manner, that he was not to be a day related to them as a co-Presbyter, and although they were well aware of the existence of the Cincinnati Presbytery, in connexion with which Dr. Beecher intended to labor, and to which, of right, and according to all propriety, his credentials should have been primarily submitted.

"We ascribe to the principles of independency, introduced through the medium of the compact already noticed, another departure of the General Assembly from the due discharge of its own constitutional duties; *first*, in conniving at an *irresponsible, voluntary* association, in assuming, to a great extent, the management of domestic missions within the Presbyterian Church; and *secondly*, in that, when the General Assembly had become convinced of the duty of giving increased energy to the exercise of their appropriate functions in this matter, nevertheless, they not merely connived at the continued exercise of the powers which the A. Home Missionary Society had usurped, but actually *encouraged* them by a recommendation in 1829, a measure which, at the time, deceived many Presbyterians as to the nature of that institution, inducing a belief that its operations and influence were compatible both with the constitution and interests of the Presbyterian Church. By these means, distractions and divisions within the church were greatly increased, &c.

"We do not hesitate to declare it as our decided opinion, that every minister or licentiate labouring as a missionary in any part of the Presbyterian Church, ought to be there only as commissioned by the General Assembly or some of its constitutional organs, directly amenable thereto, and to which alone he should report his labours, let his compensation come from what quarter it may. The church ought to do her own work, and by her own functionaries; otherwise, she puts herself at least under the indirect influence of those who do her work.

"It is in the very nature of things, that the missionaries commissioned and compensated by, and amenable and reporting to, a society independent of the church, should be under an influence from that society greater than that of the church whose ministers they profess to be; and this influence will extend to the particular churches aided, and even to the Presbytery within whose limits this irresponsible society thus operates. The influence is not the less real and powerful because it may not be seen; it is felt and is effective, and probably the more so because it operates unseen. Any person who has attentively noticed the course of things in the Presbyterian Church for the last five years, can be under no mistake as to the fact that the A. Home Missionary Society exercises a patronage within that church detrimental to her true interests, and subversive of her whole system. Without detailing, &c., we simply state, that for these four or five years, the missionaries and agents of the A. Home Missionary Society, and those known to be the exclusive adherents of that institution, have, with very few exceptions, voted and acted in a way to favor innovation and disorder in the church. Witness the arguments and votes in 1828, against re-organizing the Assembly's Board of Missions upon a more efficient plan; the bitter and vehement attack upon the report of the Assembly's Board, in 1829; the arguments and votes for several consecutive years on the subject of committee-men; the discussions and votes, in 1831, on the Barnes case; on the report of the Assembly's Board for that year; and on the election of a new Board.

"Again: let it be well observed, that the A. Home Missionary Society commissions, in its own name and by its own authority, men, nominally Presbyterian, it is true, to officiate in various parts of the Presbyterian Church, under responsibility to that institution; and, in a number of instances, these men are found labouring for months within the limits of some Presbytery, without having put themselves under its care. Now, such conduct, in a co-ordinate Presbytery, would be unconstitutional and liable to censure. See Gov., ch. 18, Digest, p. 60, &c.

"These relaxing principles and measures are undermining the stability of our Zion. To understand the nature and influence of these relaxing principles, let the proceedings of the Assembly in 1831, in the Barnes case, be contrasted with the proceedings of former Assemblies, in the cases of Mr. Balch, 1798, and of Mr. Davis, in 1810. See Digest, pp. 129, 134, 144, 148, and the Minutes of 1831 for Barnes. In Balch's case, he was required to renounce the errors charged upon him, besides acknowledging his fault in publishing them at all. In the result, Davis was deposed.

"But what a marked declension in the conduct of the General Assembly in 1831. When Barnes' case was referred by the Presbytery to the General Assembly, they evaded a decision of the question upon its doctrinal merits, and smothered the character and claims of the truth in their well known compromise.

"In conclusion, we remonstrate and testify against the following errors, which are held and taught in the Presbyterian Church, and which the General Assembly are constitutionally competent and obligated to suppress:

"1st error. That Adam was not the cov't head or federal representative of his posterity.

"2. That we have nothing to do with the first sin of Adam.

"3. That infants have no moral character.

"4. That all sin consists in voluntary acts or exercises.

"5. That man in his fallen state is possessed of entire ability to do whatever God requires him to do.

"6. That regeneration is essentially a voluntary change which the soul is active in producing.

"7. That Christ did not become the legal substitute of sinners.

"8. That the atonement is merely an exhibition of the wrath of God against sin—an expedient for enabling God to forgive it.

"9. That the atonement is general, made for all men alike," &c., &c.

The committee on the Memorial reported as follows:

"Your committee, after the most careful investigation and mature deliberation that they could bestow on the subject, have concurred in the following resolutions, which they recommend for the adoption of this Assembly, viz., Resolved,

1. That this Assembly cannot sanction the censure contained in the Memorial, against the proceedings and measures of former General Assemblies.

2. That it is deemed inexpedient and undesirable to abrogate or interfere with the Plan of Union between Presbyterians and Congregationalists in the new settlements, adopted in 1801.

3. That the previous action of the present Assembly on the subject of ordaining men, is deemed sufficient.

4. That the duty of licensing and ordaining men to the office of the gospel ministry, and of guarding that office against the intrusion of men who are unqualified to discharge its solemn and responsible duties, or who are unsound in the faith, is committed to the Presbyteries, and should any already in that office be known to be fundamentally erroneous in doctrine, it is not only the privilege, but the duty, of Presbyteries, constitutionally to arraign, condemn, and depose them.

5. That this Assembly bears solemn testimony against publishing to the world ministers of good and regular standing, as heretical and dangerous, without having been constitutionally tried and condemned, thereby greatly hindering their usefulness as ministers of Jesus Christ. Our excellent constitution makes ample provision for redressing all such grievances; and this Assembly enjoins, in all cases, a faithful compliance, in meekness and brotherly love, with its requisitions; having at all times a sound regard to the purity, peace, and prosperity of the church.

6. *That this Assembly have no authority for establishing any exclusive mode of conducting missions:* but while this *matter is left to the discretion of individuals and inferior judicatories,* we would recommend and solicit their efficient co-operation with the Assembly's Board.

7. That a due regard to the order of the church and the bonds of brotherhood require, in the opinion of this Assembly, that ministers dismissed in good standing, by sister Presbyteries, should be received by the Presbyteries which they are dismissed

to join, upon the credit of their constitutional testimonials, unless they shall have forfeited their good standing subsequent to their dismissal.

8. That, in the opinion of this Assembly, to take up and try and condemn any printed publications as heretical and dangerous, is equivalent to condemning the author as heretical; that to condemn heresy in the abstract cannot be understood as the purpose of such trial; that the results of such trial are to bear upon and seriously to affect the standing of the author; and, that the fair and unquestionable mode of procedure is, if the author be alive and known to be of our communion, to institute process against him, and give him a fair and constitutional trial.

9. That in receiving and adopting the formularies of our church, every person ought to be supposed, without evidence to the contrary, to receive and adopt them, according to the obvious, known and established meaning of the terms, as the confession of his faith; and that if objections be made, the Presbytery, unless he withdraw such objections, should not license, or ordain, or admit him.

10. That in the judgment of this Assembly, it is expedient that Presbyteries and Synods, in the spirit of charity and forbearance, adjust and settle among themselves, as far as practicable, all their matters of grievance and disquietude, without bringing them before the General Assembly and the world, as in many cases this tends to aggravate and continue them, and to spread them over the whole church, to the great grief of its members, and injury of the cause of religion."

Mr. I. V. Brown gave notice, in behalf of himself and those who may choose to unite with him, that they claim the privilege of entering their protest against the above resolutions.

Accordingly the following protest was presented, read and placed upon the minutes, sanctioned by the whole minority—thirty-eight names.

"The undersigned protest against the proceedings of the General Assembly, relative to the 'Memorial complaining of sundry grievances abroad in the church.'

"1. On account of the manner in which said memorial was treated in bringing it before the Assembly. It was committed to a committee who brought in a report, in nearly all respects adverse to the memorial, *before it was read in the house;* so that when it was read, it was heard under the influence of all the prejudice created against it by the adverse report and pre-judgment of the committee. It is believed that this method of procedure is without precedent or parallel in the proceedings of any of the ecclesiastical judicatories of our church, or of any well ordered deliberative body, of whatever kind.

"2. On account of the adoption, by this Assembly, of the first resolution submitted by the committee aforesaid, viz: '*Resolved*, That this Assembly cannot sanction the censure contained in the memorial against the proceedings and measures of former General Assemblies.' If the proceedings and measures of our General Assemblies are not to be regarded as infallible and immutable, then their equity and expediency are fairly open to the investigation and remarks of the members of the church; nor is it perceived how the redress of grievancies, arising from the acts of the General Assembly, can be obtained by an aggrieved party, if such a party may not state freely and fearlessly the ground of complaint, although this should imply, as indeed it must, in most cases, necessarily imply a censure of the proceedings which are the subjects of complaint. We fully recognize the obligations of memorialists and petitioners to address the General Assembly, in respectful language; and such language, we do conscientiously think, was used, in an exemplary manner, by the memorialists, and that they could not have laid open their grievances fairly and fully, with greater reserve than that which they maintained, and therefore that this decision of the Assembly goes to abridge the liberty which every member of our church, and every free man and Christian in our country ought to enjoy and maintain.

"3. We protest against the second resolution, as going to render permanent 'the Plan of Union between Presbyterians and Congregationalists in the new settlements,' which we consider plainly and palpably unconstitutional. We do not wish for an abrupt violation of this plan, on the part of the Presbyterian Church, but for the commencement of measures which shall result in a return to the ground of the constitution, and this without injury to, perhaps with the consent and approbation of, both the parties concerned. But regarding the second resolution as calculated, and probably intended, to perpetuate an unconstitutional transaction, we decidedly protest against it.

"4. We protest against the fifth resolution, because we view it as interfering with the liberty of speech, the liberty of the press, and with Christian duty. For any abuse of this liberty we are not advocates. But to prohibit, in all cases, the censure of authors, in connexion with their heretical publications, is in our best judgment, to throw a shield over both. For if the public are not pointed to a particular book or pamphlet, it will often not be known what publication is intended, and its very existence may be denied; and if the publication be distinctly referred to, and it bears the name of the author in the title page, (which was the case in all the instances referred to in the memorial,) then those who simply make this reference fall under the heavy denunciation of this resolution. We profess to admire the provisions of the constitution, which this resolution eulogises, as much as they do who framed and sanctioned it, and we protest against the resolution itself, because its tendency is to render difficult, and in some cases absolutely impracticable, the duty which the constitution enjoins; and thus may prove, as we have said, a shield both to the heretic and to his work.

"5. We do earnestly and solemnly protest against the seventh resolution, in which it is asserted, 'that ministers dismissed in good standing, by sister Presbyteries, should be received by the Presbyteries which they are dismissed to join, upon the credit of their constitutional testimonials, unless they shall have forfeited their good standing subsequently to their dismissal.' This resolution is in conflict with the right of a Presbytery to judge of the qualifications of its own members, which we verily believe has never before been authoritatively attacked and impaired from the time of the meeting of the Assembly of divines at Westminster, in which it was recognized, till the meeting of the present General Assembly. It is indeed in conflict with the acknowledged right inherent in the members of every society, civil as well as ecclesiastical, to judge of the qualifications of those with whom they shall be associated. But it not only contravenes a right, it also exposes the entire church to the most serious evils. It puts it in the power of a few corrupt Presbyteries to corrupt the whole church, by throwing their members into sound Presbyteries, one after another, till they become dominant in all. We view it as a virtual relinquishment and denial of one of the essential principles of all Presbyterian order and government; and as such we most solemnly protet against it. We do and must maintain that every Presbytery has an inherent and indefeasible right to determine whether it will receive into its bosom any and every member who applies for such reception. Circumstances may render it unnecessary to call this right into exercise, at least for a time, in every instance in which application is made for admission to a Presbytery. The denial of this right, we repeat and insist, is the denial of a fundamental principle of Presbyterianism.

"6. We protest against the eighth resolution, because, in our judgment, it not only establishes a principle erroneous in itself, but does, in fact, the very thing which it imputes to the memorialists. It casts censure on a former General Assembly for examining and condemning a heretical book, before the author was tried and condemned by his Presbytery. We here refer to the case of W. C. Davis. It is our firm belief that it is often imperiously a duty incumbent on the judicatories of the church to examine erroneous opinions, *in thesi;* and having carefully compared them with the standards of the church and the word of God, to condemn them in the abstract; and then, if it be thought expedient and be found practicable, (which it may not always be,) to subject those who may have promulgated those opinions to the proper discipline. To invert this order, is, in our opinion, to render discipline, in many cases, difficult, and in some impracticable, and thus to prove a protection to those who are unsound in the faith.

"We might specify some additional points in the resolutions, against which we protest; but those to which we have adverted we regard as the most objectionable. Still we feel ourselves constrained to add, that the doings of the Assembly, in regard to the memorial, adopted by eleven Presbyteries, or parts of Presbyteries, as well as by several Sessions and numerous individuals, a support greater than any other memorial has received that has ever been presented to any General Assembly in this country, is calculated deeply to grieve and wound the feelings of a large part, and we must think not an unsound or undeserving part, of the Presbyterian Church. Their pious, and as we think, their just and reasonable expectations of some redress from the Geneeral Assembly, will be utterly and hopelessly disappointed. We do, therefore, by offering this protest, most solemnly and earnestly beseech the Assembly *to pause*, to consider the probable consequences of their action on this memorial, and yet to retrace their steps, lest the adherents to the standards of our church, in their plain and obvious meaning, should find themselves constrained, however reluctantly, to resort to first principles, and make their final appeal to the great Head of the church.

"Philadelphia, June 3, 1834."

That protest is in gentle terms; in a submissive but decided spirit; it left no alternative but redress for grievances or a resort, in some shape, to first principles. The idea of abandoning the church to the desperate disposal of a company of lawless men, who had crept in unawares, and seemed resolved, in spite of every moral obligation and all reasonable dissuasions, to eat out her vitals and hold her up, with themselves, to the scorn and pity of the world as an empty shell or withered husk, never for one moment occupied the minds of the noble-hearted few who were thrown together in that memorable Assembly of the Presbyterian Church; the longest, most embroiled and most eventful which, till that day, had ever convened on American soil.

It is true, that Assembly embraced in its catalogue quite a number of nominally sound, amiable, excellent men, who made fair professions, but were too timid, too irresolute and undecided, even under the cogent circumstances then presented, to come up to the help of the Lord against his foes. But their lukewarmness could not shake the firmness of the standard-bearers in this Assembly.

Indeed the clear and startling indications of revolutionary design and hostility, in this newly created majority, rushed upon them with such power as to leave no room for hesitation. The die is cast; the church must be free! was their determined and unanimous declaration.

CHAPTER X.

Articles from the Presbyterian on the resolutions of the Assembly—Alternative presented to the minority—Proceedings of New School—Evidences of conspiracy—Moderates—The *Act and Testimony.*

THE following articles were published in the Presbyterian, bearing date, as stated, in the autumn of 1834, and were intended as criticisms upon the disorganizing measures of the preceding General Assembly. We omit the last five of these articles, which were in reply to the Repertory, in October, 1834, on the subject of the Act and Testimony. The reference to that document in these articles is more incidental than direct.

No. I.—OCTOBER, 1834.

PRESENT STATE AND PROSPECT OF THE PRESBYTERIAN CHURCH.

"Act and Testimony."

No man who regards religion at all, and especially no true Presbyterian, can be insensible to the magnitude of this subject. The nature, the importance, and the prevalence of evangelical truth, the wisdom and fidelity of the last General Assembly, and of some that preceded, the character of the minority in that body, and the propriety of their measures, and the purity, peace, and prosperity of the church at large are all involved in the discussion of this most interesting topic.

The "Act and Testimony," which it is proposed, in a few successive papers, to illustrate and commend, is a document which grew out of the condition of the Presbyterian Church, as manifested in the transactions of several successive General Assemblies, and especially at the last annual meeting of that body. Though gotten up under circumstances which gave rise to strong feeling, that instrument was adopted by the first signers in Philadelphia with as much prayerful deliberation as has usually been employed on similar great occasions, in the troublous times of the church. It was not a measure courted by the minority, but pressed upon them as a last resort, by imperious considerations.

They embraced this part of the only alternative left them, with painful reluctance; but with that firmness and promptitude which public duty and personal responsibility conspire to produce. Unspeakably more agreeable to their hearts would it have been, to find nothing in the acts of the Assembly which they could not cheerfully support. But witnessing, as they did, through the protracted period of three weeks, the adoption of a train of measures utterly inconsistent with the standards of our church, both as to doctrine and discipline—utterly illegal and indefensible in their form and tendency—they felt that they could not be faithful to the church, to themselves, nor to the great Head of the church, without making the appeal which is before you in the "Act and Testimony." They were solemnly convinced, that the time had come in which the friends of truth and order in the Presbyterian body must speak out boldly, bear testimony against error, and lift up the standard of the Lord in a *new* and *unequivocal* form.

That instrument has been assailed from many quarters and on various grounds, by policy in adversaries, from mistake among friends. Its spirit has been denounced as insubordinate and refractory, its phraseology criticised as severe and offensive, its tendency disapproved as disorganizing and schismatic. Some have pronounced it causeless and unnecessary; others have charged it with uncharitableness and illiberality. The numerous misconstructions by some, and criminations by others, with which it has been followed since its adoption, have led to a careful and impartial examination of its foundation and character. This review has produced a decided and immoveable persuasion, that the principles avowed in the "Act and Testimony," are just and appropriate, and the course of the minority distinguished by a sound, faithful, and vigilant regard to the purity and order of the church of Christ.

This document is now before the Christian public. It cannot be viewed with indifference. The matter it contains, the circumstances in which it was penned, the effect it has produced and will produce, and the manner in which the judicatories, officers, and members of the church may dispose of it, are all stamped with importance, and will form a memorable era in the annals of our great ecclesiastical body. Its advocates do not ask that it should be adopted hastily and without being canvassed; but they earnestly request that no man would reject it without full information and impartial consideration. We do honestly believe, that very many of those who appear to stand in doubt or in opposition to this measure, need only just information to transform them into friends and supporters.

Before we proceed to the illustration contemplated, it is proper to correct an erroneous impression which appears to have been artfully made by the authors and abettors of error and misrule in our church, to forestall the public mind, to facilitate their own course, and to obstruct the way of reform.

"The opposers of new doctrines and new measures," say they, "are disturbers of the peace of the church, they manifest a heresy-hunting and persecuting spirit: and all the guilt and odium of the divisions and controversies existing among us, are justly chargeable upon them!" Thus do they take it upon themselves to decide the very point in question, and to brand all whom they find in their way of innovation, with the stigma of sedition. "Oh!" say they, "if these rigid, bigotted, tenacious sticklers about doctrines and forms, would only let us alone, all things would go on smoothly and quietly, the church would be calm as a summer's sea." It is readily admitted that the enemies of truth wish nothing so ardently as to be let alone in their career, they do not like to be suspected, to have their counsels scrutinized, their errors uncovered and held up to the light. Such feelings are natural and common to all evil doers.

We admit again, that there is a limited sense in which the accusation is apparently true. As the advocates of sound doctrines, we are compelled by a sense of duty, to bear testimony against the errors of others, and sometimes openly to reprove them. Silence, in many circumstances, would be treachery to the momentous trust committed to us, and imply a participation in the mischiefs which prevail. Rebukes, they regard as the greatest offence and provocation, and in proportion to the justness of the reproof, will often be the keenness of their resentment. In this sense, we are troublers of those who violate their sacred obligations, by denying our common faith. But this is the unavoidable result of our fidelity in maintaining the truth of God. And we submit to the enlightened and candid church and world, with perfect confidence, the interesting inquiry, to which of the parties in this collision do the guilt and odium of discord belong?

We farther admit, that we are not alone in being reproached as troublesome for endeavouring to maintain the truth. Upon examination, it will be found that the charge of faction and sedition has been brought against the open advocates of truth and reprovers of error, in every age. These charges have been advanced, not only by the profligate and vulgar, the infidel and scoffer, but by men of wealth, education, and power, high in office in the churches, boasters of zeal for theological science and purity. The profane prince Ahab, who, by his apostacy "did more to provoke the Lord God to anger than all the kings of Israel that were before him," 1 Kings xvi. 33, dared to charge Elijah, the faithful servant of God, with being a "troubler of Israel." A similar accusation was alleged by the corrupt and ambitious Haman, against all the faithful servants of the true God, "scattered abroad among the people, in all the provinces of the kingdom of Ahasuerus." Esther iii., 8. The prophet Jeremiah encountered severe censures and threats on account of his fidelity in reproving the false prophets, and priests, and corrupt people of his day. Our Divine Saviour himself fell under the same denunciation! "He deceiveth the people." John vii., 12. And he was at last brought to the cross by false accusation of enmity to Cæsar. How frequently and vehemently was the apostle Paul assailed with similar opprobious and slanderous charges! Through all the subsequent periods of the church, the same practice has prevailed. Whoever has been found among clergy or laity, sufficiently honest, and bold, and faithful, to reprove, and bear testimony against errors in doctrine, has been stigmatised as factious and troublesome. We find ourselves, by these charges, placed in the best society of earth, and we willingly share their fate: but shall in no wise be deterred from pursuing the course we have chosen. We are well aware, that through the corruption of human nature, and the imperfection of Christian virtue, these unfounded allegations often prove successful, at least for a time. Popular sympathies are on the side of the accusers. A relaxed and reduced tone of theological purity, both as to truth and morality, suits the world; and a considerable portion of the church feel this sympathy so strongly, that they readily listen, and easily yield to the appeals of the disorganizing and unsound. The leaders in the majority of the last Assembly knew this fact, they seized the handle thus presented to them, and wielded it with a force and dexterity but too successful in the prosecution of their plans. The city of Philadelphia furnished decisive evidence to support these statements, and the General Assembly, in its thronged aisles, and galleries, and lobbies, confirmed the fact. This, then, is a strong hold of the majority. In their mouths, it is a convenient and imposing substitute for truth and reason. This artifice operates in two ways. It strengthens the sympathies of such as are already more than half wrong; and it drives from the ranks of opposition many who are on the whole sound men, but of a timid, hesitating temper. Thus a temporizing policy has been induced, important points at issue have been tamely and easily surrendered, for the sake of peace. But the spirit of innovation is insatiable as death—it acquires strength and boldness from concession—to attempt to compromise is to yield a victory!

Encouraged by past success, the real troublers of the church follow the minority still with the same unjust criminations. Is it true then, that in any community, professing to be governed by laws, fixed and binding in their nature, which all have voluntarily assumed and solemnly sworn to obey, that the *transgressors* of the compact are *innocent*, and the *advocates* of *honest adherence* and conformity, *criminal?* Is it more meritorious in these days of new light to destroy the truth than to defend it? or have truth and error changed sides? Has light become darkness and darkness light? Are the heretical, in the bosom of the church, discharged from all obligation to observe her standards and forms? Have their ordination vows ceased to possess binding force? Or have they entered the church, observing, nominally, the form of obligation, but secretly rejecting its spirit and denying its power.

If the charge brought against the advocates of truth be well founded, what guard is there against error? Or is there none? Has God committed his blessed truth to the winds and waves of this corrupt world without a pilot, a star, or an anchor? The minority, in this great question, believe that God has placed the most sacred guards around his truth, that he has bound his ministers by most impressive sanctions, "to be zealous and faithful in maintaining the truths of the gospel and the purity and peace of the church, whatever persecution or opposition may arise unto them on that account." Form of Gov., chap. xiv., sec. 10. And when constrained, by a regard to their own solemn engagement, and the divine command, they "lift up the standard of the Lord against the enemy, coming in like a flood," (Isaiah lix., 19,) shall they be denounced as troublers of Zion? On the same principle, may not all faithful civil officers, preservers, and promoters of justice and good order in society, be stigmatized as alarmists and disturbers? May not the very enactments of the Supreme Lawgiver be denounced by transgressors as troublesome, with equal propriety? From every just view that we can take of the subject, it is clear that they who are nobly endeavouring to support the constitution of our church, her faith and her discipline, are sustained by reason and justice. Their course is prescribed and sanctioned, not less by divine command, than by their own official pledge. Less they could not do, and maintain the character of candour, consistence, and fidelity. Let the guilt, and the awful responsibility of innovation, tumult, and animosity in the Presbyterian body, fall where they justly *should*, upon the corrupters of the purity and simplicity of our system. *They are the troublers of Zion*, and it remains for them to rescue themselves from the "curse" denounced against those who "preach another gospel." (Gals. i., 8, 9.)

A MEMBER OF NEW BRUNSWICK PRESBYTERY.

No. II.—OCTOBER, 1834.

"*Act and Testimony.*"—*Grounds of it.*

Great pains have been taken by certain leaders in the work of disorganization, and others have co-operated, in making an impression, that there is really no cause for the "Act and Testimony;" that there is no serious or alarming division in the church. Hence their incessant efforts to remove constitutional landmarks, to preserve an apparent amalgamation with the true church, by breaking down all distinctions between themselves and the pure Presbyterian body. Hence, also, their frequent cries in the General Assembly and elsewhere, "We are orthodox—we are old-school—we are true Presbyterians—we are Confession of Faith men!" This appears extremely inconsistent; for at that very moment, they were pursuing a systematic train, and passing acts which could not fail to destroy the purity and unity of the church. Enlarged charity does not prohibit us from supposing that this procedure was designed to throw dust in the eyes of the unwary, and to lead such, imperceptibly, to favour their plans. Their success in this measure is no longer matter of speculation. The question now is, shall this delusion last? It will not be difficult to exhibit to unprejudiced minds satisfactory grounds for the "Act and Testimony." Indeed, the facts and views to be presented in several subsequent essays, will lay open a train which has been for years in progress, to change materially the Presbyterian plan of church government, and to introduce theological opinions essentially at variance with the Confession of Faith.

The Western Memorial "on the present state of the Presbyterian Church," presented to the Assembly in May, 1834, furnishes a brief summary of the evidence on this subject, which existed prior to that period. We shall here present only a few of the facts there recited, referring our readers for more full information, to that important document, and, in the sequel, adding many items to the painful catalogue.

The "Plan of Union" with Congregational Churches, adopted by the General Assembly in 1801, assumes a power no where entrusted to them by the constitution. The "mutual council," an ecclesiastical tribunal then established for the government of a portion of the Presbyterian Church, and the substitution of "*committee men*" for *ruling elders*, are expedients, however well intended, most obviously repugnant to the spirit and the letter of our constitution,* and have been perverted from their original design, and persisted in so far, as to impair practically our form of government, and to threaten its very existence. For the correctness of these statements, compare that plan† with the Book of Discipline. A repeal of this plan now, when the causes which gave rise to it do not exist, has been repeatedly asked for, but in vain. This unconstitutional accommodation has been a door of entrance to anti-Presbyterian men and measures, greatly dimin-

* Form of Government, chap. xii., sec. 6.

† See Digest, p. 297.

ishing the uniformity of our character, and gradually undermining the principles of our system. Whole districts of the church are without ruling elders, know nothing of the pastoral relation between ministers and people, are supplied by teachers who have never adopted our Confession of Faith nor form of government, and are substantially Congregational in their spirit and aim, retaining for convenience sake the Presbyterian distinction. All their deviations from our constituted forms, and opposition to our standards, are openly vindicated by an appeal to the "Plan of Union." Into this prolific source of error and disunion, we ask the intelligent and candid to look, for grounds of the "Act and Testimony."

To aid the work of innovation, many devices have been employed, all accelerating its progress, and deepening its injurious effect. One of the most successful of these is, the opinion now maintained by numbers who assume the Presbyterian name, that every individual who enters our church, in adopting her standards, has a right to put his "own construction" upon any part of them, without responsibility for that construction. That this subterfuge is employed as a disguise for error, and has aided to mar both the purity and peace of our church, no intelligent and candid man, we presume, will deny.

The opinions of men, venerable for learning and piety, on the subject of adopting creeds, ought to exert great influence. The following paragraph, in relation to subscribing the articles of the established church, is extracted from a letter of Dr. Thomas Scott, author of the Commentary on the Bible:

"If by subscription be meant, an avowed assent to the truth of any proposition contained in what we subscribe, I can never subscribe these articles without telling a most audacious lie in the face of God, in a solemn and important matter of religion, for the sake of sordid lucre."

No man possessed more profoundly the confidence of the American people, than Dr. John Witherspoon. The following is his language on the subject of these subscriptions: "This is so direct a violation of sincerity, that it is astonishing to think how men can set their minds at ease in the prospect, or keep them in peace after the deliberate commission of it. The very excuses and evasions that are offered in defence of it, are a disgrace to reason, as well as a scandal to religion. What success can be expected from that man's ministry, who begins it with an act of so complicated guilt? How can he take upon him to reprove others for sin, or to train them up in virtue and true goodness, while himself is chargeable with direct, premeditated, and perpetual perjury?"* If this system of deception be permitted to re-

* Witherspoon's Works, Vol. III., p. 197.

main uncorrected in the very sanctuary of our church, what security can she have against the continual invasion of the sacred office, by unsound and disorganizing men?

The practice pursued by some Presbyteries, of ordaining young men, in one part of the church, to dispense the ordinances of the gospel in other districts, under regular Presbyterial care, has produced much evil, is at variance not less with the discreet usages of the church, than with sound expediency. Two causes have been assigned for this irregularity, to the one or the other of which it owes its origin and its prevalence; either a design to screen from constitutional scrutiny, candidates, who, from hasty preparation or weakness of intellect, are destitute of competent ministerial furniture, or to conceal corrupt opinions and prejudices on the subject of theological science and church government.

How incompatible with an honest and faithful support of the Presbyterian system, is the conduct of those Presbyteries,* who suddenly and frequently *lay hands* upon young men, even clusters of them, educated under Congregational influence and in Congregational seminaries, who know nothing about the Presbyterian system in doctrine or discipline, except the name, and are forthwith commissioned to preach the gospel and administer its ordinances, within the limits of sound Presbyteries, who are now forbidden to demur or to inquire. Is this course congenial with our ecclesiastical institutions? Must it not necessarily produce error, strife, every evil fruit? Can the friends of pure Presbyterianism, who love the church in her uncorrupted character, and feel solemnly obliged and deeply solicitous, to preserve her order from perversion and abuse, honestly stand by, in silence and inaction while the work of deterioration, in numberless instances and palpable forms, is rapidly advancing, and that under sanction of the highest authority? The resolutions in the minutes of the last Assembly, which seem to promise relief from some of these evils will be found completely nullified by other measures of the same body.

A MEMBER OF NEW BRUNSWICK PRESBYTERY.

No. III.—OCTOBER, 1834.

"*Act and Testimony.*"—*Additional grounds of it.*

The decision of the General Assembly of 1832, repeated in 1833, and confirmed in 1834, dividing the Presbytery of Philadelphia, against the determination of the Synod, was a transaction in its nature hostile to the Presbyterian system, tending to introduce, under the sanction of arbitrary power, a well digested plan to corrupt the form of our faith, to split up inferior judicatories into discordant fragments, and to divide the great body of the church, into opposing factions.

* Presbytery of Newburyport, and Third Presbytery of New York, are among those referred to.

The act referred to, contains an assumption of power, infringing the rights of inferior judicatories, and the introduction of a principle corrupting to the church.

To Synods belong the work of forming new Presbyteries, within their own bounds. The Synod has power to erect new Presbyteries, and unite or divide those which were before erected. Form of Government, chap. xi., sec. 4. In districts not claimed by Synods—in circumstances where two or more Synods have come into contact—and in cases referred to the General Assembly by Synodical advice, that body has formed Presbyteries. But after careful examination, it is affirmed that no instance can be produced from the records of the Assembly, in which this right of Synods has been questioned. Several cases are recorded in which it has been recognized and confirmed. Precedent is therefore against the assumption, as well as statute.

But, say the advocates of this arbitrary measure, "To the General Assembly belongs the power of superintending the concerns of the whole church." Form of Government, chap. xii., sec. 5. And this is a sufficient warrant for the act. Is the doctrine to be admitted, that definite designations of rights, of duties, and of powers, resting upon specific statutes, must yield to general provisions, and vague trusts? The Synod is invested, by statute, with power "to erect new Presbyteries"—the General Assembly has power "to superintend the concerns of the whole church"—therefore the Assembly may erect new Presbyteries. This is the argument. Now an argument which proves too much, proves nothing. If this inference be just, where shall we limit the power of the General Assembly? What may she not do? If this principle be admitted, is it not obvious that collision and confusion will be an immediate result? And if it be acquiesced in, who can fail to see that a concentration and accumulation of all power in the General Assembly will follow of course? It may control, at pleasure, all the measures of Synods, of Presbyteries, and church sessions. It may assume the office of admitting and disciplining church members; of educating, licensing, and ordaining candidates for the ministry. It may become a complete autocrat or despot, pervading every minute department of the church, paralyzing and practically annihilating inferior judicatories, and spreading innovation and revolution every where. Such an interpretation of our constitution, was to be expected from men ignorant of Presbyterianism, blinded and disaffected to our system by Congregational predilections. To such Presbyterians, if Presbyterians they may be called, the opinion soberly advocated in support of the above construction, that the General Assembly is a large Presbytery, the depository and source of all original powers, and that Synods and Presbyteries derive their rights from the Assembly, may appear feasible, because this scheme is approaching somewhat the New England platform of church government; but really, an attempt to support this theory, with our Book of Discipline in hand, does appear very chimerical. Against all such usurpation and confusion in the affairs of our church, we bear our testimony, and lift up the warning voice.

But the majority had a strong motive impelling them to this illegal course of action. It was to introduce what they call the "elective affinity" principle,* a principle which threatens the whole Presbyterian Church, as such, with corruption and extinction. Our form of government directs that Presbyteries shall be constituted embracing "all the ministers and one ruling elder, from each congregation, within a certain district." Chap. x., sec. 2. The "elective affinity" principle, authorizes the creation of Presbyteries, without definite boundaries, composed of men arbitrarily selected, and theologically assorted, to secure a preponderance to peculiar opinions and measures. Such a new classification was never heard of, till heresy began to appear and to become excessively impatient of constitutional restraint. The edification of the pure church demanded no such arrangement. Orthodoxy complained of no difficulty under the reign of her ancient, wise, and venerable *Formula*. She asked no indulgence, feared no evil. Why this new division, this panneling and packing, in a manner so novel, so inconvenient and unnatural? It has not happened by chance. The object is, to bring men together, theologically opposed to the standards of the church, but sufficiently coincident in views to live together and carry on the work of innovation, in which they are engaged. To support this statement, we refer to the facts developed in the memorable controversy, out of which proceeded the first prominent act of the General Assembly establishing this unconstitutional principle, the creation of the second Presbytery of Philadelphia. In this new Presbytery were embodied the individuals who had been for several years distracting the old Presbytery and the Synod of Philadelphia, by advocating and screening the heretical opinions contained in Mr. Barnes' sermon on the "way of salvation." In that struggle, they were earnest and tenacious in the highest degree. At every step, they felt that they were contending for *self*.

"Mutato nomine, de te,
Fabula narratur."

Through all the vicissitudes of that controversy, the real essence of the question never varied. It was a systematic and per-

* This *principle* is sanctioned in a resolution of the same Assembly, May 30th. "Resolved, that except in very *extraordinary* cases, this Assembly are of the opinion that Presbyteries ought to be formed with geographical limits." Ergo. In extraordinary cases, which may be imagined at pleasure, the "affinity" plan may prevail.

severing effort of those opposed to our expression of doctrine and polity as a church, to provide a sanctuary in our bosom for heretical men, and principles, and measures. And to afford them ample facilites to maintain and propagate their peculiar tenets, existing circumstances constrain us to believe, was the chief motive which governed the leaders* in the majority in the last Assembly, in their final vote upon that subject, and in many kindred resolutions recorded on their minutes. These facts are fairly deducible, from the transactions of the several judicatories participating in the controversy.

But to place the construction here presented beyond a doubt, the appellants from the Second Presbytery of Philadelphia, openly avowed, that while their cause was sustained, in part, by objections raised against technical informalities, in the proceedings of the Synod, it rested principally upon the ground of an essential and irreconcilable difference with their brethren of the Philadelphia Presbytery, respecting articles of faith. They demanded the act, which was passed, as the only means of setting them free from forms, professions, and obligations, which, with their new views, they could no longer observe. One of the appellants, (Dr. Ely,) declared, that "they had many opinions differing from their brethren of the old Presbytery, and that they differed among themselves, not too much, however, to act harmoniously together." He urged the suit for an accommodation act, after reading a list of some of his opinions, to show that they were not so enormous as had been supposed. Another, (Rev. J. Patterson,) informed the General Assembly "that he had differed from the Confession of Faith a long time, and that he had found it very difficult to get along with the Presbytery of Philadelphia." He stated very gravely, when scarcely any one else was grave, that "he had been many years engaged in selecting and bringing forward young men† for the ministry, and that he had often found it very difficult, and sometimes impossible, to get them licensed by the Presbytery of Philadelphia ;‡ they were so particular in adhering to the Confession of Faith, that he had on some occasions, plead with them earnestly to license his candidates, but had been com-

* We say "the leaders," believing that many who voted with them were actuated by different motives.

† A judicious writer in the "Southern Christian Herald," calls these appropriately, "*smuggled, contraband ministers.*"

‡ An eloquent eulogium on the purity and faithfulness of the Presbytery of Philadelphia, from the lips of an adversary ! It has been alleged that their zeal is of recent origin, simultaneous with Mr. Barnes' removal to Philadelphia. From Mr. Patterson's statement, and our own perfect knowledge, that zeal has been uniform and consistent, for more than twenty years. Let justice be done to this injured Presbytery. *Magna est veritas et prævalebit.*

pelled to send them away to be licensed by other Presbyteries, whose views accorded better with his own; and finally, that they could not live so, they must have a Presbytery to do business just as they pleased." The other appellants concurred with these statements in emphatic language. The majority of the Assembly, having perfect knowledge of these facts, sustained the appeal, sanctioning, by their decision, the principle of "Elective Affinity."

Had the majority any ground on which to protest and appeal? Let us look at this measure, to see whether the Assembly, in passing that act, came up to the high mark of their constitutional obligation. What must be the result of this new principle? Presbyteries of this spurious cast, may now be constituted, whenever suitable materials can be obtained. The disorderly, the heretical, and the discontented, have only to complain under some plausible pretext, and their separation into a distinct ecclesiastical body is sure. To these, the unsound and incompetent, refused licensure by the orthodox—and the ignorant, distorted, and fanatical of other churches and denominations, may flock, in the certain prospect of an easy passage to the sacred office. To all such Presbyterians, ambitious of distinction and power, how great will be the temptation, to quicken their zeal, and strain their resources, in multiplying candidates "*sui generis*" for the sacred ministry? They being themselves disaffected to the great principles of Presbyterian order, and turned aside from her precious faith—is it not irrational to expect that their pupils will be rooted and grounded in the doctrines of our *magna chartà?*

On the contrary, judging from experience and facts before us, may we not confidently believe that many will be precipitately pressed into the same service, entertaining theological opinions crude and deformed? Are we prepared, unresistingly, to see this revolting system carried out and perpetuated in the church? What an afflicting spectacle will she then present, torn and agitated by this great intestine division! a division which will produce alienations in families, conflicts in Presbyteries and Synods, collisions of party feeling in the important work of education, of revivals, and of missions. If union be strength, what must be the effect of all pervading discord? This evil, unless remedied, will soon find means to exert a more injurious influence on the supreme judicatory of the church.* I need not say that the plan of cutting

* "Each Presbytery consisting of not more than twenty-four ministers, shall send one minister and one elder" to the Assembly. Printed Minutes, 1833, p. 486. "Any three ministers and as many elders as may be present, belonging to the Presbytery, being met at the time and place appointed, shall be a quorum competent to proceed to business." "Of the Presbytery." Form of Government, chap. x., sec. 7. By comparing the above constitutional articles, the extent of the abuse to which the "elective affinity" principle may be carried in subdividing Presbyteries, becomes very apparent.

up Presbyteries by "elective affinity," will enable its advocates unduly to augment their numbers in that body. Already have they acquired strength by this illegal system. Time will add to their power. While to the adherents of the constitution, a corresponding privilege has been peremptorily refused.

Have the General Assembly, in passing this act, come up to the high mark of their prescribed duty, to be "a bond of union, peace, and mutual confidence, among all our churches"? The principle sanctioned organizes the Presbyterian body into two great parties. It grants to the errorists a discharge from their ordination vows; it gives them liberty to differ at pleasure; it removes the restrictions they complained of; it affords the facilities they ask for; it holds out large encouragement to every wild and daring speculator on our Book of Faith; it provides ample scope for the influx and diffusion of spurious notions, whether they proceed from constitutional peculiarities of men, their inventive fertility, their false philosophy, their pride, their prejudices, their sectarian jealousies, their infidel whims and subtleties. We are not deceived: and the intelligent of the church cannot fail correctly to estimate this point. Let it not be said in extenuation, that the differences are small. Their true nature and magnitude will hereafter form a topic of illustration. But supposing the difference to be small at present, who can justly estimate its future character and progress? This new theory is now, among us, in its first stages; it has existed hitherto under strong restraints, and in the keeping, chiefly, of men possessing some age and maturity of character, which affords a partial security against its ultimate and most deleterious results. But who can calculate the consequences of committing speculations, calling in question the fundamental truths of the gospel, to ardent young men, inexperienced, unfurnished, impetuous, and injudicious, liable to be "carried about by every wind of doctrine, by the slight of man, and cunning craftiness"? Eph. iv., 14. Ought we not to fear a sad deterioration in our system? in our faith, erasures, perversions, and engraftures? in government, collision and confusion, and following in the train, a deep defection from the vitals of christianity?

They say, the difference is "indefinite." That it is indefinite, beyond a narrow limit already ascertained, greatly aggravates the evil. It *is indefinite*, as to the number of points it may extend to, in doctrine, in morals, in discipline; *indefinite*, as to the num-

A Presbytery containing twenty-three members, and entitled to one commissioner, may be subdivided so as to secure seven votes in the Assembly. Let this Hydra loose upon the church, and you may write her destiny in the lament of the poet—

"fuit Ilium et ingens
Gloria Teucrorum."

ber of individuals, of churches, of Presbyteries, of Synods, it may infect; *indefinite*, as to the desolating mischiefs it may accomplish.

And are the minority to sit, and see, and hear, without emotion? to witness all this, or hold it in fearful anticipation, and be silent? Are we to become traitors to the church, and to her exalted Lord, by unresisting submission to this usurpation of power, prostration of rights, and legalizing of warfare? We throw ourselves into the breach, we meet the contingence, we call upon all who love the uncorrupted church to follow in this last resort, to restore her purity, and perpetuate her glory.

A MEMBER OF NEW BRUNSWICK PRESBYTERY.

No. IV.— 1834.

"Act and Testimony."—Nature and duty of the Assembly—obligations and rights of the Church.

In a great religious community, covering extensive territory, and embracing a population variegated by national extraction, by sectional jealousies, by genius, by education, and by climate, a power of decided influence, of all pervading and increasing activity, is indispensably necessary to hold this great fraternity together, to produce unity of feeling and movements, uniformity in all its prominent and essential features. A body possessing this commanding influence, the General Assembly of the Presbyterian Church was intended to be. To this end, all its constitutional designations, of power, of duty, and of responsibility, are solemnly directed. As a legislative body, as an appellate court, as a standard of theological correctness and moral purity, and as the supreme authoritative supervisor, under the Great Head of the church, its course of action and its character are immensely important. Upon its purity and fidelity hang the destinies of millions. The duty of guarding against the introduction of errors into the church, is incumbent upon private members—upon all office-bearers—and upon all inferior judicatories; but it is, with extreme solemnity and pointedness, enjoined upon the General Assembly. Chap. xii., sec. 5, Form of Government. "To the General Assembly belongs the power of deciding in all controversies respecting truth and discipline; of reproving, warning, or bearing testimony against error in doctrine or immorality in practice, in any church, Presbytery, or Synod; of superintending the concerns of the whole church; of suppressing schismatical contentions and disputations; and, in general, of recommending and attempting reformation of manners and the promotion of charity, truth, and holiness, through all the churches under their care." Here the Assembly is constituted the chief depository of conservative powers, for the church. It cannot be doubted, that, if the Assembly discharge its responsible duties faithfully, and exhibit in its various transactions, purity, wisdom, and energy, a firm and consistent adherence to constitutional laws and requirements, the effect will be visibly of the most salutary kind, in sustaining the character and improving the condition of the church. If, on the contrary, it prove tardy, vacillating, or inefficient when duty calls, if it show indifference to the church's real interest, depart from its own impressive directory, give occasion even to suspect its honesty, its influence must decline, the church's confidence in it will be shaken, the momentous trust committed to it must suffer. The moment the Assembly relaxes in the performance of its sacred guardianship, that moment the vital interests of the church are exposed to violence; the bond of union, through all its tender and delicate ramifications, is weakened. For let it be seriously called to mind, that character constitutes the *sine qua non* —the moral force—the effective existence of the Assembly. Its conduct, its acts, its decisions, are the tests, the evidence of that character, in the estimation of all intelligent and candid men.

This great ecclesiastical body is representative in its nature; Presbyteries, including the church, gave it being and constitute its body. It was established for the benefit of the whole. Its duty is clearly defined in the constitution—its rule of action is definite and immutable. Created by the will of Presbyteries, it exists at their pleasure. The obligation to obedience resting upon the church, is binding only while the original compact is preserved inviolate. We recognize in the Assembly no common law, no discretionary power. Before a new measure can be obligatory upon the church, it must be transmitted to the Presbyteries, and be sanctioned by a majority of them. Form of Government, chap. xii., sec. 6. The written constitution is the supreme law of the Assembly in all its doings. Presbyteries, and through them and with them, the great body of the church, are the constitutional expounders of law and the arbiters in every constitutional matter. Their judgment, on every subject, may be obtained by reference; when that is neglected or refused by the Assembly, the introduction of a measure before untried, of dangerous or doubtful tendency, may justify or even compel that resort, without the intervention of the Assembly. It is perfectly plain, that making that body the judge of its own actions without popular appeal, is equivalent to surrendering religious freedom altogether, and authorizing tyranny by law.

There is, of necessity, as in all human governments, a limit somewhere, at which ecclesiastical despotism begins, and passive submission is no longer a duty. When the Assembly, by unconstitutional measures, reach that point, anarchy ensues, which is the state immediately preceding revolution. The irregular and unsound proceedings of this body, becoming for years more and more suspicious and offensive, have at last brought the Presbyterian Church to this deplorable and eventful crisis. A single, or an occasional act—even a succession of measures—unwise and injurious, should not be permitted to produce results so serious, at least, till full opportunity is afforded to redress what has been done amiss. But when a series of transactions, insidiously commenced in the Assembly, is pertinaciously pursued for years, against murmurs, expostulations, and entreaties—transactions tending, if not by positive design, at least by just construction and certain operation, to introduce principles in doctrine and discipline, incompatible with received standards, infringing the rights of subordinate judicatories, of individual ministers, elders, and members of the church, and subversive of all purity and order in the system—then it becomes the imperative duty of every one solemnly to pause, and consider the nature and extent of the obligations which are binding upon the Presbyterian body.

When the General Assembly assume and exercise the right of setting aside constitutional provisions, and erecting Presbyteries on the novel principle of "*elective affinity*," as now justly explained and understood, does it not virtually, and by fair implication, discharge a portion of its ministers from allegiance to the approved standards and forms? And if a part be so discharged, for purposes of doubtful policy, or to favour heresy, can the residue be justly considered bound to obey? Is there not here then, a total disruption of the ecclesiastical compact? Again: When the Assembly attempts, directly, or indirectly, to "teach for doctrines the commandments of men," we ask, in view of the unavoidable consequences, and in the impressive language of an Apostle, "Ought we not to obey God rather than men?" Can any Presbytery, minister, elder, or member of the Presbyterian body, can any man of religious principle, in any conceivable situation upon earth, be bound in conscience, to obey that authority whose dictates conflict with the inspiration and command of God, to believe and propagate tenets which militate against his law and his truth? which are disorganizing in his moral empire, and ruinous to the souls of men?

Here let it be distinctly observed, that in political confederations, where civil right, and temporal aggrandisement, sustained by human expedients and fluctuating policy, are the governing objects, flagrant errors and evils may exist, and exist long, under various forms, and be honestly endured in quietness, without involving a violation of moral obligation on the one part, or on the other a dissolution of the compact. But in a religious community, based upon faith and piety, conscience is the great principle, which becomes the subject of administration. *It* cannot act by proxy; *it* cannot transfer to any government that allegiance which it primarily and unalienably owes to the God of conscience; *it* cannot bow in submission to any administration, not clearly ascertained to be established and acting in conformity with the known will of God, the supreme lawgiver and universal judge. Enlightened and faithful conscience, at every step of her moral action, must uprightly and freely appeal to the standard she has adopted, to ascertain her own duty, and not less to test the correctness of those under whose authority, or in concert with whom she may attempt to act. In relation to all such, whether viewed in their individual or collective capacity, her language must ever be, *unconstitutional law is illegal law, is immoral law, is no law.* The principles here stated, we hold to be founded in the nature of man, in his relation to God, in our ecclesiastical system, and in the reason of things. They are applicable to all governments, they have been recognized by the wisest statesmen and soundest jurists, in all compacts, social, civil, and sacred. Our sole object is fairly to represent the General Assembly, in organization and administration, and to test the legitimacy of its acts, by these incontrovertible principles.

To afford the Assembly the best possible aid in discharging its arduous trust, to enable it to become familiarly acquainted with the details of evil experienced or apprehended in every part of the interesting community placed in its keeping, provision is made in its constitution and rules, and sanctioned by its practice, for extending to all liberty of access, by memorial, complaint, or petition. Here originates a most critical relation. Large compilations of testimony, accompanied with deliberate suggestions to the Assembly, as to its proper policy in relation to existing evils in remote districts, anxious and importunate solicitations from important sections, and numerous individuals of the church, for the application of its influence to check errors and abuses, involve on their part privileges and rights, and on its part, obligations and duties, the neglect of *which is incompatible* with the harmony and welfare of the church. It is not in the nature of man, in his social, civil, or ecclesiastical state, to respect that authority which is indifferent alike to his rights and to his wrongs, and which closes the ear, with rebuke and repulse, against his suffering and supplicating accents. Until recently the Assembly has evinced a profound regard to the view above expressed. Its records exhibit the interesting character of a dignified, impartial, vigilant, and faithful parent of a numerous household, solicitously guarding their interests, providing for their wants, hearing complaints, warning against danger, speaking comfortably to the troubled, healing divisions, indulging no sympathies for party, no affinity for novelty, employing the wisest and the best means possible for the benefit and happiness of the whole family.

In support of these facts, we refer to the minutes of the Assembly. In 1787, the Synod of New York and Philadelphia, substantially the same body with the General Assembly, adopted the following minute: "Whereas, the doctrine of Universal Salvation and of the finite duration of hell torments, has been propagated by sundry persons in the United States of America, and the people under our care may possibly, from their occasional conversation with the propagators of such a dangerous opinion, be infected by the doctrine, the Synod take this opportunity to declare their utter abhorrence of such doctrines, as they apprehend to be subversive of the fundamental principles of religion and morality, and therefore earnestly recommend to all their Presbyteries and members, to be watchful on this subject, and to guard against the introduction of such tenets amongst our people." This is a noble example presented early by the great leaders in learning and piety in this western world. Let us see how closely and consistently it is followed up. In 1798, the General Assembly speak thus: "We take the present occasion of declaring our uniform adherence to the doctrines contained in our Confession of Faith, in their present plain and intelligible form, and fixed determination to maintain them, *against all innovations*. We earnestly wish that nothing subversive of these doctrines may be suffered to *exist*, or be *circulated* amongst the *churches*. We hope that *new explanations* of our own principles, by unusual and offensive phrases, will be cautiously guarded against, lest the feelings of Christians should be wounded, the cause of religion injured, and the enemy take occasion to triumph and blaspheme. We are extremely anxious that the peace of the church, as well as its purity of doctrine, may be preserved inviolate." In 1805, the Assembly evidences the same spirit, and firmly declares, "That it is by no means to be considered as a vulgar or unfounded prejudice, when alarm is excited by alterations and innovations in the creed of a church. There are many reasons of a most weighty kind, that will dispose every man of sound judgment and accurate observation, to regard a spirit of change, in this particular, as an evil pregnant with a host of mischiefs."*

The proceedings of the General Assembly in 1798, against the Rev. H. Balch, charged with preaching and publishing false doctrines, evince a faithful and jealous regard to the purity of the church—a high sense of duty and responsibility in that sacred body. Most diligent inquisition was made by the Assembly into his errors; his publications were laboriously examined; every thing spurious and infecting was pointedly designated for public reprobation; and the solemn mark of ecclesiastical condemnation impressed upon every article esteemed unsound and unsafe.†

* Digest, pp. 134, 137, 139—also old printed Minutes. † Digest, pp. 131, 132.

The Assembly of 1810, in their proceedings against a heretical book, published by W. C. Davis, called the "Gospel Plan," manifested the same firm and consistent zeal to purify and guard the church. They declared the doctrines asserted and advocated by that book, to be contrary to the Confession of Faith and the Word of God, and of a tendency dangerous to the souls of men.*

It cannot for a moment be doubted, that if the Assembly had continued to pursue this vigilant and faithful course, the present corrupt and deplorable state of the church would have been prevented. The conviction arises, by just inference, that the errors and distractions now existing must be traced to its unwise, unfaithful, and temporising measures.

A MEMBER OF NEW BRUNSWICK PRESBYTERY.

No. V.—NOVEMBER, 1834.

"*Act and Testimony.*"—*Additional ground—Resolutions of the Assembly.*

Evasion has been the policy of the General Assembly for several successive years, when threatening evils have been urgently pressed upon its attention. Memorials, complaints, and requests, from individuals, from Presbyteries, and from Synods, have passed unheeded, or been dismissed for reasons so slight and equivocal, as to invalidate public confidence, destroy the hope of *reform* by ordinary means, and aggravate the very evils complained of.

The history of the *Western Memorial*, stands as a striking illustration of these remarks. This was a document prepared with care, signed by many office-bearers in the church, most of whom were orthodox ministers of the gospel; it embodied a vast amount of weighty matter, and was couched in decorous and appropriate language; it neither expresses nor implies the censure of individuals, or of church judicatories, any farther than was absolutely unavoidable in telling the honest truth. This impressive communication was treated by the Assembly with marked disrespect. In violation of parliamentary precedent, of its own usages, of common sense, of common justice and courtesy, unread and unheard, it was referred to a committee, and never known to a large portion of the house till presented in the report of that committee; a report in its main character Jesuitical and unsound, hostile to the purity and order of the church, and calculated to prejudice every mind, and especially to mislead the unwary, in regard to the matter involved.

This report constitutes one of the most extraordinary ecclesiastical documents to which modern times have given birth. It bears marks of labour, and deserves attention. But it interests

* Digest, pp. 144, 148.

chiefly, as an index of the Presbyterian Church, a criterion of the theological cast of the majority of the last Assembly, and a correct devolopement of their designs. Indeed, it may be viewed as a lucid commentary upon the complex and enigmatical proceedings of several recent General Assemblies. The orthodox part of that body, and of the church in general, who have some time looked on in doubt and wonder, suspecting that all was not right with those who appeared to be carrying the *ark and testimony*, have reason to thank the *rulers* in the last Assembly for giving so full a manifesto as these resolutions afford. They are just what was needed to shed full light upon sundry previous measures, somewhat obscure; and by elucidating what was dark, they augment and confirm every suspicion that existed. In considering them, we must bear in mind the history of several past years. Events are often best interpreted by adverting to previous and attending circumstances.

The following notorious facts are admitted by candid men; that erroneous doctrinal opinions have for years existed in the Presbyterian Church, been extensively circulated from the pulpit, and in printed sermons, books, and journals; that the General Assembly have studiously avoided inquiring into this subject, resisted all modes of detection and exposure, cordially admitted men, reputed heretical, into its councils; conferred upon them its high honours and trusts; that the Assembly have, without uttering a syllable of disapprobation, connived at Presbyteries licensing and ordaining candidates known to be unsound in the faith, both reared within its own limits and coming from theological seminaries known to be at variance with our standards; that the party prompting and directing these inroads upon our constitutional faith and order, growing confident and reckless by the wide diffusion of their disorganizing influence and the increased number of their adherents, have at last reduced the propagation of heresy to system, by establishing "elective affinity" Presbyteries in various parts of the church, thus putting error out of the reach of correction, and affording every desired facility to multiply its abettors, and extend its baneful influence through the land.

The resolutions before us are a continuation of the corrupting and revolutionary process, to which we have referred in the above remarks. That they are calculated, if observed, to give it unrestrained efficacy in the church, we honestly think will abundantly appear from candid examination.

Before entering upon this review, candour requires the writer further to declare, that while he considers the majority in the last Assembly, in the aggregate, *responsible* for the acts in view, and all their injurious consequences, he has strong reason to believe, and with pleasure admits the idea, that probably a considerable part of that majority are favorable to orthodoxy, and were influenced, in their votes adverse to it, by mistaken views of the question presented, and by wrong impressions artfully made upon them. But whatever estimate may be made on this point, the measures of the majority are not altered by it, nor is their injurious effect upon the church hindered. As to all practical results in matters of this kind, they are substantially the same, whether all the actors were honestly of one heart and mind, or whether a part of them, from timidity, from misapprehension, from moderation, as it is called, or from false impressions, lent their names to assist designing leaders in accomplishing their object. It is not our duty, nor is it in our power, to separate the pure, if such there be, from the corrupt. It is the right and the duty of those who are injured by the classification to which they have consigned themselves by their own acts, to come out and remove the reproach, by a seasonable and honest correction of their error.

To discover the true import of the resolutions passed in the Assembly, on Friday, 30th of May, and marked numerically, 1, 5, 7, 8, 11, it is necessary to read them in immediate succession, as they are most obviously part of a system which has been consecutively observed through a long train of measures.

The series commences in the following terms: "*Resolved*, That this Assembly cannot sanction the censure contained in the memorial, against proceedings and measures of former General Assemblies." This is the first response given to the most numerous and respectable company of memorialists ever recognized in any ecclesiastical judicatory in the United States; a body of ministers and men as numerous and respectable as the Assembly itself. This startling resolution certainly requires elucidation.

The first idea which presents itself to the reader's mind is this: Does the General Assembly seriously pretend to enter a claim, in behalf of its counsels and the measures of its predecessors, to absolute perfection and infallibility? This is too ludicrous to be believed; and yet its language really seems to indicate a disposition to take a seat by the side of Mother Church and the Roman Pontiff. Again: does the Assembly intend to deny to individual ministers, laymen, and subordinate judicatories, the right of considering and criticising its acts? exposing what they consider errors and delinquencies? complaining of injuries done to themselves and to the church? asking at its hands, the redress of grievances arising from its own unfaithful and injurious measures? Let "the great congregation," who are deeply interested, look into this matter. This is a day of light and a land of freedom. If civil rights are dear, religious rights are much more so. Here is room for a just and wholesome jealousy. Tyranny seldom speaks out boldly and openly at first. How are errors to be detected, abuses corrected, our ecclesiastical system to be properly guarded, but by free inquiry and discussion? And shall the Assembly, which is chiefly bound to prompt and foster means of safety and improvement, be countenanced in any attempts to curtail our Christian rights and liberties? *Principiis obsta!*

But which are the "former General Assemblies" referred to in this first resolution? This is a point of consequence, and of easy solution. The letter and spirit of the *Memorial* coincide most strikingly with the measures of the General Assembly of 1787, of 1798, of 1805, and of 1810, whose transactions were particularly recited in number *five* of this series, and, indeed, this Memorial corresponds admirably with the doings of all the General Assemblies of our church who have manifested a faithful regard for purity of faith, and correctness of discipline. The resolution before us, therefore, certainly does not refer to them; for there is not the shadow of a discrepancy between them and the Memorial. To which General Assemblies, then, we ask, does this resolution refer? The answer is obvious, and cannot be mistaken. To certain more modern Assemblies, who have been successively, for years past, tampering with the disorders and errors complained of, and by evasion or connivance affording them entrance, and providing them a secure asylum in the bosom of the church. According to the true meaning of this resolution, when correctly interpreted, the memorialists are permitted, in any manner they please, to assail the *former venerable orthodox* Assemblies of the Presbyterian Church, who have been from her foundation, the defenders of her faith and purity, but they may not utter a whisper against those recent Assemblies, who have favoured importations of heresy and disorder into the bosom of the church. To *these* the last Assembly felt a peculiarly strong elective affinity—*these*, therefore, must be guarded as the apple of the eye!

We cannot help remarking farther in this connexion, that the dictators in the majority of the last Assembly, present themselves in this resolution, on another account, in a light which reflects very little credit on their sagacity, their integrity, or their consistency. They appear not to have observed, that while they are denouncing the memorialists for their implied censure against some former General Assemblies, they are themselves, in the whole tenor of their measures, making war against all the General Assemblies of our church that have convened for fifty years, excepting a very few of the most recent, in which this tender sympathy for heresy and misrule began to appear. The facts are truly degrading to the abettors of this measure, and grievous to the friends of the church; but honesty is the best policy. And we shall honestly endeavour to lay the whole of this dark business bare to the public view.

Resolution No. 5 asserts: "That this Assembly bears solemn testimony against publishing to the world ministers in good and regular standing, as heretical and dangerous, without being constitutionally tried and condemned, thereby greatly hindering their usefulness as ministers of Jesus Christ. Our excellent constitution makes ample provision for redressing all such grievances, and this Assembly enjoins in all cases, a faithful compliance in meekness and brotherly love with its requisitions, having at all times a sacred regard to the purity, peace, and prosperity of the church."

If honest constitutional investigation were really intended in this resolution, the itinerant and fluctuating condition of many of her ministers would present serious obstacles in the way of regular process. By inspecting the printed statistical tables of the General Assembly for the year 1833, it will be seen, that of eighteen hundred ministers, the whole number in the Presbyterian Church, eleven hundred are without pastoral charge, employed as professors, stated supplies, missionaries, teachers, and agents, having, in a multitude of instances, no Presbyterial connexion, in the immediate sphere of their labours. Hence it is obvious, that discipline, however much needed and desired, could not be enforced in many cases, without great difficulty and delay. Here is difficulty enough, without any augmentation from the unwise and injurious legislation of the Assembly. But we are constrained to express our belief, that the agency of the Assembly in relation to this subject, when comprehensively viewed and fully carried out, tends to encourage heresy, and to defeat discipline altogether.

This is our first objection to the fifth resolution. Having, by introducing the "affinity" system, sanctioned the introduction of unsound men into the ministry, the Assembly are perfectly consistent with themselves, in attempting to shelter them from censure, as far as possible, in their public ministry. Indeed, they would be unfaithful to their own illegitimate progeny, did they not at least attempt their protection. How is this screen to be drawn around these *holders* and *propagators of error?* Let us see. The Assembly hold themselves up as rigid champions for "*constitutional trial,*" *ad captandum,* they "enjoin a faithful compliance with the requisitions of the constitution." It often happens, when heretical artifice is at work, that men acting from the worst principles, use the same language as those professing the best. We fear it is so here. The Assembly had, a few days preceding, established the Second Presbytery of Philadelphia. The avowed object of that measure was to collect that portion of the Presbytery of Philadelphia, who differed from the Confession of Faith in theological views, in one Presbytery, where they might, unmolested by the orthodox, maintain and propagate their new opinions. The act referred to, was particularly an accommodation to Mr. Barnes, who, in his printed sermon, had denounced the "framework of faith that has been reared around the Bible," see 9th page. All this, the act of the Assembly on that subject sanctions. Now, we ask how Mr. Barnes, or any man, can be brought to "constitutional trial" in that Presbytery, while they retain their present character and claim the rights the Assembly have granted them? Will that Presbytery condemn false doctrine—any opinions which they themselves hold? This is not to be expected. Indeed, justly interpreting the measures of the Assembly, a convict at the bar of that Presbytery would have a right to appeal to the Assembly, as has already, in substance, been done, and claim the implied and pledged protection of the highest tribunal in the church, in holding the most palpable and injurious heresy. *Ab uno, omnia disce.* This is a fair specimen of the "constitutional strictness" the Assembly are about to insist on, with so much apparent honesty and zeal. To such tribunals, which are now established by the highest authority, which are multiplying through our church, and to which unsound men will unquestionably attach themselves for security, they are to be referred as the only proper tribunals to test their character and arrest their progress. And what will be the result of trial, if the farce is attempted at all, before such tribunals? Speedy acquittal will be triumphantly proclaimed, and trumpeted throughout the land, and the heretic let loose again, inspired with increased confidence, under all the advantages of alleged trial and vindication, to pursue his desolating course. On the whole, there is a striking want of candour and integrity in the whole of this matter. While the ostensible object appears to be an honest and faithful application of our judicial system for the detection and punishment of error, the real aim of this resolution, when fairly viewed, especially in connexion with what precedes and follows, may be justly pronounced, the total prevention of "constitutional trial."

2. It is a serious objection to the resolution before us, that it so decisively discourages all kinds of criticism and censure of heretical men. The reflection it intends primarily to cast upon the memorialists, for referring to heretical books and their authors, is in this essay, considered of little consequence. The writer looks to more important bearings of this intended prohibition. As we think it must be conceded, there is in the Presbyterian Church, under existing circumstances, in most cases little or no prospect of an honest trial of unsound teachers, it is the last and only refuge of the church to watch them closely; like the commended Bereans, to examine their doctrines and compare them with the true standard, to see whether these things are so, and wherever they detect dangerous error, to sound the alarm and put the people on their guard. Does this effort of the Assembly to suppress

free remark, comport with the sacred duty of the supreme guardian of truth, in the Presbyterian body? Is it competent for it to interfere with the independent and upright movements of the Christian mind in the pursuit of truth? in the exercise of faith and devotion? Is this the religious liberty of the nineteenth century? Our civil rulers, by statute unrestrictedly amenable to law, are also open to the severest animadversion of the humblest citizen. Shall our spiritual guides entrusted with immortal interests, be placed, not only out of the reach of law, but raised above the most just and necessary inquiries and complaints? Can that doctrine be consistent with the purity and safety of the church, that ministers whose *standing* may be technically *good and regular*, that is, against whom charges of heresy or schism have not been tabled before a competent tribunal, are to be considered pure and innocent until "constitutionally tried and condemned," however corrupt and disorganizing their principles and their conduct may be, in the eyes of the church and the world? What! has it come to this, that the name of *minister* may be used as a cloak for error, as a passport through the church in disseminating false doctrines to any extent, however aggravated and injurious, provided its *bearer* is so circumstanced, by the remoteness of the Presbytery to which he belongs, by its inability to act or by its unsoundness in the faith, that he cannot be brought to a regular trial and condemnation? The advice of the Apostle is worthy of regard, Rom. x., 17. "Now I beseech you, brethren, mark them which cause divisions and offences, contrary to the doctrines which you have learned, and avoid them." But according to the plan *enjoined* in the resolution, orthodox ministers, alive to the interests of the church, must be silent; the people are not permitted to complain; heretics may roam at large, scattering fire brands, arrows, and death, through the church. This injunction is followed up with the monstrous assumption, that criticising such men is "greatly hindering their usefulness as ministers of Jesus Christ!" and what consummates the preposterousness of the whole resolution is the intimation that all this silence, concealment, and submission, are required "at all times, out of sacred regard to the purity, peace, and prosperity of the church!!!"

We would not be understood to maintain that the result here anticipated, will certainly follow in every case. Where unsound ministers are found connected with orthodox Presbyteries, they may of course, be brought to regular trial. But we maintain that this will rarely be the fact. Such men will form Presbyterial connexions suited to their theological affinities. The system now in operation will tend extensively to bring every element in the body of the church, unfriendly to our faith and discipline, into combined and successful action. We have perfectly satisfactory reasons for believing that the temptation will be found too strong to be resisted. Indeed, fact has already confirmed our apprehension. Is it not mournful that the General Assembly, whose pre-eminent duty it is to defend the faith, enforce good order, and amalgamate the Christian brotherhood, should introduce principles and pass acts which invite innovation? We fondly hope that pure religion has still so deep an influence on the great body of her ministers, and so firm a hold on the popular mind, that the evils and dangers presented recently, through many channels, will inspire constitutional resistance, and produce quick *reform*.

A MEMBER OF NEW BRUNSWICK PRESBYTERY.

No. VI.—December, 1834.

"Act and Testimony."—Additional ground—Resolutions of the Assembly 7 and 8.

The last Assembly having, in their first resolution on the Western Memorial, attempted to exculpate *former General Assemblies*, which favoured the introduction of heresy into the church, and, at the same time, prospectively, to defend themselves and any future Assemblies which may pursue the same unconstitutional policy, in their *fifth* resolution, which has already passed under review, they attempt to screen heretical men from censure by prohibiting the orthodox, both ministers and people, from freedom of remark upon their doctrines and measures. It has been shown, that the remedy which they, with apparent fairness, recommend, must, under the spurious system they are studiously patronizing, in most cases where discipline is required, prove *abortive*, and that the whole scheme presented in the resolution referred to, when candidly interpreted, bears decisive marks of intended imposition on the church. The great object of the successive measures which the *majority* are striving to force upon the Presbyterian body, unquestionably is, to provide for unsound men an easy entrance, and an unmolested existence, in the bosom of the church.

The seventh resolution pursues this object in the following words: "That a due regard to the order of the church, and the bonds of brotherhood, requires, in the opinion of this Assembly, that ministers dismissed in good standing by sister Presbyteries, should be received by the Presbyteries they are dismissed to join, upon the credit of their constitutional testimonials, unless they shall have forfeited their good standing."

Until the present, it has been almost unanimously agreed, that to Presbyteries belongs inherently the right to superintend the migrations of ministers through the church, and, by personal examination, to test the theological soundness of any belonging to sister Presbyteries, who may apply for admission. The above resolution urges a new theory and corresponding practice, that ministers of our own denomination should be received in all the Presbyteries of our church on a mere Presbyterial *certificate*. To the full introduction and ultimate establishment of the "affinity system," it, no doubt, appears extremely important to its abettors, that every obstacle, both in the constitution and habits of the church, should be removed with all practicable speed. With this end obviously in view, the measure here recommended is no less artful and daring than some that have preceded. Under the plausible disguise assumed, every man of penetration and candour will detect a deadly assault upon the great fundamental barrier of the Presbyterian Church against heresy. It is true, as implied in this resolution, that orthodox Presbyteries, in the legitimate exercise of their rights, are formidable to heretical men and their devices; and the church will at once perceive, since these Presbyteries are now marked out as victims of heretical rapacity, how inconceivably important it is to preserve and perpetuate them in their unimpaired purity and power.

To this insidious attempt of the Assembly to make a Presbyterial certificate an *exclusive voucher* for character and standing in the Presbyterian Church, we hold the following objections:

1. It is a palpable violation of the constitution of the church, which declares, (Form of Government, chap. x., sec. 8,) "The Presbytery has power to ordain, to install, to remove, and to *judge* ministers." The power, without limitation, of judging ministers, is vested in the Presbyterial body, it is, indeed, a divine, original, and essential right, which, except in case of appeal, has never been alienated or transferred to any other body, and can never be either limited or destroyed but by the exercise of unlawful power and criminal violence. Take away from Presbyteries this primary, fundamental right, and the divine fabric of Presbyterianism suffers a radical change; its essential character and peculiar glory at once pass away; it degenerates into a mere human device, and ours is no longer the Presbyterian Church, founded upon the simple, but grand and beautiful platform of the New Testament, organized by our blessed Lord.

Gospel ministers, from the moment they commence their trials for the sacred office, till they finish their earthly course, are subject to the jurisdiction and disposal of the Presbytery. Their geographical locations, their public exhibitions, their deportment, their migrations through the church, and "the report of them that are without," 1 Tim. iii., 7, are proper subjects of inquiry and adjudication in the Presbyterial body, both in regard to its own constituent branches and to those of other Presbyteries soliciting membership. On a judicious and faithful discharge of this trust, depends, in a great measure, the purity of the church. Corrupt Presbyteries and "false teachers" may be prevented from infecting her purer districts by the instrumentality of this constitutional guard.

2. Making the Presbyterial certificate sufficient evidence of ministerial character and standing, without farther examination, will let in upon the church a wide spreading and desolating flood of error. Every one must see, that this measure is just what the party in the Presbyterian Church, opposed to her faith and discipline, now need to enable them, without restriction or delay, to pervade, to occupy, and to infect every portion of the church, by their unsound and disorganizing men. They have already erected unconstitutional Presbyteries on the affinity principle. They have learned from the cases of Dr. Beecher, Mr. Barnes, and others, that certificates of dismission from such bodies, are not considered valid by orthodox Presbyteries. Hence, they have only to constitute these dismissions sufficient vouchers, by laying violent hands on the power of Presbyteries, and their emissaries of every grade will at once have free course. This omnipotent outfit can easily be obtained from the Third Presbytery of New York, the Second Presbytery of Philadelphia, the Presbytery of Cincinnati, or from some other affinity Presbytery; and, according to the plan now proposed, it must prove a passport through the land, and its bearer may demand instantaneous admission, without examination, in any and every Presbytery in the church. Since the flag protects its bearer, Arminians, Pelagians, Emmonites, Unitarians, and all the litters of errorists now invited to flock hither, will be enabled to march at pleasure under this irresistible safeguard.

This is a plain and honest exposition of the resolution under consideration. It seems really astonishing that a sufficient number of men could be found in the General Assembly, willing to offer such an egregious *insult* to the *understanding* and *integrity* of the Presbyterian Church! to her *understanding*, by presuming she could be duped into a tame acquiescence! to her *integrity*, by supposing she would not have honesty and firmness enough to repel the aggression! yet this is the indubitable fact. Here it is—let every man examine and decide for himself.

3. The measure proposed must exert a deteriorating influence on the character and usefulness of gospel ministers.

1. Publishing to the world the fact that gospel ministers are no more accountable to Presbyteries for theological sentiments, must tend to inspire them with indifference to intellectual improvement, theological purity, and official standing. We admit, that ministers should supremely regard higher motives and weightier sanctions, connected with their holy vocation; but, in every day experience, we are inclined to think, a sense of constant amenableness to the brethren, in the frequent changes and migrations to which ministers may justly look forward, operates with very

many as a paramount motive to diligence in acquiring knowledge, in cultivating correct views, and in much of the detail of official duty. This motive it is now proposed to supersede.

2. The resolution before us is calculated to degrade the ministers of the gospel, by impairing that noble elevation of mind and self-respect which conscious integrity and purity inspire in the honest unsophisticated ambassadors of Jesus Christ. The course here recommended prompts them systematically to walk in a disguise, to *shun the light lest their errors should be reproved;* men who, above all others in the world, should be open and communicative, this resolution teaches and urges to cover themselves from the view of the church by a veil of concealment; no longer to repose for a standing in the church and a passage through it, upon tested and proved sincerity, truth, and honour, but to rely upon a mere scrap of paper, a pitiable *Pass*, signed by a moderator and clerk, it may be, of some remote, obscure, and unsound Presbytery! If that can be obtained, all is well. *Talents*, and *learning*, and *piety*, and *orthodoxy*, and *morality*, and *discreet zeal*, are stale commodities; it may be with such Presbyteries, out of fashion and of no value, but the *Pass* is omnipotent in their view.

3. This system will necessarily destroy kind feeling and harmonious action among brethren wherever it is attempted in practice. In a pure and peaceful state of the church, instances may rarely occur in which a resort to catechetical examination may be deemed necessary. But the power to examine, and, of course, the right of deciding as to the expediency of exercising that power, are both vested in the Presbyterial Assembly. Now we ask, what fair motive a candid, undesigning minister, on removing to a different part of the Presbyterian Church, can have for declining this colloquial interview with his brethren? He stands, in the sight of God and man, bound by the most sacred pledge to conform to the standards of the church. The proposed examination is intended to ascertain the fact, whether or not his doctrinal views tally with the Confession of Faith. The peace of the church, the honour, the usefulness, and comfort of the candidate supposed to be applying for admission, and the fidelity of the Presbytery, whose powers are called in question, all demand that this great question of orthodoxy should be settled before this new connexion is ratified. Ought the candidate to decline this interview? On the contrary, should he not court an opportunity to disclose his opinions, particularly on points in regard to which he knows painful suspicions and controversies exist? Does truth seek evasion and concealment? Is purity afraid of the touchstone?

But the bearers of these Presbyterial vouchers will say, "We are orthodox, and your insisting on examination implies a suspicion of our soundness." True, but will declining examination remove the suspicion? Is refusing investigation the best mode of deciding character? To this query common sense and universal experience furnish a decisive negative. Therefore, we say, the course recommended will certainly increase suspicion, and destroy all confidence among brethren. The happiness and usefulness of ministers depend very much upon their union in spirit, in council, in effort; and these can be based only upon union in faith, in affection, and in object. These unions must be real, sincere, voluntary, they cannot be coerced. Now, it is evident, that an attempt to *press* ministers into *Presbyteries* against *their* will, must produce jars and animosities, greatly retarding the work of the ministry, and distracting the body of Christ. The practical influence of *Pass* ministers may, therefore, be considered neutralized in orthodox districts, except in propagating heresy and promoting divisions. Men wearing the badge, which betrays a want of confidence in themselves, cannot expect the confidence of the church, and we have no doubt that the great body of enlightened, free, and independent people, constituting the Presbyterian body, will despise and resist this unkind, unfaithful, and impotent effort, forcibly to impose upon them and their children an order of men, who, meanly and under suspicion, shrink from the very test of faith and character which they have solemnly sworn to observe.

Resolution 8. "That, in the opinion of this Assembly, to take up, and try, and condemn any printed publication as heretical and dangerous, is equivalent to condemning the author as heretical; that to condemn heresy in the abstract, cannot be understood as the purpose of such trial; that the results of such trial are to bear upon and seriously to affect the standing of such author; and that the fair and unquestionable mode of procedure is, if the author be alive and known to be in our communion, to institute process against the author, and give him a fair and constitutional trial."

The *majority* having, as appears in their previous enactments, attempted to throw a shield over men of their own caste, and to provide for them an open and safe way through the church, in this resolution are exerting their skill to erect a *defence* around their *spurious* publications. That this is the object of the resolution cannot be doubted, and that it is, *prima facie*, a suspicious transaction, is equally clear. The commonly received opinion among writers, publishers, and readers is, that all books and pamphlets issued from the press are public property, additions to the existing mass of knowledge; that they are intended for the moral and literary use of the public; that, of course their matter and manner are proper subjects of criticism and approbation or censure; that no man is precluded from the privilege of examining publications, or forming and expressing an opinion of them, favourable or unfavourable; that publications purporting to discuss deeply interesting topics, in theoretical and practical religion, are pre-eminently engrossing and impressive to the public mind; and, that all men who regard truth and morality, as individuals and as collective communities, have not only a right, but are peculiarly obligated to influence the issues of the press, by freedom of discussion, conducted on independence of opinion. These truths we hold to be incontrovertibe in a free government, exclusive of all considerations of friend or foe, time or place, sect or denomination. What there is in the nature or circumstances of the heretical books referred to in this resolution, entitling them to exemption from the liabilities incident to all literary publications in this land of freedom, we are wholly unable to conceive. If they bear any relation to the Presbyterian Church, so as to create in her a responsibility for their character, the more obvious and cogent are the motives impelling the church, and all her members and judicatories, to recognize them and deal with them according to their merits; if they do not sustain this relation, then, on the principles of common justice, they are to be regarded with other literary productions, as fit subjects of commendation or rebuke. The mere circumstance, that the *umpire* appealed to is within the church, whatever may be the fact in regard to others, affords to those professing allegiance to that church no just ground of complaint. The opinion, that because the authors of these books belong to the Presbyterian body, therefore the books themselves are of right exempt from censure within the pale of this church, appears to us totally unsound; a mere fetch to screen heresy in the abstract from merited condemnation.

On the supposition, that this ecclesiastical connexion, which is very remote, if it exist at all, is to protect unsound books in the manner announced by the majority, it was certainly incumbent upon them to suggest some other mode of arresting the mischievous influence exerted by heretical publications. The remedy they propose is contained in the concluding proposition of this resolution: "The fair and unquestionable mode of procedure is, if the author be alive and known to be in our communion, to institute process against the author, and give him a fair and constitutional trial." To the adoption of this course, we must beg leave to oppose the following considerations:

1. It is opposed to the constitution of our church.

"The Presbytery has power to condemn erroneous opinions, which injure the purity or peace of the church." Form of Government, chap. x., sec. 8. "To the General Assembly also belongs the power of reproving, warning, or bearing testimony against error in doctrine." Chap. xii., sec. 5.

What is it, in the common acceptation of terms, "to take up, and try, and condemn any printed publication as heretical and dangerous," or, "to condemn heresy in the abstract," but to bear testimony against it—the specific and momentous service our form of church government so repeatedly enjoins? With those who *sincerely and correctly* regard the constitution of our church, the course proposed in this resolution will be considered both insubordinate and nugatory.

2. The example of the General Assembly may be urged in opposition to this new process against spurious books.

Here we refer to General Assemblies which had character and weight, defying all suspicion of sympathy, except for the truth; Assemblies which, in all their measures, exemplified both the spirit and the letter of the constitution, and spoke the words of truth and consistency. We assert, without fear of contradiction, that it has been the practice of the judicatories of the church, until an insidious predilection for heresy crept in, to condemn errors in the abstract, and to bear testimony against unsound publications of Presbyterian ministers. Many instances might be adduced from the annals of the church: the proceedings of the Assembly, A. D. 1810, in the case of W. C. Davis, whose book was "taken up, and tried and condemned," is in the knowledge of many now living. The transactions of pure and impartial General Assemblies, here referred to, furnish an authoritative *precedent*, which unadulterated Presbyteries will continue to respect and observe. "We cannot sanction," and we are fully persuaded that the church in general will not sanction "the censure contained in this resolution against proceedings and measures of former General Assemblies."

3. The "fair and unquestionable mode" of testing a printed book, "is to give it a fair and constitutional trial," *on its own merits*, having no regard to its author, its sectarian relation, or any explanation, gloss, or comment, except so far as is requisite to bring it to the proper standard.

Every volume is supposed to contain the opinions of its author on the subject it treats. The reader has a right to infer, that its sentiments have been carefully considered, judiciously arranged, accurately expressed, so as to convey the writer's mind clearly to the reader. Every book is intended to improve the public mind. With a view to this, it aims to inform and impress it, it invites public examination, it labours to guide and elicit public opinion. In no other way could any publication accomplish a useful purpose. Taking up a book, therefore, and trying it on its own merits, by the criterion it professes to regard, is most manifestly falling in with the very design of all intelligent authors. If the result of such trial be favorable to the character of the work, the author will not, probably, cavil at the process. If otherwise, the result may, indeed, bear upon and seriously affect, not only the standing of the work, but the character of the author; the fault, however, is his own, and he must receive the sentence which justice awards to his incompetence, his indiscretion, or his unsoundness.

It places both the book and its author in a very undesirable light, to say that the former cannot be understood without having recourse to the latter. This would involve the absurd consequence, that all decision is to be suspended respecting a work intended for general instruction, except so far as the author's powers of ubiquity might enable him to be present with his book, to enlighten its obscurity and adapt it to human comprehension, by oral illustration.

Besides, to minds operating according to the common laws of reason, one would suppose it to be very apparent, that a much more definite and just estimate could be formed of any man's opinions upon a given subject, from a treatise *written* deliberately in specific phrase, than from oral discussion or extempore harangue, which is always attended with excitement, frequently with ambiguities, and very often, under circumstances here supposed, with deceptive popular arts. We believe, therefore, that the claims of truth and justice will be better maintained by testing the book, than by trying its author.

4. The course of procedure here recommended, *i. e.* commencing process against the author, as an immediate and general resort, appears to us incompatible with fidelity to the church and the interests of truth. Cases may occur, in which this form of process might prove convenient and efficient, the book and its author existing near together and being equally amenable to judicial investigation. But in general this mode will be liable to serious embarrassments, injurious to the cause of truth. It is an easy work, quickly performed any where, to take up and examine a work, and pronounce an opinion of its merits. But the trouble and difficulty which attend instituting and conducting the trial of a gospel minister are in general so great, the responsibility so impressive, and the odium often artfully connected with prominence in this agency, so repulsive, that frequently a prosecutor cannot be found. Should this occur in the case of a heretical author, it is obvious, his spurious and corrupting publication would escape deserved condemnation.

If however, this difficulty, through the zealous devotedness of some friend of truth and purity, should be remedied, and the incipient steps of process be taken, from the probable remonstrances of the tribunal appealed to, and, it may be, the absence of the defendant from the place of trial, and many other impediments often occurring in such transactions, it is obvious there must be much delay, which will afford the heretical production an opportunity uninterruptedly to pursue its work of infection and moral death. Besides, an artful man, with influential friends, warm *affinity* advocates, by various subterfuges, cavils and appeals, may induce such procrastination as in a great measure to defeat the end of trial.* Should the investigation result in the conviction of the author, his book must still, by proper process, be involved in the general condemnation, or its malign influence would still be felt with undiminished force. Now from these remarks, can any impartial man fail to perceive, that the form of process urged in the resolution, tends necessarily to impede the course of justice, to give heretics dangerous advantages in the church, and to screen unsound and injurious publications from merited censure? When a house is discovered to be on fire, our first object is to extinguish the flames, and preserve surrounding property from the destructive element. Afterwards, if judged expedient, the incendiary may be pursued, and brought to justice at leisure. What would be thought of the man who should deliberately advise the multitude not to disturb the fire, but go in pursuit of the individual who applied the torch? They would exclaim with one voice, he is insane or an accessory to the conflagration.

5. From preceding illustrations, it is obvious that the *fair trial* here again so specially recommended, should the innovations threatened take effect, can rarely, if ever, be had, in spite of our excellent forms, and the utmost vigilance of orthodox men. And we are irresistibly brought to the conclusion, that a persuasion of this fact was a chief motive with the dictators in the majority, in so repeatedly urging this procedure. Let not the church be gulled by such imposture! Let intelligent and impartial men candidly survey the course of policy here proposed, and they cannot fail to discover "graves which appear not, and the men that walk over them are not aware of them," "whited sepulchres, which indeed appear beautiful outward, but are within full of dead men's bones, and of all uncleanness."

A MEMBER OF NEW BRUNSWICK PRESBYTERY.

No. VII.—December, 1834.

"*Act and Testimony*."—*Additional Ground—Resolution of the Assembly* 11.

"*Resolved*, That this Assembly cherish an unabated attachment to the system of doctrines contained in the standards of their faith, and would guard with vigilance against any departures from it; and they enjoin the careful study of it upon all the members of the Presbyterian Church, and their firm support, by all scriptural and constitutional methods."

* This was strikingly exemplified in the trial of Mr. Duffield.—Ed.

To a plain man, ignorant of the previous transactions of the last General Assembly, and unacquainted with the imposing speciousness which generally marks the incipient stages of revolution, this resolution would appear quite artless and honest. Indeed, it seems adapted to make a favourable impression upon the inexperienced and unwary. But its impression upon the more enlightened, thinking, and inquisitive, if we mistake not, will be very different. Till we reach this stage, in the adventurous crusade of the majority of the last Assembly, their *To Pan* is distinctly visible. Here the unity of the drama, at least in appearance, suffers interruption. There is an incoherence which needs solution—a chasm which must be filled by *truth.*

The character of any religious assembly must be desperate, when it is compelled to become its *own eulogist!* Never before, we believe, did any General Assembly stand in this predicament before the public. "Let another man praise thee, and not thine own mouth—a stranger, and not thine own lips." Prov. viii., 2. If the majority, whose exclusive work this is, felt the need of vindication from some seen or apprehended accuser, they ought to have found a more appropriate—a less suspicious advocate! The old adage still has fitness and force, "Self-praise is no praise!" Indeed, to common, unsophisticated minds, it implies one of two things; a work of conscience betraying guilt, or a work of artifice, aiming at deception. Often, both these operations combine in producing this result.

But, to avoid the difficulty and injustice of determining, on abstract principles, the merits of a measure possessing connexions and bearings unusually multifarious, we shall present an outline of the case, with its most material circumstances, that every observer may judge for himself.

The resolutions constituting the theme of some preceding strictures, were pushed through the Assembly with such an air of impetuosity and triumph, as indicated clearly that they were introduced, not for discussion, but for immediate adoption, as the result of decision in previous conclave. An irresistible conviction, from the evidence of their senses, rushed upon the minority, that the orthodox church was in the hands of her adversaries; that the spirit of heresy and misrule had become predominant. But, unwilling to continue under an impression so humiliating and painful, and supposing it possible that some of the above decisions were induced by causes not likely to operate in other circumstances, it was judiciously determined to test the Assembly on the same subject *in thesi.* And, for this purpose, the Rev. Mr. Jennings proposed the following resolution: "That this Assembly, in accordance with a previous resolution, which allows this body to condemn error in the abstract, and in accordance with our form of government, which gives the General Assembly the privilege of warning and bearing testimony against error in doctrine—does hereby bear solemn testimony against the following errors, whether such errors be held *in* or *out* of the Presbyterian Church, viz.: 'That Adam was not the covenant head or federal representative of his posterity; that we have nothing to do with the first sin of Adam; that it is not imputed to his posterity; that infants have no moral character; that all sin consists in voluntary acts and exercises; that man, in his fallen state, is possessed of entire ability to do whatever God requires him to do, independently of any power or ability imparted to him by the gracious operations of the Holy Spirit; that regeneration is the act of the sinner; that Christ did not become the legal substitute and surety for sinners; that the atonement of Christ is not strictly vicarious; that the atonement is made as much for the non-elect, as for the elect.'"

In this resolution, the heretical opinions which have become so prevalent and injurious in the churches, are presented in a form detached from all personal and party reference, divested of every circumstance, exciting and offensive. The timid and moderate, the boasted lovers of peace and extreme toleration, who refused their assent to a public testimony, when these errors were exhibited in connexion with names, classes, and localities in the church, are here deprived of this popular plea. The resolution invites them to bear testimony against heresy *in the church or out of the church*. With a call thus favourably presented, enforced by views of the dangerous nature and alarming extent of these errors, pressed by motives drawn from precedent in the long list of former venerated Assemblies, and urged by cogent arguments and appeals from many quarters, it was supposed that no man, who in the slightest degree loved the church, regarded her faith, and felt his responsibility, would hesitate to comply. Thus an opportunity was offered the General Assembly to redeem its character, to re-inspire confidence in both ministers and churches, to impress the world with a sense of its purity, fidelity, and zeal, by lifting up this standard of the Lord against the *enemy of truth* and righteousness, *coming in like a flood!* There could be invented no more impartial, seasonable, and conclusive test of theological character. But the introduction of this resolution produced immediately, in the leaders of the majority, visible excitement and determined resistance. *These opinions must be screened*, was the declaration of every eye, of every movement, of every accent, from that part of the house occupied by its opposers. The most inveterate hostility to the solemn and impressive duty urged, was manifested in a manner that would admit of no apology. Indeed recollecting past transactions, and especially the letter and spirit of the resolutions immediately preceding, it is impossible to resist the impression, that a strong heretical bias, a close affinity for the errors then before the house, an invincible determination to shelter them from just censure at all hazards, prompted the resistance and arts employed to defeat the motion.

The following fact already before the public, is entitled to the highest consideration, as constructive evidence. When this resolution was under consideration, a distinguished member* of the majority arose in his place, and pointing to this document in the hands of a member, addressed the chair in these emphatic and memorable words: "Moderator, I am ready to put my hand to the doctrines contained *in that paper*. And, if this be heresy, I am free to confess, so worship I the God of my fathers." Now, we ask, in what manner an orthodox Assembly, zealous of its purity, of its honour and usefulness, and of the soundness and safety of the vast community to be influenced by its example, would have received such a declaration from one of its members? For example, the Assembly of 1798—1805—of 1810? They would instantly have exclaimed, in an unanimous burst of indignation—heresy, heresy! What need of further evidence? But mark the difference in this instance. This *specific* and *daring* avowal of false doctrine, is received by the majority, in general, with exultation. The leaders exchange a look of triumph. Many previous decisions had proved that all power was in their hands. Any motion from the minority would, therefore, have been worse than useless. The desperate author of this heretical assumption not only passed with impunity, but was hailed as a *champion* by his *fellow theologians*, who clustered around to cheer his triumph over the *orthodox minority*, over the *Confession of Faith*, and over *the Bible!*

To throw this subject out of the house was now the paramount object. On motion for indefinite postponement, the first evasive expedient attempted, there being some demur, then followed the resolution at the head of this article.

If we believed the heretical dogma, "That regeneration is the act of the sinner," and that the majority intended this resolution as *a penitential renovating exercise*, very loudly called for in their case, we might treat it with more indulgence; but on every other principle, we hold it liable to very serious objections. Every one must remark, in this measure, an undeniable evasion of an important public duty. The Assembly, as the supremely efficient and responsible tribunal in such matters, are solemnly called upon to bear testimony against notoriously prevalent and dangerous errors; they flee from the point, and make proclamation of their

* Dr. D. Lansing, of New York.

own theological purity, a subject not at all in question before the house! But on the supposition that the Assembly were perfectly pure, how is that fact, existing in a negative inoperative form, unknown except through its own proclamation, to correct the alarming evils presented in Mr. Jennings' resolution? Does not every eye discover evasion, subterfuge, and incongruity here?

> "Humano capiti, cervicem pictor equinam
> Jungere si velit."

And is that Assembly to be accounted pure and faithful, which trifles so egregiously with the religious interests of the church, and of the world; like children in the juvenile sport called "Cross questions and silly answers!" How are the interests of our holy religion to be defended and fortified against destructive errors, but through the faithful warnings of the General Assembly and subordinate judicatories? Supineness and evasion, always deleterious in the guardians of public faith and piety, are doubly criminal, when corrupting theories are boldly advanced, and the most precious and essential principles of the gospel are assailed under imposing sanctions. We consider these interests too grave to be disposed of in this light and evasive manner.

But, unhappily, there exists in this transaction, matter involving charges much more serious than a neglect of public duty; even bringing into question the morality of the resolution and the correctness of those who sustained it by their suffrage.

1. We remark, that the assertion contained in the first clause of the resolution, is opposed to a multitude of irrefragable facts, the principal of which our illustration requires us to recapitulate.

The majority in the last Assembly have passed acts in theory and practice sanctioning the affinity principle, and that by the exercise of power not delegated to the Assembly. They have, in substance, censured the Western Church, and through them the whole orthodox body, for daring to complain of the temporizing policy of previous Assemblies, and of their unwise and injurious enactments. They have refused to alter the "Plan of Union" with Congregational Churches, which has proved a fertile inlet to heresies and disorders, and is no longer necessary as an accommodation. They have refused to consider and act upon the numerous and flagrant heresies in the church, referred to, *in extenso*, in the Western Memorial. They have passed an act prohibiting the orthodox, both ministers and people, from criticising and complaining of *false teachers* in the church, thus seriously threatening our religious liberties. They have organized such a system, and produced such a state of things in the church, as secures to unsound ministers, if they choose to avail themselves of it, total exemption from discipline. They have issued an injunction requiring all Presbyteries to afford such men free course through the church, whatever their reputed standing may be, on the exclusive ground of a Presbyterial certificate, *alias* an *affinity pass.* They have pronounced a *veto* upon the constitutional practice hitherto prevalent, of condemning heresy in the *abstract*, thus affording positive protection to all disorganizing, heretical infidels, and demoralizing publications, in the Presbyterian body.

In the face of all these facts, to which we invite candid attention, the majority resolve, "That this General Assembly cherish unabated attachment to the system of doctrines contained in the *standards* of their faith!" Now before the first proposition in this resolution can be received as true, we must believe that the majority devised and adopted the several successive measures above recited, skilfully arranged all their several parts in an unbroken train, admirably adapted the whole, as we have seen, to the purpose of letting in, propagating, and protecting heretical principles, teachers, and books, all without design, *by mere chance*, without the remotest intention, directly or indirectly, to countenance error. Every one, with prodigious sageness of look, will here exclaim, "What a most adroit, seasonable, long-winded, comprehensive, and prolific *chance* that was!" Why, we might add, it would require no greater effort of this long dormant and much decried principle, now becoming so astonishingly sagacious and active, to produce a little world like ours, at least a church, with galleries and columns, seats and hearers, and some Beman or Lansing, Owen or Wright, profoundly lecturing on human *perfectibility*, the *march of mind*, *flood of light*, *new divinity*, modern improvements in the Bible! And why not, (for it has vast resources,) in this fortuitous way, pounce on a theological seminary, with hall and chapel, books and funds, teachers and pupils, all easily fitted by a little metamorphose, for splendid affinity operation? I say, before we can believe the first declaration in this resolution, we must believe all this—"*Hic labor, Hoc opus!*"

But as this is a point of great magnitude, let us look carefully into the terms and import of this resolution. *It appeals to a standard of purity, and implies a statute* of limitation. The terms abated and *unabated* are relative; they refer to that standard of faith. The resolution claims for the majority, undeviating conformity to that standard, both as abstractly portrayed in the formulary, and as practically exhibited in the action of previous General Assemblies. It cannot refer to the Assemblies very recently preceding, for that would be deceptive, because these are considered as having exhibited an *abated* standard of purity. They must then, in point of time, refer to periods of unquestioned soundness. So that they assume for themselves, universally, the highest degree of theological perfection. To maintain the assertion as stated, what they assume for the Assembly in the aggregate, they assume for every individual of that body, for it would be dishonest to claim it for all in universal terms, with an understanding that there existed exceptions in individual cases; this would be acknowledging the falsity of the general assertion. They must therefore intend to declare that the Assembly, collectively and individually, without exception, were perfectly sound, that there had been, and there was, no leaning to heresy, that no member on the floor was chargeable with this delinquency. Now let the evidence before us be reviewed, let the notorious fact be contemplated, that Dr. Lansing, a few moments previous to the passing of this act, had openly avowed and assumed the heretical opinions contained in Mr. Jenning's resolution, and yet this majority proclaim that their "attachment to the standards of our faith is unabated!" and add, "that they would guard with vigilance against any departures from it!" Who can possibly believe this? Did they endeavour, in any manner, to *guard* that heretical member against *departing from the faith?* Did they reprove his conduct? Is there any evidence that they considered it a departure at all, or in itself an error? Would any spectator, and there were many scores present, conclude that the majority considered Dr. Lansing's creed, in the slightest degree unacceptable? On the contrary, would not the inference unquestionably be, that they who controlled and gave character to the decisions of the house, intended to *countenance* such expressions of religious belief as he employed, and to give them a decisive *sanction?* Are we not thus fairly authorized to consider the majority as carrying out, in this act, their previous indications of theological opinion? They had been already, weeks, devising plans, passing acts, cultivating and exerting party discipline, all evidently to favour this very theological *farrago*, and, now, when a member rises and avows it as *his own*, in their presence, and under implied approbation, they are pursuing a steady and consistent course, to *countenance* and *sustain* error, to make *heresy* the *character*, and revolution the law, of the church.

This *schedule* of false doctrine goes out, so far as the last Assembly can give it currency, as a part of our theological system, an appendage of the Confession of Faith. It was announced on the floor of the Assembly, and then and there, without opposition from the ruling party, *acquiesced in*. If it may be proclaimed triumphantly, without rebuke, in the face of the highest authority, it may, of course, be the theme of popular declamation through all the churches in our land. And shall this majority, notwithstanding all these undeniable and irresistible facts, which establish their unsoundness, their unfaithfulness, and their guilt, be permitted, in the crowning act of apostacy from the faith, and defection from duty, by proclamation through the land, to assert their purity and innocence? What man, acquainted with the nature of truth and the laws of evidence, can possibly believe the assertion which it presumes to utter?

2. Our second charge against the proclamation is, that it attempts to make others believe what facts disprove.

We consider it a serious matter to lead men to believe what is not true. The object of this measure undoubtedly is, to make the church and others believe that the majority were, as a body and as individuals, theologically pure; that they were, without exception, good Presbyterians, particularly *in love* with the standards, making good use of their power in the Assembly, and anxious to promote the good of the Presbyterian Church. Their ulterior object evidently was to ingratiate themselves with the public, to conciliate the regard of the church, and to settle the mooted point whether they were sound in the faith and worthy to be trusted. Now, as the testimony against them was very formidable, and augmenting every day, we cannot but think that modesty, delicacy, and kindred virtues, should have disposed them to speak of their own character and standing, if at all, in very different language. It is neither honourable nor grateful, to assert, and declare, and proclaim, in the face of obstinate facts and insurmountable evidence. Whether the majority had full confidence or not, in the truth of their assertion, it is clear that very few, if any, beside themselves, believe it; and we cannot suppress the suspicion, that they never would have issued this declaration, had they not thought it needed confirmation. If there had existed no evidence implicating them, except the case of Dr. Lansing, that is sufficient to convict them of false statement and of culpable remissness in screening a transgressor, *taken in the very act;* his words, spoken and assumed, constituting the charges, and they, in common with scores of others, being the witnesses. To us, it appears decidedly wrong, to utter and circulate, as true, what known facts cannot fail to render exceedingly questionable. And all will concur in pronouncing it a crime of no ordinary magnitude, to assert and publish to the world, as fact, what we ourselves know not to be true. It will not, therefore, be considered strange, that the minority should repel with abhorrence, a measure which called upon them to bear part in a declaration which they consider as false as any thing ever published to the world.

3. The mutilated state of the Assembly's minute in connexion with this resolution, is sufficient to impeach the integrity of the whole transaction.

Whenever the records of a legislative body cease to give a true history of its proceedings, it becomes an object of suspicion, and the higher the pretensions of that body to moral purity, generally, the greater is the implied evidence of its guilt. We are aware, that ordinarily, the adoption of a substitute excludes the original motion; and we are no advocates for burthening minutes with all the primary and secondary motions to which business often gives origin in our ecclesiastical judicatories. It is too obviously just to admit of doubt, that every substitute, to come within the limits of propriety and *order*, ought to be a modification of the original motion, and retain, at least, some of its essential features. Admit the contrary, and you afford the designing the right at any moment, to arrest the most seasonable and important discussion, exerting the most salutary influence upon public religion and morals, to which he and his accomplices may feel an occult repugnance; to divert the attention of the house, under specious pretexts, to matters totally irrelevant, even of an opposite or hostile nature; and then to make a record which shall not exhibit a trace of the grand and interesting question thus artfully and injuriously evaded. In this supposed case, we have a fair outline of the transaction of the majority in the instance before us. Mr. Jennings moves the Assembly to bear evidence against certain palpable errors; another member moves a substitute of a spirit and object totally different. The latter is carried and inserted in the minutes; the former, the rejection of which so deeply implicates the character of the house, is forcibly expunged from the records, and the majority pertinaciously insist on excluding every vestige of it. Is this true history? Is there not here a serious mutilation of our ecclesiastical record? suppression of a most important fact, which the church should know, and which the world should see? The minority urged them to fill up their record, to tell the *whole* truth. But all their appeals on the ground of *right*, of *expediency*, and of *courtesy*, were peremptorily refused. We can discover for their concealment and distortion, no justifiable motive. If they desired thus to save themselves from apprehended reproach, and to procure for their exculpatory resolution more kind reception, they have failed. For this dark, fore-boding chapter in their history has come to light and pronounced its sentence—*Tekel.*

Finally, all will agree that the time and circumstance in which this declaration appeared were all well selected. The majority had now in their legislative capacity, accomplished all that appeared necessary and practicable, to introduce and confirm the affinity system. They saw the Assembly much agitated, the public mind much perturbed, repeated protests and numerous acts of testimony indicating resistance by appeals to the people, the fountain of power. Hence they hasten precipitately to reach the public ear and forestal the public mind with this surprising and disgusting tale: "*Resolved*, That this Assembly cherish unabated regard to the doctrines contained in the standards!" If the eyes of the church can be blinded, the fears of the watchmen on the wall of Zion quieted, the great body of Christians lulled to repose a little longer, all will be well. Usurped power, encroaching heresy, the well digested and combined system of perversion and corruption which has been partially developed in these successive illustrations, will make rapid advances, and speedily defy all attempts at correction and *reform.*

It cannot be concealed from those disposed to look and listen with candour, that the Presbyterian Church have almost, if not entirely, reached this deplorable crisis. It remains with the sound and faithful in this great community to decide whether the evil already felt shall be redressed, and those justly feared find a remedy. To us it appears infallibly certain, that nothing but pious and united, prompt and energetic action, among the sincere friends of truth and order, according to the spirit of the gospel, and our ecclesiastical *regime*, can renovate our contaminated system, and restore our abused and degraded church to that purity of character, to that healthful vigour in operation, to that elevated, beneficent, and holy destiny, which the faith and prayers of God's people, reposing on his promises, have till this trying hour with confidence anticipated.

A Member of New Brunswick Presbytery.

Although the New School had as yet achieved no settled victory, it could not be said that they had effected nothing, for they had acquired prodigious power; they had seized the citadel, and were preparing for the pillage; and if not effectually checked, they would soon have subjugated the whole Presbyterian ecclesiastical domain to their ravages. Attacked, as the church was, in every vital point, by inveterate drilled battalions, from hundreds of ambuscades, what prospect could she entertain of escape? Does marble wear away by perpetual attrition? Do the everlasting hills grow less from falling showers, sweeping winds, and other causes which incessantly act upon them? Then from the combined force of all the agencies employed with vigor by the unsleeping, untiring energy of New School men, the church must be reduced very soon, if not already, to a desperate state.

The alternative presented to the minority was obvious and very imperative; they must be justly exposed to the charge of timid and perfidious default in duty, or issue a wide spreading proclamation to alarm the slumbering churches.

It was calculated, by the minority in the Assembly, that unless the most prompt and energetic measures were adopted to call forth, at the earliest hour possible, such united effort from the body of the church, to sustain their action during the protracted and painful struggle against superior numbers, powers, and arts, in the Assembly of 1834, there would remain to the orthodox Presbyterian body, very little prospect of their ever regaining their rightful ascendancy, or successfully pursuing the end of their organization. Discoveries were made during this meeting of the Assembly, of hostility to the ancient and venerable church and standards; fixed designs and determinations, with all practicable speed, to overturn the whole ecclesiastical fabric: of usurping absolute dominion over it; perverting its principles, embezzling its funds, remodelling its institutions and ordinances, and transforming its whole organization into a structure of a different kind. These indications produced effects the most startling and rousing to the true-hearted few found in the minority. A weighty responsibility was felt pressing upon them; and before them, lay a profound difficulty in deciding their course. For, although they believed that the conspiracy was confined to a few master spirits, yet full evidence was afforded, by the unanimity which marked their measures, that the leaders had acquired the confidence of their adherents, who stood ready to follow wherever they pointed the way.

The New School sympathies displayed by the leaders in this defection from the Presbyterian Church and standard, in the house and in the streets, in the most confidential interviews on matters of highest moment, destroyed all confidence in their fidelity to the church. Considering many of the excellent laymen involved in this difficulty, sound and discreet men if left to themselves, but deceived and misled by their infatuated dictators, the condition of the church was very critical and interesting, and under the most favourable aspect, called loudly for immediate and energetic remedial action.

As evidence of the existence, and an illustration of the nature of the conspiracy in progress, let us look at the features of it, as progressively developed, which were prominent and could not be hidden. Dr. Beecher, the Magnus Apollo, was placed at Walnut Hills, near Cincinnati, to instruct, arrange, and dispose of their agents to the best advantage. Every New School operator in the land, and especially in the West, was looking with intense anxiety, to the arch-leader in this formidable combination, for directions; watching his movements, receiving his mandates, executing his will, from St. Louis to Boston. In their action, there was, of course, great order, concert, and efficiency, considering how expanded and comprehensive the plan was they were pursuing, the number of agents employed, the variety in their capacities and qualifications, from education, sectional interests and feelings, physical and moral powers and sympathies. With some, the enlargement and successful management of the Presbyterian Education Society, was a prime motive and aim; with others, the American Board of Missions, the Home Missionary Society, &c. Some were busily engaged in selecting young men for training to their purpose, building up academies, colleges, and seminaries; collecting funds from Presbyterian congregations to aid their Eastern institutions and operations; superintending the press, conducting correspondence, attending conventions and ecclesiastical judicatories, to forward their schemes. All was life and activity, and untiring zeal among them, and the whole enterprize was marked by features of hostility to the Presbyterian Church, as the unique object. Any attempt, however constitutional, discreet, and absolutely necessary to correct or restrict these flagrant and growing evils, would be immediately denounced and branded with the offensive charges of "intolerance, tyranny, oppression, persecution, ultraism," or some such odious epithet. But the hour of decision appeared to be unquestionably approaching.

The cool, temporising, and conciliatory course which some good men advocated as a general resort, the minority believed would have speedily consummated the threatened catastrophe in our church, which her subtle foes had *banded together* to realize. This Fabian policy was what they courted and expected, and were secretly resolving to make available for their ignoble purpose. Moderates, as to their reliableness, are generally very doubtful. They cannot be counted on as certain in the season of storm and peril. The same elements of organic or integral formation, which made them moderates at first, are still embodied in their constitutions, and ready for action, if at all, only according to their own peculiar genius and temperament, and extremely difficult to be enlisted and relied upon in a critical cause, where decisive and energetical action are imperiously demanded.

In this emergency, we had all sorts of tempers mixed up in the small and anxious group. The crisis was novel—the interest involved momentous—everlasting results seemed to hang upon the developments of every hour. On surveying the little company, we saw in the midst of us some sweet and amiable Melancthons, with all his listlessness and inefficiency; there was also here and there a timid, vacillating, and unreliable Erasmus; but there was need of more than one Calvin, with his French penetration and fire, quick insight, and indomitable candour and ardour, and above all a Luther of immoveable courage and constancy, whom nothing could elude, nothing intimidate, nothing resist, to head the comparatively small and trembling phalanx of vanquished but determined defenders of the faith, and of the church of Christ. By a wise and merciful Providence, *he* was furnished for the occasion, in full panoply, and fulfilled the task demanded with triumphant power. We knew that chieftain had enemies, whether from envy of his talents or achievements, we would not decide. But we fully believed, that posterity would do justice in spite of envy or of hate, to the minds that conceived, and to the pen that executed, the *immortal Act and Testimony*, and that even the present indifferent and opposed ecclesiastics of our denomination, if there should be such to any considerable amount, would soon see cause to change their minds and retrace their steps.

CHAPTER XI.

Act and Testimony flew rapidly—New School opposed to it—Princeton Repertory dissented—Explanations of the views of its supporters—Statement of its origin—Character drawn by the Repertory, October, 1834.

This imperishable bill of Presbyterian wrongs and rights, grievances and protestations, dangers and reliefs, was ushered forth about the close of the Assembly. The document flew with telegraphic despatch, and was received with enthusiastic approbation by those who saw the sufferings of the church, and felt the ardent impulse for deliverance and reform. That the New School, at whose counsels and machinations it aimed a fatal blow, should sympathize with such a manifesto, and at such a crisis, it would have been more than folly to anticipate. It poured denunciations like repeated peals of thunder, upon their plans and efforts to divide, impair, and overthrow that very church which they had bound themselves, by the most sacred vows, to cherish and protect. Alarmed at this sudden and decided, though brief and earnest, exposure of their perfidious and distracting plans and measures, they summoned all their instrumentalities through the land, to pervert the *Act and Testimony*, to weaken its force by creating opposition, to cover its framers and advocates with opprobrium, to magnify every symptom of popular dissatisfaction they could discover; with boldness and effrontery to add to the crime of their heresies, the guilt of denying them; throughout the whole church, in their assemblies, tribunals, and journals, with indefatigable cries, complaints, and importunities, to rouse their co-workers to come forth and sustain the work, which they had, as they thought, and there was too much reason to apprehend, already hopefully begun.

As the course pursued by the minority, under these trying circumstances, was criticised by some timid, wavering souls in and out of the Assembly, then and afterwards, and their solemn annunciation to the churches unsparingly condemned by the *Repertory*, a journal of high standing at Princeton, which united with the New School in inflicting heavy censures upon the minority, it is deemed necessary and expedient, to present, in addition to what were published at the time, some remarks explanatory of the views and motives by which this minority were governed in their acts.

In the first place, it cannot be denied that the minority in the Assembly of 1834, were pressed by peculiar responsibilities. The General Assembly, by the constitution of the church, being a representative body, charged with the interests of the whole church, must in her aggregate capacity, be profoundly obligated to superintend and guard those interests. Whenever the Assembly, organized under constitutional rules, transcends her legitimate powers, or declines to perform most obvious duties for the protection of the church, or takes measures to create a policy, the necessary operations of which would be, if persisted in, to undermine and overturn the whole ecclesiastical system—a vast responsibility must, of course, devolve upon the minority, if there be such, in the house. This has been decided to be the fact, in all similar and co-ordinate institutions among civilized men. They, the minority in such cases, became then the only true representatives and guardians of the Presbyterian Church; duties of vast importance devolved upon them; they owed a service of surpassing magnitude, proportioned to the clearness of their perceptions and the strength of their convictions, to their constituents; a crisis occurred which they did not, could not, anticipate—neither could they receive any instructions how to meet it. It would not suffice as an excuse for inaction, to themselves, to the church, or to the world, to say, let all alone; this majority, through the constituted channels, and at the ordinary time, will give an account of themselves to the church, which can take effective measures to correct abuses or neglects; because the majority, in such cases, according to all experience, never will fully report their transactions, their secret and deceptive conclaves, and their artful mutilation of the subjects and the rule of action in the house, and the uncandid spirit which in many instances pervades their records, with intention to mislead; they never gather up and spread out before the public eye, the mischievous and pernicious operations of their agents, in all their numbers and gradations, the circulation of false doctrines and promotion of disorderly measures in the church. Men who stay at home and do nothing, depending upon Congregationalists, either through the church, or in her advisory councils, to give them information of the evils they are propagating in various ways, with great zeal and perseverance, through the land, may take for granted, that they are never to know the truth, till it is too late to redeem the church. Cases in which insidious workers in society expose their own misdeeds to public view, are extremely rare, and not in accordance with the ruling passions of human nature. Hence it was that the minority felt bound to issue an alarm to the churches. But, in addition, the minority, consisting of about forty individuals, realized that they had rights, as well as obligations, personal and peculiar to themselves. Laying aside their representative character and responsibility, it was competent for them to speak out, in solemn accents, to their brethren in the Lord, both ministers and laymen, and implore immediate aid in this period of calamity and peril. They had individually great interests at stake. In their persons, and in their official capacities, they wielded power, if faithful, but invited rebuke and dishonour, if idle or neglectful. It could not be banished from their minds, that hundreds of thousands of sound and anxious Presbyterians, either then did, or soon would, look imploringly to them, under God, for relief in this tremendous emergency, and that a far greater number, including the youth and rising generations, would be exposed to fatal infection from the corrupt miasma, with which the church and the whole land were threatened, from the success of New School principles and measures.

The minority felt persuaded that their public announcement was sanctioned by parliamentary precedent in all countries; by frequent appeals to the public in the House of Congress; by similar resorts in our legislative assemblies and judicial tribunals; and that no harm could possibly result from their testimony, unless by abuse of its spirit or perversion of its terms. That the crisis for such a process had truly arrived, no living and candid man could doubt, after fairly estimating the facts of the case now on record. The church had actually passed over to the possession of her enemy, in whose hands skillful efforts had been employed to erect munitions of art and power, almost defying approach on every side. In this condition of jeopardy and alarm, paramount motives sprang up from the sympathies, especially for the theological seminary at Princeton. It must be saved, and this is the most direct and effectual method, was the language of every heart and tongue. Her libraries, her professors, her edifices, her stones, and her dust, were dear to the minority, many of whom had lent their feeble aid in laying the corner stones and in carrying up the walls of that noble religious light house for God; in placing the professors in those consecrated chairs for the edification of Zion. These were all, in the estimation of the minority, if not permanently already, in a fair way to be fully at the disposal of the invaders. They had already cast lots, if not for their garments, at least for their chairs and their honours.

These professors were viewed as the protegees of the church. The minority felt, that to them, in all their delicate relations and vicissitudes, the Presbyterian branch of the Church of Christ, now suddenly cast upon their care, had given a solemn pledge of protection. That sacred pledge they resolved to maintain inviolate, if possible, to the last, through darkness and storm. Their attachment and devotion, founded in public vows and testimonials, already becoming hoary with age, had been cemented and confirmed by the affectionate intercourse of many years. On this subject it is pleasant to say, the minority claimed, deserved no monopoly; the whole church sympathized in the happy sensibility. The minority felt their insufficiency in such an emergency, but resolved, in solemn consultation, that if they could not wholly remove the danger, they would at least try to mitigate the shock, by faithfully exhibiting the alarming posture of the church, to the whole body and to the whole world, in a brief and sententious call for every friendly heart and hand to join in the general rescue. (The preceding remarks exhibit the circumstances and feelings of the minority, in the document called the Act and Testimony.) In that hour of solemn emotion, the idea of being deterred from discharging this most imperative duty, by the fear that possibly some individuals, scattered through the church, in less favourable circumstances for knowing the truth, might not choose to act in concert, or even might prefer to hazard all and join the enemy, never occurred to the mind of the minority. If it had, it would either have prompted to stronger action, or have been at once pronounced an extreme position, not likely to be assumed by honest and intelligent Old School Presbyterians.

If it was right, as the minority honestly believed then, and more confidently maintain now, after testing the appropriateness and power of their appeal, to cry aloud and spare not, to show the people at large the transgressions of their temporary rulers, and to proclaim the danger which threatened the church, let it be remembered, that in times of great public consternation and apprehension, the men who first feel the impulse and sound the trumpet, are not apt to study the graces of diction, or to strive to make their language, snatched in the moment of tumult and agitation, quadrate with the minute and wire-drawn rules of grammar, taste, or fancy, nor can they spend time, when a moment lost may lose a crown, to court an adaptation of their empassioned style to the popular opinions, passions, and caprices, which, in the ardent simplicity of their hearts, they either realized not at all, or kindly supposed could not but coincide with their own. Such and similar considerations must apologize satisfactorily to the very critical and censorious, for some peculiarities of style, thought, and phrase, found in the *Act and Testimony* For the general character and merit of this document, we may appeal to the Biblical Repertory itself, and quote its language with pleasure and with triumph. See No. for October, 1834.* "The history of this document we understand to be as follows: The proceedings of the last General Assembly of our church being in many cases *much* disapproved of, by *a large* minority of that body, a meeting was called in Philadelphia, to which all those ministers and elders were invited who sympathized with this minority in their opinions and feelings. Among other acts of this meeting, a committee was appointed to draft a public declaration to the churches, of the views and wishes of those then present. The result of this appointment was the publication of a paper entitled an *Act and Testimony*. It is impossible for any man to read this document without being deeply impressed with respect for its authors. It is pervaded by a tone of solemn earnestness, which carries to every heart the conviction of their sincerity, and of their sense of the importance, as well as the truth, of the sentiments which they advance. The fear of God, reverence for his truth, and love for his church, seem clearly to have presided over the composition of this important document. In addition to these intrinsic claims to the respect of those to whom it is addressed, the fact that it has received the sanction of so large a number of the best ministers of our church, demands for it the most serious consideration."

If this testimony from the pen of an opposer, be true as stated, the *Act and Testimony* has nothing to fear from men. What is there pronounced on this humble instrument, seems to be uttered with great apparent solemnity and candour. How what follows in a long and painful train is to be reconciled with this brief and solemn eulogy, the present historian candidly acknowledges his utter incapacity to tell.

* As the paper here referred to is destined to last while the church exists upon earth, it is of some importance that the *history* of it, begun in the Repertory, should be enlarged and completed. The truth is believed to be:

1. A committee of five were appointed by the minority to draw the document. Dr. Wm. Engles, Chairman.

2. By request, Rob't I. Breckenridge drew the paper, and reported it to the committee, without a name prefixed, and without the specifications of errors annexed.

Dr. Engles, the Chairman, prefixed the name, *Act and Testimony*.

By request, we understand, Dr. Hodge added the specifications of error or false doctrine.

3. Dr. Engles suggested the signing of the Act and Testimony through the churches, and sending the signatures weekly to his office in Philadelphia, merely to give interest and diffusiveness to the circulation of the Act and Testimony. With this the committee had nothing to do.

CHAPTER XII.

Act and Testimony at large—Article in opposition in full, without comment, from Repertory, October, 1834—Its effect in the vicinity, and on the Churches—In the Presbytery of New Brunswick—Temper and course of the New School—Convention to meet in Pittsburgh, May, 1835—Church exposed—Despondence abroad—Efforts to encourage—Extreme Despondence—Dr. Alexander, though prudently silent at home, discovered to lean to the Orthodox company—Evidence of it stated here, and visible in his action in the Assembly.

"*To the Ministers, Elders, and Private Members of the Presbyterian Church in the United States:*

"Brethren, beloved in the Lord:—In the solemn crisis to which our church has arrived, we are constrained to appeal to you in relation to the alarming errors which have hitherto been connived at, and now, at length, have been countenanced and sustained, by the acts of the supreme judicatory of our church. Constituting, as we all do, a portion of yourselves, and deeply concerned as every portion of the system must be in all that affects the body itself, we earnestly address ourselves to you, in the full belief that the dissolution of our church, or what is worse, its corruption in all that once distinguished its peculiar testimony, can, under God, be prevented only by you.

"From the highest judicatory of our church we have, for several years in succession, sought the redress of our grievances, and have not only sought it in vain, but with an aggravation of the evils of which we have complained. Whither, then, can we look for relief, but first to Him who is made head over all things, to the church, which is his body, and then to you, as constituting a part of that body, and as instruments in his hand to deliver the church from the oppression which she sorely feels?

"We love the Presbyterian Church, and look back with sacred joy to her instrumentality in promoting every good, and every noble cause, among men; to her unwavering love of human rights; to her glorious efforts for the advancement of human happiness; to her clear testimonies for the truth of God, and her great and blessed efforts to enlarge and establish the kingdom of Christ our Lord. We delight to dwell on the things which our God has wrought by our beloved church, and by his grace enabling us, we are resolved that our children shall not have occasion to weep over an unfaithfulness which permitted us to stand idly by, and behold the ruin of this glorious structure.

"'Brethren,' says the Apostle, 'I beseech you by the name of our Lord Jesus Christ, that ye all speak the same thing, and that there be no divisions among you, but that ye be perfectly joined together, in the same mind and in the same judgment.' In the presence of that Redeemer by whom Paul adjures us, we avow our fixed adherence to those standards of doctrine and order, in their obvious and intended sense, which we have heretofore subscribed under circumstances the most impressive. In the same spirit, we do therefore solemnly acquit ourselves in the sight of God, of all responsibility arising from the existence of those divisions and disorders in our church, which spring from a disregard of assumed obligations, a departure from doctrines deliberately professed, and a subversion of forms publicly and repeatedly approved. By the same high authority, and under the same weighty sanctions, we do avow our fixed purpose to strive for the restoration of purity, peace, and scriptural order to our church, and to endeavour to exclude from her communion those who disturb her peace, corrupt her testimony, and subvert her established forms. And to the end that the doctrinal errors of which we complain may be fully known, and the practical evils under which the body suffers be clearly set forth, and our purposes in regard to both be distinctly understood, we adopt this *Act and Testimony.*

" *As regards Doctrine.**

"1. We do bear our solemn testimony against the right claimed by many, of interpreting the doctrines of our standards in a sense different from the general sense of the church for years past, whilst they still continue in our communion. On the contrary, we aver that they who adopt our standards, are bound by candour and the simplest integrity, to hold them in their obvious accepted sense.

"2. We testify against the unchristian subterfuge to which some have recourse, when they avow a general adherence to our standards *as a system,* while they deny doctrines essential to the system, or hold doctrines at complete variance with the system.

"3. We testify against the reprehensible conduct of those in our communion, who hold, and preach, and publish Arminian and Pelagian heresies, professing, at the same time, to embrace our creed, and pretending that these errors do consist therewith.

"4. We testify against the conduct of those who, while they profess to approve and adopt our doctrine and order, do never-

* To sustain the accuracy of the following specifications, we are happy in being able to quote the authority of Dr. Hodge, who kindly consented to become the drawer of this most important feature of the *Act and Testimony,* on the request of the committee appointed to prepare the document. But in all the memorials and testimonies on this subject, presented to the General Assembly at different times and from various parts of the church, there is a substantial agreement in regard to the nature, as well as extent, of the alleged heresies, pervading the whole.

theless, speak and publish, in terms, or by necessary implication, that which is derogatory to both, and which tends to bring both into disrepute.

"5. We testify against the following, as a part of the errors which are held and taught by many persons in our church:

"1. Our relation to Adam. That we have no more to do with the first sin of Adam, than with the sins of any other parent.

"2. Native depravity. That there is no such thing as original sin; that infants come into the world as perfectly free from corruption as Adam was when he was created; that by original sin, nothing more is meant than the fact, that all the posterity of Adam, though born entirely free from moral defilement, will always begin to sin when they begin to exercise moral agency, and that this fact is somehow connected with the fall of Adam.

"3. Imputation. That the doctrine of imputed sin and imputed righteousness, is a novelty and is nonsense.

"4. Ability. That the impenitent sinner is by nature, and independently of the aid of the Holy Spirit, in full possession of all the powers necessary to a compliance with the commands of God; and that, if he laboured under any kind of inability, natural or moral, which he could not remove himself, he would be excusable for not complying with God's will.

"5. Regeneration. That man's regeneration is his own act; that it consists merely in the change of our governing purpose, which change we must ourselves produce.

"6. Divine Influence. That God cannot exert such an influence on the minds of men as shall make it certain that they will choose and act in a particular manner, without destroying their moral agency; and that, in a moral system, God could not prevent the existence of sin, or the present amount of sin, however much he might desire it.

"7. Atonement. That Christ's sufferings were not truly and properly vicarious.

"Which doctrines and statements are dangerous and heretical, contrary to the gospel of God, and inconsistent with our Confession of Faith. We are painfully alive, also, to the conviction, that unless a speedy remedy be applied to the abuses which have called forth this Act and Testimony, our theological seminaries will soon be converted into nurseries, to foster the noxious errors which are already so widely prevalent, and our church funds will be perverted from the design for which they were originally contributed.

"*As regards Discipline.*

"The necessary consequence of the propagation of these and similar errors amongst us, has been the agitation and division of our churches and ecclesiastical bodies; the separation of ministers, elders, and people, into distinct parties, and the great increase of causes of alienation.

"Our people are no longer as one body of Christians; many of our church sessions are agitated by the tumultuous spirit of party; our Presbyteries are convulsed by collisions growing out of the heresies detailed above, and our Synods and our Assembly are made theatres for the open display of humiliating scenes of human passion and weakness. Mutual confidence is weakened; respect for the supreme judicatory of the church is impaired; our hope that the dignified and impartial course of justice would flow steadily onward, has expired; and a large portion of the religious press is made subservient to error. The ordinary course of discipline, arrested by compromises in which the truth is always loser, and perverted by organized combinations to personal, selfish, and party ends, ceases altogether, and leaves every one to do what seems good in his own eyes. The discipline of the church, rendered more needful than ever before, by the existence of numberless cases, in which Christian love to erring brethren, as well as a just regard to the interests of Zion, imperiously call for its prompt, firm, and temperate exercise, is absolutely prevented by the very causes which demand its employment. At the last meeting of the General Assembly, a respectful memorial, presented in behalf of eleven Presbyteries, and many sessions and individual members of our church, was treated without one indication of kindness, or the manifestation of any disposition to concede a single request that was made. It was sternly frowned upon, and the memorialists were left to mourn under their grievances, with no hope of alleviation from those who ought to have at least shown tenderness and sympathy, as the nursing fathers of the church, even when that which was asked was refused to the petitioners. At the same time, they who first corrupted our doctrines, and then deprived us of the means of correcting the evils they have produced, seek to give permanent security to their errors and to themselves, by raising an outcry in the churches against all who love the truth well enough to contend for it.

"Against this unusual, unhappy, and ruinous condition, we do bear our clear and decided testimony, in the presence of the God of all living; we do declare our firm belief that it springs primarily from the fatal heresies countenanced in our body; and we do avow our deliberate purpose, with the help of God, to give our best endeavours to correct it.

"*As regards Church Order.*

"We believe that the form of government of the Presbyterian Church in the United States, is in all essential features in full accordance with the revealed will of God; and therefore, whatever impairs its purity, or changes its essential character, is repugnant to the will of our master. In what light, then, shall we be considered, if, professing to revere this system, we calmly behold its destruction, or connive at the conduct of those engaged in tearing up its deep foundations? Some of us have long dreaded the spirit of indifference to the peculiarities of our church order, which we supposed was gradually spreading amongst us, and the developments of later years have rendered it most certain that as the perversion of our doctrinal formularies, and the engrafting of new principles and practices upon our church constitution, have gone hand in hand, so the original purity of the one cannot be restored without a strict and faithful adherence to the other. Not only then for its own sake do we love the constitution of our church, as a model of all free institutions, but as a clear and noble exhibition of the soundest principles of civil and religious liberty; not only do we venerate its peculiarities, because they exhibit the rules by which God intends the affairs of his church on earth to be conducted; but we cling to its venerable ramparts, because they afford a sure defence for those precious, though despised doctrines of grace, the pure transmission of which has been entrusted as a sacred duty to the church.

"It is, therefore, with the deepest sorrow, that we behold our church tribunals, in various instances, imbued with a different spirit, and fleeing, on every emergency, to expedients, unknown to the Christian simplicity and uprightness of our forms, and repugnant to all our previous habits. It is with pain and distrust, that we see sometimes the helpless inefficiency of mere advisory bodies contended for and practiced, when the occasion called for the free action of our laws; and sometimes the full and peremptory exercise of power almost despotic practiced in cases where no authority existed to act at all. It is with increasing alarm, that we behold a fixed design to organize new tribunals, upon principles repugnant to our system, and directly subversive of it, for the obvious purpose of establishing and propagating the heresies already recounted; of shielding from just process the individuals who hold them, and of arresting the wholesome discipline of the church. We do therefore testify against all these departures from the true principles of our constitution; against the formation of new Presbyteries and Synods, otherwise than upon the established rules of our church, or for other purposes than the edification and enlargement of the Church of Christ; and we most particularly testify against the formation of any tribunal in our church upon what some call principles of elective affinity; against the exercise by the General Assembly, of any power not clearly delegated to it; and the exercise even of its delegated powers for purposes inconsistent with the design of its creation.

"*Recommendations to the Churches.*

"Dear Christian Brethren—you who love Jesus Christ in sincerity and truth, and adhere to the plain doctrines of the cross, as taught in the standards prepared by the Westminster Assembly, and constantly held by the true Presbyterian Church; to all of you who love your ancient and pure constitution, and desire to restore our abused and corrupted church to her simplicity, purity, and truth, we, a portion of yourselves, ministers and elders of your churches, and servants of one common Lord, would propose most respectfully and kindly, and yet most earnestly:

"1. That we refuse to give countenance to ministers, elders, agents, editors, teachers, or to those who are in any other capacity, engaged in religious instruction or effort, who hold the preceding or similar heresies.

"2. That we make every lawful effort to subject all such persons, especially if they be ministers, to the just exercise of discipline, by the proper tribunal.

"3. That we use all proper means to restore the discipline of the church, in all its courts, to a sound, just, Christian state.

"4. That we use our endeavours to prevent the introduction of new principles into our system, and to restore our tribunals to their ancient purity.

"5. That we consider the Presbyterial existence, or acts of any Presbytery or Synod formed upon the principles of elective affinity, as unconstitutional, and all ministers and churches voluntarily included in such bodies, as having virtually departed from the standards of our church.

"6. We recommend that all ministers, elders, church sessions, Presbyteries, and Synods, who approve of this Act and Testimony, give their public adherence thereto, in such manner as they shall prefer, and communicate their names, and, when a church court, a copy of their adhering act.

"7. That inasmuch as our only hope of improvement and reformation in the affairs of our church depends on the interposition of Him who is King in Zion, that we will unceasingly and importunately supplicate a Throne of Grace for the return of that purity and peace, the absence of which we now sorrowfully deplore.

"8. We do earnestly recommend that on the second Thursday of May, 1835, a convention be held in the city of Pittsburgh, to be composed of two delegates, a minister and ruling elder, from each Presbytery, or from the minority of any Presbytery, who may concur in the sentiments of this Act and Testimony, to de-deliberate and consult on the present state of our church, and to adopt such measures as may be best suited to restore her prostrated standards.

"And now, brethren, our whole heart is laid open to you and to the world. If the majority of our church are against us, they will, we suppose, in the end either see the infatuation of their course, and retrace their steps, or they will at last attempt to cut us off. If the former, we shall bless the God of Jacob; if the latter, we are ready, for the sake of Christ, and in support of the testimony now made, not only to be cut off, but, if need be, to die also. If, on the other hand, the body be yet in the main, sound, as we would fondly hope, we have here, frankly, openly, and candidly, laid before our erring brethren, the course we are, by the grace of God, irrevocably determined to pursue. It is our steadfast aim to reform the church, or to testify against its errors and defections until testimony will be no longer heard. And we commit the issue into the hands of him who is over all, God blessed for ever. Amen.

Ministers.

James Magraw,	David R. Preston,
Robert I. Breckenridge,	William Wylie,
James Latta,	William M. Engles,
Ashbel Green,	Cornelius H. Mustard,
Samuel D. Blythe,	James C. Watson,
S. H. Crane,	William L. Breckenridge,
J. W. Scott,	John H. Symmes,
William Latta,	David McKinney,
Robert Steele,	George Marshall,
Alexander A. Campbell,	Ebenezer H. Snowden,
John Gray,	Oscar Harris,
James Scott,	William I. Gibson,
Joshua L. Wilson,	William Sickles,
Alexander McFarlane,	Benjamin F. Spilman,
Jacob Coon,	George D. McCuann,
Isaac N. Candee,	George W. Janvier,
Robert Love,	Samuel G. Winchester,
James W. McKennon,	George Junkin.

Elders.

Samuel Boyd,	Geo. Morris,
Edward Vanhorn,	H. Campbell,
W. Dunn,	Thos. McKeen,
James Algeo,	James Wilson,
James Agnew,	D. B. Price,
Henry McKeen,	C. Hotchkiss,
Charles Davis,	Chs. Woodward,
W. Wallace,	W. A. G. Posey,

A. D. Hepburn,	James Carnahan,
Jos. P. Engles,	Moses Reed,
Js. McFarren,	James Steele,
A. Symington,	George Durfor,
A. Bayles,	John Sharp,
Wm. Agnew,	Isaac V. Brown.

"Philadelphia, May 27, 1834."

The following article extracted from the Biblical Repertory, October, 1834, is inserted at full length, without comment, viz., Art. VI., p. 505.

"*The Act and Testimony.*

"The history of this document we understand to be as follows: The proceedings of the last General Assembly of our church being in many cases much disapproved of by a large minority of that body, a meeting was called in Philadelphia, to which all ministers and elders were invited who sympathized with this minority in their opinions and feelings. Among other acts of this meeting, a committee was appointed to draft a public declaration to the churches, of the views and wishes of those then present. The result of this appointment was the publication of a paper, entitled an *Act and Testimony.* It is impossible for any man to read this document without being deeply impressed with respect for its authors. It is pervaded by a tone of solemn earnestness, which carries to every heart the conviction of their sincerity, and of their sense of the importance, as well as the truth, of the sentiments which they advance. The fear of God, reverence for his truth, and love for his church, seem clearly to have presided over the composition of this important document. In addition to these intrinsic claims to the respect of those to whom it is addressed, the fact that it has received the sanction of so large a number of the best ministers of our church, demands for it the most serious consideration. It is, therefore, natural, that those who feel the truth and weight of a great portion of the statements of this document, and yet withhold from it their signatures, should feel desirous of letting their brethren know the grounds on which they act. We believe that most of the sentiments of this *Act and Testimony* meet a ready and hearty response from the great majority both of our ministers and elders; and yet we presume it will not be signed by any thing like a moiety of either. Why is this? Is it because they fear to assume the responsibility of such an act? This is very easily said, but we believe that the number of those who are nervous enough to be influenced by such a consideration, is very small. There is often much more courage in not acting, than in acting; and still more frequently in moderation, than in violence. It is generally easy and safe, in cases of controversy, to take sides decidedly and through good and evil, with one part or the other. If you are sure of decided opponents, you are equally certain of warm friends. The unfortunate individuals who belong to neither side, are cared for by neither, and blamed, if not abused, by both. Though there may be imbecility, indecision, and timidity, which prevent a man's knowing what to think, or saying what he knows, there may also be firmness in standing alone, or in that unenviable position when neither sympathy nor approbation is to be expected. It is humbling to think of good men as being so deficient in the fear of God, and so sensitive to the opinions of their fellow men, that they withhold their approbation of the avowal of truth from the base fear of man; we are, therefore, slow to attribute such a motive, or to believe in its extensive influence. There must be some other and better reason why such a document as the Act and Testimony has not received, and is not likely to receive, the sanction of more than a small minority of our churches. We pretend not, of course, to know the reasons which have influenced the conduct of so many individuals, but we know that the following considerations have had a decisive weight on the minds of many, and presume that these and similar views have influenced the course of others.

"In the first place, this document has been perverted from its true and legitimate purpose as a Testimony, into an invidious test act. This evil has resulted from two sources, partly from the form and nature of the act itself, in some of its essential features; and partly from the use that has been made of it in some of our leading religious journals. It would seem to be a very obvious principle, that any individual member of a body has a right to address his fellow members on subjects affecting their common interests. If he thinks that errors and disorders are gaining ground among them, it is more than a right, it is a duty, for him to say so, provided he has any hope of making his voice effectually heard. If such be the case with an individual, it is equally obvious that he may induce as many as he can to join him in his warnings and counsels, that they may come with the weight due to numbers acting in concert. Had the meeting in Philadelphia, therefore, been contented to send forth their solemn testimony against error and disorder, and their earnest exhortation to increased fidelity to God and his truth, we are sure none could reasonably object. Their declaration would have been received with all the respect due to its intrinsic excellence, and to the source whence it proceeded. But when it is proposed to 'number the people,' to request and urge the signing of this Testimony as a test of orthodoxy, then its whole nature and design is at once altered. What was the exercise of an undoubted right becomes an unauthorized assumption. What was before highly useful, or at least harmless, becomes fraught with injustice, discord, and division. What right have I to publish a declaration on truth and order to the churches, and call upon every one to sign it on pain of being denounced as a heretic or revolutionist? Surely many sound and good men may well take exception at some of my modes of expression, or demur at some of my recommendations, without forfeiting all claims to confidence. It may be said that no one is required to sign this *Act and Testimony* against his own will, and that there is no denunciation of those who decline. It ought, however, to be considered that this is a necessary result of the call on the part of the meeting, and in the body of the Act itself, for a general signing of the document, like a new league and covenant, that it should act as a test. Such in fact, no doubt, was its design. The authors of this feature of the plan, at least, designed to make it the means of ascertaining the number and strength of those who thought with them, and of uniting them in a body, capable of acting with concert. If such is the very nature and purport of the Act, it necessarily follows, that refusing to the test, or to join the league, must be regarded as an act of hostility. The very design of the effort is to make neutrality impossible. Our first objection, then, is, that it is not what it professes to be, a Testimony, but a test. Had it been signed only by the chairman and secretary of the meeting by which it was issued, or by the individual members, its whole nature would have been different. As it is, it is a test, and must operate unfairly and injuriously, subjecting some to unjust suspicions, and dividing those who, on every principle of duty, ought to be most intimately united.

"But, leaving this objection out of view, and admitting that it was right to adopt this extra-constitutional method of ascertaining and rallying the friends of truth, we think there are specific objections against this docnment, which show that it is unfit to answer this purpose. We have already said, and said sincerely, that it is impossible to read this Testimony without being deeply impressed by the seriousness of its tone, the weight and truth of the great part of its sentiments, and the decided ability and skill with which it is drawn up. It evinces in every line the hand of a man accustomed to legal precision and accuracy of phrase. Yet it was neccessarily prepared in a hurry, probably at a single sitting, and read at a general meeting, in which the careful weighing of every clause was out of the question. Considering these circumstances, instead of being surprised that there are instances of unguarded statement, or unwise recommendations, our wonder is, that the blemishes of both classes are not tenfold more numerous. But is it not obvious that a document that was to be put forth, not only as a Testimony, but a test, which the friends of truth were to be required to sign, or forfeit their character as such, and which was designed to rally as large a number as possible of those who were of the same heart and mind, should be most carefully and solemnly considered, and every thing avoided which might cause the well affected to hesitate or refuse? Were we ever so much in favour of such a measure, we are free to confess, that there are statements in this Act and Testimony, in which we could not concur, and recommendations of which we highly disapprove. Of course, however anxious we might be to join in this enterprise, we should still be obliged to submit to have our names cast out as evil.

"It is not our purpose to go over this document and criticise its various parts. We shall merely refer to a few of the passages, which we think must be stumbling blocks in the way of all but the most determined.

"The very first paragraph is sufficiently startling. It stands thus: 'BRETHREN IN THE LORD:—In the solemn crisis to which our church has arrived, we are constrained to appeal to you in relation to the alarming errors which have hitherto been connived at, and now at length have been countenanced and sustained by the acts of the supreme judicatory of our church.' The first question suggested by this paragraph is, whether in fact such a crisis has arrived in our church, as to justify such avowedly revolutionary measures, as the present document recommends? If such is the state of the church, desperate remedies may be justified, if in themselves wise and well directed. This point, however, we must at present waive. The statement to which we would now call the attention of our readers, and at which we should hesitate long, and sign at last, if sign we must, with a slow and shaking hand, is the declaration, that the highest judicatory of our church has at length countenanced and sustained alarming errors. These errors, of course, are those specified in the document itself. Is it then true, that the highest judicatory of our church has 'countenanced and sustained' the doctrine, that we have no more to do with the sin of Adam than with the sins of any other parent—that there is no such thing as original sin—that man's regeneration is his own act—that Christ's sufferings are not truly and properly vicarious? How serious the responsibility of announcing to the world that such is the case! How clear and decisive should be the evidence of the fact, before the annunciation was made and ratified by the signatures of such a number of our best men. Surely something more than mere inference from acts of doubtful import should be here required. We do not pretend to be privy to the grounds on which this serious charge is made; but we are sure that no conscientious man would set his name to it, without having evidence to produce the painful conviction that such was the fact. Such evidence ought to have been detailed. We do not know, and we suppose the churches generally do not know, what this evidence is. How then can they sign this document? How can they be expected to take the responsibility of one of the most serious annunciations ever made to the churches? We do not believe it to be true. We have not the least idea, that one-tenth of the ministers of the Presbyterian Church would deliberately countenance and sustain the errors specified above. And if not done deliberately and of set purpose, it should not be announced as having been done at all. We may put upon acts an interpretation very different from what they were intended to bear, and thus be led to assert as fact what is very far from the truth.

"We see that some, in adopting the Act and Testimony, apparently impressed with the solemnity of the step they were about to take in sanctioning this introductory paragraph, refer, in justification of the charge which it involves, to the rejecting of a series of resolutions, calling upon the Assembly to denounce these and various other errors. But is the inference a necessary, or even a fair one, from declining to consider these resolutions, which required the Assembly to condemn certain errors, whether 'held in or out of the Presbyterian Church,' to the sanctioning of these errors themselves? During the sessions of the last General Assembly in Scotland, a motion was made and rejected, relative to the devising of some measures for securing the better observance of the Sabbath. Must we infer from this rejection, that the body in question countenanced Sabbath-breaking?* A few years ago, when petitions were circulated in reference to Sunday mails, many, especially after the failure of the first attempt, refused to sign them. Are such persons to be regarded as in favour of the desecration of the Lord's day? The mere rejection, or rather refusal, to entertain the resolutions referred to, cannot, of itself, therefore, afford evidence of the disposition of the Assembly to countenance these errors. We do not know the history of the case, but there may have been something in the circumstances under which they were introduced, to account for their being set aside. We have heard, indeed, the warmest friends and advocates of the Act and Testimony regret exceedingly the manner in which they were brought forward. As far as our informant, a leading member of the minority in the last Assembly, knew, it was without consultation, to any extent, either as to their form or mode of being presented. Yet, what more difficult and delicate task, than the framing of doctrinal propositions, to be affirmed or denied by the supreme judicatory of a church? If these resolutions were hastily prepared, carelessly arranged, or loosely expressed,

* The rejection arose, we believe, from the wish to await the issue of the Parliamentary proceedings on the subject.

this alone would be reason sufficient to account for the Assembly's passing them over. As they have been published in the religious papers, the churches may judge on this point. For ourselves, we are not surprised at their rejection. Instead of wondering that a majority of the Assembly did not vote for them, we wonder that any considerable number of voices was raised in their favour, so various are the errors they embrace, and so different in degree; some of them serious heresies, and others opinions (at least as we understand the resolutions) which were held and tolerated in the Synod of Dort, and in our own church from its very first organization. Is it to be expected that, at this time of the day, the Assembly would solemnly condemn all who do not hold the doctrine of a limited atonement? We do not believe that the penman of the Act and Testimony himself, whatever his private opinion on the doctrine may be, would vote for these resolutions. And it is too notorious that many of his most active and zealous cooperators deny this, and still more important points, to allow for a moment the supposition that they could intelligently have given such a vote. Surely then, the rejection of propositions, for which at no period of the history of the church, perhaps, a tenth of its ministers could have voted, is no adequate proof that the Assembly 'countenanced the alarming errors' contained in this Act and Testimony. We are not now attempting to decide whether the Assembly did or did not countenance these errors, but we say, the evidence on which we could be induced to subscribe the solemn declaration that they did, must be very clear; and that no such evidence is exhibited to those who are called upon to join in the accusation. As before said, we do not believe that the errors quoted above from this document, or any others which it specifies, (unless it be that on the doctrine of imputation) are held or approved by one-tenth of the ministers of the Presbyterian Church. And we consider it a very serious affair to have the corruption of such a body of Christians asserted and proclaimed through both hemispheres.

"As a proof of disregard of discipline, the Testimony refers to the treatment, by the Assembly, of a memorial sent up from several Presbyteries, sessions, and individual members. It may be supposed that the manner in which this paper was disposed of, furnishes evidence that the Assembly countenanced the errors above mentioned. This memorial, however, is not sufficiently known to make this the ground of a general signature of the Act and Testimony. We are very far from feeling called upon to justify all acts of the Assembly, or to apologize for them. Our feelings always, and our judgment generally, were with the minority in that body. There were things in the doings of the Assembly, which we disapprove of as much as any of the signers of this document. The manner in which this memorial was treated, is one of the acts which we think much to be regretted. But the single point now is, whether this treatment furnishes evidence sufficient to authorize the authentication of the charge contained in the first paragraph of the Act and Testimony. Let any one look over this memorial, and ask whether it was reasonable to expect the Assembly, in the present state of the church, to meet its demands. It is a long document, which concludes by requesting,

"1. 'That the 'Plan of Union between Presbyterians and Congregationalists in the new settlements' be wholly abrogated, &c.

"2. That Presbyteries be restrained from ordaining, licensing, or dismissing men, not to labour in their own bounds, but in the bounds of other Presbyteries.

"3. That the Assembly resume the sole direction of Missionary operations within the bounds of the Presbyterian Church, to the exclusion of non-ecclesiastical associations.

"4. That the Assembly bear solemn testimony against the many errors preached and published in the church.

"5. That various points of order and discipline should be decided; as, 1. Whether one Presbytery must admit a member coming from any other with clean papers. 2. Whether a judicatory may not examine and express an opinion of a book, without first commencing process against its author, when a member of their own body. 3. Whether in adopting the Confession of Faith as a system, the candidate 'is at liberty to reject as many particular propositions as he pleases,' &c.

"6. That the Assembly disannul the act of the Assembly of 1832, dividing the Presbytery of Philadelphia, and disavow the principle that Presbyteries may be founded on 'the principles of elective affinity.'*

"Here is matter enough to occupy a deliberative assembly for months. That all these points should be taken up, and properly considered, was therefore not to be expected. And as many of these requests are in direct opposition to measures carried with the full concurrence and approbation of the prominent signers of the Act and Testimony, who now request the Assembly to undo what they themselves have done—it was as little to be expected, that, if considered, they could be granted. Though we think that the number and weight of the signatures to this memorial were such that the Assembly ought to have paid more attention to their plea, and granted many of their requests, we are far from being convinced that it was a desire to countenance or sustain the errors specified in the Act and Testimony, which led to the

* For the sake of brevity we have not quoted these demands at length, but contented ourselves with giving the substance of each.

course pursued. It is a very prevalent, and in itself a reasonable feeling, that church-courts should not legislate *in thesi*, or pronounce on doctrines in the abstract; that it is best to wait until the points come up for decision in the usual course of judicial proceedings. This feeling is so strong in some of the soundest and best men of our church, as of itself to induce them to vote against many of the demands made in this memorial. It is not, however, possible to know the motives which influenced different individuals in taking the course which the Assembly pursued with this document. It is sufficient, that this course does not afford proof of the charge brought in the first paragraph of the Act and Testimony; and this point we think as clear as it can well be made. Were there no other reason, therefore, for not signing this document, the character of that paragraph we think sufficient.

"There is another ground of serious objection to be found in the fifth of its eight recommendations to the churches. The signers say, 'We would propose, that we consider the Presbyterial existence and acts of any Presbytery or Synod formed upon the principles of elective affinity, as unconstitutional, and all ministers and churches voluntarily included in such bodies as having virtually departed from the standards of our church.' This, it is to be observed, is not an expression of the opinion, that the existence and acts of such bodies are unconstitutional, but a recommendation that they be so considered, and, of consequence, so treated. This is the only interpretation which we are able to put upon this passage. If this be its meaning, it must be seen at once, that it is a very serious step. For the members of any community, civil or ecclesiastical, to meet together, and recommend to their fellow members, to consider and treat the acts of the constituted authorities as unconstitutional and void, is an extreme proceeding, to be justified only by a necessity which authorizes the resolution of the society into its original elements. It is a deliberate renunciation of an authority which every member of the community has bound himself to respect. It is, therefore, the violation of a promise of obedience which can only be excused by proving that it is an extreme case, to which the promise was never intended to apply, and is not in its nature applicable. In civil governments this procedure is inceptive rebellion; in ecclesiastical governments it is the first step in schism. To take this step, is either a virtue, or a crime, according to the presence or absence of a justifying cause. That it must, however, be a very serious cause which will justify the disregard of obligations voluntarily assumed, and promises deliberately given, will of course, be admitted. That it is not competent for any individual, within the limits of the extreme cases just supposed, to judge for himself of the unconstitutionality or the constitutionality of the acts of the constituted authorities of the community to which he belongs, is too obvious to need remark. Every one sees that there would be an end of all government, if every member of a community were allowed to recognize or disregard a law at option; or by a simple assumption of its unconstitutionality to escape from the obligation to obedience. We cannot but regard, therefore the recommendation of this document, that churches and ministers consider certain acts of the Assembly unconstitutional, as a recommendation to them to renounce their allegiance to the church, and to disregard their promises of obedience. Whether this recommendation be justifiable or not, depends of course on the exigency of the case. Those who do not think the act complained of, sufficiently heinous and destructive to dissolve the bonds of their allegiance, cannot sign this Act and Testimony; while those who regard it as a case of life or death, may feel at liberty to give the advice in question.

"Though we are of the number of those who disapprove the plan of constituting Presbyteries on the principle complained of, and think that it was, at least, never contemplated by the constitution, yet we are unable to discover so much evil in the measure as to justify the dissolution of the church, or the disregarding of the obligation we are all under to obedience. The plan recommended in this document necessitates a schism of the church, and perhaps was designed so to do. The Assembly have passed an act which these signers refuse to recognize. Either the Assembly must retract, or the signers must secede. One or the other of these results must take place, unless we are to have the confusion of two churches, with two sets of ministers and members, not recognizing each other's acts or ecclesiastical standing, all included in the same body. How can such a state of things exist? The Assembly's Second Presbytery of Philadelphia, we will suppose, ordains a man to the ministry. As their constitutional existence is denied, the validity of this ordination, as a Presbyterial act, must also be denied. This leads to a denial of the candidate's ministerial acts, at least ecclesiastically considered. He is to those who adopt this recommendation, a layman, and can do nothing which a layman may not perform. Will they recognize his baptisms? his introduction and dismission of church members? This evil may be bearable, while there are but two or three individuals in this situation; but it must increase every month or year, until the whole church is a chaos. Such seems the necessary result of acting on the plan recommended, unless schism be at once resorted to. This result, indeed, seems to have been distinctly in view when the act was prepared. The signers say, 'If the majority of our church are against us, they will, we suppose, in the end, either see the infatuation of their course, and retrace their steps, or they will, at last, attempt to cut us off.' That is to say, 'we have assumed such a position that things cannot remain as they are; the Assembly must either retrace their steps, or the church be divided.' Division, then, is the end to which this enterprise leads, and at which, we doubt not, it aims;* and division for what? As far as this document is concerned, it is division which is to result from not recognizing the existence and acts of certain Presbyteries and Synods. This is the only effective provision in the whole act. All its other recommendations may be adopted, and no division occur; but if this be acted upon, division is inevitable. Is the church then prepared to divide, because one portion thinks that A. B. C. may lawfully be united into a Presbytery, on the ground that they wish to be so united; and the other that A. B. C. and D. may be thus united, because they live within the same geographical lines? The motive for the wish, in the former case, does not affect the principle. It may be a corrupt motive, or a good one. Some individuals in Philadelphia wished to be set apart into a Presbytery, it was said, because they differed from the standards to which the majority of their Presbytery adhered. Other individuals in Cincinnati wished to be set apart in like manner, it was said, because they adhered to the standards, while the majority of their brethren were unsound. Admit both these suppositions to be correct, and both requests to have been granted, and we have two elective affinity Presbyteries, the one formed from a desire to evade the operation of the constitution, and the other to give it its full force. We think the principle is a bad one; but it is clear it may operate one way as well as the other, and that it is not to be viewed as a device designed to form a secure retreat for heresy. The fact is, that the members of our Presbyteries are so much intermixed, especially in our cities, where not only ministers, but even churches frequently change their location, that the necessity of definite geographical limits has never been strenuously insisted upon. As the geographical is the obvious, and, in ninety-nine cases out of a hundred, the most convenient principle of division, and the one which the constitution directs to be followed, it is clear that it ought to be adhered to. But can any one prevail upon himself to say, that the church must be split to pieces, because, in a single case, another principle has been adopted? The fact is, that this matter is, comparatively speaking, altogether insignificant; and it never would have attracted the least attention, were it not for the supposed motive which led to the adoption of the elective affinity principle. Had a Synod constituted twelve ministers, resident in one city,

* Since writing the above, we see that this intention is denied, in the Presbyterian. We have heard other signers of the Act and Testimony, however, very distinctly avow their desire to effect a division of the church.

all of them equally distinguished for soundness of doctrine and purity of life, six into one Presbytery, and six into another, simply because it had been so requested, would the whole church be agitated, when it was ascertained that the members of the one body were not separated geographically from those of the other? This no one can believe. It is not, therefore, the simple principle in question, however generally admitted to be incorrect, that is the cause of this deep and extended feeling. If this be true, it ought not to be thrust forward as a test principle. The church ought not to be called upon to deny the constitutional existence of bodies constituted on this plan, and by this denial, render schism unavoidable. Brethren agreed in doctrine and views of order and discipline, united in heart and effort, ought not to be thrust asunder, because, on such a point as this, they cannot agree.

"We can hardly persuade ourselves that reflecting men can consider this matter, viewed as an abstract constitutional point, of sufficient importance to justify schism. Yet this is really the issue made and presented in the Act and Testimony. Refusal to retract on this point was the great offence of the last Assembly. As soon as this refusal was known, preparation was made for issuing this manifesto. We do not doubt, as already said, that the real ground of offence, the true cause of the present excitement, is not this insignificant question, but the impression as to the motive which governed the decision of the Assembly. Still this is the question as here presented. It is not pretended that the Assembly formally sanctioned the errors enumerated in this document. It countenanced and sustained them, by the erection of the Second Presbytery of Philadelphia, and by the refusal to consent to its dissolution. These are the acts, therefore, which are the grounds of complaint, and which the churches are called upon to disregard. The issue, therefore, is upon a constitutional point of very minor importance.

"Our second specific objection, then, to this Act and Testimony is, that it recommends a disregard of the regular authority of the church which we are bound to obey; and that the ground of this recommendation is, in our opinion, altogether insufficient. The consequence of adopting the proposed course, must be either to divide the church on a constitutional question of little comparative moment, or to produce a state of the greatest confusion and difficulty. A third objection, and the only other of this kind we shall mention, is founded on the eighth and last recommendation, viz. 'We do earnestly recommend, that on the second Thursday of May, 1835, a convention be held in the city of Pittsburgh, to be composed of two delegates, a minister and ruling elder from each Presbytery, or from the minority of any Presbytery, who may concur in the sentiments of this Act and Testimony, to deliberate and consult on the present state of our church, and to adopt such measures as may be best suited to restore her prostrated standards.' The objections to this recommendation are nearly the same urged against the one already considered. It is essentially a revolutionary proceeding. It is an appeal from the constitutional government, to the people in their primary bodies. When this is done, merely for the expression or formation of a public sentiment, which may exert its legitimate influence upon the regular authorities, there is no ground of complaint. Analogy is to be found to such a course in the public meetings and conventions under our civil government, which are perfectly consistent both with the theory and regular action of our institutions. But the case before us is very different. A large meeting first declare certain acts unconstitutional, and resolve not to submit to them. They invite others to join in this refusal, and to send delegates to meet in general convention to adopt ulterior measures. They first take a step which brings them necessarily into collision with the government, and then call on all of like mind to unite with them. The analogy is so complete between this case and that which recently convulsed our whole country, and threatened the existence of our political institutions, that none can fail to perceive it. There can, therefore, be no invidiousness in making the allusion. An act of the general government was pronounced by the people of one of the states, to be unconstitutional and consequently void. They deliberately resolved to refuse to submit to it. Whether this was right or wrong, it was regarded by the country as creating a necessity for one of two things; either that the act should be repealed, or the Union dissolved by secession or war. It was indeed, in itself, a conditional dissolution of the Union. The condition was the repeal of the offensive act. If this was refused, the union was at an end. When, under these circumstances, the state in question proposed to call a convention of all who agreed with her in opinion as to the grievance complained of, did not every one regard the proposal as a step in advance, as a measure designed and adapted to make the breach more certain and serious? Of this there can be no doubt. Public sentiment was overwhelmingly against the wisdom and lawfulness of the course of this aggrieved member of our Union. The remedy, as extra-constitutional and revolutionary, was deemed disproportioned to the malady. Yet it was on all hands admitted that there might be evils, which, being intolerable, would justify this dissolution of political society, and the disruption of all existing bonds of political duty and allegiance. So in the case before us, if the evils complained of are such as justify the dissolution of the church, and the disregard of the solemn obligations by which we have bound ourselves together, then the case is made out. The propriety of the Act and Testimony is vindicated. The point now before us, however, is, the true nature of its recommendations. We say they are extra-constitutional and revolutionary, and should be opposed by all those who do not believe that the crisis demands the dissolution of the church. If such a crisis be made out, or assumed, then all the rest is a mere question of the ways and means.

"We do not believe that any such crisis exists. That there has been much disorder of various kinds within our bounds, that there has been a good deal of erroneous doctrine preached and published, and that many judicatories have been criminally remiss in matters of discipline, we do not doubt. These are evils with regard to which the churches should be instructed and warned, and every constitutional means be employed for their correction. But what we maintain is, that there has been no such corruption of doctrine or remissness in discipline as to justify the division of the church, and consequently all measures having that design and tendency are wrong and ought to be avoided.

"To exhibit fully the grounds of this opinion, would require us to review the origin and progress of the present difficulties, and consequently render it necessary for us to enter into historical details too extensive for our limits, and inconsistent with our present object. We must, therefore, be contented with the remark, that the burden of proof rests on those who assert that such a crisis does exist. This proof has not yet been exhibited. Until it is, we can only say, that we do not believe there is any call for the extreme measures proposed in the Act and Testimony.

"We believe, indeed, that there are a number of men in our church, who hold doctrinal opinions which ought to have precluded their admission, and who should now be visited by regular ecclesiastical process. But we believe this number to be comparatively small. We have never doubted that there was serious ground of apprehension for the purity of our church. Considering the ease with which men are introduced into our communion, who, not being brought up among us, know nothing and care nothing about Presbyterianism, it is very evident that we must have a constant accession of unsound, and even hostile men, if our judicatories are not faithful to their vows. We have often wondered, indeed, at the facility with which decided Congregationalists, so born and educated, become Presbyterians. We rejoice to see that there is a general Congregational Association formed in the state of New York. Those brethren who really prefer the Congregational system, may now indulge that preference, instead of being forced to submit to the painful necessity of joining a church, with whose distinctive organization they are unacquainted, or to which they are unfriendly. This is the main evil, which it requires nothing but honesty on the part of the Presbyteries effectually to prevent. We are happy in knowing that at least one case has occurred, in which a Presbytery, where there is not, to our knowledge, a single adherent of the *Old School*, has deliberately, and almost unanimously, refused to ordain a candidate who held the popular errors on depravity and regeneration. There are not wanting other decisive and cheering intimations that the portentous union between the New Divinity and the New Measures, which threatened to desolate the church, has, at least for the present, done its worst. The latter, but scarcely the lesser, of this firm of evils, is, to all appearance, dead. Its course doubtless will be marked by melancholy memorials for generations. But as the great mass of the wisdom and piety of the country (we are speaking of the north and east) were found decidedly arrayed against it, we trust the church will be spared such another visitation. And even as to the other member of the firm, we hope the shout of victory from its advocates was rather a mistake. If we may credit what we hear, the novelty being over, the wonder is on the decline. It is said, that out of the immediate sphere of the origin of the theory, its friends are very few, and very far between.

"But let it be supposed that in all this we are mistaken, that the corruption in doctrine, and remissness in discipline, are far more extensive than we imagine. Let it even be admitted, that the General Assembly, after having long connived at alarming errors, has at length countenanced and sustained them. Let every thing be admitted which we have endeavoured to disprove. Still, the case of the Act and Testimony is not made out. The necessity or propriety of schism does not appear. Is Christ divided? If the head be one, should the body so easily be separated? Is not the visible union of the people of God, as the expression of their spiritual union to each other and the Lord Jesus, a solemn obligation? To what a lamentable condition would the church be reduced, if, on every occasion of disappointment or excitement, or even of serious mistake, injustice, or error, her members were to separate into distinct communions? We are not about to advocate a spurious liberality, or defend a spirit of compromise with remissness or error. We merely wish to state, that the division of a church of Jesus Christ is a very serious thing, expressly forbidden in the word of God,* and only to be justified by the most obvious necessity.

"What then constitutes a necessity for schism, and makes that crime a virtue? We venture to answer, that no man is at liberty to labour for a division of the church to which he belongs, unless

* 1 Cor. i., 10.

he and others are called upon either to profess what they think erroneous, or to do what they think wrong. As the duty of preserving the unity of the church is obvious and admitted, the seceders must make out that they are free from this solemn obligation. But what can free them from the solemn obligation of duty, but the interference of some stronger obligation? So long as the standards of any church remain unaltered, its members profess the same faith which they avowed when they joined it. I do not profess to hold or to teach what A. B. or C. may be known to believe, but I profess to believe the Confession of Faith of the church to which I belong. It matters not, therefore, so far as this point is concerned, how corrupt a portion, or even the majority, of the church may be, provided I am not called upon to profess their errors. Instead of my mere ecclesiastical connexion with them being a countenancing of their errors, it may give me the best opportunity of constantly testifying against them. Who have done so much to render conspicuous and odious the errors and unfaithfulness of the clergy at Geneva, as the orthodox and pious portion of their number? The individuals who previously seceded, left the body in quietness behind them, and lost in a great measure their ability both to promote the truth and to oppose error. As another illustration, let us refer to the church of Scotland. Every one knows the long controversy between the orthodox and the moderate parties in that body. Had Dr. Witherspoon, and the faithful men who acted with him, lifted the standard of division, what would have been the present state of that church? In all probability it would be little better than that of Geneva. All the resources of the body, all its institutions, its corporate existence and privileges, would have been basely (shall we say?) delivered up to the enemy as a contribution to his means of promoting and perpetuating error. By the faithful adherence of these men to their posts, after one defeat had followed another in rapid and long succession, the church has been saved. The pious and orthodox portion have gained the ascendancy, and are now shaking off the trammels of patronage and other antiquated corruptions, and wielding the whole of her resources for the advancement of truth. Blessings will rest forever on the memory of Witherspoon, because he was not a preacher of secession. If others in that land of our ecclesiastical fathers had been equally wise; if the numerous body of evangelical men split up into the sects of Burghers, Anti-Burghers, &c., were now united with their former brethren, what an army would they form! Would any one be so infatuated as to urge the pious and devoted members of the Protestant Church in France to secede from their brethren, and give up their institutions at Strasburg and Montauban, to be perpetual nurseries of error? Or would any one counsel the orthodox Germans to forsake their stations on the plain, where they can meet their enemies on equal terms, and go down into the deep and narrow valley of dissent?

"What has become of the Morristown Presbytery? What has become of the True Reformed Dutch Church, which not only seceded from their highly respectable and orthodox brethren, but had well nigh excommunicated them? How completely has the wave of oblivion blotted them out! They have disappeared from the visible ranks, at least, of the hosts of the church. Are they doing more good, or preventing more evil now, than in their former connexion? We think their example should serve at once as a warning to any who are disposed to secede from among us, and as a rebuke to those who appear anxious to precipitate a similar crisis in our church.

"We cannot see, then, how anything is to be gained, for the cause of truth, by secession; but we see how much will be lost. We shall gain no advantage in opposing error; but only lose our facilities for promoting truth. Instead of manifesting fidelity to the cause of the Redeemer, we shall deliver up the post committed to our keeping. Until, therefore, the standards of the church are altered, or its members are in some way called upon to profess error, or to do wrong, their motto should be, 'STAND FAST; HAVING ON THE WHOLE ARMOUR OF GOD.'

"We have now performed a painful, though, as we think, an imperative duty. We have come out openly against brethren in whose doctrinal views we coincide, whose persons we love, whose character and motives we respect, with whom we have ever been associated, and fondly hope ever to continue united. The grounds on which we have felt constrained to bear this testimony, may be very briefly stated.

"As we have already said, it is at all times the privilege, and often the duty, of the members of a community, to spread their views on important practical subjects before their fellow members. How constantly is this done in political matters. If such be the privilege of every individual, it is especially incumbent on those who are connected with the periodical press. The very end and object of that press is the diffusion of practical knowledge, and the discussion of important points of truth and duty. We confess, however, that we have had other motives for the course which has been taken. We, in common with that large class of our brethren who do not belong to the number against whom the Testimony is directed, and yet have not joined in the Act, have felt annoyed by the urgency which has been used to obtain signatures, and the serious censure lavished on those who refuse their names. It was necessary, as a matter of self vindication, that the grounds of this refusal should be publicly stated. It should be known, that it was not fear for the consequences of the Act, nor insensibility to the evils complained of, but disapprobation of the nature and tendency of the measure. It is with a sincere desire to cooperate in the prevention of the evils, which we think must ensue from the prosecution of the course proposed, that we have lifted up our voice against it. Let the facts and reasons here presented pass for what they are worth. Let brethren give them a candid consideration. Let them ask themselves, if when, as they suppose, error and disorder are coming in like a flood, they should turn their backs on the enemy, and leave a weakened and discouraged remnant to continue the battle. What if they are defeated, not once or twice, but many times? Constancy and truth always ultimately prevail. Let us only be careful that it is for truth we struggle, and that our weapons are not carnal, but spiritual, and there is no ground for apprehension. In every church there are fluctuations. Sometimes truth and piety predominate, at others, error and irreligion. When darkest, it is nearest light. In a church like ours, we think, there is no excuse for abandoning the regular constitutional methods of proceeding. Every man can free himself from responsibility for the errors of his brethren, if he cannot have them corrected. He has all the means that others have to secure predominance for his own views, and if they are correct, he may confidently hope for their success. Let but the friends of truth be humble, prayerful, faithful, and active; let them adhere to each other and to the church, and then, whether in the majority or minority for the time being, they will be most effectually serving their Master and his cause."

Before proceeding further in the narrative, we think it proper to say, that much as the course of the Repertory was regretted, deeply, indeed, as it was disapproved by most of the prominent men in the church, there existed in the public mind in general, no doubt that the theological principles of the professors were unchanged. As a friendly and favourable solution of their course, many believed it was based upon mistaken views as to the extent of defection in the church; upon a wrong impression as to the design of the Act and Testimony, and its probable influence as a remedy for the evils prevalent in the church. The professors flattered themselves that the evils complained of were not so extensive as alleged, that the leprosy was more superficial, and susceptible of cure by being let alone, than the minority could possibly realize, forming their opinion from much more thorough intercourse with ministers and people.

Had these very respectable gentlemen understood their position as their friends did, and estimated the object and character of the *Act and Testimony* correctly, and permitted it to pass on its own merits, without any expression of opinion, it would have been well. This was desired and expected. Indeed, taking into consideration that the document, as soon as printed, was in wide circulation, thousands having stood ready to catch it from the press, it was immediately and positively beyond revocation. Hence the article in the Repertory could not possibly have any salutary influence on the measure in progress.

The article from the Repertory, above inserted, was generally, even by those who sided with the professors, considered an unfortunate production; and it produced more surprise, alarm, and heart-felt pain among the Old School men, than any thing previously issued upon the subject. Through the popularity of the journal and the supposed writers in it, its central location in the bosom of the church, its being sustained by the oldest seminary in the Presbyterian body, patronized by one of the oldest, largest, and most intelligent Presbyteries in the United States, it exerted a strong influence in dividing the orthodox, and in bringing every thing to a point of jeopardy. Thus it greatly aggravated and protracted the difficulties then existing in the church.

The first and immediate effect of that article was seen with astonishment, in dividing and paralyzing the Presbytery of New Brunswick, which ought to have been foremost in sustaining the action of the minority in the General Assembly of 1834, as their manifesto was intended, almost exclusively, to save from New School rapacity, the seminary located centrally within its bounds. This unhappy measure of a majority of the Presbytery, proceeded from the influence of one or more of the professors over a large number of the junior members, who had been connected with the seminary under their care, and hence were, with great ease, subjected to their control.

When this fact was made public, the churches, to a considerable extent around, experienced a serious shock, and responded to it with unfaltering disapprobation. In the various modes of condemnation they employed on this occasion, the elders of the churches, in some cases, were more prompt and decided than the ministers, and in some instances, did not hesitate to reprove the vacillation and tardiness of their pastors, by openly avowing their approbation of the *Act and Testimony*, and by giving to it their public signature. The unwise and unhappy course pursued by the seminary, through their *organ*, was hailed with triumph and exultation by the New School, as, in their opinion, admirably adapted to strengthen their cause and extend their influence widely through the churches. It is recited and plead now, by Mr. Judd, as one of his strong vindications of the New School inveteracy. They gave this document warm support and extensive circulation. In their disorganizing and mischievous periodicals of every grade, they spread it out on their pages with triumph, fraternizing, with apparent sincerity, with this new and unexpected accession of Princeton allies. Indeed, they used this apparently congenial instrument with great diligence and adroitness, to subserve their own evil purposes; of course without the desire or design of its authors.

After the rising of the Assembly of 1834, great interest was manifested through the church on the subject of the convention invited in the *Act and Testimony* to meet in Pittsburgh in May, prior to the General Assembly, which had recently resolved to hold its next annual meeting in that city. The New School were excessively hostile to that measure, very justly fearing that its influence might be unfavourable to their plans. The sympathizers with the Princeton dissent, in general, assumed the same position, and by their action undesignedly greatly strengthened the power of the New School party. Even in the Presbytery of New Brunswick, a majority denounced the convention as a caucus, and succeeded in preventing that Presbytery from sending a delegate to represent them in that important conservative meeting of the church for consultation.* Already an impression of discouragement and despondence, as to the result of the impending conflict, began to affect the minds of many adherents of the Old School body. The trustees of the theological seminary were engaged in the laudable enterprise of collecting funds to endow and establish that institution at Princeton. Many who had either subscribed to that fund, or resolved to participate in its accumulation, seeing the success attending New School movements, and the lukewarmness prevalent at Princeton, declined contributing until the result could be more certainly predicted. Even the trustees of the seminary, not knowing how soon, and how totally, the whole institution, with its professors, edifices, libraries, funds, and assets *en masse*, might pass into the hands of the New School, gave distinct intimations to their agents and collectors to suspend their operations, considering it much better that the funds in hand or in prospect should remain in possession of the donors, than be placed within reach of the rapacious foe. And what cannot but be regarded as remarkable, while the condition and prospects of the church generally, and of the seminary in particular, were hanging in this state of torturing suspense, the opposers of the *Act and Testimony* some time continued their hostility to that document, and the general relief measures contemplated.

So imminently exposed was the whole interest of the Presbyterian Church considered, in consequence of the successes attending New School artifice and encroachment, that a company of gentlemen were designated by a large and respectable number of the

* The member who attended that convention from this Presbytery, went at the suggestion of the minority in Presbytery.

Old School, to proceed in a noiseless and unobserved manner, to wait upon the professors at their homes, to reason and remonstrate with them on the subject of their position, if possible to induce them to concur with their brethren in the public action of the church. These gentlemen, agreeably to the arrangement made for them, assembled at Princeton in the autumn of 1836, and met the professors in Dr. Hodge's study, whither they had been invited to repair. At this conference, the three professors of the seminary attended, and the Rev. J. W. Alexander was also present. The following members of the Old School deputation were in attendance; Rev. Dr. James Blythe, of South Hanover, Indiana, Dr. C. C. Cuyler, of Philadelphia, Dr. George Junkin, of Easton, Pennsylvania, Dr. W. W. Phillips, of New York, and last and least, the humble penman of these pages.

Nothing important or decisive was exhibited in this interview. The parties, respectively, with much moderation, stated their views, but without any decisive result. In the course of these remarks, a gentleman in company took liberty to observe, that to him there did not appear to be any great or serious obstacles between them, and that it really seemed very deplorable that so great an interest should be left in suspense when the only difference appeared to be a mere matter of church policy. After an interim of silence, perhaps five minutes in duration, the Rev. James W. Alexander, then comparatively a young man, in a very unassuming and respectful manner, repeated the suggestion, that there was really very little difference or distance between the parties, and manifested a strong desire that an entire reconciliation should take place. He urged very gently, that the parties both desired the same thing, and they differed merely as to the best manner of accomplishing it. This, said he, is not a sufficient ground upon which to jeopardize so great an interest; wise men do not act in this manner. In a strain somewhat like this, and of very little greater extent, this remarker did more, probably, towards adjusting the difficulty, than any one who had preceded him. The tone, as well as temper of his remarks, seemed a little above his years, and that gave to them a peculiar emphasis. After considerable deliberation on the subject among the assembled delegates, though labouring under a disappointment which they all greatly regretted, it was resolved to entrust the church a while longer amidst appalling contingencies, to her watchful and gracious owner and keeper, without attempting any change in their system of action, and to press it on with all possible zeal and vigor. The minuteness of this detail is intended to show the extreme despondence on the state and prospects of the church, which had seized the minds of many who were supposed to be as well informed as any others on the subject, and thus in some measure to vindicate the orthodox body in general, for the measures they ultimately adopted to relieve the church.

Although the professors, and a majority of the Presbytery of New Brunswick who acted in concert with them, were still considered as belonging to the Old School in reality, yet their conduct was highly disapproved as tending to produce suspicion, and to weaken their influence, and to impair the standing and usefulness of the seminary. To illustrate and confirm the preceding statement, we introduce the following incident. In a neighbouring city lived a rich, intelligent, and very devoted elder of the Old School body, of Scotch origin, education, and form of religion. His zeal for the church was as strong as any other layman's. In common with many of less distinction, he had received an impression that very probably the church, through the indefatigable and unscrupulous action of the New School, and this unhappy diversion of the Professors and others in and about Princeton, would in a short time go into New School possession and control. He was not in favour of disgracing the Presbyterian name, and scandalizing Christianity, by a protracted warfare with such desperate men as he saw in the field labouring for the captivity of our Zion.* He occupied a first rate post for intelligence, and well knew the inveteracy of the assailants, and honestly believed that they would never relinquish their object till the church was in their power, and the seminary plundered of its sacred spoils. He was, consequently, very solicitous that the Princeton delegation should ascertain whether the theological gentlemen there, who had seconded the revolt from the Act and Testimony, were determined to persist in their course. Unless some favourable indications should be given, he and others like-minded, had resolved to abandon Princeton immediately to the control of the adversary, and take measures instantly to establish another seminary, on grounds entirely out of their reach. For this purpose, the money was ready in bank; a beautiful site, with appropriate grounds and edifices, was selected; the principal officers for the institution were designated from among the most prominent in our church, and every thing ready for action. But the delegates did not, on the whole, consider the condition of the seminary at Princeton, exposed as it was, sufficiently desperate to warrant so great a sacrifice and so decisive a change at that time. In this feeling our highly respected friends in New York cordially acquiesced.

The following remarks and quotations are inserted to explain the public character and position of Dr. A. Alexander, so far as

* The distinguished gentleman here referred to was the Hon. *Robert Lenox*, of Wall Street Church, New York.

connected with the reform measures in the Presbyterian Church, adopted by the successive General Assemblies of 1830 to 1838.

From the year 1830 to 1837, the friends of Dr. Alexander, knowing his peculiar situation and great influence, felt anxious to discover his opinions on the great question pending in the church. Being very silent or uncommunicative on the subjects involved, very little was known with certainty in regard to his private thoughts. Hence he was involved indiscriminately and most reluctantly in the feeling which circulated to some extent, unfavourable to the course pursued by most of the Princeton theologians. Public opinion was unavoidably involved in suspense by this want of light or evidence on the subject, in regard to several of these gentlemen.

It is exceedingly gratifying to the writer, to find himself able to shed much light on this interesting chapter of our history, by extracts from the "Life of Dr. Alexander" by his son, recently published, New York, 8 vo., by Charles Scribner, 145 Nassau street, a channel of intelligence on every subject treated, and especially upon this, of the most important and unsuspected character. And what renders this testimony the more agreeable to the writer, is the fact that all the items of knowledge which he had collected from long and familiar intercourse with the Professor and other authentic sources, in regard to this matter, and even most of the hypothetical opinions he had entertained from partial indications, find in these brief extracts from Dr. Alexander's biography, illustration and support.

On page 473, he says: "That there exists a difference in opinion in the church, in reference to certain doctrinal points, and as to the precise import of the act adopting the Confession of Faith, by candidates, at their licensure and ordination, cannot be denied or concealed." Again: "We wished it to be understood, that we were the determined opponents of all those in our communion who manifested a leaning towards Arminian or Pelagian opinions in theology, or who discovered a disposition to invade the principles of Presbyterian Church government, or to exchange them for those of the Congregational system. Against these, and against all who manifested a desire to favour them, we have lifted our voice from time to time." Several of these extracts are such as were copied by Dr. Alexander's biographer, either from private notes or published essays.

On page 475, early as the year 1831, he writes to a former pupil: "My mind is full of gloomy apprehensions respecting the affairs of our church, since the meeting of the last General Assembly. I cannot foresee whither we shall be driven. I had never suspected that the new men and new measures would so soon prevail in the supreme judicatory of our church. . . .

The burden and heat of the day will soon come upon the young men, who will have great need to be strong, to preserve the ark of the Lord from falling into the hands of the Philistines. Quit yourselves like men." In a letter to Rev. W. S. Plumer, he writes: "Stand up bravely for the religion of your fathers, which is also ours by deliberate choice, as well as inheritance." In 1834, he says: "If it is now found that our differences are so wide that we cannot live in peace, let us peaceably agree to separate into two distinct denominations." Some time after, from surveying the conflicts likely to result from division, he uses the following language, page 476: "Upon mature deliberation, therefore, we declare our sentiments to be opposed to all schemes which tend to the division of the Presbyterian Church." But soon, from counter views, his mind is changed: "Our church cannot proceed much farther under her present organization. The General Assembly ought not to be long continued in its present form. . . . *It* is *necessary*, for our *very existence*, that we should separate." Page 477.

These few short extracts indicate with sufficient clearness the course Dr. Alexander pursued through the trying season here referred to. He believed separation of such discordant elements unavoidable—indeed necessary—and yet took no active part in the measures leading to it, except urging on, as above, junior ministers in the church. He never signed the *Act and Testimony*, which was the grand entering wedge of reform in the church. But it is not known to the writer, that, by any public act or expression, he ever opposed or disapproved it. And nothing is more certain—the minutes of the decisive Assembly of 1837 fully prove and record the fact—that he was among the foremost, if not the very first, to suggest and carry out several of the triumphant measures in general, which arose out of the Act and Testimony, and were substantially based upon it. It is a sufficient reason for the Doctor's not signing that document, that he was daily surrounded with a cluster of gentlemen, most of whom were unfriendly to it, from whom a gentleman of his delicate sensibility and refinement of feeling, standing in the relation he sustained, would naturally desire not to *appear* to differ.

As the Presbytery of New Brunswick has been seriously censured, as a body, for its opposition to the *Act and Testimony*, the incipient reform measure commenced in the Assembly of 1834, justice to this Presbytery requires the introduction into this narrative, of the two extracts following, from their minutes, in October, 1836, and October, 1837.

Extract from the Minutes of the Presbytery of New Brunswick, Freehold, October 4th, 1836, *viz:*

"Mr. I. V. Brown introduced summary resolutions on the state of the church, which were read and committed to Dr. Miller, Mr. Brown, D. V. McLean, Studdiford, Stryker, and Wynkoop."

The committee to whom were referred the resolutions introduced by Mr. Brown, reported; the report was amended and adopted, and is as follows, viz:

"I. *Resolved,* That in the opinion of this Presbytery, the Rev. Albert Barnes, in his Notes on the Epistle to the Romans, has published opinions materially at variance with the Confession of Faith of the Presbyterian Church, and with the word of God, especially with regard to original sin, the relation of man to Adam, and justification by faith in the atoning sacrifice of the Redeemer; that the manner in which he has controverted the language and doctrines of our standards, is highly reprehensible, and adapted to pervert the minds of the rising generation from the simplicity of the gospel plan; and that the work referred to, in its amended form in a late edition, contains representations which cannot be reconciled with the letter or spirit of our public standards, and of the Sacred Scriptures; especially as Mr. Barnes has declared that he does not wish it to be understood, that in his verbal alterations he has changed a single sentiment.

"II. *Resolved,* That this Presbytery, in superintending the theological education of Mr. Barnes, saw no satisfactory evidence that he was unsound in the faith; and in taking his obligation for licensure, they *supposed* him to be *candid and honest,* in receiving the standards of our church without reservation, according to the obvious import of the constitution. They cannot, therefore, but view with surprise, deep regret, and disapprobation, the following declarations, contained in his pretended vindication: 'I have not changed my views materially since I was licensed to preach the gospel. In the theological seminary at Princeton, my views, which were the same as now, were fully known; by the Presbytery of New Brunswick, by which I was licensed, they were, or might have been, fully known.' The Presbytery, in tenderness to Mr. Barnes, forbear to make any remark on these assertions, and leave them to a candid and discerning public, to draw the unavoidable inference.

"III. *Resolved,* That the right to private construction of articles, asserted by ministers of our communion in the ordination engagement, the practice openly advocated by many, of adopting the standards of our church 'as a system and for substance of doctrine,' and the plan of making mental reservations in that solemn service, with a view to 'examining the language and forming an opinion' afterwards of the doctrines received, are errors which derive no countenance either from the constitution of our church, or her practice, while *uncorrupted—errors* which this Presbytery have, not only with undeviating uniformity avoided sanctioning or in the slightest degree tolerating within our body, but which they consider as uncandid and dishonest, by whomsoever practiced; as inconsistent with a right understanding of the terms of our ordination vow; as opening a door for corruption and disorder in the church; and as a violation of the spirit of the constitution, which declares, chap. xxviii, sec. 4, that 'an oath is to be taken in the plain and common sense of the words, without equivocation or mental reservation.'

"IV. *Resolved*, That whereas the Presbyterian Church in the United States, in their constitution and form of government, and in repeated declarations made through their representatives, have solemnly recognized the importance of the missionary cause, and their obligation, as well as right, to promote it by all means in their power; and whereas their acknowledgment and declaration have never gone forth to the full extent of the obligations imposed upon them by the head of the church; and whereas this Presbytery solemnly believe, that one principal object in the constitution of the church, by the Lord Jesus Christ, was the diffusion of divine truth through the earth, and the 'preaching of the gospel to every creature,' through the instrumentality of united effort by the church, in her organized capacity; therefore, whilst this Presbytery would unfeignedly rejoice in the goodness of the Lord, manifested in employing the instrumentality of others to send salvation to the heathen, at the same time earnestly desirous to cooperate in this great work, to fulfil, at least in part, their own obligation, and to answer the just expectations of the friends of Christ in other denominations, and in other countries, in obedience to what is believed to be the command of Christ, Presbytery hereby declare their opinion that the Presbyterian Church in these United States, in its nature and constitution, is a missionary society, whose object is to aid the conversion of the world to God; and that every member of the church is a life member of said society, bound to do all in his power for the accomplishment of this object; that the organization of the Presbyterian Church is such, that the General Assembly is her proper organ in the missionary work, possessing every qualification, and affording every facility, for its successful prosecution, without external conflict or internal confusion; that the act of the majority in the late Assembly, refusing to ratify the adoption of the Western Board of Foreign Missions, agreeably to an arrangement made with the Synod of Pittsburgh by the preceding General Assembly, manifests a want of good faith with that body, and fidelity in observing contracts; exhibits a want of kindness to the large and respectable minority in that General Assembly, and to the multitudes at large who loudly maintain the right and claim the privilege of conducting Foreign Missions, by the General Assembly, as the proper organ.

"V. *Resolved*, That this Presbytery do now become, and declare themselves to be auxiliary to the Western Board of Foreign Missions, under the care of the Synod of Pittsburgh, and recommend said Board to the liberal patronage of the churches in connexion with this Presbytery.

"VI. *Resolved*, That this Presbytery, solemnly considering the distracted and increasingly unhappy condition of our beloved church, desire to designate, as the basis of their opinions, herewith communicated, some of the principal causes to which the painful and threatening evils experienced and apprehended in the church, may, and must justly, be traced.

"First: The introduction and propagation of doctrines, by ministers in our connexion, essentially at variance with our system of faith and with the word of God; the evidence of which exists in numerous sermons, pamphlets, and papers, issued within our bounds, and by ministers in our connexion; in a long train of legislative and judicial acts of successive General Assemblies, and inferior judicatories; the result of which has been the injury of the cause of truth, by sheltering heretical books and teachers, and especially in the extensive diffusion of Mr. Barnes' unsound publications, which have recently obtained the sanction of a majority of the supreme judicatory of our church, whose annals have thus become the *history*, and whose authority the safeguard of Arminian and Pelagian heresy.

"Secondly: The unconstitutional efforts of several successive General Assemblies to favour the introduction of false doctrines and to screen their propagators, by authorizing the erection of Presbyteries on the principle of 'elective affinity,' which is repugnant both to the letter and spirit of our organization and government.

"Third: The Assembly's giving their sanction to the disorganizing assumptions advanced recently in an elaborate plea before them, that candidates may and of right ought to be admitted to the holy office, materially 'differing in opinion from our known standards in doctrine, worship, and government,' on the ground of scruples, neither avowed by themselves, nor sanctioned by existing rule, on competent authority; that the Confession of Faith may be received and signed, 'for substance of doctrine, or for system,' with reservations.

"Fourth: The open avowal, by the majority of the last Assembly, that *that body* is not competent, and has *no right* to conduct missionary operations, accompanying this declaration with an act refusing to confirm the contract of a previous Assembly's committee, for the transfer of the Western Foreign Missionary Board, thus depriving the orthodox body of the privilege of serving God and their generation, according to the constitution of the church and the dictates of their own hearts, at the same time affording alarming evidence of a design to supersede the boards and institutions of our church, and substitute for them, and impose upon the Presbyterian body, an unconstitutional and inefficient system. This Presbytery, therefore, do in the fear of God, solemnly declare it as their deliberate judgment, that they can see no prospect of our being able to accomplish the great objects for which the church was founded, and for which Christian fellowship ought to be cherished, *by the continuance of the discordant parts of the Presbyterian Church in one body.*

"*Resolved*, That the foregoing resolutions be printed in the Presbyterian, and New York Observer."

Extract from the Minutes of the Presbytery of New Brunswick, at Trenton, October, 1837.

"The committee appointed to examine the printed minutes of the last General Assembly, brought in their report, which, after amendment, was adopted, and is as follows, viz:

"That although in ordinary circumstances, it might be deemed unnecessary, if not unsuitable, for Presbyteries to express judgments on the proceedings of the highest judicatories of the church, yet as the doings of the last Assembly have been made the subject of much animadversion, and even of great severity of censure, on the part of some other Presbyteries, it may be due to truth and justice to express the opinion of this Presbytery in regard to some of the most prominent acts of that body. This becomes the more advisable, because the expressed opinions of the inferior judicatories may furnish an important indication of the course most proper to be pursued in future. Therefore,

"I. *Resolved*, That agreeably to the judgment expressed by this Presbytery, at its stated meeting in April last, the Plan of Union adopted by the General Assembly of 1801, was formed without any legitimate authority; that it was entirely unconstitutional; that its operation for a number of years past, has been injurious to the interests of the Presbyterian Church; and that the last Assembly, in abrogating that Plan, fulfilled an obvious and important duty to the churches under its care.

"II. *Resolved*, That although we respect and love the Congregational Churches, and desire to maintain Christian intercourse with them, yet in the judgment of this Presbytery, the incorporating of churches formed on Congregational principles with the Presbyterian Church, was an unnatural union, which could not fail of interfering with the orderly and comfortable operation of our system, and ought to be regarded as such, at whatever time, or by whatever means, it was formed, and which ought by no means to be continued.

"III. *Resolved*, That upon the principles of the preceding resolutions, the Synod of the Western Reserve never had any constitutional connexion with the Presbyterian Church; and therefore, that the General Assembly, in declaring said Synod no longer connected with our body, formed a decision equally just and conformable to the spirit of our form of government.

"IV. *Resolved*, That in the judgment of this Presbytery, the act of the General Assembly, declaring the Synod of Utica, Geneva, and Genesee to be no longer connected with our body, was equally just and proper with the act of the Assembly in the case of the Western Reserve; for whether the said three Synods derived their origin from the Plan of Union of 1801, as many of their churches doubtless did, or, as has been alleged, chiefly from the act of the Assembly of 1808, by which two large bodies of Congregational ministers and churches were received, retaining their Congregational character as constituent parts of the then Synod of Albany, they cannot be considered as occupying, on account of this alleged origin, any more favourable ground than the Synod of Western Reserve. On the contrary, the act of 1808, being a still more palpable and extraordinary violation of our ecclesiastical constitution, than even the plan of 1801, the former furnishes a basis even less tenable than the latter, for the support of a Presbyterian body. To which may be added the notorious fact, that a large number of the churches and ministers composing the said Synod, were not only Congregational when first irregularly introduced into the Presbyterian Church, but still retain that form of government.

"V. *Resolved*, That in the judgment of this Presbytery, the decision of the General Assembly, in declaring that the four Synods disowned, never had been constitutionally united with the Presbyterian Church, and cannot now be considered as connected with our body, ought by no means, to be rescinded, nor any part of those Synods to be restored to membership with the General Assembly, in any other way than that pointed out by the Assembly, on page 445 of its printed minutes, viz. 'By any Presbytery, if such there be, strictly Presbyterian in doctrine and order, and by any individual churches and ministers of like character, separating themselves from their Congregational neighbours and making application, with proper evidence of their character and wishes, as the case may be, either to the next General Assembly, or to some convenient Presbytery or Synod, authorized to take order thereon.'"

CHAPTER XIII.

The danger of having Literary Journals connected with Theological Seminaries—General character and influence of the Assembly of 1834—Public sentiment—Controversy between the General Assembly and the Home Missionary and Presbyterian Education Societies—Dr. J. L. Wilson's four propositions.

A serious impression had occupied many minds a long time, that while much good might be anticipated from the Repertory,* published at Princeton, under patronage of the Seminary, and as its organ, that, managed as it has been, some corresponding evils might spring from the same source. A few years past, some good men think, have in part realized these apprehensions. It is possible, by slow degrees, and without design, even with a view of extended usefulness, to invert the natural order, and even the studied arrangement of things, so far as to make the power which was intended to be subordinate, become not only co-ordinate, but supreme; or, at least, to exhibit quite serious advances towards accomplishing this inversion.

And here, to guard against misapprehension of the following incidental remarks, let it be observed, that there is a tendency around all literary institutions to concentrate talent and influence, by many instrumentalities. Theological institutions are by no means exempt from these unavoidable or contingent susceptibilities. Place a man of intellectual vigor and moral worth where you please, and employ him as you choose, he becomes a centre of attraction and influence. A pastor of a church, of intelligence and sound discretion, may, in a few years, make himself a little monarch among the people of his charge, and to some extent around. This shows, among other things, the importance of permanence in the pastoral relation.

A theological professor of ordinary merit, grows naturally and certainly into great influence and authority, and it is desirable, to a considerable extent, that he should. As his acquaintance through the church extends, his character, his appropriate literature and labours, become better and better known and appreciated; his pupils multiply and scatter through the church, and over the land, proclaiming his worth and his praises, which is right, widely among the masses. The professor derives, of course, great accessions of credit and power, from all these universally pervading channels of influence, as a scholar, a gentleman, a sage, a saint, an orator, a philosopher, a critic, &c., &c. All very well for the good

* It appears from "Alexander's Life," that Dr. Hodge was, from the beginning, the Editor of that publication.

of the institution, and, perhaps, of the man; for practical purposes, fictitious capital is often as good as real.

While the above process has been proceeding, and these literary efforts or interests have been successfully advancing, the professor, of course, begins to extend the range of his views with the estimate of his powers, and sometimes comes to the conclusion that nothing is so sacred or so elevated, as to be placed beyond his reach. Thus he gradually forgets, or transcends his proper sphere, and this is the charge that has been brought against the Repertory. For some time, the suggestion that this excellent journal has not confined itself strictly, perhaps, within its proper limits, but systematically, and without any justifiable motive or useful result, criticised and condemned the solemn acts and adjudications of the General Assembly as the supreme guardian of the Presbyterian Church.

Now, when it is considered that this seminary belongs to the General Assembly, is under its constant supervision and control, that the professors of the institution were appointed by her, are dependent upon her, in all things amenable to her, have been instructed by her as to every prominent and important act, is it wonderful that the question should be asked, in good earnest and great kindness, "Shall the church control the seminaries, or the seminaries control the church?" Suppose, for a moment, that the seminaries, north, south, east, and west, and many others as is probable will be created, to the number of scores, so far as we can see ahead, and each possess its learned and ambitious faculty, its literary and theological journal, taking annually the same liberty to criticise, dissect, reverse, condemn, the laboured and solemn opinions, instructions, and decisions, sent out to the church by her sovereign authority, through the land—can harmony be rationally anticipated among these rival institutions, or the General Assembly be reverently regarded as the bond of union and peace in the Presbyterian body? Is there not reason to fear that battles of books, of journals, of critics, of professors, of theories and speculations, of doctrines and governments, of baptisms and rites, of forms and modes, may spring up and greatly annoy the church? Who can foresee what conflicts between rival seminaries, jealousies between sectional districts, ecclesiastical functionaries, and various powers and interests, may start into being? Competition will arise, in criticising the measures of the Assembly, in testing her decisions, correcting her errors, reproving her neglects, or commending her zeal and fidelity; all originating in the Repertories within her bosom, and to be referred to the ambition, arrogance, or presumption and folly, of the editors or contributors to these theological journals. Will such exhibitions tend to establish the General Assembly in her constitutional power, her calm and temperate mode of action? to confirm and perpetuate our noble ecclesiastical system in all its peculiar and salutary principles and rules? or will it not rather contribute to render our supreme council a timid, feeble, vacillating, and inefficacious machine, either exercising tyrannical power, or unduly yielding to the paramount influence of some monthly or quarterly within her own limits, more popular and formidable than others, in this unnatural and unwarrantable crusade against the mother of us all?

Besides, it is a very grave and important question, what is to be the probable influence of this state of things, in progress of years, upon the real character of didactic and polemic theology, and kindred topics, through the Presbyterian Church, and our country at large. The general character of the age we live in, and of the land we inhabit, the constitution, the habits, and ruling passions of our increasing population, are evidently favourable to progress, invention, novelty. That old systems of truth and order have grown stale with time, is the remark frequently made: their foundations must be broken up, and new theories and speculations, often at the expense of truth, built upon them. The mind of multitudes of men, in church as well as state, possessing genius, talent, and learning, have become restless and impatient under the hitherto dominant and salutary restrictions of literary taste and theological authority. There is a general relaxation of obligation and respect for the established and venerated standards of truth, now visible through the whole of society, in every department of science, of philosophy, and of morals and religion.

Now, if the channels of inquiry, discussion, and criticism, of theory and speculation on sacred topics, are thrown widely open, as at present, and if the spirit of competition, thirst for distinction or pre-eminence, and the desire of developing new systems, schemes, and shades of truth, be prompted by large facilities and license, to engage in this ambitious rivalry between the organs and professors of co-ordinate institutions, whose characters, number of students, strength and resources, standing and influence, are all to be graduated by the result of this contest, who can anticipate justly the effects likely to spring from these conflicts? Can uniformity, harmony, happy union and success, be rationally expected long to prevail in the great Presbyterian body, when competitions, jealousies, and animosities, are every where actively at work? The truth is, our seminaries, if possible, should be kept out of this vortex. Some have long maintained, at least in private circles, that even the professors of our seminaries should have extremely little, if any thing, to do with ecclesiastical legislation, or the action of the General Assembly. It has always appeared as a matter, the propriety of which might be well contested, the frequent attendance of professors at the sessions of the General Assembly, entering warmly into all her measures, her debates, controversies, her appeals, and agitations, whether of public or private interest. And we are greatly strengthened in this impression, by the opinion of at least one of the venerable professors, who has, we doubt not, by order of the Master of all assemblies, left his chair at Princeton vacant recently, to go up higher, even to the General Assembly of the first born.

It cannot be doubted, that the system of theological education and training, upon which the church is relying to sustain her multiplying exigencies and expanding enterprise, must undergo a considerable change; from the vastness of our national territory, and widening of the missionary field at home and abroad, it is evident there must be a proportionate extension of educational means, and multiplication of theological institutions. The restless and enterprising spirit of the age we live in, and the very air we breathe, will engender elements of difficulty profusely, and cast dangers into the bosoms of these seminaries. It will be no easy, no unimportant work, to place them, and to maintain them under salutary control, a control and discipline as much needed, and perhaps more, by the faculties and professors, as by the students. From secular, mere literary institutions, we may infer something in regard to theological. Now is the time to settle principles, ascertain limits, fix laws, form habits, on this great and commanding subject, which, if neglected now, may rend the church, and prove disastrous to the great moral and religious interests of this western world. Prove all things—hold fast that which is good.

In regard to the general character and influence of the Assembly of 1834, the spectators who then gave their attendance and pronounced their opinion, and multitudes in and out of the church, who have since observed the result of that long and solemn meeting, have not hesitated to declare their honest conviction, that through the influence of Divine Providence, it was more than any other specific instrumentality employed, the effective means of producing that happy expurgation of the Presbyterian family, which was consummated in 1837. If the New School triumph in the Assembly of 1834 was evil, it was short. In the Assembly of 1835, which met at Pittsburgh, the convention invited by the Act and Testimony, so effectually restrained the power of the New School, that they obtained no signal victory in that Assembly, but were checked in their progress, and cast into such a position as very speedily led to their entire ejection from the church. The so much abused minority of 1834, and their momentous *Act and Testimony*, were the principal means of bringing deliverance and triumph.

A controversy between the General Assembly, by her constituted Missionary Boards, and the American Home Missionary Society, and the Presbyterian Education Society, for supremacy and exclusiveness in the management of their business within the bounds of the Presbyterian Church, had been progressing for several years with increasing warmth. These societies had no sanction for existence and operation within the limits of the Presbyterian body; neither were they at all responsible to the Assembly for their conduct. They were called *voluntary* societies, because they claimed perfect independence of all control, and assumed the right of acting according to their own sovereign pleasure, in opposition to the boards of the church, in concert with spurious Presbyteries, who were engaged in training, licensing, and ordaining young men, unsound in the faith, to be located and employed by these voluntary societies at pleasure, through the wide expanse of the Presbyterian field, to propagate their heresies, promote disorder, and sow the seeds of Congregationalism through the churches. To expose and impair this infecting system of operation, about this period, (1832) Dr. Joshua L. Wilson, of Cincinnati, who may justly be styled the father of Presbyterianism in the West, a man of decided talents, purity, power, and untiring zeal in the cause of truth, attempted to establish against the voluntary societies, the four following propositions, viz:

"I. The Lord Jesus Christ has committed the management of Christian missions to his church.

"II. The Presbyterian Church, being one great family of the church of Jesus Christ, is by her form of government, organized into a Christian Missionary Society.

"III. The American Home Missionary Society is not an ecclesiastical, but a civil institution.

"IV. By interference and importunity, she disturbs the peace, and injures the prosperity, of the Presbyterian Church."

A convention from twenty Presbyteries met in Cincinnati in the month of November next ensuing. A majority of the convention decided against "a united agency of Home Missions for the West," and in "favour of the General Assembly's mode of conducting missions." Of this decision, the minority complained. They published a report to the Presbyteries in the valley of the Mississippi, in which they say that the "Synod of Pittsburgh had a controlling influence in the convention;" "that the votes of that Synod carried every question." They also complained, that the "official influence of the Board of Missions was employed to prevent union in the West."

Mr. Judd's account of the effect of these measures is amusing, viz:

"This determined opposition to the American Home Missionary Society, (Judd, p. 100,) hastened the general controversy respecting the most eligible method of conducting the various benevolent operations of the church. Most who were in favour of conducting them by boards especially of the General Assembly, became more decided and zealous in support of their peculiar policy, and increasingly hostile to the operations within the bounds of the Presbyterian Church, of societies organized and conducted upon the *voluntary* principle. The advocates for conducting all the benevolent operations of the church by boards under ecclesiastical supervision, increased in number, and their policy became more and more *exclusive and intolerant.* Hence those who were from *principle,"** (*Congregationalists,* i. e. New School men,) "in favour of voluntary societies, were laid under the necessity of abandoning their conscientious preferences, or of defending them. A sense of duty constrained them to adopt the latter course." The following twenty pages of Mr. Judd's volume are employed in detailing the disgraceful and disgusting contest into which the voluntary societies had compelled the Assembly to engage, to exclude these voluntary intermeddlers from their Presbyteries and congregations, and to prevent, if possible, their constant interference with all the business of the church. It is really amusing to see Mr. Judd, in the midst of his tirade against the Assembly for not tolerating the gross New School innovations and assaults upon Presbyterian order, in connexion with missions, writing about "conscientious preferences," "being laid under the necessity of defending them." What secret or open power, argument, or influence, could possibly justify their hostile and rapacious acts against the Presbyterian Church? It was their own deliberate, voluntary, self-moving preference for New England men and measures. They *came in among us, but they were not of us.* Their hearts, their affections, their aims, their efforts, were all directed to New England. They hated the Presbyterian Church, and they intended and laboured hard to destroy it. *By their fruits, ye shall know them.* But they have failed, and we give thanks to God for the deliverance.

CHAPTER XIV.

Convention called to meet in Pittsburgh, by Act and Testimony—Their action—Memorial.

THE convention called by the signers of the Act and Testimony, together with the minority of the last General Assembly, and

* This admission, of itself, is sufficient to condemn the whole course of the New School party.

others, in May, 1834, met in the Second Presbyterian Church of Pittsburgh, on the 14th of May, 1835. The Rev. John Witherspoon was called to the chair, and Rev. I. V. Brown and the Rev. Thomas Alexander, were appointed secretaries *pro tem.* The convention was opened by prayer, about fifty delegates being present, which number was increased by additions at subsequent meetings. The Rev. Dr. Ashbel Green was elected president, and took his seat accordingly. The convention appointed and observed the 18th inst., as a day of fasting, humiliation, and prayer, with special reference to the objects for which they assembled.

The committee, previously appointed for the purpose, on the manner of addressing the General Assembly, reported: 1. That the only expedient form is that of respectful memorial and petition. 2. That a committee be appointed to prepare such memorial, when the convention shall have decided the points to be embodied therein.

The great object contemplated in calling the convention was not less appropriate than important, that of collecting information on the state of the church, through all the channels and from all the sources which might be laid open at the meeting, and presenting that intelligence to the Assembly, with a memorial based upon it, suggesting some principal measures required to terminate or diminish the evils prevalent in the churches. If wrong information had been received, and thereby wrong impressions made, it was esteemed very desirable to correct these errors, and this meeting appeared well calculated to afford the means. On the other hand, if the truth had been only partially reported, and that small portion very imperfectly circulated, this meeting furnished a well adapted remedy. The memorial addressed to the Assembly was their principal measure, and, in substance, appears in the minutes of that Assembly. The convention passed several resolutions, having a direct and salutary bearing upon the condition of the church, which we shall insert without comment.

In connexion with the memorial from the minority of the Cincinnati Presbytery, on the state of the church in Western Ohio, the convention resolved:

"1. That the operation of any missionary society within the Presbyterian Church, and not responsible to her judicatories, is an infringement of her rights, and inconsistent with her integrity and peace.

"2. That the operation of any education society within the bounds of the Presbyterian Church, for the training of her ministry, independent of her ecclesiastical judicatories, is a usurpation of the rights of the church, and ought to be resisted, as tending to undermine her own education board, and the independence of her ministry.

"*Resolved*, That the subjects contained in the above resolutions be referred to the committee on addressing the Assembly.

"*Resolved*, That the committee appointed to draft a memorial to the assembly, make such a statement relative to the formation of ecclesiastical judicatories, on what has been called the principle of 'elective affinity,' as shall express the disapprobation of this convention, of all action on that principle, by any judicatory of this church, and our desire, that the evils which have already been produced, by acting on said principle, may be redressed.

"*Resolved also*, That the right of examining, and after examination of receiving, or refusing to receive, any minister, licentiate or candidate, whether from foreign bodies or from Presbyteries of our own church, however sustained by credential, is inherent in every Presbytery, and is essential to its well-being.

"*Resolved*, That the subject of doctrinal errors, existing in the Presbyterian Church, and also, that of the repeal of the resolution of the last General Assembly, touching the right of judicatories, to try and condemn heretical publications, be also referred to said committee as proper to be inserted in the memorial."

Sundry other resolutions contempleting the same object, we omit the insertion of, to secure space for the following highly important and impressive resolve:

"*Resolved*, That the committee on the memorial be instructed to present to the General Assembly, the solemn conviction of this convention; that the Presbyterian Church owes it as a sacred duty to her glorified Head, to yield a far more exemplary obedience, and that in her distinctive character as a church, to the command which he gave at his ascension into Heaven—'go ye into all the world and preach the gospel to every creature.' It is believed to be among the causes of the frowns of the great head of the church, which are now resting upon our beloved zion, in the declension of vital piety and the disorders and divisions that distract us, that we have done so little, comparatively nothing, in our distincttve character as a church of Christ, to send the gospel to the heathens, the Jews and the Mahommedans. It is regarded as of vital importance to the welfare of our church, that foreign as well as domestic missions, should be more zealously prosecuted and more liberally patronized, and that as a nucleus of foreign missionary effort and operation, 'The Western Foreign Missionary Society should receive the countenance, as it appears to us to merit the confidence of those who cherish an attachment to the doctrine and order of the church to which we belong."'

After some discussion, the above document was committed to Rev. Messrs. Blythe, Cuyler and Witherspoon, with instructions to present it to the notice of the General Assembly, in whatever way was deemed best.

As closely connected with the object in view, the convention unanimously passed the following resolutions:

"1. That the thanks of this house be given to those editors of religious papers who, by giving publicity to '*The Act and Testimony*,' and other documents connected with the same, have contributed to the furtherance of the views of this convention, in reference to the much desired reform in the church.

"2. That this convention are deeply impressed with the conviction, that the *Act and Testimony* prepared by some of the minority of the last General Assemby, in connexion with other brethren, and since that time so extensively adopted, has been under the smiles and blessings of God, of marked and extensive benefit to our beloved church.

"3. That we recognize our obligations in the most lively gratitude to God, for the care of providence in bringing together the members of the convention, in health and safety, and in an especial manner for uniting us together in the most harmonious accord in all the measures that have been discussed and adopted."

After passing these acts, and spending some time in prayer and praise to God, the apostolic benediction was pronounced, and the president declared the convention finally dissolved.

Having already stated with sufficient fulness and clearness, most of the prominent points which were referred to the committee to draft the memorial, with powers and instructions, we refer the reader to the act of the General Assembly on the memorial, which exhibits that document without any material change.

CHAPTER XV.

General Assembly in Pittsburg, May, 1835—Memorial received from the Convention—Resolutions accompanying and based upon it.

In the General Assembly which met in the first Presbyterian Church, of Pittsburgh, on the 21st of May, 1835, the Rev. Wm. W. Phillips, D. D, was chosen Moderator.

The following record embraces, substantially, the memorial presented to the General Assembly, by the convention, an account of which precedes.

"The committee to whom was referred the memorial and petition of a number of ministers and ruling elders of the Presbyterian Church, and certain other papers relating to the same or kindred subjects, beg leave to report—that they have endeavoured to deliberate on the said memorial and petition, and other papers committed to them, with all that respect which the character of those from whom they come, could not fail to inspire; and with all the calmness, impartiality and solemnity, which the deep importance of the subjects on which they have addressed the Assembly, so manifestly demands.

"In approaching the consideration of these weighty subjects, the committee deemed it to be an obvious duty, to exclude from their views all those principles which result from the wishes or plans of different parties in the church, and to take for their guide, simply the word of God, which we consider the only infallible rule of faith and practice; and those public formularies, by which we have solemnly agreed and stipulated with each other, to be governed in all our proceedings. The moment we depart from these, we are not only exposed to all the evils of discord, but also run the risk of destroying those bonds of union by which we have been so long bound together as an ecclesiastical body. There is certainly no portion of the visible church, in which a harmonious accordance with the same adopted formularies, and a uniform submission to the same rules of truth and order, are so essential to the maintenance of ecclesiastical peace and to cordial co-operation, in promoting the great purposes for which the church was founded, by her king and head, as among the churches of our denomination. The committee, indeed, by no means expect, and do not suppose, that the Assembly would think of enforcing that perfect agreement of views in every minute particular which, in a body so extended as the Presbyterian Church, has perhaps never been realized. But that an entire and cordial agreement in all the radical principles of that system of truth and order, which is taught in the Holy Scriptures—which is embodied in our confessions of faith and form of government, and which every minister and elder of the Presbyterian Church has solemnly subscribed and promised to maintain, may not only be reasonably expected, but must be, as far as possible, secured, if we would maintain the 'unity of the spirit,' in the bonds of peace and love. This, it is presumed, the General Assembly will be unanimous in pronouncing. If this be not so, it is in vain that we assemble from year to year; in vain that we hope for intercourse, either pleasant or edifying. Our judicatories must be scenes of discord and conflict, and the ties which bind the several parts of our extended body to each other, can scarcely fail of being ties to strife and contention.

"Under convictions which these general principles are adapted to impress, the committee most deeply feel the importance of some of the conclusions to which they are constrained to come; and although some of these conclusions are at variance with several acts of the last General Assembly, yet they cannot doubt that they make an essential part of the Presbyterian system, and of course cannot be abandoned, without seriously endangering both the comfort and the safety of our beloved church.

"The committee, therefore, as the result of their deliberations on the documents committed to them, would most respectfully recommend to the Assembly the adoption of the following resolutions, viz:

"I. *Resolved,* That in the judgment of this General Assembly, it is the right of every Presbytery, to be entirely satisfied of the soundness in the faith, and the good character in every respect, of those ministers who apply to be admitted into the Presbytery as members, and who bring testimonials of good standing from sister Presbyteries, or from foreign bodies, with whom the Presbyterian Church is in correspondence; and if there be any reasonable doubt respecting the proper qualifications of such candidates, notwithstanding their testimonials, it is the right, and may be the duty of such Presbytery to examine them, or to take such other methods of being satisfied in regard to their suitable character, as may be judged proper; and if such satisfaction be not obtained, to decline receiving them. In such case, it shall be the duty of the Presbytery rejecting the applicant, to make known what it has done, to the Presbytery from which he came, with its reasons; it being always understood that each Presbytery is, in this concern, as in all others, responsible for its acts to the higher judicatories.

"II. *Resolved,* That in the judgment of this General Assembly, it is the right, and may be the duty, of any judicatory of our church, to take up, and if it see cause, to bear testimony against any printed publication, which may be circulating within its bounds, and which in the judgment of that judicatory may be adapted to inculcate injurious opinions; and this, whether the author be living or dead—whether he be in the communion of our church or not—whether he be a member of the judicatory expressing the opinion, or of some other—a judicatory may be solemnly called upon to warn the churches under its care, and especially the rising generation, against an erroneous book, while the author may not be within the bounds or immediately responsible, at their bar; and while even, if he were thus responsible and within their reach, they might not think it necessary to arraign him as a heretic. To deny our judicatories, as guardians of the churches, this right, would be to deny them one of the most precious and powerful means of bearing testimony against dangerous sentiments, and guarding the children of the church against that '*instruction which causeth to err.*' The writer of such a book may reside at a distance from the neighborhood in which his work is circulating, and supposed to be doing mischief, or he may be so situated, that even if it be proper to commence process against him, it may not be possible to commence, or at any rate, to issue that process within a number of months. In the meanwhile, if the right in question be denied, this book may be scattering poison, without the possibility of sending forth an effectual antidote. Indeed, it may be indispensably necessary, in cases which may easily be imagined, to send out such a warning, even though the author of the book were fully acquitted from the charge of heresy.

"III. *Resolved,* That the erection of church courts, and especially of Presbyteries and Synods, on the principle of '*elective affinity;*' that is, judicatories not bounded by geograpical limits, but having a chief regard in their erection to diversities of doctrinal belief, and of ecclesiastical policy, is contrary both to the letter and the spirit of our constitution, and opens a wide door for mischiefs and abuses, of the most serious kind. One such Presbytery, if so disposed, might, in process of time, fill the whole church with unsound and schismatic ministers, especially if the principle were adopted, that regular testimonials must of course secure the admission of those into any other Presbytery. Such a Presbytery, moreover, being without geographical bounds, might enter the limits and disturb the repose of any church into which it might think proper to intrude, and thus divide churches, stir up strife, and promote party spirit and schism, with all their deplorable consequences. Surely a plan of procedure in the church of God, which naturally and almost unavoidably tends to produce effects such as these, ought to be frowned upon, and as soon as possible terminated by the supreme judicatory of the church; therefore—

"IV. *Resolved,* That from and after the meeting of the Synod of Philadelphia, in October next, the Synod of Delaware shall be dissolved, and the Presbyteries constituting the same, shall be then and thereafter annexed to the Synod of Philadelphia; and that the Synod of Philadelphia, thus constituted by the union aforesaid, shall take such order concerning the organization of its several Presbyteries as may be deemed constitutional and expedient; and that said Synod, if it shall deem it desirable, make application to the next General Assembly for such a division of the Synod as may best suit the convenience of all its Presbyteries, and promote the glory of God.

"V. *Resolved,* That while this General Assembly fully appreciate, and deeply deplore, the many painful evils which result from the present division in our church, in respect to the method of conducting domestic missions, and the education of beneficiary candidates for the ministry, they are persuaded that it is not expedient to attempt to prohibit, within our bounds, the operation of the 'Home Missionary Society' or of the 'Presbyterian Education Society,' or any other voluntary association not subject to our control. Such an attempt would tend, it is believed, to increase rather than to diminish the existing evils. The Assembly, however, is persuaded that it is the first and binding duty of the Presbyterian Church to sustain her own boards, and that voluntary associations, operating within the bosom of the Presbyterian Church, and addressing themselves to her members and congregations, are bound upon every principle, both of moral and ecclesiastical obligation, neither to educate nor to send forth as Presbyterians, any individuals known to hold sentiments contrary to the word of God, and to the standards of the Presbyterian Church.

VI. "*Resolved,* That this Assembly deem it no longer desirable that churches should be formed, in our Presbyterian connexion, agreeably to the plan adopted by the Assembly, and the General Association of Connecticut, in 1801; therefore resolved, that our brethren of the General Association of Connecticut be, and they hereby are respectfully requested to consent, that said plan shall be, from and after the next meeting of that association, declared to be annulled; *and resolved,* that the annulling of said plan shall not in anywise interfere with the existence and lawful operations of churches, which have already been formed on this plan.

"VII. *Resolved,* That this General Assembly see no cause, either to terminate or modify the plan of correspondence, with the associations of our Congregational brethren in New England. That correspondence has been long established. It is believed to have been productive of mutual benefit. It is now divested of the voting power, which alone could be considered as infringing the constitution of our church, by introducing persons clothed with the character of plenary members of the Assembly. It stands at present, substantially, on the same footing with the visits of our brethren from the Congregational Union of England and Wales; and in the present age of enlarged counsel and of combined effort, for the conversion of the world, ought by no means to be abolished. Besides, the Assembly are persuaded, that amidst the increasing and growing intercourse, between the Presbyterian and Congregational Churches, it is desirable to have that intercourse regulated by compact, and of course, that it would be desirable to introduce terms of correspondence, even if they did not already exist.

"VIII. *Resolved*, That while this General Assembly has no means of ascertaining to what extent the doctrinal errors, alleged in the memorial to exist in our church, do really prevail, it cannot hesitate to express the painful conviction, that the allegation is by no means unfounded; and at the same time, to condemn all such opinions as not distinguishable from Pelagian or Arminian errors, and to declare their judgment, that the holding of the opinions referred to is wholly incompatible with an honest adoption of our Confession of Faith. That this is the case, will be doubted by none, who impartially consider the statements of that Formulary, contained in chapter VII, sec's 3rd and 4th; chapter VII, sec. 2nd; chapters VIII, IX, X, sec. 1st and 2nd; chapter XI, sec. 1st, which statements must of course be interpreted, in their plain, obvious and hitherto acknowledged sense. Against the doctrinal opinions therefore, above alluded to, the Assembly would solemnly lift a warning voice, and would enjoin upon all our Presbyteries and Synods to exercise the utmost vigilance in guarding against the introduction and publication of such pestiferous errors."

The following highly important missionary resolution, presented substantially to the Assembly for their consideration, by the convention immediately preceding, was adopted, viz:

"The committee on the paper submitted to them, in relation to the Western Foreign Missionary Society, recommend the adoption of the following resolutions, viz:

"I. That it is the solemn conviction of this General Assembly, that the Presbyterian Church owes it as a sacred duty to her glorified Head, to yield a far more exemplary obedience, and that in her distinctive character as a church, to the command which he gave at his ascension into heaven, 'Go ye into all the world and preach the gospel to every creature.' It is believed to be among the causes of the frowns of the great Head of the church, which are now resting upon our beloved Zion, in the declension of vital piety, and the disorders and divisions that distract us, that we have done so little, comparatively nothing, *in our distinctive character* as a church of Christ, to send the gospel to the heathen, the Jews, and the Mahomedans. It is regarded as of vital importance to the welfare of our church, that foreign as well as domestic missions, should be more zealously prosecuted and more liberally patronized, and that as a nucleus of foreign missionary effort and operation, the Western Foreign Missionary Society should receive the countenance, as it appears to us to merit the confidence, of those who cherish an attachment to the doctrines and order of the church to which we belong.

"II. *Resolved*, That a committee be appointed to confer with the Synod of Pittsburgh, on the subject of a transfer of the supervision of the Western Foreign Missionary Society, now under the direction of that Synod, to ascertain the terms on which such transfer can be made, to devise and digest a plan of conducting foreign missions, under the direction of the General Assembly of the Presbyterian Church, and report the whole to the next General Assembly."

CHAPTER XVI.

The Assembly met in Pittsburgh, May 19, 1836, earnestly contend with the New School assailants, for their right to conduct missions—Controversy warm and lasting—Orthodox views presented—Resolutions offered—Overruled by New School men—Their artifice—Pertinacy—Triumph—Exultation—Protest drawn by Dr. Miller—The Church in the power of her foes.

WE here insert a very material part of the records of the Assembly which met in Pittsburgh on the 19th day of May, 1836.

The arrogant usurpations and encroachments of the New School, through the whole course of this Assembly, confirmed the impressions which their corrupt measures in preceding years had implanted deeply in the breasts of honest and true Presbyterians. Here, having mustered their full force, they resolved, by the most violent and reckless action, if possible, to occupy the citadel of the church, and so to fortify themselves in that position as to defy all attempts to dislodge them. Mistaken in their calculations, they could not see that they were preparing a precipice for themselves, opening a volcano whose speedy eruption would throw them, in fragments and scattered clusters, with painful and disgusting exhioitions, from within and from without, to every wind, as the just recompense of their long and audacious crusade against that church which they had solemnly sworn, before earth and heaven, forever to maintain and vindicate.

The question was now to be decided, whether or not the

Presbyterian Church should continue to exist and control her legitimate business according to her own constitution, usages, and earnest wishes, or be given up to the lawless management with which they saw themselves threatened by the New School party. A few brief records will remove the disguise from the intruders, and display the full deformity of their designs.

On Wednesday, 27th of May, the following document was presented to the Assembly, viz:

"The committee to whom was referred the report of the committee appointed by the last Assembly, on the subject of a transfer of the Western Foreign Missionary Society to the General Assembly, and also the overture from the Synod of Philadelphia, on the subject of foreign missions, report:

"That the attention of the last Assembly was called to the subject of foreign missions, by the following overture, on page 31 of printed minutes: 'That it is the solemn conviction of this General Assembly, that the Presbyterian Church owes it as a sacred duty to her glorified Head, to yield a far more exemplary obedience, and that in her distinctive character as a church, to the command which he gave at his ascension into heaven, 'Go ye into all the world, and preach the gospel unto every creature.' It is believed to be among the causes of the frowns of the great Head of the church, which are now resting upon our beloved Zion, in the declension of vital piety, and the disorders and divisions that distract us, that we have done so little, comparatively nothing, in our distinctive character as a Church of Christ, to send the gospel to the heathen, to the Jews, and to the Mahomedans. It is regarded as of vital importance to the welfare of our church, that foreign as well as domestic missions should be more zealously prosecuted, and more liberally patronized; and that as a nucleus of foreign missionary effort and operation, the Western Foreign Missionary Society should receive the countenance, as it appears to us to merit the confidence, of those who cherish an attachment to the doctrines and order of the church to which we belong.'"

"The Assembly feeling the force of the suggestions contained in this overture, and believing it to be a very important part of their appropriate work, to spread the gospel throughout the world, adopted the overture in the form of a resolution, together with the following, viz:

"'*Resolved*, That a committee be appointed to confer with the Synod of Pittsburgh on the subject of a transfer of the Western Foreign Missionary Society, now under the direction of that Synod; to ascertain the terms on which such transfer can be made; to devise and digest a plan of conducting foreign missions, under the direction of the General Assembly of the

Presbyterian Church, and report the whole to the next General Assembly.'

"From this it appears that the proposition to confer with the Synod, and to assume the supervision and control of the Western Foreign Missionary Society, originated in the Assembly.

"At that time, the Western Foreign Missionary Society was in a prosperous condition, enjoying the confidence, and receiving the patronage of a considerable number of our churches, having in their employ about *twenty* missionaries, and their funds were unembarrassed. The committee having conferred with some of the members of that society, and finding that the proposal was favourably regarded by them, indulging the hope that an arrangement might be definitely made with the Synod, at their next stated meeting, by which the Assembly would be prepared to enter on the work at their present session, brought the subject again before the Assembly, when it was, after mature deliberation,

"'*Resolved*, That the committee appointed to confer with the Synod of Pittsburgh, on the subject of the transfer of the supervision of the Western Foreign Missionary Society to the General Assembly, be *authorized*, if they shall approve of the said transfer, to ratify and confirm the same with the said Synod, and report the same to the next General Assembly.'

"The committee thus appointed and clothed with full powers to ratify and confirm a transfer, submitted the terms on which they were willing to accept it, to the Synod of Pittsburgh, at their Sessions last fall. The members of the committee not being present at the meeting of the Synod, and there being no time for further correspondence, the Synod (although they would have preferred some alteration of the terms,) were precluded from proposing any, on the ground that such alteration would vitiate the whole proceedings, and therefore acceded to the terms of the transfer, which were proposed by the committee of the Assembly, and solemnly ratified the contract on *their part.* Feeling themselves bound by the same, and trusting to the good faith of this body, they have acted accordingly, and have made no provision for their missionaries now in the field, for a longer time than the meeting of this Assembly, having informed them of the transfer which has taken place, and of the new relation they would sustain to this body, after their present Sessions.

"It appears, then, to your committee, that the Assembly have entered into a solemn *compact* with the Synod of Pittsburgh, and that there remains but one righteous course to pursue, which is, to adopt the report of the committee appointed last year, and to appoint a Foreign Missionary Board. To pause now, or to annul the doings of the last Assembly in this matter, would be obviously a violation of contract, a breach of trust, and a departure from that good faith, which should be soundly kept between man and man, and especially between Christian societies; conduct which would be utterly unworthy of this venerable body, and highly injurious to the Western Foreign Missionary Society.

"The committee beg leave further respectfully to remind the Assembly, that a large portion of our churches (being Presbyterians from conviction and preference,) feel it to be not only consistent, but their solemn duty in the sight of God, to impart to others the same good, and in the same form of it, which they enjoy themselves, and to be represented in heathen lands, by Missionaries of their own denomination. They greatly prefer such an organization as this contemplated, and which shall be under the care of the Presbyterian Church, and cannot be enlisted so well in the great and glorious work of sending the gospel to the heathen under any other form. Already, with the blessing of the great Head of the church on the efforts of the Western Foreign Missionary Society, in this form of operation, has a missionary spirit been awakened among them to considerable extent, and an interest in the cause of missions been created, never before felt by them. They have furnished *men* for the work, and are contributing cheerfully to their support in the foreign field.

"As one great end to be accomplished by all who love the Redeemer, is to awaken and cherish a missionary spirit, and to enlist all the churches in the work of evangelising the world; as every leading Christian denomination in the world has its own foreign missionary board, and has found such distinct organization the most effectual method of interesting the churches under their care in this great subject; as such an organization cannot interfere with the rights or operation of any other similar organization, for the field is the world, and is wide enough for all to cultivate, as it is neither desired nor intended to dictate to any in this matter, but simply to give an opportunity of sending the gospel to the heathen by their own missionaries, to those who prefer this mode of doing so, giving them that liberty which they cheerfully accord to others, your committee cannot suppose for a moment, that this General Assembly will, in this stage of the proceedings, refuse to consummate this arrangement with the Synod of Pittsburgh, and thus prevent so many churches under their care, from supporting their missionaries in their own way. From this view of the case, they recommend to the Assembly the adoption of the following resolutions, viz:

"1. *Resolved*, That the report of the committee appointed by the last Assembly to confer with the Synod of Pittsburgh on the subject of a transfer of the Western Foreign Missionary Society to the General Assembly, be adopted, and that said transfer be accepted on the terms of agreement therein contained.

"2. *Resolved,* That the Assembly will proceed to appoint a Foreign Missionary Board, the seat of whose operations shall be in the city of New York."

The intelligent reader cannot fail to perceive that the preceding minute contains an argument, and a thread of special pleading in favour of the missionary system of operation, proposed by the Assembly to the Synod of Pittsburgh. The question will at once be asked, why this defence or vindication, so formal and serious, of a measure not yet completely confirmed, is interwoven with the report and resolutions under consideration by the Assembly. The answer is obvious. It was well known that the New England party, who were present with all their strength, had resolved to make a most inveterate attempt to defeat the happy arrangements so successfully made with the Synod of Pittsburgh, in the missionary work. Well, we ask again, why did the New School combine all their strength in this manner, and direct their venom against this wise, and holy, and benevolent missionary enterprise? The answer is, that they might monopolize and engulph this great work in their Home Missionary Society, and bring the whole Presbyterian Church, in her length and breadth, with all her talents, resources, and capacities, to throw off their Presbyterian responsibility, name, and spirit, to become the tools, the abettors, the convenient, dependent instruments of alien organizations, and thus, at once the victims and the slaves of the New School party.

A few more lines will reveal the secret, and confirm the fact, which, on the best grounds, are anticipated in the preceding documents.

Thursday morning, the Assembly took up the report to the last Assembly, on the transfer of the Western Foreign Missionary Society, the order of the day.

Dr. Skinner, one of the committee who dissented from this report, made a counter report, which was read, and is as follows, viz:

"Whereas, the American Board of commissioners for foreign missions, has been connected with the Presbyterian Church from the year of its incorporation, by the very elements of its existence; and whereas, at the present time, the majority of the whole of that board are Presbyterians; and whereas, it is undesirable that there should be *any collision,* at home or abroad; therefore,

"*Resolved,* That it is *inexpedient* that the Assembly should organize a *separate* foreign missionary institution."

Here the New School unmask themselves; our anticipation is realized; the design of the adversary to subvert the Presbyterian

Church altogether, is laid bare. A brief analysis of Dr. Skinner's motion would present the matters contained in it before us in the following aspect. The American Board of commissioners "connected with the Presbyterian Church from its incorporation, by the elements of its existence." The fact is, there were individuals of the Presbyterian Church connected with that board from the beginning. But who were these individuals? Who authorized that connexion? What was their character, in ecclesiastical sympathy, policy, and intercourse? They were, with very few exceptions, of the same cast with those who were then supporting Skinner in his motion, New England, Congregational, New School men, anti-Presbyterian advocates of the *voluntary principle.*

Again: Skinner's resolution says, at present, "a majority of the whole of that board are Presbyterians." If true, this fact shows how far the spirit of apostacy and defection from the Presbyterian family had already penetrated; what power it had acquired over our own members, and what dangers it was threatening to the true church; for the fact still remains unshaken, that although most of them might have been nominally Presbyterian, their hearts, their affections, their influence, their contributions, and their efforts, were all directed and devoted to a foreign land; to an institution, in every feature, in all its designs, its movements and influences, hostile to the Presbyterian system; this, they sought to abolish, and for it to substitute their own.

Again, Skinner says, "it is undesirable that there should be *any collision** at home or abroad." Here is exhibited the kind, liberal, *pacific* spirit of the men who charge the orthodox body with intolerance, for maintaining their own standards! They tell us plainly, they *mean to contend;* they are ready for war; they never intend to relinquish the purpose of triumph and monopoly, power and spoils, without a bloody struggle. We do not doubt it; we have tested their principles, we have already witnessed their rancour and violence, we have seen their character sufficiently developed to put this matter beyond doubt. But are we to be frightened and deterred by such threats? Must Presbyterians sacrifice all to the cruel invaders and plunderers of their church, without an effort to repel them? Have they no distinctive principles and forms to contend for? Have they no duties to perform, to the trusts and responsibilities confided? to the flocks committed to their care? to the Saviour who bled for them? to the God who will judge them?

Again: Skinner's resolution asserts, "it is inexpedient to organize a separate foreign missionary society." Who can fail to admire the modesty of this summary, or conclusion of the whole

* Here is their threat of open warfare. As the Yankees in New York said, "they meant to fight it out."

matter? This Boston association is competent to explore and embrace the whole earth; to perform the desired errand of mercy to all mankind; to penetrate all lands and oceans, mountains, rivers, islands, and continents. They will occupy the whole field of the world themselves; they will leave nothing undone that ought to be done; our name is legion, for we are many. God needs no other instrumentality in fulfilling the Saviour's command, "Go preach the gospel to every creature," than these New School apostates from Presbyterianism.

The motion was made and carried on the top of a hill, from which it will be distinctly visible to millions of honest eyes, to the ends of the earth, and till the end of time. Another fact in this disgraceful recapitulation must not be omitted. The motion of Dr. Skinner, the mover well knew, if carried, came with an unrelenting, coercive power, of simple majority, to compel the Assembly to violate a sacred contract, made by her solemn appointment and sanction, with the Synod of Pittsburgh, to secure the transfer of the Western Foreign Missionary Society to the Assembly. Can any candid, judicious man upon earth, presume to say that the Presbyterian Church were bound, in the slightest degree, to submit to acts and measures of New School origin, so arbitrary, insolent, and oppressive, when the alleged preference was based, not upon the superior excellence or efficiency of the New School missionary system, but upon open and inveterate hostility to the avowed Presbyterian plan of conducting missions as a church.

On Friday, at two o'clock. P. M., the vote was taken on the question to postpone the report of the committee, to take up the report of Dr. Skinner, and was decided in the negative by the following vote, viz: 133 in favour of postponing, and 134 in the opposition, giving to the Presbyterian Church organization, one single vote majority.

The New School, still determined as death upon their object, on the resumption and extended discussion of the subject of transferring the Western Missionary Society to the General Assembly, on the main question of adopting the report, called for the previous question, which gave a majority of four votes in favour of Skinner's motion.

The following protest was introduced and ordered to be entered on the minutes, viz:

"The undersigned do solemnly protest against the decision of the General Assembly, whereby the report of the committee of the last General Assembly, respecting the Western Foreign Missionary Society was rejected, for the following reasons:

"1. Because we consider the decision of the Assembly, in this case, as an unjustifiable refusal to carry into effect a solemn contract with the Synod of Pittsburgh, duly ratified and confirmed under the authority of the last Assembly.

"2. Because we are impressed with the deepest conviction, that the Presbyterian Church, in her ecclesiastical capacity, is bound, in obedience to the command of her divine Head and Lord, to send the glorious gospel as far as may be in her power, to every creature; and we consider the decision of the Assembly in this case as a direct refusal to obey this command, and to pursue one of the great objects for which the church was founded.

"3. Because it is our deliberate persuasion, that a large part of the energy, zeal, and resources of the Presbyterian Church cannot be called into action in the missionary cause, without the establishment of a missionary board by the General Assembly. It is evident that no other ecclesiastical organization, by fragments of the church, can be formed, which will unite, satisfy, and call forth the zealous co-operation of those in every part of the church, who wish for a general Presbyterian board.

"4. Because, while the majority of the Assembly acknowledges that *they* had a board which fully met all the wants and wishes of themselves, and of those who sympathized with them; they refused to make such a division as would accord to us a similar and equal privilege, thereby, as we conceive, refusing that which would have been only just and equal, and rejecting a plan which would have extended greatly the missionary spirit, and exerted a reflex beneficial influence on the church, thus indulged with a board agreeable to their views.

"5. Because, to all these considerations, urged with solemnity and affection, the majority of the Assembly were deaf, and have laid us under the necessity of protesting against their course; of complaining that we are denied a most reasonable, and, to us, most precious privilege; and of lamenting that we are laid under the necessity of resorting to plans of ecclesiastical organization, complicated, inconvenient, and much more adapted, on a variety of accounts, to interfere with ecclesiastical harmony, than the proposed board would have been.

Pittsburgh, June 9, 1836. *Signed.*

Samuel Miller—*the writer*,
James Lenox, &c."

In all, Orthodox, 87 names—New School, 91.

The passage of Dr. Skinner's resolution, was the consummation of New School ambition for the present moment; a full exhibition of the proscriptive tyranny and violence of their designs. It seems scarcely possible, that any company of men whose reason was not dethroned, could become so infatuated as to suppose that the Presbyterian Church would submit to such an outrage; that they would permit strangers and aliens, of another creed, another policy, another name, another spirit, who had, under false pretences and broken vows, *crept in unawares*, concealing their ingress, multiplying their numbers, magnifying their powers, fortifying their positions, with untiring zeal and in an increasing progress, to take away from the Presbyterian body, to snatch rapaciously from their very bosom, that work of benevolence and evangelization, which was the governing and distinguishing designation and ascension command of her gracious sovereign. But this triumphant act of spoilation, these infatuated and desperate men actually attempted, and well nigh succeeded in accomplishing; with a deliberate coolness, callousness, air of triumph and exultation, rarely witnessed. So that at the church door, after the Assembly adjourned, the great apostle of New School propagandism in the West, so flushed with the victory, and so confident of ultimate triumph in their revolutionary progress, exclaimed aloud, in vulgar terms, "That's the last kick of Presbyterianism!" There you may read the character of Dr. Beecher. Poor creatures; they really calculated, with a majority of only four votes, that "they had fought it out;" that they had won the battle; that the struggle was over; that the church was truly under their control; that its various boards, already organized or in contemplation, would be either abolished, or changed to suit their Congregational schemes, and transferred to another region, to be directed and conducted as aliens and strangers might prefer.

But the giant church was only slumbering; half awake, the foe had obtained only partial possession of her active available means, in such a tremendous emergency. She heard their war whoop and saw the desolation and havoc of the assailants; she heard their whispers and caught their secret counsels and designs for the future, as they floated in the breeze—their self gratulation and triumph in their past and future progress. "The last kick of Presbyterianism!"—that delicate and refined morceau of wit, of New School delicacy—of their apostolic piety and devotion, startled many of the church's sleeping sons from their unseasonable repose. Thus the passage of the despotic resolution above recited, and the manner in which it was promulged and made the theme of insolent boast and triumph, aided in producing the speedy discomfiture and total banishment of the New School party from Presbyterian record.

The church now clearly perceived, that their liberties, in Christ Jesus, were violently assailed; that an attempt was made to impair their honour and high standing in the christian world, that the most choice, direct and animating path of duty and usefulness opened to them as a church, by their great leader, was obstructed; that the solemn dictates of their consciences were paralized by arbitrary and coercive power, requiring them to sacririfice their deep sense of obligation to obey the Saviour, and to become subservient to the will and caprice of an alien band, who had by corrupt and lawless means, and for corrupt and lawless purposes, attempted to acquire dominion over them; these sacrifices they were not prepared to make.

CHAPTER XVII.

New York Address—Opinions of Mr. Barnes—Strictures upon his writings—Favourable Notices of Dr. Junkins' Testimony—Dr. Miller's rejected Resolution—Protest in connexion—A powerful host in support on record—Unitarian Sentiments in regard to the New School, and their opinions.

"An address to the ministers, elders and members of the Presbyterian Church in the United States," was issued A. D. 1836, by "a committee appointed by members of the last General Assembly, at Pittsburg, to prepare and circulate a publication on the state of the church, and particularly on the two great subjects, which had occupied the attention of the Assembly, viz:—The Barnes' case and the Foreign Missionary Question." This document, abounding in lucid intelligence, powerful argument and convincing appeal, to the understanding and heart of all honest and sensible men, stands among the most important papers published in that day of contest, for the church's purity and safety; foremost and highest in eloquence, integrity and power. We shall endeavour to convey to the reader a just idea of that document by inserting some extracts. It is a matter of regret that it cannot be placed entire in the hands of every reader in our land.

The following observations should be stamped upon the front of every religious society in the world, and make a permanent lodgment there:

Page 4. "To the successful maintainance of the truth of God—to union of effort in its maintainance, creeds, confessions of faith, are indispensable. It is readily conceded, that the Bible is the only infallible rule of faith and practice; the ultimate standard by which every doctrine and every spirit must be tried. But it is well known, that men interpret the Bible very differently, and that all the errorists that have ever disturbed the church, have professed to receive it as their text-book. The Arian, the Socinian, the Pelagian, and the Arminian, if you believe them, all find their several systems in the Bible; so that a simple profession of faith in the Bible, it appears, is a very vague matter, and something more definite and explicit is evidently necessary to ascertain the religious sentiments of men. Accordingly, the church has never been without her confession of faith, her avowed creed. The Presbyterian Church has her forms of doctrine, her confession of faith and catechisms, which constitute her public standards. On entering the Presbyterian Church, every minister of the gospel is required solemnly to avow, that the doctrines of these standards are the doctrines which he holds and approves; he is required to answer in the affirmative, the following among other questions, viz: Do you sincerely receive and adopt the confession of faith of this church, as containing the system of doctrine taught in the Holy Scriptures? Mark this language. It is not, do you receive 'for substance of doctrine,' 'with considerable latitude of interpretation,' the confession of faith of this church? Nor is it, do you receive the 'system' of doctrine which this confession teaches? It is more explicit still. Do you sincerely *receive* and adopt *the confession of faith* of this church, as containing the system of doctrines taught in the Holy Scriptures? as containing the accredited principles of christianity, arranged in systematic order, according to their mutual bearings and dependence? This is the simple naked question, and were all who answer this question to do so in good faith, sincerely and candidly, then would the name of Presbyterian be an intelligible and sufficient passport throughout our bounds; then would a certificate of the fact, that an individual, before any Presbytery in the land, had received our standards, at once make us acquainted with his doctrinal sentiments, and commend him to our confidence, for we should then all speak the same thing, and be perfectly joined together in the same mind and in the same judgment!

"But if in answering this question, men are not sincere and candid, if when they say, they *sincerely* receive and adopt the *confession of faith* of this *church*, they receive it merely as a 'system,' distinguished from and in preference to other systems, and reserve to themselves the right of construing its language, to mean something different from that which it has been uniformly understood to mean, then it is plain that we have no common standards—no bond of union—and that it is impossible to know what are the doctrines held by those nominally connected with us."

Another kindred paragraph is weighty and appropriate to this point. "Creeds, confessions of faith, to answer their true and legitimate purpose, must be *honestly* received; and here we are constrained to believe, is one fruitful source of our distractions as a church, a *lack* of honesty in the reception of our standards. Although they have professed to receive our standards, they do not consider themselves bound by that act to receive all the doctrines contained in them, nor to construe the language in which they are expressed, in the sense in which it was manifestly employed by those who framed them. Their gigantic and independent minds are not to be *tramelled* by *frame-works* of faith, that men have invented; without any regard to the solemn vows which they have voluntarily come under, they publish to the world their unhallowed speculations, their crude and undigested theories. Instead of withdrawing in a peaceable and orderly manner from a church, whose formularies they have never honestly adopted, they remain to destroy its unity and interrupt its harmony. Under the name and cloak of Presbyterianism, they disseminate sentiments which lead directly to Arminianism, Pelagianism and Socinianism. These are the men, who, in our judgment, have caused divisions among us, for we are a divided church, as really divided as though we were called by different names, and existed under different organization. The schism has come already, and let those men who have come into our church, by professing to receive our standards, when, in fact, they did not believe them, in their plain and obvious import, answer for it, for they are its authors. These remarks, it is painful, exceedingly painful, for us to make, but we are persuaded they are well founded. If any think them severe, it is our conscientious conviction, it is only the severity of *truth*."

This address contains a critical and just exposition of Barnes' heresies, incorporated in his sermon on the *Way of Salvation*, in his Notes on the Epistle to the Romans, and in all his theological publications. The account it furnishes of his errors and the evidence against them, exhibited in his trial before the Presbytery of Philadelphia, and in the laborious and faithful investigation of Dr. Junkin, in his memorable prosecution so ably conducted, will be handed over to the church universal, in the present day, and down to all future generations, as a monument of Mr. Barnes' rashness, folly and guilt, in his wide and numerous departures from the faith delivered to the saints.

Notwithstanding the New School influence ultimately brought to operate in favour of Mr. Barnes, both in the Presbytery and Synod of Philadelphia, so extensively as to exonerate him in a great measure from his corruptions in doctrine, fully proved on most incontestible evidence, yet the predominant party, in their triumph, greatly impaired their character and standing in public estimation, so as to facilitate and hasten their downfall.

The following resolution, presenting the doctrinal question in a form entirely separate from all matters of church order, was introduced by Dr. Miller, to obtain the real sense of the house in this unembarrassed manner, on the charge of heresy, viz:

"*Resolved*, That while this General Assembly has thought proper to remove the sentence of suspension, under which the

Rev. Mr. Barnes was placed, by the Synod of Philadelphia, yet the judgment of this Assembly is, that Mr. Barnes, in his Notes on the Epistle to the Romans, has published opinions materially at variance with the Confession of Faith of the Presbyterian Church, and with the word of God, especially with regard to original sin, the relation of man to Adam, and justification by faith in the atoning sacrifice and righteousness of the Redeemer. The Assembly consider the manner in which Mr. Barnes has controverted the language and doctrine of our public standards, as highly reprehensible, and as adapted to pervert the minds of the rising generation from the simplicity and purity of the gospel plan. And although some of the most objectionable statements and expressions which appeared in the earlier editions of the work in question, have been either removed, or so far modified or explained, as to render them more in accordance with our public formularies; still the Assembly considers the work, even in its present amended form, as containing representations which cannot be reconciled with the letter or spirit of our public standards; and would solemnly admonish Mr. Barnes again to review his work; to modify still farther the statements which have grieved his brethren, and to be more careful in time to come to study the purity and peace of the church."

This motion was rejected by a vote of 122 to 109. The decision proves the existence of a marked and irreconcilable opposition in fundamental theological sentiments between this majority and the minority, against the decision of the Assembly. On this resolution, the following protest was presented, signed by one hundred leading or prominent ministers and elders, in the Presbyterian Church. The number of signatures would have been much larger, had not the Assembly been daily diminished, by frequent applications for leave of absence. The protest is in few words, but full of import, from the pen of Dr. Miller; while it exhibits the falseness of Mr. Barnes, it shows the sentiments of the Rev. and venerated writer in their true character.

"Whereas, the General Assembly of the Presbyterian Church, did by their vote, on the 7th instant, reject a resolution, disapproving some of the doctrinal statements contained in Barnes' Notes on the Romans, which resolution, especially under the peculiar circumstances of the case, the undersigned considered of high importance to the church with which we are connected, to the cause of our Lord and Saviour Jesus Christ, and to the just exhibition of His grace and truth, we, whose names are subscribed feel constrained in the name of the great Head of the church, solemnly to protest against said decision, for the following reasons, viz:

1. Because we believe that the constitutional standards of the

church, in their plain and obvious meaning, and in the sense in which they have always been received, are the rule of judgment by which all doctrinal controversies are to be decided; that it is the duty of the church to maintain inviolate her doctrine and order, agreeably to those standards: to bear her decided testimony against all deviations from them, and not to countenance them even by implication. Yet in the above decision, there was, we believe, a departure from our constitutional rule, a refusal to bear testimony against errors, with an implied approbation of them, and a constructive denial that ministers of the gospel, in the Presbyterian Church, are under solemn obligations to conform in their doctrinal sentiments, to our Confession of Faith and Catechisms.

"2. Because the errors contemplated in the aforesaid resolution, do not consist merely nor chiefly in inaccurate or ambiguous expressions and mistaken illustrations, but in sentiments and opinions respecting the great and important doctrines of the gospel, which are utterly inconsistent with the statement of those doctrines made in the Confession of Faith, and revealed in the word of God. We sincerely and firmly believe, that Mr. Barnes has denied, and that in a sneering manner, that Adam was the covenant head of the human race; that all mankind sinned in him as such, and were thus brought under the penalty of transgression; that Christ suffered the penalty of the law when he died for sin, and that the righteousness of Christ is imputed to believers for justification. These and similar doctrinal views, we regard as material deviations from our standards, as dangerous in themselves and as contravening some of the leading principles of our system, such as man's complete dependence and the perfect harmony of justice and grace, in the salvation of the sinner.

"3. Because this expression of approbation of his opinions was passed after, as we believe, it had been clearly and sufficiently proved to the Assembly, that Mr. Barnes had denied these important truths, and had expressed opinions respecting original sin, the nature of faith and the nature of justification, which cannot be reconciled with our standards; and after, instead of retracting any of his doctrinal opinions, he had declared expressly before the Assembly, and published in the preface to the last edition of his Notes on the Romans, that he had not changed, but held them still, and was determined to preach them till he died.

"For these reasons, and for the glory of God, that we may preserve a conscience void of offence, we request that this, our solemn protest, may be entered on the minutes of the Assembly."

As this protest, in connection with Dr. Miller's rejected resolution, brings the truth and reality of Mr. Barnes' obstinate and determined violation of several leading and fundamental doctrines of the gospel, and of the fixed purpose of the New School party now predominant in the Assembly, as appears from the vote of the house, to sustain and vindicate him in his false doctrines, it is thought highly expedient to record here the names of those who had signed the protest, when it was presented to the Assembly, that the church and the world may see what kind of testimony stands against him in this connexion, viz:

W. W. Phillips, J. McElroy, James Hoge, Samuel S. Davis, Francis McFarland, Joseph Smith, James McCurdy, Jacob F. Price, W. L. Breckinridge, H. M. Koontz, P. I. Sparrow, Robert Johnson, Joseph Harleson, John H. Culbertson, W. P. Alrich, J. S. Wilson, T. C. Stuart, J. McClintock, Nathaniel Tod, Alex'r R. Curry, Geo. Anderson, James McFarren, John Banin, John M. C. Bartly, Sam'l McQuestin, Wm. James, Ananias Platt, Duncan McMartin, Edwin Downer, H. M. Hopkins, James V. Henry, Russel I. Minor, Wm. Marshall, James Lenox, Samuel Boyd, W. Wallace, (N. Y.) Sam'l Miller, B. Ogden, James Seabrook, Jacob Castner, Joseph Campbell, James Kennedy, John Stinson, Samuel Henderson, I. Coulter, Joel Stoneroad, N. Ewing, James Alexander, Jos. D. Ray, Rob't Highlands, John Miller, I. Eaton, Rob't Porter, Jos. McFarren, C. Valandingham, Alex'r Write, R. Johnson, James Wilson, E. Rowland, Archibald Hanna, Jno. Elliot, W. Wallace, (Lon.) Rob't Smith, J. S. Galloway, S. Scovil, B. E. Swan, G. Bishop, Wm. Dun, M. G. Wallace, J. S. Weaver, S. Donnell, B. F. Spilman, W. A. S. Posey, J. S. Berryman, D. S. Tod, Lewis Collins, W. Williamson, James Wharey, John McElhenney, Thos. Baird, E. W. Caresthans, Arch'd McCallum, R. H. Kilpatrick, J. S. McCutchan, F. A. Ogden, A. A. Campbell, I. Ingram, S. B. Luvers, J. Le Roy Davies, Thos. L. Dunlap, Eugenius A. Nesbit, G. T. Snowden, Horace S. Pratt, John H. Vancourt, F. H. Porter, Thos. R. Borden, T. C. Stuart, John R. Hutchinson, D. Morrow, J. H. Gray.

If the history of this melancholy transaction could stop here, it would be a happy pause for the honor of poor fallen man, and especially for the christian ministry; but the truth must be told. A paper was presented to the Assembly, professing to be an answer to the above protest, prepared by Drs. Skinner and Allen, together with Mr. Brainerd, and recorded on the minutes. When the motion was made to insert it there, an excellent member from the South remarked, that we might as well say white was black. But the facts of the case being already quite fully before the reader, no comment is necessary; the paper will proclaim its own unhappy character. The signers to it say:

"1. That by their decision they do not intend to, and do not, in fact, make themselves responsible for all the phraseology of Mr. Barnes, some of which is not sufficiently guarded, and is liable to be misunderstood, and which we doubt not Mr. Barnes, with reference to his usefulness and the peace of the church, will modify so as to prevent, as far as may be, the possibility of misconception." It is painful to believe it, and yet such is the fact, as is well known to all who were in the Assembly, that Dr. Skinner, the chairman who presented this paper, did identify himself with Mr. Barnes, and declared, "that no man could have more accurately expressed his own sentiments; that he fairly represented the New School brethren; that if Mr. Barnes were condemned, *they* would be condemned." Dr. Peters declared that he not only approved of the doctrines, but of the language employed by Mr. Barnes. "When I heard," said he, "of the sentence of his suspension, I regarded it as a blow struck at one half of the Presbyterian Church; I shall not vote to restore him on the ground of toleration; he has a right to be a minister in our connexion; if any one is to be tolerated, it is the prosecutor. Yes sir, the time has come when the question is, whether such men are to be tolerated in the Presbyterian Church! No sir, I do not even condemn his (Barnes') indiscretions. It is time to have the question settled," (it has since been settled, quite decisively,) "whether in this nineteenth century we may exercise the liberty of using language adapted to the age!" And yet, after such expressions as these, (and this is a fair sample) these men have the audacity to place on their records, which they knew would meet the public eye, "that they do not intend to, and do not make themselves responsible for Mr. Barnes' phraseology," &c., &c., and they proceed to say:

"2. Much less do the Assembly adopt as doctrines consistent with our standards, and to be tolerated in our church, the errors alleged by the prosecutor, as contained in the book on the Romans. It was a question of fact, whether the errors alleged are contained in the book; and by the laws of exposition, in conscientious exercise of their own rights and duties, the Assembly have come to the conclusion that the book does not teach the errors charged." Wonderful! They were slow in coming to that conclusion, and better for them had they never pretended to at all.

Thus every kind of denial, perversion and subterfuge, is resorted to by them to conceal their obliquities, and if it were possible, to recover public confidence. But it is too late; their falseness is so glaring and manifold that it cannot be covered over. And they allow their errors and attempted frauds and impositions, no chance to escape detection; for in every meeting, in their speeches, their public transactions, they never fail to ensure their renewed enactment and condemnation, by endeavouring, as in the case now under review, to make the worse the better prove; to clothe palpable falsehood and error in the habiliments of truth.

The following is a specimen of the language of the Christian

Examiner, (a leading *Unitarian paper,*) for March, 1836, page 69, concurring with the orthodox opinion on this point, in regard to the New School. "On the atonement, our author's (Mr. Barnes') views are far in advance of those of the church to which he belongs. Though he maintains that Christ was, in some sense, 'a *substitute* in the place of sinners,' he denies a strictly and fully vicarious atonement, and makes the Saviour's death important chiefly as an illustration of the inherent and essential connexion between sin and suffering."

Again, page 70, "On the subject of man's nature, capacities, and duty, our author is sound and lucid. The idea of hereditary depravity he spurns, as unworthy even a passing notice. He asserts repeatedly, that men sin only '*in their own persons, sin themselves,* as, indeed, how *can* they *sin,* in any *other* way?' The imputation of Adam's transgression, he treats as a scholastic absurdity. Of the figment of Adam's federal headship, and the condemnation of his posterity for partnership in his sin, Mr. Barnes says, 'there is not one word of it in the Bible.' It is a mere philosophical theory, an introduction of a speculation into theology with an attempt to explain what the Bible has left unexplained." How gratifying it must be to the pride and ambition, to the talents, learning, moral purity, and devotion of Mr. Barnes and all his sympathizers, to be thus eulogized and commended, or shall we rather say, held up sarcastically to the derision and contumely of an indignant public by such men as the *Unitarians!*

Hear the Unitarian brethren of the New School type again: "In conclusion, we would say, that while our orthodox brethren publish and circulate, and receive with favour, such books as these 'Notes,' we most cordially extend to them the right hand of fellowship, even though they refuse to return it. We regard them as fellow-labourers with us for the overthrow of time-hallowed absurdities, for the cleansing of the Christian creed 'from whatever defileth and maketh a lie.'" This must be, to the New School, cheering language, coming, as it does, from one of the most infidel, polluted, and corrupting sources in our degenerate world.

As an instance of the most glaring artifice, we recite the following resolution of the majority in the last Assembly. After labouring, for many days, by every means they could invent and employ, to screen Mr. Barnes, to throw censure and reproach upon orthodox men, and sound judicatories, to sustain and confirm in the church heretical sentiments and disorganizing measures, and discovering that the public could not be blinded in regard to these palpable acts of dishonesty and corruption, they fabricate and adopt, as a last resort in this connexion, the following revolting declaration, which excited, at the time of its passage, inexpressible astonishment and grief, to all who heard it, or have been heard to speak of it, viz: "So far is the Assembly from countenancing the errors alleged in the charges of Dr. Junkin, that they do cordially and *ex animo*, adopt the Confession of our church, on the points of doctrine in question, according to the obvious and most prevalent interpretation; and do regard it as a whole, as the best epitome of the doctrines of the Bible ever formed. And this Assembly disavows any desire, and would deprecate any attempt, to change the phraseology of our standards, and would disapprove of any language of light estimation applied to them; believing that no *denomination can prosper* whose members permit themselves to *speak slightly* of its formularies of doctrine, and are ready to unite with their brethren in contending earnestly for the faith of our standards." Here we are compelled to pause in amazement, not knowing which to admire most, the fabricators or their fiction. On reviewing the course of Mr. Barnes' sympathizers and advocates, the history of which is before us on the preceding pages, for several years, the following facts appear: 1. They admit that he used the language and uttered the sentiments alleged. 2. They refused to censure either himself or his heretical sentiments, or to bear testimony against them, or any errors akin to them at all. 3. They adopted and approved his peculiar and heretical terms, identifying themselves and declaring their amalgamation with him in his unsound course of exposition and remark on the word of God, and the standards of the church. 4. They deny altogether that Barnes' language teaches heresy, or deviates from the fair, usual, and honest expression of the Confession and Catechisms of the church. Fifthly, and finally, they profess, without proposing the slightest alteration in their past declarations, to adopt the Confession of our church as it stands, *ex animo*, to laud its phraseology, its high and exalted pre-eminent standing among the formularies of past ages and the present time. Now, is it wonderful that these men, as a body, should have forfeited the confidence of both the church and the world? that they should be considered unreliable and desperate in their public course, striving to sustain themselves, and to buoy up their prostrate and ruined reputation, by fraudulently forcing under it, a foundation of dissolution and rottenness? Ought it to be surprising, if the great mass of Presbyterian ministers and people, of a totally different faith and spirit, the standards of our church being the touch-stone, after being compelled, with painful conflicts and lamentations, to associate in trials, in business, in responsibilities, for many years, without a possibility of deliverance, that they should now feel the urgent necessity of throwing off this humiliating, burdensome, and most painful connexion? How could it be otherwise? Are our lives to be unceasingly vexed, and finally worn out, in perpetual strife and suffering?

The address of the Pittsburgh committee, published at New York, 1836, on the missionary question, is able and conclusive. But having already filled several pages with this interesting discussion, and placed the subject in as clear a light as was found practicable, we do not think it is necessary to add any thing to what is already written upon this subject.

CHAPTER XVIII.

The Convention of Ministers and Elders which met in Philadelphia before the Assembly of 1837—The Testimony and Memorial presented to them, and their Memorial and Address to the Assembly based upon them—Committee appointed on this Memorial.

The convention of Presbyterian ministers and ruling elders, recommended by the committee appointed by the minority of the last General Assembly, met agreeably to appointment in the Sixth Presbyterian Church, May 11th, 1837, immediately preceding the Assembly.

The roll embraced one hundred and twenty-six, from every part of the Presbyterian Church. This number was augmented by new accessions, and the Rev. George A. Baxter, of Virginia, was chosen President.

The convention met frequently, and sometimes even during the session of the General Assembly. The condition, dangers, and prospects of the church were solemnly and ably discussed, after which, and on the most mature and deliberate consideration, the following document was adopted and presented to the General Assembly.

"*Testimony and Memorial.*

"When any portion of the Church of Jesus Christ is called in his providence to take a step which may materially affect their Master's cause, and influence for good or ill the destinies of large portions of mankind through successive generations, it is a very plain, as well as solemn duty, to state clearly the reasons of their conduct, the evils of which they complain, the objects at which they aim, and the remedies which they propose. This convention, consisting of one hundred and twenty-four members, of whom one hundred and twelve are delegated by fifty-four Presbyteries, and twelve by minorities in eight other Presbyteries, all of which members are ministers or ruling elders of the Presbyterian Church in the United States of America, after mature deliberation, full consultation with each other, and earnest prayer to God for direction, have agreed on the following memorial, and do hereby respectfully lay it before the General Assembly now in session, and through it before all the churches and the whole world, as our solemn, and, as we trust, effective Testimony against evils which faithfulness to God, and to the world, will no longer permit us to endure.

"That we have not been rash and hasty, nor manifested a factious opposition to errors and disorders, which were only of small extent or recent introduction, is manifestly proven by the fact that these evils have been insidiously spreading through our church for many years, and that they have at length become so mature and so diffused, as not only to pervade large portions of the church, but to reign triumphantly over the body itself, through successive General Assemblies. On the other hand, that we have not been wholly faithless to our Master and to truth, we appeal to the constant efforts of some through the press and pulpit; to the firm and consistent course of some of our Presbyteries and Synods; to the faithful conduct of the minorities in the Assemblies of 1831, 2, 3, 4, and 6; to the Act and Testimony; to the proceedings of the conventions of Cincinnati in 1831, and Pittsburgh in 1835, and to the noble Assembly of 1835.

"We contend especially and above all for *the truth*, as it is made known to us of God, for the salvation of men. We contend for nothing else, except as the result or support of this inestimable treasure. It is because this is subverted that we grieve; it is because our standards teach it, that we bewail their perversion; it is because our church order and discipline preserve, defend, and diffuse it, that we weep over their impending ruin. It is against *error* that we emphatically bear our testimony; error, dangerous to the souls of men, dishonouring to Jesus Christ, contrary to his revealed truth, and utterly at variance with our standards. Error, not as it may be freely and openly held by others, in this age and land of absolute religious freedom: but error, held and taught in the Presbyterian Church, preached and written by persons who profess to receive and adopt our Scriptural standards; promoted by societies operating widely through our churches; reduced into form, and openly embraced by almost entire Presbyteries and Synods; favoured by repeated acts of successive General Assemblies, and at last virtually sanctioned to an alarming extent by the numerous Assembly of 1836.

"To be more specific, we hereby set forth in order, some of the doctrinal errors against which we bear testimony, and which we and the churches have conclusive proof, are widely disseminated in the Presbyterian Church.

"*In relation to Doctrine.*

"1. That God would have been glad to prevent the existence of sin in our world, but was not able, without destroying the moral agency of man; or, that for aught that appears in the Bible to the contrary, sin is incidental to any wise moral system.

"2. That election to eternal life is founded on a foresight of faith and obedience.

"3. That we have no more to do with the first sin of Adam than with the sins of any other parent.

"4. That infants come into the world as free from moral defilement as was Adam, when he was created.

"5. That infants sustain the same relation to the moral government of God in this world as brute animals, and that their sufferings and death are to be accounted for, on the same principles as those of brutes, and not by any means to be considered as penal.

"6. That there is no other original sin than the fact that all the posterity of Adam, though by nature innocent, or possessed of no moral character, will always begin to sin when they begin to exercise moral agency; that original sin does not include a sinful bias of the human mind, and a just exposure to penal suffering; and that there is no evidence in Scripture, that infants, in order to salvation, do need redemption by the blood of Christ, and regeneration by the Holy Ghost.

"7. That the doctrine of imputation, whether of the guilt of Adam's sin, or of the righteousness of Christ, has no foundation in the word of God, and is both unjust and absurd.

"8. That the sufferings and death of Christ were not truly vicarious and penal, but symbolical, governmental, and instructive only.

"9. That the impenitent sinner is by nature, and independently of the renewing influence or almighty energy of the Holy Spirit, in full possession of all the ability necessary to a full compliance with all the commands of God.

"10. That Christ never intercedes for any but those who are actually united to him by faith; or that Christ does not intercede for the elect until after their regeneration.

"11. That saving faith is the mere belief of the word of God, and not a grace of the Holy Spirit.

"12. That regeneration is the act of the sinner himself, and that it consists in a change of his governing purpose, which he himself must produce, and which is the result, not of any direct influence of the Holy Spirit on the heart, but chiefly of a persuasive exhibition of the truth analogous to the influence which one man exerts over the mind of another; or that regeneration is not an instantaneous act, but a progressive work.

"13. That God has done all that *he can do* for the salvation of all men, and that man himself must do the rest.

"14. That God cannot exert such influence on the minds of men, as shall make it certain that they will choose and act in a particular manner, without impairing their moral agency.

"15. That the righteousness of Christ is not the sole ground of the sinner's acceptance with God; and that in no sense does the righteousness of Christ become ours.

"16. That the reason why some differ from others in regard to their reception of the gospel is, that they make themselves to differ.

"It is impossible to contemplate these errors without perceiving that they strike at the foundation of the system of gospel grace; and that, from the days of Pelagius and Cassian to the present hour, their reception has uniformly marked the character of a church apostatizing from 'the faith once delivered to the saints,' and sinking into deplorable corruption. To bear a public and open testimony against them, and as far as possible to banish them from the 'household of faith,' is a duty which the Presbyterian Church owes to her Master in heaven, and without which it is impossible to fulfil the great purpose for which she was founded by her divine Head and Lord. And this Convention is conscious that in pronouncing these errors unscriptural, radical, and highly dangerous, it is actuated by no feeling of party zeal, but by a firm and growing persuasion that such errors cannot fail in their ultimate effect, to subvert the foundation of Christian hope, and destroy the souls of men. The watchmen on the walls of Zion would be traitors to the trust reposed in them, were they not to cry aloud, and proclaim a solemn warning against opinions so corrupt and delusive.

"*In relation to Church Order.*

"Believing the Presbyterian form of government to be that instituted by the inspired apostles of the Lord, in the early church, and sanctioned, if not commanded, in the scattered notices contained in the New Testament, on the general subject, our hearts cling to it as to that order approved by revelation of God, and made manifest by long experience, as the best method of preserving and spreading his truth. When that truth is in danger, we hold but the more steadfastly to our distinctive church order, as affording the best method of detecting and vanquishing error. That any form of administration should totally prevent evil, is manifestly impossible while men continue as they are; and it is no small praise to the institutions of our church, that they so nearly reach this result, as to be incapable of regular action in the hands of those who are themselves corrupt. They live with and for the truth; to spread error, they must be perverted; and before a general apostacy, Presbyterian order must always perish.

"Thus it has been in these evil times. Abundant proof is before this convention, and indeed before the whole world, that the principles of our system have been universally departed from, by those who have departed from our faith; and that generally that has been done with equal steps. Or if, as there is reason to fear, some portions of the church still hold the external form of Presbyterianism, and deny the power of its sacred doctrines, they are those only, who, in attaching themselves to us, have either evaded subscription to our creed, or subscribed without believing it. It is enough that any system should exclude honest errorists, and speedily detect, if it cannot *exclude, those who are otherwise.*

"Among the departures from sound Presbyterian order, against which we feel called on to testify, as marking the times, are the following:

"1. The formation of Presbyteries without defined and reasonable limits, or Presbyteries covering the same territory, and especially such a formation founded on doctrinal repulsions or affinities; thus introducing schism into the very vitals of the body.

"2. The refusal of Presbyteries, when requested by any of their members, to examine all applicants for admission into them, as to their soundness in the faith, or touching any other matter connected with a fair Presbyterial standing; thus concealing and conniving at error, in the very strong hold of truth.

"3. The licensing of persons to preach the gospel, and the ordaining to the office of the ministry such as not only accept of our standards merely for substance of doctrine, and others who are unfit and ought to be excluded for want of qualification, but of many even who openly deny fundamental principles of truth, and preach and publish radical errors as already set forth.

"4. The formation of a great multitude and variety of creeds which are often incomplete, false, and contradictory of each other, and of our Confession of Faith and the Bible; but which even if true are needless, seeing that the public and authorized standards of the church are fully sufficient for the purposes for which such formularies were introduced, namely, as public testimonies of our faith and practice, as aids to the teaching of the people truth and righteousness, and as instruments for ascertaining and preserving the unity of the Spirit in the bonds of peace; it being understood that we do not object to the use of a brief abstract of the doctrines of our Confession of Faith, in the public reception of private members of the church.

"5. The needless ordination of a multitude of men to the office of evangelist, and the consequent tendency to a general neglect of the pastoral office; frequent and hurtful changes of pastoral relations; to the multiplication of spurious excitements, and the consequent spread of heresy and fanaticism, thus weakening and bringing into contempt the ordinary and stated agents and means, for the conversion of sinners, and the edification of the body of Christ.

"6. The disuse of the office of ruling elder in portions of the church, and the consequent growth of practices and principles entirely foreign to our system; thus depriving the pastors of needful assistants in discipline, the people of proper guides in Christ, and the churches of suitable representatives in the ecclesiastical tribunals.

"7. The electing and ordaining ruling elders, with the express understanding that they are to serve but for a limited time.

"8. A progressive change in the system of Presbyterial representation in the General Assembly, which has been persisted in by those holding the ordinary majorities, and carried out into detail by those disposed to take undue advantage of existing opportunities, until the actual representation seldom exhibits the true state of the church, and many questions of the deepest interest have been decided contrary to the fairly ascertained wishes of the majority of the church and people in our communion; thus virtually subverting the essential principles of freedom, justice, and equality, on which our whole system rests.

"9. The unlimited and irresponsible power assumed by several associations of men under various names, to exercise authority and influence, direct and indirect, over Presbyters, as to their field of labour, place of residence, and mode of action in the difficult circumstances of our church; thus actually throwing the control of affairs in large portions of the church, and sometimes in the General Assembly itself, out of the hands of the Presbyteries into those of single individuals or small committees located at a distance.

"10. The unconstitutional decisions and violent proceedings of several General Assemblies, and especially those of 1831, 2, 3, 4, and 6, directly or indirectly subverting some of the fundamental principles of Presbyterian government, effectually discountenancing discipline, if not rendering it impossible, and plainly conniving at and favouring, if not virtually affirming as true, the whole current of false doctrine which has been for years setting into our church, thus making the church itself *a principal actor in its own dissolution and ruin.*

"*In Relation to Discipline.*

"That a state of affairs even approaching to that over which we now mourn, should obstruct the exercise of discipline, may not only be easily supposed, but unhappily, the very evils which rendered it imperatively necessary, conspired to prevent the possibility of its regular exercise. A church unsound in faith is necessarily corrupt in practice. Truth is in order to godliness, and when it ceases to make us pure, it is no longer considered worthy of being contended for.

"With the woeful departures from sound doctrine, which we have already pointed out, and the grievous declensions in church order heretofore stated, has advanced step by step, the ruin of all sound discipline in large portions of our church, until in some places our very name is becoming a public scandal, and the proceedings of persons and churches connected with some of our Presbyteries, are hardly to be defended from the accusation of being blasphemous. Amongst other evils, of which this convention and the church have full proof, we specify the following:

"1. The impossibility of obtaining a plain and sufficient sentence against gross errors, either *in thesi*, or when found in books printed under the name of Presbyterian ministers, or when such ministers have been directly and personally charged.

"2. The public countenance thus given to error, and the complete security in which our own members have preached and published in newspapers, pamphlets, periodicals and books, things utterly subversive of our system of truth and order, while none thought it possible (except in a few, and they almost fruitless attempts) that discipline could be exercised, and therefore none attempted it.

"3. The disorderly and unseasonable meetings of the people, in which unauthorized and incompetent persons conducted worship in a manner shocking to public decency; females often leading in prayer in promiscuous assemblies, and sometimes in public instruction; the hasty admission to church privileges, and the failure to exercise any wholesome discipline over those who subsequently fall into sin, even of a public and scandalous kind; and by these and other disorders, grieving and alienating the pious members of our churches, and so filling many of them with rash, ignorant and unconverted persons, as gradually to destroy all visible distinction between the church and the world.

"4. While many of our ministers have propagated error with great zeal, and disturbed the church with irregular and disorderly conduct, some have entirely given up the stated preaching of the gospel, others have turned aside to secular pursuits, and others still, while nomina y engaged in some part of christian effort, have embarked in .he wild and extravagant speculations which have so remarkably signalized the times, thus tending to secularize and disorganize the very ministry of reconciliation.

"5. The formation in the bosom of our churches and ecclesiastical bodies, of parties ranged against each other, on personal, doctrinal and other questions, strifes and divisions amongst our people, bitter contentions amongst many of our ministers, a general weakening of mutual confidence and affection, and, in some cases, a resort to measures of violence, duplicity and injustice, totally inconsistent with the christian name.

"*Method of Reform.*

"Such being the state of things in the Presbyterian Church, we believe that the time is fully come for the adoption of some measures, which shall speedily furnish relief from the evils already referred to. Under this conviction, we present ourselves respectfully before you, praying you to lose no time, in so adjusting the important matters at issue, as to restore at once purity and peace to our distracted church. We are obliged to record our most solemn and settled belief, that the elements of our present discord are now too numerous, too extensively spread and essentially opposed, to warrant any hope that they can, in any way, be composed, so long as they are compressed within the limits of our present ecclesiastical organization. Mutual confidence is gone, and is not to be restored by any temporizing measures. This is a sad, but a plain truth. It is a result over which the church has long mourned, and at which the world has scoffed, but for the production of which we, and those who agree with us, cannot hold ourselves responsible, firmly believing, as we do, that we are in this controversy contending for the plain and obvious principles of Presbyterian doctrine and polity. In a word, it needs but a glance at the general character, the personal affinities, and the geographical relations of those who are antagonists in the present contest, to be satisfied that our present evils have not originated within, but have been brought from without, and are, in a great degree, the consequences of an unnatural intermixture of two systems of ecclesiastical action, which are in many respects entirely opposite in their nature and operation. Two important families in the great christian community, who might have lived peacefully under different roofs, and maintained a friendly intercourse with each other, have been brought beneath the same roof, and yet without an entire incorporation. Contact has not produced real union, except in a comparatively few instances; on the contrary, original differences of opinions and prejudices, in relation to the principles of government and order, in many points of great practical moment, have for a number of years, been widening instead of narrowing, and those who would have been friendly as neighbors, have at last, by being forced together into the same dwelling, after many and painful conflicts, furnished abundant evidence of the necessity of some effectual remedy. We cannot consent to meet any longer upon the floors of our several judicatories, to contend against the visible inroads of a system, which, whether so designed or not, is crippling our energies, and which, by obvious but covert advances, meances our very existence. We are in danger of being driven out from the home of our childhood.

"While, however, we complain and testify against the operations of this unnatural, unwise and unconstitutional alliance just referred to, we wish it to be distinctly understood, that we do it chiefly because of our sincere belief that the *doctrinal purity* of our ancient Confession of Faith is endangered, and not because of the preferences we have for a particular system of mere church government and discipline. We hold the latter to be important mainly from their relation to the former. Hence, we wish it to be distinctly understood, that we have not, nor do we wish to have, any controversy with the system of congregational church government upon its own territory. Towards the churches of New England, which stand fast in the faith once delivered to the saints, towards the distinguished and excellent brethren in the Lord, in those churches, who are now testifying against the errors which are troubling *them*, as they are troubling *us*, we entertain the most fraternal esteem and affection. Let there be no strife between us, and there will be none, so long as there is no effort made by either body to intrude upon the domestic concerns of the other. We want no more than to be allowed the fair and unimpeded action of our own ecclesiastical principles. We desire to stand upon our own responsibility, and not to be made involuntary sharers in the responsibility of other bodies and systems of action, with which we cannot entirely harmonize. We desire to perform our Master's work upon principles which we prefer, because they are the first principles of our own ecclesiastical system of government, recognizing at every step the propriety and necessity of responsibility, and refusing to commit to any man, or body of men, large and important trusts, without the right of review, control, and if needs be, speedy correction.

"These being our views, we earnestly urge upon the attention of the Assembly, the following items of reform:

"1. While we wish to maintain as heretofore, a friendly correspondence and interchange of annual visits, with the evangelical associations of New England, we are anxiously looking to the General Assembly, in the hope and belief that it will take into immediate consideration the plan of union adopted by the Assembly of 1801, (See Digest, p. 297, 298) and that it will perceive in the original unconstitutionality and present pernicious operations of that plan, reasons for its immediate abrogation.

"2. While we desire that no body of Christian men of other

denominations, should be prevented from choosing their own plans of doing good; and while we claim no right to complain should they exceed us in energy and zeal, we believe that facts too familiar to need repetition here, warrant us in affirming that the organization and operations of the so called American Home Missionary Society, and American Education Society, and its branches, of whatever name, are exceedingly injurious to the peace and purity of the Presbyterian Church. We recommend accordingly, that they should be discountenanced, and their operations, as far as possible, prevented, within our ecclesiastical limits.

"3. We believe that every Church, Presbytery or Synod now in nominal connexion with this Assembly, but which is not organized on Presbyterian principles, should be immediately brought into order, dissolved, or disconnected from the Presbyterian Church.

"4. We believe that it is highly important, that, at the present time, Presbyteries should be directed to examine henceforward all licentiates and ministers applying for admission from other denominations, on the subjects of theology and church government, as well as personal piety and ministerial qualifications, and to require of them an explicit adoption of the Confession of Faith and Form of Government.

"5. We desire that immediate measures be taken, in order that such members of any Presbytery as hold any of the errors, or practice any of the disorders now testified against, may be subjected to discipline; that such Presbyteries and Synods as tolerate them, may be cited and tried, and such of these bodies as are believed to consist chiefly of decidedly unsound or disorderly members may be separated from the Presbyterian Church, provision being made at the same time for the re-union of orthodox churches, private members, or ministers, who may be found in any of them, with other convenient bodies.

"6. As these are times of high and dangerous excitability in the public mind, when imprudent or partisan men may do great injury, especially when they have facilities for operating on a large field, this convention is of opinion that the General Assembly ought to make known to our national societies, not previously noticed in this memorial, that the Presbyterian Church expects of them great caution in the selection of their travelling agents, and that it ought to be regarded as peculiarly unkind in any of them to give to the correspondence or general bearing of their institutions, a bias against the strictest order, and soundest principles of our beloved branch of the Church of Christ.

"*Conclusion.*

"And now we submit to the highest tribunal of our church, to all our brethren beloved in the Lord, and to the generation in which our lots are cast, a Testimony which we find ourselves unable to weaken or abridge, and keep a good conscience towards God and man. We have performed a duty to which the providence of God has shut us up. We have done it, in reliance on his grace, and in view of his judgment bar. Whatever the issue may be, we rejoice in the sense of having discharged a great and imperative obligation, manifestly required at our hands, and all whose issues ought to promote the purity, the peace, and the unity of the Church of Christ.

"The whole responsibility of future results is from this moment thrown first upon the General Assembly now in session, and afterwards upon the whole church. The Assembly will, of course, pursue such a line of conduct as will appear to acquit it before earth and heaven. The destinies of the Presbyterian Church, as now organized, are in its hands, and our Saviour will require a strict account concerning it. The great body of the church must needs rejudge the whole action of the Assembly, and on her judgment we repose, with a sacred assurance, second only to that which binds our hearts and souls in filial confidence to her glorious Lord. For ourselves, the hardest portion of our work is past. Hearts which the past has not broken, have little need to fear what the future can bring forth. Spirits which have not died within us in the trials through which we have been led, may confidently resign themselves to His guidance, whose words have rung ceaselessly upon our hearts, '*This* is the way, walk ye in it,' and whose cheering voice comes to us from above, 'Fear not, it is I.'

By order of Convention.

"Geo. A. Baxter, *President.*
"C. C. Cuyler, *Vice President.*

"Thos C. Baird, }
"Horace S. Pratt, } *Clerks.*

"Philadelphia, May 18, 1837."

The preceding memorial presents a synoptical view of the deeply interesting subjects which were discussed by this convention, and the results and conclusions of that large and distinguished company of pastors and elders, convened from all parts of the Presbyterian body, to collect and exhibit intelligence, to detect dangers, and suggest remedies, on the state of the church. That this Testimony, with the character it bears, and at the time it was presented, should exert a strong influence on the public mind, and on the transactions of the General Assembly then in session, it would be very reasonable to believe.

CHAPTER XIX.

Meeting of the Assembly of 1837, Philadelphia—Organization—Memorials presented—Resolutions of Assembly—Abrogation Act passed—Majority thirty-three votes—Committee of ten from each party, on voluntary division of Church—Assembly engage in prayer—Report of the committee of majority—Committees agree on some points—Not on others—Their correspondence—Papers in numerical order—Committee on state of the Church discharged—True reasons for the failure of friendly division—Synod of Western Reserve declared out of the Presbyterian Church—So also, Synods of Utica, Geneva, and Genessee—Cases of orthodox individuals and churches provided for—Testimony against heretical opinions.

THE General Assembly of the Presbyterian Church met agreeably to appointment in the Central Presbyterian Church, Philadelphia, May 18th, 1837. Rev. David Elliot, D. D., was elected Moderator. Testimony in various forms, memorials, complaints, and petitions, on the subject of corruptions and abuses in the church, were presented from the Presbytery of Lancaster, the Presbytery of Albany, Presbytery of New Brunswick, and especially a "Memorial and Testimony," from the large and important convention of delegates from all parts of the church, then in session in the city of Philadelphia. This memorial was committed to Dr. *A. Alexander*, Mr. Plumer, Dr. A. Green, Dr. Baxter, Dr. Leland, Mr. Lowrie, and Mr. Lenox. The committee reported on that part of the memorial relating to the connexion existing between the Congregational and Presbyterian Churches, and recommended the adoption of the following resolutions offered by the chairman:

"1. That between these two branches of the American Church, in the judgment of this Assembly, there ought to be maintained sentiments of mutual respect and esteem, and for that purpose no reasonable efforts should be omitted to preserve a perfectly good understanding between these branches of the Church of Christ.

"2. That it is expedient to continue the plan of friendly intercourse between this church and the Congregational Churches of New England, as it now exists.

"3. But as the Plan of Union adopted for the new settlements in 1801, was originally an unconstitutional act on the part of that Assembly, these important standing rules having never been submitted to the Presbyteries, and as they were totally destitute of authority, as proceeding from the General Association of Connecticut, which is invested with no power to legislate in such cases, and especially to enact laws to regulate churches not within her limits; and, as much irregularity and confusion have arisen from this unnatural and unconstitutional system of union, therefore it is resolved, that the act of the Assembly of 1801, entitled 'A Plan of Union,' be, and the same is hereby abrogated." Digest, pp. 297—9.

The subject of these resolutions, and especially that of the third in order, was, after long and serious discussion, adopted by the Assembly, by a majority of thirty-three votes.

By this decision, the root and origin of the calamities which had so long and so deplorably afflicted the church, were so far removed out of the way, that the Assembly immediately began to exert her utmost skill with great moderation to devise and apply some appropriate system, to terminate amicably all connexion with the party whose action had been for a long time so seriously adverse to the interests of the church, and annoying to the orthodox body.

In reference to that part of the report of the committee on the memorial, relating to disorders in practice, and errors in doctrine, tolerated in the church by inferior judicatories, a resolution was passed, to cite to the bar of the next Assembly, such inferior judicatories as shall appear to be charged by common fame with such irregularities as are referred to in said *memorial.* And it was farther resolved, to take the proper steps for carrying out such a process. For this purpose, it was pronounced essential by a decision of the house, to appoint a special committee to ascertain what inferior judicatories are thus charged by common fame, to prepare charges and specifications against them, and to digest a suitable plan of procedure in the matter, and report, &c.

Subsequent action of the Assembly on this subject rendered it unnecessary for this committee to meet and report, according to appointment.

A suspension of the action of this committee was occasioned by the following motion of Mr. Breckinridge, in pursuance of previous notice, viz: To appoint a committee of ten members, on the state of the church, of whom an equal number shall be from the *majority* and *minority* of the vote on the resolutions to cite nferior judicatories, to inquire into the expediency of a voluntary division of the Presbyterian Church. Dr. Junkin and Mr. Ewing, on the part of the majority, and Messrs. A. Campbell and Jessup, on the part of the minority, were appointed to nominate each five members of the committee on the preceding resolution. Dr. Junkin and Mr. Campbell, from the committee to nominate this committee of ten on the division of the church, respectively reported the following nomination, viz: Mr. Breckinridge, Dr. Alexander, Dr. Cuyler, Dr. Witherspoon, and Mr. Ewing, on the part of the majority, and Dr. McAuley, Dr. Beman, Dr. Peters, Mr. Dickinson, and Mr. Jessup, on the part of the minority.

The Assembly engaged in prayer on behalf of this committee, and of the subject referred to them. This large and respectable committee, appointed on Saturday, May 27th, met several times, corresponded frequently on the subject entrusted to them, and held the whole matter under profound and solemn advisement till the following Tuesday, when the Rev. Dr. Alexander, *chairman* of the committee, with instructions, reported, that they had not been able to agree and requested to be discharged. Both portions of the committee then made separate reports, which were entered upon the minutes, and are as follows, viz:

To those persons who desire to understand thoroughly the nature of this interesting matter, we offer no apology for inserting the documents, literally and at full length, as they came from the hands of the committee. And it cannot but be regarded as a very important matter, to exhibit in this record, the evidence, as well as the nature, of the disposition manifested by the majority, in this negotiation, to effect a division of the church on just principles and in an amicable manner.

"*Report of the Committee of the Majority.*

"The committee of the majority, from the united committee on the state of the church, beg leave to report:

"That having been unable to agree with the minority's committee, on any plan for the immediate and voluntary separation of the New and Old School parties, in the Presbyterian Church, they lay before the General Assembly the papers which passed between the committees, and which contain all the important proceedings of both bodies.

"These papers are marked 1 to 5, of the majority, and 1 to 4, of the minority. A careful examination of them will show that the two committees were agreed in the following matters, namely:

"1. That of the propriety of a voluntary separation of the parties in our church, and their separate organization.

"2. As to the corporation funds, the names to be held by each denomination, the records of the church, its boards and institutions.

"3. It will farther appear, that the committees were entirely unable to agree on the following points, namely:

"1. As to the propriety of entering at once, by the Assembly, upon the division, or the sending down of the question to the Presbyteries.

"2. As to the power of the Assembly to take effectual initiative steps, as proposed by the majority; or the necessity of obtaining a change in the constitution of the church.

"3. As to the breaking up of the succession of the General

Assembly, so that neither of the new assemblies proposed should be considered this proper body continued; or that the body which should retain the name and institutions of the General Assembly in the Presbyterian Church, in the United States of America, should be held in fact and law, to be the true successors of *this* body. While the committee of the majority were perfectly disposed to do all that the utmost liberality could demand, and to use in all cases such expressions as should be wholly unexceptionable, yet it appeared to us indispensable to take our final stand on these grounds.

"For, *first*, we are convinced, if any thing towards a voluntary separation is done, it is absolutely necessary to do it effectually and at once.

"*Secondly*, as neither party professes any desire to alter any constitutional rule whatever, it seems to us not only needless, but absurd, to send down an overture to the Presbyteries on this subject. We believe, moreover, that full power exists in the Assembly, either by consent of parties, or in the way of discipline, to settle this, and all such cases; and that its speedy settlement is greatly to be desired.

"*Thirdly*, in regard to the succession of the General Assembly, this committee could not, in present circumstances, consent to any thing that should even imply the final dissolution of the Presbyterian Church, as now organized in this country; which idea, it will be observed, is at the basis of the plan of the minority; insomuch, that even the body retaining the name and institutions, should not be considered the successors of this body.

"*Finally*, it would be observed from our fifth paper, as compared with the fourth paper of the minority's committee, that the final shape which their proposal assumed, was such that it was impossible for the majority of the house to carry out its views and wishes, let the vote be what it might. For if the house should vote for the plan of the committee of the majority, the other committee would *not* consider itself or its friends *bound* thereby, and voluntary division would therefore be impossible in that case. But if the house should vote for the minority's plan, then the foregoing insuperable objections to that plan being supposed to be surmounted, still the *whole case would be put off*, perhaps indefinitely.

"A. ALEXANDER, C. C. CUYLER, &c., &c."

"*Report of the Committee of the Minority.*

"The subscribers, appointed members of the committee of ten on the state of the church, respectfully ask leave to report, as follows, to wit:

"It being understood that one object of the appointment of said committee, was to consider the expediency of a voluntary division of the Presbyterian Church, and to devise a plan for the same, they, in connexion with the other members of the committee, have had the subject under deliberation.

"The subscribers had believed that no such imperious necessity for a division of the church existed as some of their brethren supposed, and that the consequences of division would be greatly to be deprecated. Such necessity, however, being urged by many of our brethren, we have been induced to yield to their wishes, and to admit the expediency of a division, provided, the same could be accomplished in an amicable, equitable, and proper manner. We have accordingly submitted the following propositions to our brethren on the other part of the same committee, who, at the same time, submitted to us their proposition, which is annexed to this report.

"*No.* 1 *of the Majority.*

"The portion of the committee which represents the majority, submit for consideration:

"1. That the peace and prosperity of the Presbyterian Church, in the United States, require a separation of the portions called respectively, the Old and New School parties, and represented by the majority and minority in the present Assembly.

"2. That the portion of the church represented by the majority, in the present General Assembly, ought to retain the name and the corporate property of the General Assembly of the Presbyterian Church, in the United States of America.

"3. That the two parties ought to form separate denominations, under separate organizations; that to effect this, with the least delay, the commissioners in the present General Assembly, shall eleet which body they will adhere to, and this election shall decide the position of their Presbyteries, respectively, for the present; that every Presbytery may reverse the decision of its present commissioners, and unite with the opposite body, by the permission of that body, properly expressed; that minorities of Presbyteries, if large enough, or if not, then in connexion with neighbouring minorities, may form new Presbyteries, or attach themselves to existing Presbyteries, in union with either body, as shall be agreed on; that Synods ought to take order and make election on the general principles already stated, and minorities of Synods should follow out the rule suggested for minorities of Presbyteries, as far as they are applicable."

"*No.* 1 *of the Minority.*

"Whereas, the experience of many years has proved, that this body is too large to answer the purposes contemplated by the constitution, and there appear to be insuperable obstacles in the way of reducing the representation; and whereas, in the extension of the church over so great a territory, embracing such a variety of people, difference of view in relation to important points of church policy and action, as well as theological opinion, are found to exist;

"Now, it is believed, a division of the body into two separate bodies, which shall act independently of each other, will be of vital importance, to the best interests of the Redeemer's kingdom; therefore,

"*Resolved*, That the following rules be sent down to the Presbyteries, for their adoption or rejection, as constitutional rules, to wit:

"1. The General Assembly of the Presbyterian Church, in the United States of America, shall be and it hereby is divided into two bodies; the one thereof to be called the General Assembly of the Presbyterian Church, in the United States of America, and the other, the General Assembly of the American Presbyterian Church.

"2. That the Confession of Faith and form of government, of the Presbyterian Church of the United States of America, as it now exists, shall continue to be the Confession of Faith and form of government of both bodies, until it shall be constitutionally changed and altered by either, in the manner prescribed therein.

"3. That in sending up their commissioners to the next General Assembly, each Presbytery, after having, in making out their commissions, followed the form now prescribed, shall add thereto as follows, viz: That in case a majority of the Presbyteries shall have voted to adopt the plan for organizing two General Assemblies, we direct our said commissioners to attend the meeting of 'The Presbyterian Church of the United States of America,' or 'The American Presbyterian Church,' as the case may be. And after the opening of the next General Assembly, and before proceeding to other business, than the usual preliminary organization, the said Assembly shall ascertain what is the vote of the Presbyteries; and in case a majority of said Presbyteries shall have adopted these rules, then the two General Assemblies shall be constituted and organized, in the manner now pointed out in the form of government, by the election of their respective moderators, stated clerks, and other officers.

"4. The several Presbyteries shall be deemed and taken to belong to that Assembly with which they shall direct their commissioners to meet, as stated in the preceding rule. And each General Assembly shall, at their first meeting, as aforesaid, organize the Presbyteries belonging to each, into Synods. And in case any Presbytery shall fail to decide, as aforesaid, at that time, they may attach themselves, within one year thereafter, to the Assembly they shall prefer.

"5. Churches, and members of churches, as well as Presbyteries, shall be at full liberty to decide to which of said Assemblies they will be attached; and in case the majority of male members in any church, shall decide to belong to a Presbytery, connected with the Assembly to which their Presbytery is not attached, they shall certify the same to the stated clerk of the Presbytery which they wish to leave, and the one with which they wish to unite, and they shall, *ipso facto,* be attached to such Presbytery.

"6. It shall be the duty of Presbyteries, at their first meeting after the adoption of these rules, or within one year thereafter, to grant certificates of dismission, to such ministers, licentiates, and students, as may wish to unite with a Presbytery attached to the other General Assembly.

"7. It shall be the duty of church sessions, to grant letters of dismission to such of their members, being in regular standing, as may apply for the same, within one year after the organization of said Assemblies under these rules, for the purpose of uniting with any church attached to a Presbytery under the care of the other General Assembly; and if such session refuse so to dismiss, it shall be lawful for such members to unite with such other church, in the same manner as if a certificate were given.

"8. The boards of education and missions shall continue their organization as heretofore, until the next meeting of the Assembly; and in case the rules for the division of the Assembly be adopted, those boards shall be, and hereby are transferred to the General Assembly of the Presbyterian Church, in the United States of America, if that Assembly, at its first meeting, shall adopt the boards as their organizations, and the seats of any ministers or elders, in those boards, not belonging to that General Assembly, shall be deemed to be vacant.

"9. The records of the Assembly shall remain in the hands of the present stated clerk, for the mutual use and benefit of both Assemblies, until, by such an arrangement as they may adopt, they shall appoint some other person to take charge of the same; and either Assembly, at their own expense, may cause such extracts and copies to be made thereof, as they may desire and direct.

"10. The Princeton Seminary funds, to be transferred to the Board of Trustees of the Seminary, if it can be so done legally, and without forfeiting the trusts upon which the grants were made; and if it cannot be done legally, and according to the intention of the donors, then to remain with the present board of trustees, until legislative authority be given for such transfer. The supervision of said Seminary, in the same manner in which it is now exercised by the General Assembly, to be transferred to and vested in the General Assembly of the Presbyterian Church, in the United States, to be constituted. The other funds of the church to be divided equally between the wo Assemblies.

"Pass a resolution suspending the operation of the controverted votes, until after the next Assembly."

Being informed by the other members of the committee, that they had concluded not to discuss in committee the propositions which should be submitted, and that all propositions, on both sides, were to be in writing, and to be answered in writing, the following papers passed between the two parts of the committee:

"*No. 2 of the Minority.*

"The committee of the minority make the following objections to the proposition of the majority:

"1. To any recognition of the terms 'Old and New Schools,' or 'majority and minority,' of the present Assembly; in any action upon the subject of division, the minority expect the division, in every respect, to be equal, no other would be satisfactory.

"2. Insisting upon an equal division, we are willing that that portion of the church which shall choose to retain the present boards, shall have the present name of the Assembly; the corporate property which is susceptible of division, to be divided, as the only fair and just course.

"3. We object to the power of the commissioners, to make any division at this time, and as individuals, we cannot assume the responsibility.

"*No. 2 of the Majority.*

"The committee of the majority having considered the paper submitted by that of the minority, observe:

"1. That they suppose the propriety and necessity of a division of the church may be considered as agreed on by both committees, but we think it not expedient to attempt giving reasons in a preamble; the preamble, therefore, is not agreed to.

"2. So much of No. 1, of the plan of the committee of the minority, as relates to the proposed names of the New General Assemblies, is agreed to.

"3. Nos. 1 to 8, inclusive, except as above, are not agreed to, but our proposition, No. 3, in our first paper, is insisted on.

But we agree to the proposition in regard to single churches, individual ministers, licentiates, students and private members.

"4. In lieu of No. 9, we propose that the present stated clerk, be directed to make out a complete copy of all our records, at the joint expense of both the new bodies, and after causing the copy to be examined and certified, deliver it to the written order of the moderator and stated clerk of the General Assembly of the American Presbyterian Church.

"5. We agree in substance to the proposal in No. 10, and offer the following as the form in which the proposition shall stand:

"That the corporate funds and property of the church, so far as they appertain to the Theological Seminary at Princeton, or relate to the professors' support, or the edcation of beneficiaries there, shall remain the property of the body retaining the name of the General Assembly of the Presbyterian Church, in the United States of America; that all other funds shall be equally divided between the new bodies, so far as it can be done, in conformity with the intention of the donors, and that all liabilities of the present Assembly shall be discharged in equal portions by them; that all questions relating to the future adjustment of this whole subject, upon the principles now agreed on, shall be settled by committees, appointed by the new Assemblies, at their first meeting, respectively; and if these committees shall not agree, then each committee shall select one arbitrator, and these two, a third, which arbitrators shall have full power to settle, finally, the whole case in all its parts; and that no person shall be appointed an arbitrator who is a member of either church; it being distinctly understood, that whatever difficulties may arise, in the construction of trusts, and all other questions of power, as well as right, legal and equitable, shall be finally decided by the committees or arbitrators, so as in all cases to prevent an appeal by either party, to the legal tribunals of the country.

"*No. 3 of the Minority.*

"1. We accede to the proposition to have no preamble.

"2. We accede to the proposition No. 4, modifying our proposition No. 9, in relation to the records and copies of the records; the copy to be made within one year after the division.

"3. We assent to the modification of No. 10, by No. 5 of the propositions submitted, with a trifling alteration in the phraseology, striking out the words, 'shall remain the property of the body retaining the name of the General Assembly of the Presbyterian Church, in the United States of America,' and inserting the words, 'shall be transferred, and belong to the General

Assembly of the Presbyterian Church, of the United States of America, hereby constituted.'

"4. We cannot assent to any division by the present commissioners of the Assembly, as it would in no wise be obligatory on any of the judicatories of the church, or any members of the churches. The only effect would be, a disorderly dissolution of the present Assembly, and be of no binding force or effect upon any member who did not assent to it.

"5. We propose a resolution, to be appended to the rules, and which we believe, if adopted by the committee, would pass with great unanimity, urging in strong terms, the adoption of the rules by the Presbyteries; and the members of the minority side of the committee, pledge themselves to use their influence, to procure the adoption of the same, by the Presbyteries.

"*No.* 3 *of the Majority.*

"The committee of the majority, in relation to paper No. 2, observe:

"1. That the terms 'Old and New School,' 'majority and minority,' are meant as descriptive, and some description being necessary, we see neither impropriety nor unsuitableness in them.

"2. Our previous paper, No. 2, having, as we suppose, substantially acceded to the proposal of the minority, in relation to the funds, in their first paper, we deem any farther statement on that subject, unnecessary.

"3. That we see no difficulty in the way of settling the matter at present, subject to the revision of the Presbyteries, as provided in our first paper, under the third head; and as no 'constitutional rules' are proposed, in the way of altering any principles of our system, we see no constitutional objection to the execution of the proposal already made. We therefore adhere to the plan as our final proposal. But, if the commissioners of any Presbytery should refuse to elect, or be equally divided, then the Presbytery which they represent, shall make such election, at its first meeting after the adjournment of the present General Assembly.

"*No.* 4 *of the Majority.*

The committee of the majority, in reply to No. 3, of the minority's committee, simply refer to their own preceding papers, as containing their final propositions.

"*No.* 4 *of the Minority.*

"The committee of the minority, in reply to No. 3, of the majority, observe, that they will unite, in a report to the Assembly, stating that the committee have agreed, that it is expedient that a division of the church be effected, and in general, upon the principles upon which it is to be carried out, but they differ as to the manner of effecting it.

"On the one hand, it is asked, that a division be made by the present Assembly, at their present meeting; and on the other hand, that the plan of division, with the subsequent arrangement and organization, shall be submitted to the Presbyteries for their adoption or rejection.

"They will unite in asking the General Assembly, to decide the above points, previous to reporting the details; and in case the Assembly decide in favor of immediate division, then the paper No. 1, of the majority, with the modifications agreed on, be taken as the basis of the report in detail.

"If the Assembly decide to send to the Presbyteries, then No. 1, of the minority's papers, with the modifications agreed on, shall be the basis of the report in detail.

"The committee of the minority cannot agree to any other propositions than those already submitted, until the above be settled by the Assembly.

"If the above proposition be not agreed to, or be modified and then agreed to, they desire that each *side* may make a report to the Assembly, to-morrow morning.

"*No.* 5 *of the Majority.*

"The committee of the majority, in answer to No. 4, &c., reply, that understanding from the verbal explanations of the committee of the minority, that the said committee would not consider either side bound by the vote of the Assembly, if it were against their views and wishes, respectively, on the point proposed to be submitted to its decision, in said paper, to carry out in good faith, a scheme which, in that case, could not be approved by them; and under such circumstances, a voluntary separation being manifestly impossible, this committee consider No. 4, of the minority, as virtually a waiver of the whole subject. If nothing further remains to be proposed, they submit that the papers be laid before the Assembly, and that the united committee be dissolved."

The committee on the state of the church was discharged.

After the discharge of this committee, whose report is fully presented above, the whole subject of a voluntary division of the Presbyterian body, was indefinitely postponed.

From these papers, it will be seen, that the only question of any importance, upon which the committee differed, was that proposed to be submitted to the decision of the Assembly, as preliminary to any action, upon the details of either plan. Therefore, believing that the members of this Assembly, have neither a constitutional, nor moral right, to adopt a plan for the division of the church, in relation to which they are entirely uninst ructed by the Presbyteries; believing that the course proposed by their brethren of the committee, to be entirely inefficacious, and calculated to introduce confusion and disorder into the whole church, and instead of mitigating to enhance the evils which it proposes to remove, and regarding the plan proposed by themselves, with the modifications thereof, as before stated, as presenting in general, the only safe, certain and constitutional mode of division, the subscribers do respectfully present the same to the Assembly, for their adoption or rejection.

"THOS. MCAULEY, N. S. S. BEMAN, O. PETERS, &c."

The candid and judicious reader of the propositions, the correspondence, and the reports of the committees, in the General Assembly of 1837, on the state of the church, and on the subject of an amicable division, may, from the pages here recorded, obtain a good insight into the real character and aim of the parties at issue. The orthodox had been rendered so unhappy by the encroaching and distracting measures of the New School for years past, that they were most honestly and earnestly desirous of accomplishing a separation without conflict or tumult, that their committee were prepared, and, indeed, substantially instructed and authorized, to exercise the highest Christian liberality, and to make every lawful sacrifice to effect the object in view. It is, therefore, submitted, whether the records of their transactions do not fully award to them the high character of fidelity to the principles avowed, and to the accommodating spirit professed. We most deeply regretted the failure of the magnanimous effort to avert most aggravated evils, both experienced and apprehended, in this voluntary and peaceful manner. The committee of the majority had a herculean task to perform. All the interests of the church, under God, were entrusted to them, and they had wily adversaries to treat with, and to watch and to guard against, every step.

Candid reviewers cannot but see, that the negotiation failed through the unreasonable, and, as appears, the designing positions insisted on by the minority's committee. They demanded delay, that the matters might be sent down to the Presbyteries, on the pretence, that the Assembly had no power in herself to act on the subject; they alleged unwillingness to assume the responsibility of immediate decision; they avowed openly, that neither they nor their division of the church, would be bound by any action of the Assembly touching the division of the church at that time; they insisted that the constitution of the whole church should be entirely changed and reorganized, to bring themselves, it may have been, upon a parallel with the original and true church; they required that the whole institution of the Presbyterian Church should be so broken up as to leave no vestige of it; to destroy the identity of the body, the true succession to the General Assembly; that no remaining fragments of the wreck should be afterwards considered the proper body of the Presbyterian Church heretofore existing. What could be more monstrous? Design, artifice, renewed and protracted warfare, stand out prominently in every feature of this dark, foreboding exhibition. It was absolutely impossible that the majority could coincide with such an absurd and shocking plan of proceedure. The idea of treating upon such terms, was not for a moment entertained. And the alluring prospect died away, leaving among the orthodox, many spirits deeply afflicted at the failure.

The subject of the "Abrogation" of the unconstitutional and injurious "Plan of Union" of 1801, from which all our evils sprang, had been several days* under more absorbing and solemn consideration than ever before; and the minds of the Old School seemed to be conducted, as if by an inspiring ray, to the adoption of this incontestible principle, that if "the Plan of Union of 1801," the source of all our church difficulties and unhappiness were dried up, the streams of strife and bitterness would cease to flow out; if the foundation of the corrupt and nauseating mass of New Schoolism be removed, the whole superstructure erected upon it must fall to the ground; for a house which has no foundation cannot stand.

Here, the original motion, which had been for several days before the house for consideration, but postponed from time to time, was introduced in the following terms, viz:

"*Resolved*, That by the operation of the abrogation of the 'Plan of Union of 1801,' the Synod of the Western Reserve *is*, and is *hereby declared* to be no longer a part of the Presbyterian Church in the United States of America;" which was decided in the affirmative by a majority of twenty-seven votes.

The Assembly prosecuted, to great extent, a discussion of the resolution offered respecting the operations of the American Home Missionary Society, and of the American Education Society, within the bounds of the Presbyterian Church. After this long debate, the resolution passed in the affirmative, in the following words, viz: "That while we desire that no body of Christian men, of other denominations, should be prevented from choosing their own plans of doing good; and while we claim no right to complain, should they exceed us in energy and zeal, we believe that facts too familiar to need repetition here, warrant us in af-

* See Minutes of the Assembly for 1837, pp. 420—437.

firming, that the organization and operations of the so called American Home Missionary Society, and American Education Society, and its branches, of whatever name, within our bounds, are exceedingly injurious to the peace and purity of the Presbyterian Church. We recommend, accordingly, that they should cease to operate within any of our churches."

The following resolutions were carried by large majorities:

"1. That in consequence of the abrogation, by this Assembly, of the 'Plan of Union of 1801,' between it and the General Association of Connecticut, as utterly unconstitutional, and, therefore, null and void from the beginning, the *Synods of Utica, Geneva*, and *Genessee*, which were formed and attached to this body, under and in execution of said 'Plan of Union,' be, and are hereby declared to be out of the ecclesiastical connexion of the Presbyterian Church of the United States of America, and that they are not, in form or in fact, an integral portion of said church.

"2. That the solicitude of this Assembly on the whole subject, and its urgency for the immediate decision of it, are greatly increased by reason of the gross disorders which are ascertained to have prevailed in those Synods, as well as that of the Western Reserve, against which a declarative resolution, similar to the first of these, has been passed during the present Sessions, it being made clear to us, that even the 'Plan of Union' itself, was never consistently carried into effect by those professing to act under it.

"3. That the General Assembly has no intention, by these resolutions, or by that passed in the case of the Synod of Western Reserve, to affect, in any way, the ministerial standing of any members of any of said Synods, nor to disturb the pastoral relation in any church, nor to interfere with the duties and relations of private Christians, in their respective congregations; but only to determine and declare, according to the truth and necessity of the case, and by virtue of the full authority existing in it, for that purpose, the relation of all said Synods, and all their constituent parts, to this body, and to the Presbyterian Church in the United States.

"4. That inasmuch as there are reported to be several churches and ministers, if not one or two Presbyteries, now in connexion with one or more of said Synods, which are strictly Presbyterian in doctrine and order, be it therefore further resolved, that all such churches and ministers as wish to unite with us, are hereby directed to apply for admission into those Presbyteries belonging to our connexion, which are most convenient to their respective locations; and that any such Presbytery as aforesaid, being strictly Presbyterian in doctrine and order, and now in connexion with any of said Synods, as may desire to unite with us, are hereby directed to make application, with a full statement of their cases, to the next General Assembly, which will take proper order thereon."

Here the Assembly resumed the consideration of that part of the report of the committee on the memorial of the convention, which relates to doctrinal errors. The following preamble and resolution were both adopted by a large majority, viz:

"As one of the principal objects of the memorialists is, to point out certain errors, more or less prevalent in our church, and to bear testimony against them, your committee are of opinion, that as one great object of the institution of the church was to be a depository and guardian of the truth; and as by the constitution of the Presbyterian Church in the United States, it is made the duty of the General Assembly to testify against error, therefore,

"*Resolved*, That the testimony of the memorialists concerning doctrine, be adopted as the testimony of this General Assembly, as follows, viz:

"'1. That God would have prevented the existence of sin in our world, but was not able, without destroying the moral agency of man; or, that for aught that appears in the Bible to the contrary, sin is incidental to any wise system.

"'2. That election to eternal life is founded on a foresight of faith and obedience.

"'3. That we have no more to do with the first sin of Adam than with the sins of any other parent.

"'4. That infants come into the world as free from moral defilement as was Adam, when he was created.

"'5. That infants sustain the same relation to the moral government of God in this world as brute animals, and that their sufferings and death are to be accounted for, on the same principles as those of brutes, and not by any means to be considered as penal.

"'6. That there is no other original sin than the fact that all the posterity of Adam, though by nature innocent, or possessed of no moral character, will always begin to sin when they begin to exercise moral agency; that original sin does not include a sinful bias of the human mind, and a just exposure to penal suffering; and that there is no evidence in Scripture, that infants, in order to salvation, do need redemption by the blood of Christ, and regeneration by the Holy Ghost.

"'7. That the doctrine of imputation, whether of the guilt of Adam's sin, or of the righteousness of Christ, has no foundation in the word of God, and is both unjust and absurd.

"'8. That the sufferings and death of Christ were not truly vicarious and penal, but symbolical, governmental, and instructive.

"'9. That the impenitent sinner is by nature, and independently of the renewing influence or almighty energy of the Holy Spirit, in full possession of all the ability necessary to a full compliance with all the commands of God.

"'10. That Christ does not intercede for the elect until after their regeneration.

"'11. That saving faith is not an effect of special operation of the Holy Spirit, but a mere rational belief of the truth, or assent to the word of God.

"'12. That regeneration is the act of the sinner himself, and that it consists in a change of his governing purpose, which he himself must produce, and which is the result, not of any direct influence of the Holy Spirit on the heart, but chiefly of a persuasive exhibition of the truth analogous to the influence which one man exerts over the mind of another; or that regeneration is not an instantaneous act, but a progressive work.

"'13. That God has done all that he *can* do for the salvation of all men, and that man himself must do the rest.

"'14. That God cannot exert such influence on the minds of men, as shall make it certain that they will choose and act in a particular manner, without impairing their moral agency.

"'15. That the righteousness of Christ is not the sole ground of the sinner's acceptance with God; and that in no sense does the righteousness of Christ become ours.

"'16. That the reason why some differ from others in regard to their reception of the gospel is, that they make themselves to differ.'"

Against all these errors, whenever, wherever, and by whomsoever taught, the Assembly solemnly testified, warning all in connexion with the Presbyterian Church against them. They enjoined it also upon all inferior judicatories, to adopt all suitable measures to keep their members pure from opinions so dangerous, and especially to guard with great care the door of entrance to the sacred office.

In regard to the report of the committee on that part of the memorial which relates to church order, the Assembly adopted the following preamble and resolutions, viz:

"Whereas, it is represented to the Assembly, that the following disorders and irregularities are practiced in some portions of the Presbyterian Church, without determining the extent of them, the Assembly would solemnly warn all in our connexion against them; the principal of which are as follows, viz:

"'1. The formation of Presbyteries without defined and reasonable limits, or Presbyteries covering the same territory, and especially such a formation founded on doctrinal repulsions or affinities; thus introducing schism into the very vitals of the body.

"'2. The licensing of persons to preach the gospel, and ordaining to the office of the ministry such as not only accept our standards merely for substance of doctrine, and others who are unfit and ought to be excluded for want of qualification, but of many who openly deny fundamental principles of truth, and preach and publish radical errors as already set forth.

"'3. The formation of a great number and variety of creeds which are often incomplete, false, and contradictory of each other, and of our Confession of Faith and of the Bible; but which even if true are needless, seeing that the public and authorized standards of the church are fully sufficient for the purposes for which such formularies were introduced, namely, as public testimonies of our faith and practice, as aids to the teaching of the people truth and righteousness, and as instruments for ascertaining and preserving the unity of the Spirit in the bonds of peace; it being understood that we do not object to the use of a brief abstract of the doctrines of our Confession of Faith, in the public reception of private members of the church.

"'4. The needless ordination of a multitude of men to the office of evangelist, and the consequent tendency to a general neglect of the pastoral office; frequent and hurtful changes of pastoral relations; to the multiplication of spurious excitements, and the consequent spread of heresy and fanaticism, thus weakening and bringing into contempt the ordinary and stated agents and means, for the conversion of sinners, and the edification of the body of Christ.

"'5. The disuse of the office of ruling elder in portions of the church, and the consequent growth of practices and principles entirely foreign to our system; thus depriving the pastors of needful assistants in discipline, the people of proper guides in Christ, and the churches of suitable representatives in the ecclesiastical tribunals.

"'6. The unlimited and irresponsible power assumed by several associations of men under various names, to exercise authority and influence, direct and indirect, over Presbyters, as to their field of labour, place of residence, and mode of action in the difficult circumstances of our church; thus actually throwing the control of affairs in large portions of the church, and sometimes in the General Assembly itself, out of the hands of the Presbyteries into those of single individuals or small committees located at a distance.

"'7. A progressive change in the system of Presbyterian representation in the General Assembly, which has been persisted in by those holding the ordinary majorities, and carried out in detail by those disposed to take undue advantage of existing opportunities, until the actual representation seldom exhibits the true state of the church, and many questions of deepest interest have been decided contrary to the fairly ascertained wishes of the majority of the church and people in our communion; thus virtually subverting the essential principles of freedom, justice, and equality, on which our whole system rests.'"

CHAPTER XX.

Dr. Alexander's resolutions to correct New School disorders—Protest of New School against the Abrogation Act—Committee to reply—Their answer, long, minute, and able.

As an additional subject of great and vital importance, showing the zeal and pertinacity of the New School, in their aims and efforts to subdue the church to their power, we might here record the fact of their dividing and subdividing Presbyteries, possessing their views, so as to multiply their aggregate number and increase their strength in the General Assembly. To remedy this disorderly and corrupt artifice, the following resolutions were offered by Dr. A. Alexander, viz:

"1. That no commissioner from a newly formed Presbytery shall be permitted to take his seat, nor shall such commissioner be reported by the committee on commissions, until the Presbytery shall have been duly reported by the Synod, and recognized as such by the Assembly; and that the same rule apply when the name of any Presbytery has been changed.

"2. When it shall appear to the satisfaction of the General Assembly, that any new Presbytery has been formed for the purpose of unduly increasing the representation, the General Assembly will, by a vote of the majority, refuse to receive the delegates of Presbyteries so formed, and may direct the Synod to which such Presbytery belongs, to reunite it to the Presbytery or Presbyteries to which the members were before attached."

To see the unfairness of this New School measure, for the correction of which Dr. Alexander's resolutions are intended, let us suppose a case, parallels to which, on a small scale, can be designated in the history of New School artifice, to swell their numbers and their influence in church judicatories. By the constitution of the church, every Presbytery, consisting of twenty-four members or less, down to three, according to the last established ratio of representation, is entitled to one commissioner to the General Assembly.* Now, if a New School Synod should desire

* Form of Government, chap. X, sec. 7.

and resolve on such a course of action, they may make out of one Presbytery, containing twenty-four members, eight Presbyteries, each entitled to a seat in the General Assembly. Now the whole original Presbytery of twenty-four members, being restricted by the constitution to one clerical representation in that body, by this artful subdivision their ratio of representation and power in the General Assembly, are augmented in the proportion of one to eight. The case supposed is an extreme one, but the disorderly and corrupting principle or practice is fairly exhibited and has been successfully attempted.

The protests entered by the minority in the General Assembly, against the measures passed by the majority, to correct the disorders and abuses prevailing in the church, are so numerous and destitute of strength, that passing by the whole train of them, and the answers to them, we shall transfer from the minutes of the Assembly, pages 458—462, the answer recorded there to the protest of the minority against the abrogation of the "Plan of Union" of 1801. As the protest of the minority, in all its material points, is referred to, and discussed at some length in the answer, the protest is omitted, but can be seen on the minutes, at page 454.

The committee to whom it was referred to answer that protest, state that "The reasons of protest are numbered from 1 to 6. No. 1 is the principal, and, therefore, we prefer leaving it to the last, and commencing with No. 2. 'We protest,' say the minority, 'against the resolution referred to, because the Plan of Union adopted by the General Assembly of 1801, was designed to *suppress and prevent schismatical contentions and for the promotion of charity*, or, in the language of the plan itself, "with a view to prevent alienation, and to promote union and harmony."' To this, a sufficient answer is found in the broad and undeniable fact, that the Plan of Union 'has been a principal means of dividing the church, and this General Assembly, into two parties; and has been the main source of those schisms which for many years have distracted our Zion.' Whilst it is admitted, that in some instances, it may have beneficially affected certain localities, it has laid the deep foundation of lasting confusion, and opened wide the floodgates of error and fanaticism. For proof of this, we have only to refer to the recorded votes of the last and the present General Assemblies, from which it abundantly appears that the representatives of churches formed on this plan, have always opposed the boards of education and of missions, and the efforts towards reform, and the suppression of errors and of schismatical contentions.

"No. 3. 'Because it declares the said "Plan of Union" to have been totally destitute of authority, as proceeding from the General Association of Connecticut, which is invested with no power to legislate in such cases.'

"In reply to this let it be remarked, first, that the protestors, seeming to admit that the General Association of Connecticut had no power and authority to bind their churches, yet insist that the General Assembly could make a treaty or covenant that should be binding on the other side; and the brethren, in arguing the case, did insist on the 'Plan' being of the nature of a covenant, (although no such term is contained in it,) and yet one of the parties to this covenant had no authority to make a contract, and to make it obligatory on their churches. That is, a contract, treaty, or covenant, can exist, and be and continue for ever, binding in right and in law upon one party, whilst the other party, having no power or authority to bind themselves, and those for whom they plead its benefits, never could be bound. That is, a treaty or covenant may exist, without a mutual obligation, or a consideration stated.

"Secondly: The protestors, without distinctly affirming it again, seem willing that the reader of their protest should believe, that the General Association of Connecticut had power to bind their churches; that their acts participate of the nature of ecclesiastical authority. 'By acceding to the said stipulations,' say they, 'the said Association relinquished whatever right it had to the direction and regulation of the members of its own churches in the new settlements.' Now these remonstrants know perfectly well, that the General Association of Connecticut never had, never claimed, and never exercised any right at all 'to the direction and regulation of the members of its own churches,' even in Connecticut itself, much less 'in the new settlements.' The right of counsel and advice is the utmost stretch of their power and authority. And this General Assembly might give counsel and advice to the churches of Connecticut, and should it be founded in truth, it is just as binding upon those churches as the counsels of their own General Association, *i. e.* it comes *divested* entirely of all ecclesiastical *authority.*

"Thirdly: The resolution of abrogation is alleged to be 'a breach of faith, and wholly void and of no effect.' This is begging the question; it goes on the assumption that faith was plighted of right, and the treaty, so called, lawfully constituted; which we have supposed to be the very point in question.

"Fourthly: 'Because it denominates the "Plan of Union" unnatural, as well as unconstitutional, and attributes to it much confusion and irregularity.' A sufficient answer to this is found in the preceding; to which may be added a single remark as to irregularity, viz: that upon inquiry of brethren who came in upon this 'Plan,' it appeared from their own showing, to the abundant conviction of this General Assembly, that there were some members on the floor, deliberating and voting on the very resolutions in question who had never adopted the Confession of Faith of this church."

No. 5. The fifth reason of protest is, that the resolution was concocted and brought before the Assembly, by members of this body, who had previously consulted in the form of a convention, and memorialized this body on the subject; and that a majority of the committee to whom the memorial was referred, were members of the convention.

As to the former, let it suffice to say, that it is the right of every free man, and the duty of every Christian, before entering upon any great and important measure, to "ponder the path of his feet," because, "in the multitude of counsellors there is safety." How the name convention, any more than the name "caucus," should utterly vitiate their counsel, it may be difficult to discern.

As to the latter, it may be remarked, that in all deliberative bodies, the principle is settled, that large committees ought to be selected, in proportion to the respective party views that may be entertained on the subject committed. The wisdom of the rule is obvious to common sense, and the moderator of this Assembly simply carried out the rule in this case.

No. 6. The sixth reason of protest is, "because the debate on the subject was arrested, by an impatient call for the previous question. The Assembly was thus forced to a decision, without any proper evidence of the existence of the alleged irregularities, and before the subject of errors in doctrine, had been decided on in the Assembly."

Here remark, first, the call for the previous question was not impatient; it was asked for, and seconded by a majority of the house, not in the spirit of violence, and unjust oppression of the minority; nor, secondly, was there any unreasonable curtailment of debate. The resolution was discussed two whole days, a period of time, perhaps, more extended than was ever before allotted or allowed by any General Assembly, to any single naked resolution. And, thirdly, the brethren of the minority occupied the floor more than one half of the time. And on another resolution, when the discussion was arrested by the previous question, it was just at the close of two long speeches, by the minority, and after they had consumed more than five hours in debate; whereas, the majority had not occupied the floor two hours and a half. So utterly groundless is the insinuation, that a cruel and unjust use has been made of the previous question.

"The Assembly was thus forced," say the protestors—"the Assembly was forced!" "Forced"—by whom? undoubtedly by itself; "forced" to do as it wished to do; "forced" to decide by a strong vote, on a subject which had been discussed two whole days! Strange coercion, this!

But, fourthly, the resolution in question was passed before the doctrinal errors were condemned. This is true. But it is also true, that the "Assembly was thus forced," by the opposition of the minority, to pass by the doctrinal discussion, because they could not have it in the order recommended by their committee. Certain alleged errors were offered by the minority, which they refused to have put in their proper place, but insisted upon having, first of all, a decision upon them as amendments; which attempt, had it been successful, would have precluded their discussion, except upon a vote of reconsideration, which requires two-thirds; and thus, the majority would have been completely, as to these alleged errors, in the power of the minority. Hence they were laid on the table, to be taken up at a future time.

We now proceed to No. 1. The principal reason of protest is in these words, viz: "Because the said act is declared, in the resolution complained of, to have been *unconstitutional*."*

In opposition to the resolution declaring the Plan of Union unconstitutional, it would appear most reasonable, that the protestors should affirm its constitutionality; *i. e.*, that the constitution covers and provides for it. This ground, however, the protestors have not ventured to take. On the contrary, they explicitly admit, that the constitution makes no provision for said act; "it is," say they, "neither specifically provided for, nor prohibited in the constitution."

A remark or two will show, that in this they have abandoned the ground, for

1. The constitution of the Presbyterian Church, like that of our national union, is a constitution of specific powers, granted by the Presbyteries, the fountains of power to the Synods and the General Assembly.

2. No powers, not specifically granted, can lawfully be inferred and assumed by the General Assembly, but only such as are indispensably necessary to carry into effect those which are specifically granted.

* Several writers of ability and discrimination, have written in support of this declaration, and probably there is no point, respecting which the honest and sensible portion of our church are more fully satisfied, than that now before us; but as the committee who prepared this answer, was one of peculiar ability, candor and zeal, and as they have added some important ideas to the mass presented by others, thus strengthening and deepening the general impression in regard to this fundamental principle, we think it is important to insert the whole answer in this public record. It is believed to have been written by Dr. Geo. Junkin, and bears marks of his mind and his pen.

3. Therefore, the burden of proof lies upon those who affirm, that the Assembly had power to enact this "Plan of Union." They admit that there is no specific grant of such powers; they are bound then to prove, that its exercise was indispensably necessary, in order to carry out some other power specifically granted. Now we search in vain for any such proof in the protest. There is, we believe, but a single effort of the kind. This effort is made in view of two distinct and distant clauses in our book. (Form of Gov't, chap. XII, sec. 4.) The General Assembly "shall constitute the bond of union, peace, correspondence and mutual confidence, among all our churches." But surely here is no power granted to constitute a bond of union with churches of another denomination. It has exclusive reference to all "our churches;" and yet the protestors refer to this as authority for forming a union with a denomination not holding the same form of government.

An equally unsuccessful attempt is made, upon chap. 1, sec. 2, where the book affirms, "that any Christian church or union, or association of churches, is entitled to declare the terms of admission into its *communion*." And the protestors assert here, that the General Assembly exercised this power in forming the "Plan of Union," and so declared the "terms of admission into the communion, into the Presbyterian Church, proper to be required in the frontier settlements."

On this statement, two remarks seem requisite: First, the settling of the terms of communion, we had thought was the highest act of power; an act beyond the reach of the General Assembly itself; an act which the constitution itself provides, shall be done only by a majority of the Presbyteries. When, we ask, did the Presbyterian Church "declare the terms of admission into its *communion?*" Most assuredly, when the constitution was adopted. And yet the protestors, in this case, aver that the "Plan of Union," is a declaration of the terms of admission into our communion! Could they affirm more directly its unconstitutionality.

The other remark is, that the Plan of Union does not prescribe the terms of admission into the communion of the Presbyterian Church. It prescribes the way in which Congregationalists may remain out of this church, and yet exercise a controlling and governing influence over its ecclesiastical judicatories.

In the entire absence of all proof, that the power exercised in forming the Plan of Union, was indispensably necessary to carry out a power, specifically granted, and in the face of their own admission, that such power is not specifically given to the General Assembly, we conclude that the act in question was without any authority, and must be null and void.

The next thing worthy of notice, is the criticism on the phrases, "constitutional rules," and "obligatory on all the churches." This Plan of Union, it is argued, is not of the nature of constitutional rules, obligatory on all the churches, and therefore, it was not necessary that it should have been sent down, and have received the sanction of a majority of the Presbyteries. In presenting this argument, the protestors admit, that if the plan did embrace constitutional rules, the Assembly had no power to enact it. The book (Form of Gov., chap. XII, sec. 6) declares: "Before any overtures or regulations proposed by the Assembly to be established as constitutional rules, shall be obligatory in the churches, it shall be necessary to transmit them to all the Presbyteries, and to receive the returns of at least a majority of them, in writing, approving thereof."

This was not done with the Plan, and the only question before us is, whether it is an alteration of the constitution. This Assembly affirms, that it is a radical and thorough change of the entire system. On which remark—

1. Our book describes our church courts, viz: The Church Session, the Presbytery, the Synod and the General Assembly; and in chapter IX, it defines "the Church Session to consist of the pastor, or pastors and ruling elders, of a particular congregation," and intrusts to these, as permanent officers, the government of that church. But the Plan of Union provides for no such thing. It expressly dispenses with the Church Session, and leaves the government in the hands of the people, or of a temporary committee.

Again: chap. X, sec. 2. "A Presbytery consists of all the ministers and one ruling elder, from each congregation within a certain district." But the Plan of Union abrogates this provision. It does not merely pass it by, but absolutely repeals and nullifies it. According to the Plan, a Presbytery may have committee men, less or more in it, and may have not a single elder. The book further states, that "every congregation, (*i. e.*, of Presbyterians as before described) which has a stated pastor, has a right to be represented by one elder; and every collegiate church, (*i. e.*, a church with two or more ministers) by two or more elders, in proportion to the number of pastors." Here, it is perfectly obvious, that the principle of equal representation in Presbytery, is aimed at. The same is true of a Synod, chap. XI. "The ratio of the representation of elders, in the Synod, is the same as in the Presbytery;" that is, every congregation governed by its own Session, shall be represented in Presbytery and Synod. But the Plan provides for Congregational committee men, sitting and acting, and voting in Presbytery, although it also provides that the congregation he represents, shall not be under the government of the Presbytery, and no appeal shall be taken from it to the Presbytery, even by a minister, unless the church agree to it. Thus the power of government is in the hands of men, over whom that government does not extend. It is surely not necessary to proceed farther, to show that the Plan is an abrogation of the fundamental principles of the Presbyterian system; and yet the protestors say, it does not contain constitutional rules. No, verily, but it is a mass of unconstitutional usurpations, resulting from an overstretch of power. By the criticism of the protest, it is denied that the Plan contains constitutional rules; whereas, in the first sentence of the instrument itself, it is called "a Plan of Government for the Churches, in the New Settlements.' And the second sentence runs thus, "Regulations adopted by the General Assembly, &c." Now, if regulations are not rules, language has lost its meaning; and if regulations, containing "a Plan of Government for the Churches," are not intended to be binding, and do not touch the constitution, we are utterly at a loss to see how rules and regulations could be expressed. The article in question has been called "a Plan of Union," "a contract," "a covenant," none of which phrases are found in the document itself. It declares itself to be "regulations," containing "a Plan of Government for the churches." Now, the General Assembly never had the power to establish "regulations," and a new "Plan of Government;" the Plan is therefore null and void.

But we are told, that these governmental regulations were not binding on "all the churches." Were they not, indeed! Have they not given rise to heterogenous bodies, who have come up here and bound us almost to our undoing? Have they not bound with green withes, this body and its boards of education and missions? Have they not well nigh shorn us of the locks of our strength, and forbidden us to go forth into the fields of missionary conflict against the foes of our God and King? Surely these protestors will not say the regulations are not binding upon all the churches.

But again, we are told in the protest, they are of long standing and have acquired the force of common law. Does long use constitute law? Then it would follow, that concubinage and polygamy exist of moral right.

Again, we are told that this "Plan of Government" was in existence twenty years prior to the last adoption of our constitution, and the inference is, that therefore it is binding, and was viewed as a contract to be kept in good faith. The fair inferences from the fact, however, ought to be, that this "Plan of Government" was not submitted to our Presbyteries, by the General Assembly, and is therefore not binding; and that this neglect was owing to the circumstance that it was then little known, and its evils were not all developed.

Again, we are told in the protest in reference to this new "Plan of Government," that its omission of elders being expressly provided for and designed, does not "vitiate the organization, for there must then be numerous churches among us, in which there are no deacons, for the same reason pronounced unconstitutional." And we are free to confess, that if the constitution made the deacon a ruling officer in the church, he must be found in our ecclesiastical courts, and his absence would nullify their constitutional existence. This, however, is not the case. The deacon's office, in the New Testament, and in our book, is limited to "serving tables." The argument, therefore, is lame and shows its eastern birth.

Again, this protest affirms, that the argument against this "Plan of Government for the Churches," because it was not submitted to the Presbyteries, strikes equally against the theological seminaries, the boards of education and of missions, and also against the admission of the Presbyteries of the Associate Reformed Synod, into this church.

Let us touch these in their order; and first, the theological seminaries. Here again, if these protestors can show that these seminaries are, in the language of our book, "constitutional rules, obligatory on the churches," or even, in the language of their favorite plan, "regulations" and "a Plan of Government for the Churches in the New Settlements," we will give up the argument, and Princeton and the Western Seminaries, and all. But if, as every one knows, the constitutions and regulations of these seminaries, have nothing to do with the government of the churches any more than the private regulations of a private clergyman, for his private class of students, then is this argument null and void from the beginning. As to the power in the Assembly to organize a seminary, it may be found in the book, (Form of Gov. chap. XII, sec. 5) under the general power of "superintending the concerns of the whole church," none of which concerns is of more vital importance, than that of providing an efficient ministry; also, to them belongs the power of "promoting charity, truth and holiness, through all the churches under their care." Now, the training of a pious and orthodox ministry, is the most effectual mode of accomplishing this work, and clearly places theological seminaries within the Assembly's power.

The same remarks are relevant and true, in reference to the board of education.

As to the board of missions, "the superintending of the concerns of the whole church," cannot be carried out without missions, and the Form of Government, chap. XVIII, expressly provides for them, and grants to the Assembly power over this very business; it reads thus: "The General Assembly may, of their own knowledge, send missions to any part, to plant churches or to supply vacancies; and for this purpose, may direct any Presbytery to ordain evangelists or ministers, without relation to any particular churches." How utterly unreasonable then for the protestors to deny the Assembly's power, to institute a board of missions.

As to the Mason Library and the Associate Reformed Churches, it may be necessary only to remark, that the two Presbyteries of New York and Philadelphia, the only parts which came into this Presbyterian Church, were from their beginning *Presbyterian*, according to the strictest order, holding the same identical Confession of Faith and Presbyterian Form of Church Government; it is, therefore, difficult to perceive how the admission, by the General Assembly, of strict and rigid Presbyterians, into their connexion, could be either extra or unconstitutional. The act of their admission did not create "regulations" and a "Plan of Government for the Churches," as did the Plan in question; it was not an "overture or regulation for establishing constitutional rules, obligatory upon the churches," and therefore its transmission to all the Presbyteries was not necessary.

Finally: The unconstitutionality of the "Plan of Union for the Government of the Churches, in the New Settlements," abrogated by this resolution, is farther demonstrated by a reference to Form of Government, chap. XII, sec. 1, which says: "The General Assembly is the highest judicatory in the Presbyterian Church; it shall represent, in one body, all the particular churches of this denomination;" and subsequently, it defines the ratio of representation. Now, it has been proved on the open floor of this General Assembly, by the protestors themselves, that the Synod of the Western Reserve, which was formed on this "Plan of Government," and which contains one hundred and thirty-nine particular churches, has only from twenty-four to thirty Presbyterian Churches in it; and yet, that Synod claim a right to twenty representatives here! Whom do these twenty represent? Certainly not "particular churches of this denomination," as our book says. No, but Congregational Churches, which by the terms of our book, and the whole representative spirit of our system, have no right to be represented here, and to judge and vote here, under a constitution which they deny to be binding upon themselves. With no greater impropriety would unnaturalized foreigners claim the right of franchise in our country, and of eligibility to office in our legislatures, our supreme judicial tribunals, and the executive departments of our states and of the nation. Besides, it has been shown by themselves here, that this "Plan of Government" has been here violated, by those claiming privileges under it, sending men to the Assembly who had never adopted our constitution.

We therefore conclude, that the reasoning of the protestors is fallacious; the "Plan of Government," adopted in 1801, is, and ever has been unconstitutional, and therefore this General Assembly ought to declare, as it has done in the resolution protested against, that it is, from the beginning, *null and void.*

CHAPTER XXI.

Mortification and designs of the exscinded company—Considerations on the pecuniary terms offered by the majority—Estimate of the claims of the New England body.

On considering the situation of the New School party, after their ejection from the Presbyterian Church, it must be perceived that they had cause for profound and cutting mortification. They had hoped and looked for protracted warfare, relying upon their skill and prowess, to turn the tide again in their favour. But when they found themselves, in the midst of their buoyant and delusive anticipations, suddenly and irresistibly struck with this masterly and statesmanlike *coup de main*, placing them universally and entirely without the limits of our ecclesiastical connexion, desperation took the place of their deceptive illusion. Had they peacefully acquiesced in the measure, knowing, as must necessarily have been the fact, that their whole habitual and determined course of action was absolutely uncongenial and irreconcilable with the elements, the structure, integral features of the Presbyterian body, which, sickened and distracted with their anomalous and incurable disorders, had, as a last resort, cast them out, as an heterogeneous and intolerable incubus, to seek some new and congenial associations, they might have exhibited some traits of dignity, self-respect, and Christian decorum, which would have deterred them from the unlawful and undermining struggles in church and state with which they now stand convicted and stigmatized through the whole Christian world.

In this sudden and overwhelming change of circumstances, their first attempt was, by an intrigue as degrading as it was shallow, disorderly, and violent, to regain, by arrogant demands, their standing in the church, which, from pure disgust, had disowned and repudiated them. At the same time, they manifested a strong desire to monopolize the loaves and fishes, a moiety of which had been gratuitously offered to them, at the last meeting of the General Assembly, on an amicable arrangement then proposed for dividing the church. In their perfect infatuation and extravagant aims, they hoped to place themselves in a higher sphere, under a new name, for the gratification of their pride and ambition, and for the admiration of the present generation; but through the entire failure of all their schemes and efforts, they have become sensible that the want of pure faith, true consistency, and sound discretion, have brought upon them the frown of Divine Providence, and the disapprobation and disgust of all good men; for it is an immutable truth, "The face of the Lord is against them that do evil."

On inspecting the pecuniary account, it will be seen that the terms offered to the New School, by the General Assembly of 1837, in their proposed compromise, were large and liberal, far beyond what justice would require. In dividing the funds susceptible of division, on lawful principles, no more equitable standard to be governed by could probably be suggested, than the relative numbers of the respective parties. On examining the lists, it will be found that the New School numbered and claimed at most about five hundred ministers, which would leave in the Presbyterian Church about one thousand four hundred and fifty ministers, and, including ministers abroad and Presbyteries who have not reported, would enlarge the amount to fifteen hundred. Hence, on the foundation of justice, leaving out of view every opposing consideration, the largest amount of the disposable funds which the New School could at all pretend to claim, would be one-third, or less. But the overture for pacific adjustment shows that the Old School assented to the proposal of an equal division. This is considered, on the part of the majority, evidence of strong desire, not only to do full justice, but to extend great favour to the weaker party, at the moment of separation.

In ascertaining the correct state of this account, and striking a balance, it is of no small importance to inquire which of these parties contributed most to the accumulation of the funds in question. Some facts may be collected from unquestionable ecclesiastical records, for our guidance on this subject. Before the New School were fully formed and recognized in the church, a portion of these funds were already in hand. Nothing is more fully susceptible of proof, if not already impressed on every man's memory, than the fact that far the greater part of the whole amount was contributed by the Presbyterians of the old stamp. The New School, even when few in number, in general, never would, and never did, give a pro rata proportion of their church funds to the General Treasury, and that proportion rather decreased, than increased with their growth. Their sympathies for New England, the A. B. C. F. Missions, the Home Missionary Society, the

Presbyterian Education Society, and other minor institutions, began early and increasingly to distort their feelings and their charitable energies in the church; so that of the moneys raised in the churches for benevolent purposes, fractions and reserves were kept back for the avowed purpose of indulging their acknowledged predilections for New England societies. In the Synod of New Jersey, this practice was kept up for many years, and openly advocated by men of some popularity and distinction,* who, from personal influence, procured a heavy vote in favour of this course of action. Warm debates and struggles often agitated the Synod on this subject.† The contributions which swelled the amount of the funds in question, came chiefly from the Old School churches, and Old School pastors, in the principal cities, large towns and villages, and opulent country congregations, who were, for a long time, almost universally free from New School obliquity. In settling this question, or forming a correct opinion upon the subject, it is right to embrace in our view, the notorious fact, that the deformed and dishonest devotion of the New School to New England societies, prompted them to such measures in collecting money, from pure Presbyterian districts, as to impair the resources of the church, and divert them into foreign channels. The feelings and affections of the honest and unsuspecting people, were, in many cases, alienated from their own church to serve another; the regular operations of sound Presbyteries were deranged by the artful and disorganizing interference of strangers. Agents of New England societies overran the whole church, to collect money, and awaken sympathy for rival institutions. It seemed of little avail to complain of such men as trespassers, disturbing the church, filching her treasures, disaffecting her congregations, interfering with her boards, seizing upon funds which properly belonged to the uncorrupted Presbyterian Church. These were the men who had come in among us "unawares" on the platform of 1801. They were bound by solemn sanctions to build up the Presbyterian Church; but, behold, instead of contributing to her aggrandisement, they are constantly robbing it; instead of strengthening her, they make it their chief work to weaken and distract her, to block up the channels of order, and introduce confusion. Now, had these intruders been faithful to their vows, and used as much zeal to enrich and adorn the church as they have to impair and destroy her, had they honestly performed the work assumed, faithfully discharged their duty, given their funds in good measure and good season, how much fuller would have been her treasury, how much more strong and

* Such men as the very excellent and respected Dr. Samuel Fisher.

† In this, the writer cannot be mistaken, having frequently participated in these controversies.

elevated would the church have appeared at this day. But these are the men, after all their neglect, their misapplication of Presbyterian funds, their hostility and overt acts against the church, who come forward and unblushingly demand her property; even call the whole church into a civil court, with very little object in view, but to make a vain and empty show of themselves and to embezzle the funds, acquired in the manner stated, before a New School judge, who seemed inclined very strongly to help out their dishonest enterprise. All this they performed or attempted, after having, by their heretical departures for many years from the standards of the church which they had sworn to support; after labouring incessantly, for a long period, to divide, corrupt, and overthrow the church, by encroaching, deranging, and subversive measures, secret and insidious, or open and daring, as the preceding history fully proves.

The principle has been long and firmly established by the decisions of the highest judicial tribunals in Europe and America, that in cases of intestine commotion and division, and ultimate separation of parties in ecclesiastical bodies, on the ground of heresy,* the orthodox portion, of course, retain the name, the organization, the power, the *property*, and the rights pertaining constitutionally to the original body. The intruders, the dissenters, or revolutionists, forfeit every claim to estate or property, personal or real, except so far as the pure and uncontaminated adherents of the orthodox principles and policy, may voluntarily choose to differ, as a matter of gratuitous favour.

* The Presbyterian Church case was not one of that kind. There was no charge of heresy. Hence, Judge Gibson, in delivering the opinion of the court, (see Judd, p. 203,) distinctly states: "We were called, however, to pass, not on a question of *heresy*, for we would have been incompetent to decide it, but on the regularity of the meeting, at which the trustees were chosen. That the Old School party succeeded to the privileges and property of the Assembly, was not because it was more Presbyterian than the other, but because it was stronger." This decision was controlled merely by the amount of numbers, and comparative strength of parties. The questions of orthodoxy and order were only incidentally referred to in the decision, though *fully established in the evidence.* Had both been embraced in the enquiry, the New School would have been more overwhelmingly cast down. They complain that they were not tried. They moved the suit upon a mere question of law, because they were afraid to go into the merits of the case. Thus it is clearly seen, that the judgment of the court was pronounced upon a principle entirely different from that on which the Abrogation rested. Both were just and appropriate. Either sufficient to warrant and sustain the decision issued upon it. And if both are viewed together, and the fact of heresy is superadded, on what ground would the miserable ejected party then stand? But they are all, substantially, comprehended in these historic illustrations and results.

CHAPTER XXII.

The design and attempt of the New School, by intrigue and violence, if necessary, to substitute their mockery in the place of the constitutional organization of the General Assembly of 1838—Their riotous conduct —Their suit before *Nisi Prius* in Philadelphia, to obtain the church bodily.

Facts justify the belief, that the exscinded Synods, by their leaders, intended, if possible, first of all, to regain their places in the Presbyterian body. Though it is really difficult to conceive how their pride, their self-respect, and their wounded honour, could allow them to think for a moment of desiring to associate again with a company of men, who had so unceremoniously, as they alleged, cast them out of their union, as unworthy of it, or unfit for it. But an interim of a year between the last and the next General Assembly, gave them a full opportunity to devise a plan of procedure, which they thought better adapted to their views. This plan, succeeding disclosures proved to consist of a covered design, by art and violence combined, by one of the grossest instances of humbuggery the world can show, to effect a substitution of themselves, *en masse,* for the orthodox body, and manœuvre the majority entirely out of the house, they remaining as the sole possessors. For this purpose, they had agreed to congregate in numbers in the General Assembly, at the opening of their meeting in Ranstead Court, rudely to rush upon them, to interrupt their regular proceedings, throw them into disorder, and, in the confusion of the moment, created by themselves for the purpose, to get up a mock organization of their own corrupt materials; thus to prostrate and extinguish the General Assembly of the Presbyterian Church, if possible, altogether, call themselves by the same name, claim to be the true body, seize upon whatever property of the church they could lay their hands upon, and sue for the balance wherever their rapacity failed to reach it.

In the prosecution of this desperate scheme, their first step was to procure an adviser in the premises: and it is to be regretted, that they hit upon a man of so little wit, discretion, or integrity, to dictate in this very critical emergency. The plan of the conspiracy* being arranged by their "counsel," as they pronounced

* The following extract from Dr. Judd's book, p. 164, confirms facts stated above. The writer being located in the seat immediately in the rear of Mr. Cleaveland, had a near and distinct view of the paper from which he read, and could even have read it himself, and is fully confident, therefore, that this document differs considerably, in length and substance, from the original, which could not be obtained. "As the commissioners from a large number of Presbyteries have been denied their seats in this house,

him, "learned in the law," the scene of development selected was the floor of the General Assembly, in the church of Ranstead Court, at about three o'clock, P. M., on the opening of the Assembly. Their conscript fathers, their Cataline and Cethegus, &c., &c., all being designated, enrolled, and instructed; are promptly present at the decisive hour; though personally visible, yet perfectly disguised, and their designs covered with midnight darkness, except as to a few old side men, who may have had some knowledge of what was to follow. A multitude, of all characters, sexes, and ages, appeared anxiously crowding round, some in the gallery, and some in the church below, as if some intimation had been given *them* of the exhibition intended, or that their aid, in some way, might be needed to carry out the conspiracy. Now, without any outbreak, or overt act disturbing the meeting, on a simple disclosure, or detection of the fact, that such a brigand, under concealment, banded together, under a mischievous written article or bond of union, of an absent leader, with matured designs to interrupt one of the most solemn assemblies upon earth, to derange, to supplant, to overthrow, the whole Assembly: to usurp their powers, to occupy their places, to invalidate their trusts, to seize their property; what opinion would be formed by intelligent, upright, impartial judges, of such a company of assailants, so organized and circumstanced? especially when it is recollected that the great majority of this Assembly were ministers of Jesus Christ, met by his authority, and upon the business of his earthly kingdom, commencing their proceedings under their *own established rules and usages?* Would they not consider the purity of the hall occupied, profanely invaded? the conscientious rights of the Assembly unrighteously impugned? the principles of order and decency, by law secured to all religious bodies of men, completely outraged? But what shall we think, when these combined assailants, throwing off their disguise, assuming their true character, and each beginning to perform the part secretly assigned him, in the tumultuous drama, by reading their own documentary history of their combination, making mo-

and as we have been advised by counsel learned in the law, that a constitutional Assembly must be organized at this time and place, he trusted it would not be considered an act of discourtesy, but merely of necessity, if we now proceed to organize the Assembly of 1838, in the fewest words, and in the shortest time, and with the least interruption practicable. I therefore move, that C. N. S. Beman, from the Presbytery of Troy, take the chair." This rude and disorderly assault upon the General Assembly, struck them like an armed force, in the midst of their regular proceedings, in the organization of the body, in strict conformity with the letter of the Book of Discipline, established rules, and prescribed order. The Assembly, of course, suspended action in perfect astonishment, and allowed the disorderly, tumultuous intruders, to get through with their mock-movement, when they resumed business.

tions, stamping feet, uttering conflicting and unearthly sounds, from all sexes, ages, positions, and directions, overwhelming all business, impressing the quiet and orderly assembly with astonishment and dismay, following up this profound and appalling confusion, amidst shouts and screams, making motions and calling for votes, with a violent rush, exhibiting in numbers and violence, the extent of the revolutionary movement, which had clandestinely gained access to the house—would not any sane discreet man, on beholding these extravagant and unparalelled exhibitions, be impressed with the belief that the actors were rather a company broken loose from a lunatic asylum, or a state penitentiary, than an association of grave and dignified ministers of any church? This plain statement will show that the object which they were vainly labouring to accomplish, was that of forcing themselves back, on some principle not fully disclosed, into that church and Assembly of which they had recently been declared, on account of their false principles and disorderly conduct, to be no longer members, or of seizing the whole church as their own.

In the honest state of New Jersey, they would have been called a mob; they would have been characterized as rioters, legally liable to indictment, punishable with fines and imprisonment, for clandestinely and violently disturbing a religious Assembly.

The idea of attempting gravely to analyze and discuss the course of such a band of lawless intruders step by step, to decide its constitutional course and procedure, in common sense, law, or justice, is perfectly preposterous. And if the counsellors, whose opinions they have so boastfully spread out before the public, had honestly declared to them, as they certainly ought when application was made for their opinions, that they had acted like a company of outlaws, and could expect no protection or indulgence from the legal tribunals of the land, they would have saved the courts of Pennsylvania from much burdensome labour, the applicants from expense and disgrace, and themselves from extensive and justly merited *disapprobation*.

But the task of a formal legal investigation, they forcibly, under the sanction of legal advisers, imposed upon the court of Nisi Prius, in Pennsylvania, with a view to justify their tumultuous and disorderly conduct, and to secure the spoils of the church they there sought to destroy. This resort to law, before a secular tribunal, was in violation of the fundamental principle of Protestantism, viz: That the Church of Jesus Christ is independent of the civil power, and not amenable, while she commits no civil offence, to the bar of Cæsar. Honest devotion to this fundamental principle of religious liberty and gospel religion, inspired the Free Church of Scotland, in its defence and establishment of this sacred foundation, in defiance of the secular arm.

To make this appeal to Cæsar successful, a jury was obtained in the court of *Nisi Prius,* of an order well adapted to the end pursued. As the Old School have always protested against litigation, or acknowledgment at all, of civil power in ecclesiastical affairs, Dr. Judd pronounces it very inconsistent in the Old School to "apply to the court for a new trial, after the decision against them in the court below." After having violently, and according to the rules of the church, illegally compelled them to appear before a civil tribunal, which was considered by the public generally *prejudiced* against them, and in which, in the course of trial, one of the eminent advocates of the prosecutors attempted to *increase* that *prejudice*, as was manifest to every observer, could it possibly be regarded as unreasonable or unrighteous, that the Old School party, injured and oppressed as they were, should be willing to let the same court, more fully assembled, review the case, examine the evidence, and reverse or sustain the sentence, as appeared to them to be right?

That suit, once commenced, based upon false history and numerous charges wholly insupported by evidence, in violation of a long train of unimpeachable ecclesiastical records, the idea of compromise, concession, of retreat, of surrendering funds, to a company possessing no claims to them, was entirely futile. At the crisis when negotiation was attempied, the New School refused a spontaneous bona fide offer of a full half of the whole property of the church, legally disposable, and upon that broad and immovable fact, we leave this branch of the subject in controversy, to the estimate and decision of an impartial public. It might justly be added, that the mischiefs this party had been doing, and attempting in the Presbyterian Church, for twenty years preceding the abrogation, and the mighty, sweeping desolation they intended, could they only acquire the requisite power, are matters so much of public notoriety, as to expose their designs and graduate their turpitude, in the most ample manner. Instead, therefore, of sustaining their spurious and unchristian litigation, the whole company ought to have been reached, under a criminal process, for disturbing the peace of the church, and introducing disorder and confusion into the house of God.

CHAPTER XXIII.

Court in Banc—Judge Gibson presiding, &c.—Explanatory remarks—Arguments of the Hon. John Sergeant—Three points particularly discussed. 1. The principles of religious freedom and the rights of conscience; the argument by implication, denying the jurisdiction of the court, in ecclesiastical and spiritual matters. 2. Justifying the organization and proceedings of the General Assembly of 1837. 3. A vindication of Dr. Elliott, and the party who supported him, in the Assembly of 1838.

At first glance, it seems very absurd, to set men whose heads and hearts are habitually and laboriously occupied, with the intricacies and quibbles of civil law, to investigate questions of a purely moral and spiritual nature; and such a measure assumes a more unwarrantable and repulsive character, when the fact is recognized, that the constitutions of both church and state prohibit it. The constitution of Pennsylvania declares, "that every man shall worship God in his own way—that no human authority, in any case whatever, can control or interfere with the rights of conscience." But the relators (as the New School are technically called in this suit) have forcibly introduced this controvery to a civil tribunal. After refusing a liberal proposal by the Old School, to compromise the matters in controversy, they pressed it into the court of Nisi Prius, in Pennsylvania; and its presentment for argument in the Supreme Court of this state, is a matter of course, as well as of right, on the part of the respondents. The New School are therefore the responsible party, and to be censured for all the scandal to religion, and inflammatory effects among the parties, that may result from this process.

The fruitless attempt made, 1837, in Ranstead Court, by these parties, to divide and separate amicably, shows the impropriety and impracticability of their remaining together, and if once separated, of ever uniting or coming together again, peaceably. There was an irreconcilable opposition in their integral elements, their ideas, their habits, their objects, and universal tendency of mind, character and life, which must forever prevent their harmonizing and constituting a uniform homogeneous body. There seemed to exist insurmountable, moral and conscientious differences, which neither party was willing to sacrifice. The same causes, or irreconcilable discrepancies, which prevented their agreeing to divide, prevented their continuing together, and must secure their permanent separation. A division must take place. That separation which the parties could not, or would not effect, no other power has a right to compel or enforce. This would violate the rights of conscience and impair religious liberty. Where, then, shall an umpire be found to settle this religious controversy? Civil power, the arbiter in civil disputes, has no right to intermeddle with spiritual interests and moral obligations. Calming the tumult—harmonizing these discordant elements, must be left to the religious community itself, however heterogeneous the mass and difficult the work. They must recur to their own constitution and laws; search into the facts and principles of their previous organization and action; apply the law and testimony, and form a separation, according to the whole collected and concentrated body of facts and circumstances. A majority of the whole is the only power recognized in our ecclesiastical constitution, to perform this work; and with the result of its action no power upon earth has a right to interfere, or can intermeddle without disorganizing the church of Jesus Christ, paralysing the rights of conscience, subordinate only to the Lord of conscience, and expelling religious liberty from the world.

Now, the interference of civil authority in the case before us, is especially inexcusable, as the respondents had performed no act in violation of civil rights, making them amenable to a civil tribunal. Nothing is more notorious than that they had transgressed no laws of the country; they could not, therefore, be interfered with by the tribunals of the country. They must be left to the moral and spiritual discipline of the church. But suppose, in spite of all these views, an appeal is made to the civil tribunal, before which we now stand? How is this Bench, with all its profound learning, to decide or prescribe the proper course for the church, in the difficult crisis to which she is reduced? Only by assuming the place of the General Assembly. But who gave them a right to erect themselves into an ecclesiastical tribunal? The constitution of this state positively forbids it. And after the civil court has acted, what is to give their decree a binding force? They cannot touch the rights nor the power of conscience, but by rousing its voice and its indignation against them, if they interfere with the church's sovereign decision. To produce acquiescence in their action, if adverse, their only resort is civil power, fines, and bars and bolts, all hostile, if not fatal, to the rights of conscience, and to the liberty wherewith Christ has made us free. And yet here we are as a religious body, prosecuting a great religious object, before a civil court.

With these sentiments in our hearts, we responded to the relators in the court of *Nisi Prius;* by compulsion, and with the same sentiments we appeared before the Supreme Court, driven by necessity to that last resort, in civil law, not of *free men* in Christ Jesus, but of common citizens, or secular men, in the community. We hope the world around us, and the court above us, and all observers of our course, will form a right estimate of the Old School body, in joining this issue with our pursuers, to redress our multiplied grievances, under this constrained appeal to Cæsar.

This case, as presented to the Supreme Court of Pennsylvania, was not only in itself important, complex and difficult, but altogether novel in its character, very little attention having been paid to questions of conscience, in the practice of the American courts.

The only parallel case recited by Mr. Sergeant, in his argugument before the Court in Banc, denying the power of civil courts to interfere with the spiritual interests of the church, or disavowing on the part of civil tribunals, their right of jurisdiction in ecclesiastical and spiritual affairs, was the record of a case in the Supreme Court of Delaware, showing the opinion of that court to be, Chief Justice Johns presiding, "that no power shall, or ought to be, vested in or assumed by any magistrate, that shall in any case interfere with, or in any manner control the rights of conscience, in the free exercise of religious worship," or by implication, in managing and conducting their spiritual and religious affairs, agreeably to the free and conscientious dictates of their own minds and hearts.

The entire and permanent separation of church and state, is of unspeakable importance and absolute necessity, to the freedom and stability of all our institutions; and no man better qualified than Hon. John Sergeant, to discuss and establish upon its right principles, this great question of religious liberty and the rights of conscience, it is honestly believed, could be selected from the American bar. Here, from constitution, deep reflection, fixed habit, and experience as a pre-eminently learned christian advocate, he was at home. This great question of religious freedom for hundreds of millions of people, in these rising states, absorbed all his sympathies, elicited all his powers of thought and ratiocination, and prompted him to that great effort, which proved him to be the champion of religious liberty and the rights of conscience.

The clear conceptions, the powerful reasonings and impressive conclusions, exhibited in his argument, are of inestimable value, for the influence they must exert upon the minds of all sober thinking people. We therefore, with pleasure, present in these pages as much of Mr. Sergeant's masterly argument as our limits will allow. In that part which relates to the rights of conscience and religious freedom, we use his language closely. On some other topics, we have been compelled to abbreviate and condense the argument, however, honestly retaining the true meaning and import of the speaker. Those wishing to examine the whole discussion, may have that pleasure, by referring to the "Church Case," I vol., 8 vo., by the Rev. Samuel Miller, Jr.

Mr. Sergeant's Argument.

"May it please your Honours, the counsel for the relators have told us, that such a decision (confirming the judgment of the court below) would be productive of peace; that it would bring together again those who are so widely separated. But, that has been tried; they were together, and after all that has been disclosed, in the course of the trial of this cause, I think every one ought to be very cautious in cherishing a desire to force them together again. If I understand the subject, this is the main ground of our portion of the objection made to the decision of the court and jury; that the rights and the powers of the General-Assembly, the highest and the final judicatory of the Presbyterian Church, as well as of all its subordinate judicatories, are purely spiritual and moral. It so happens, that deeming them to be matters between every man and his own conscience, in which no human tribunal has the authority to interfere, we consider an attempt to force us into any religious connexion whatever, a direct violation of our most sacred rights. We suggest now, that such an attempt would be unconstitutional and inconsistent with spiritual liberty; that it would strike at the root of the great principle of our institutions, namely, that spiritual concerns are not to be interfered with by the civil power. These parties can never come together again by consent, never in the world, but of their own free choice. The idea of forcing one mass of people to sit at the same spiritual table with another, implies, in the first place, the power of searching into the hearts of men, for without it, who can tell the consequences of such an union? I take it, then, that the position of the learned counsel is not correct. I go for freedom, for no force from any quarter. We shall presently see whether, notwithstanding all that we have suffered in name and character, we are not the real champions of spiritual liberty. I believe we are. And at the same time, it will appear, whether the effort of the minority is not to deprive us of that liberty, to force us into an association with those whom we do not choose to be with; whether their prominent object is not to compel us to abandon all our rights, or what is equivalent, to give up the great right of choosing our associates. An effort in itself strongly repulsive.

"This is the most dangerous power that a civil tribunal has ever been called upon to exercise. Your Honours have enough to do, enough of trouble and perplexity, in determining those cases upon which you must decide. What you are here called to do, is to open for the subjects of your inquiry and labour, a new source of conflict and litigation, of unknown extent. None can define its limits, or control the spirit of discord, which it will pour forth. We have warned our opponents—not threatened, as has been intimated—we have warned them of the litigation that would follow their proceedings; but it is for litigation that they seem to have sought. Every church, Presbytery, and Synod in the land must decide this question for itself; that is as plain as it can be. Nay, every individual in the land must engage in the contest, and how will you limit the violent spirit of litigation, if the law is once thrown open to these parties? Observe what effects it has already produced. The minority of the Assembly of 1838 have certainly done a great deal, if they have accomplished what the charge of his Honour, Judge Rogers, decides that they have accomplished. If the matter be not too serious to joke about, following the example of those who have preceded me, in some degree, though, perhaps, speaking more innocently, I would say, that the proceeding by which the minority in that Assembly claim to have manœuvred the majority out of doors, was one of the greatest practical hoaxes ever seen or heard of. I mean to say, that no man can look seriously at the thing, uninfluenced by any respect to who shall succeed at last, but he must so regard it. I do not speak now of the decision of the law. So the *facts* strike me, and so they must, I think, strike every one. I say that these gentlemen, if they succeed here, will have accomplished a great deal; but the rest that they will have to do, what remains to be accomplished, they will find more difficult, weightier, more distracting. Let us tell them, that much trouble and confusion would be avoided, if the admonition—I will not quote scripture—the admonition to let spiritual bodies decide on spiritual questions, were duly observed. I intend to show, before I have done with the case, that this is an attempt to strip the General Assembly of that power; to place it in the hands of the tribunals of the land; and so to place it, in a manner, I will not say to the shame of religion, but to the disparagement and disgrace of its ministers, so far as disparagement and disgace can be brought upon those holy officers. What length of years, what venerable character, what stock of service or of merit, will ever serve as a shield? The very first act of power performed by the new body, which met in the First Presbyterian Church, was to direct a bolt at the head of the only remaining trustee, of those originally incorporated by the act of 1799. Their first act was an act of rough exscision. The first exercise of their newly obtained power, was aimed at him who had held his office from 1799 to 1898—forty years lacking one. Your Honours may see in this the spirit with which we are threatened; you may see it even in the argument of the cause in this court. All must grant, that in my learned friend's remarks upon Dr. Elliott's text, and in his offer to furnish him with a more appropriate one, the same spirit is manifested, not originating in him, but within the compass of the supposed triumphant party, who, flushed by their fancied victory, begin immediately to claim cognizance of the conscience and the heart, and charge Dr. Elliot with having, while in the performance of a solemn religious service, in the very presence of his Maker, used that text from impure motives. From the beginning to the end of the trial of this case, I am sorry to say it, but say it because I felt it, during the short time that I was able to be in court, I felt, and I am sure my colleagues felt—I hope my clients did not feel—that we were *in the midst of a pelting tempest, a torrent against which it seemed almost vain to make resistance.* The same spirit, may it please your Honours, has been manifested in the course of this discussion, and if at last, the Assembly of 1838 and the Old School party, are condemned, it will be, not because of their acts, but because we have undertaken to know what is in their hearts, and judge that we may have discovered there, sinister motives and designs. We, I have said, are the true champions of spiritual liberty and of the rights of conscience, and however much we may have suffered, if our cause is just, it must prevail; all must come back to the plain ground of the constitution and laws, and leave such disputes as this, which cannot be adjusted by the civil power, to the tribunals of the church, and to Him who shall be the final judge of all.

"Now, may it please your Honours, the general question which is presented in this case is, whether we are not entitled to have a new trial. Great interests are confessedly involved in it. The question, as regards our country, is one of vast magnitude; in some aspects of it, none greater can arise; and certainly there can be none in which the respective champions of the two parties are entitled to greater consideration, as regards their motives, characters, and lives. The respect due to them, I mean not to violate. I do not mean to speak a single word of any member of the New School party, personally disparaging, or calculated to wound needlessly his feelings. I am not instructed so to speak, nor would I, if I were; I will endeavour in my reply to the arguments which we have heard, to maintain this principle inviolate, treating with the utmost respect the opinions of our opponents, so far as it may be practicable, and with respect unlimited the opinion of his Honour, Judge Rogers. Yea, more, I will in the beginning, say, that the learned judge had a most difficult and arduous task to perform. Not on account of the mere novelty of the case, though this made it essential that there should be time and opportunity for cool discussion and careful consideration. Look at the great amount of evidence contained in this paper book, that has been laid before your Honours. He must search out and gather from all this mass, and from the contrarient statements of the bar, the precise facts of the case to which the law was then to be applied. And what were his means for the performance of his remaining duty? Was he to turn to the common law? That could give him little aid; and our own statute law none at all. This case introduced an entirely new system of laws, and, though thoroughly instructed in all the principles of the law of the land, his Honour was required to gather, from the scattered fragments suddenly laid before him, in the heat and hurry of the trial, the whole law of the Presbyterian Church, a church which has a common law, and a statute law of its own, and a complete form of government, not framed, however, like ours, in the exact distribution of distinct powers. One while a witness occupied the stand and gave in his testimony; then a little was read from one pamphlet, and then a little from another; then a rule of order, and then an article from the constitution. Here was thrown in the history of a Synod, and there a map containing the names of certain judicatories without their boundary lines. Amid all this, his Honour must suddenly catch up just what was necessary to the case, undisturbed by the din and conflict below, so that he might at last instruct the jury as to the law that was to govern their verdict. I will not say, may it please your Honours, that it was impossible for him to comprehend the matter to his own satisfaction, in the course of a single trial; I will not undertake to measure the utmost reach of human intellect; but I will undertake to say, that I trust and believe that there is no judge on this bench, who would not desire the ground thus gone over, to be reviewed; and that if he has fallen into any error, it might be corrected. I do not doubt it; and, therefore, I now address his Honour as freely as I do any of his associates, under the perfect conviction that if he should see any error, he will not be the last to correct it. Now, we desire the opportunity of another trial, and the grounds of our application have been already, in some degree, disclosed. We undertake to show from the history of the cause, that several parts of our defence were not allowed to have that weight which should have been allowed them. I go farther, and say, that when the case went to the jury, and even before it went to them, there was a manifest prejudice in their minds against us; from what source arising, it is not necessary for me to say. If the fact, that the verdict was rendered by a jury so influenced and so prejudiced, be substantiated, that, of itself, will be a sufficient ground for demanding a new trial. I say, also, that the whole investigation, so far as it has been conducted, and the decision, to the extent to which it has gone, is a manifest violation of our constitution, I mean the constitution of the church, of spiritual liberty, and of the rights of conscience. I have already adverted to this point; for an illustration of which I must thank Mr. Randall. He has told us, that the effect of your Honour's adding your sanction to the verdict of the jury, would be to force together the two parties in this controversy. Now, if I may be allowed a few words more, in reply to this, I will endeavour to suggest some views of the subject, arising out of it, tending to show the propriety, in fact the necessity, of a strict adherence to the constitutional principle to which I have referred.

"In the first place, and this must already have suggested itself to your Honour's mind, there are great difficulties and embarrassments in the way of inquiries like that in which we are now engaged, as the present case must bear witness. Is it fit that this court should entertain an appeal from the General Assembly? I do not mean now to inquire, whether it is fit that such an appellate jurisdiction, when it belongs to a civil court, should be exercised. If your jurisdiction be established, you must take cognizance of the appeal. I speak of the difficulty, nay, of the impossibility of arriving at a right conclusion in such a case. Need I point out the grounds of difficulty? I will call your attention for a moment to the resolutions of the Assembly of 1837, which have given rise to this proceeding; to either one, that repealing the *Plan of Union*, or that exscinding the four Synods, or to both. Why, if an appeal be taken in regard to those acts, to this tribunal, your Honours must put yourselves in the place of the General Assembly itself, and decide what you would have done in a similar case, whether, under the same circumstances, you would have pursued the same course. In this investigation, the very first blow has been aimed at the intentions and motives which governed those whose acts are called in question. They are charged with pride, a lust for power, a desire to appropriate to themselves the funds of the church; every thing opprobrious and vile has been heaped upon them, and, if finally, our opponents effect their purpose, it can be only because those acts are to be considered as done not honestly, but with some sinister design. How can your Honours undertake to decide this point?

"Again, passing by the gross injustice which was done us in the out-set, I come to another point; and here, I mean to be explicit. His Honour, Judge Rogers, no doubt in the press and hurry of the proceeding, after distinctly admitting that *the act abrogating the Plan of Union* was one which the *Assembly* had *a right to perform*, goes on to characterize that act as unjust. No doubt, in the discussion of the case at the bar, one side had maintained that it was an unjust act, and the other that it was just. This, probably, led his Honour to inquire, not only whether the act was lawful, but also as to the other point debated. Now, I mean to contend, and, therefore, have brought this view before you, that where an act is not unlawful, a court has no right to inquire into the motives which influenced that act. And for this reason; that to decide as to a man's motives, you must place yourself exactly in his position, and take the same views of every thing that he does. Else you cannot judge properly. If the General Assembly has a right to do any act, it is accountable to no human tribunal for the manner in which it may choose to exercise this right. It is a fundamental doctrine, that so long as any one keeps within the precincts of his legitimate powers, he cannot, in law, be affected, by his thoughts, words, or deeds. Your Honours have seen, that in another part of the charge to the jury, that relating to the organization of the Assembly of 1838, the learned judge has in a like manner, treated Dr. Elliott, the clerks, and a portion of the Old School party; inquiring into their motives, characterizing acts otherwise right, from the motives with which they were performed, as a conspiracy. I do not know whether a conspiracy had been charged upon us, even in the discussion at the bar. Certainly such a charge could not be applicable, it being once decided that our acts were lawful—such as we had a right to perform.

"There is great cause here, for the court to ponder deeply and examine well the ground on which they stand; and another reason may be added to those already mentioned. Before your Honours arrive at the end of this case, I am persuaded you will find that if these parties are left to themselves, the public at large, and the friends of religion, will not have more cause to deplore the result, than has been furnished in the present investigation. They were in their own proper arena, two parties contending for what they considered their respective rights; one remained upon the ground while the other betook themselves to another place. The latter have appealed to a court of law, and, drawing their adversaries out of their ordinary and appropriate place, have compelled them to join in conflict and strife of a mere temporal tribunal, where are commonly dealt with matters that engage the feelings and arouse the passions, there is no telling how far the inflammation may extend. Whatever may be the result, or the influence of this proceeding, if hereafter it be found that it has brought scandal on religion, if, indeed, that be in the power of man, which I do not believe, or disparagement upon its professors and ministers, this cannot be imputed to us. Those who brought the case here, are alone responsible for the issue. And if they have raised the shout of victory once, they may possibly yet see the time, as they advance in life, as the shadows of their closing day lengthen, and the distance before them becomes contracted, when they may have occasion to mourn the events that have separated them entirely from these good men. In the course of the events of this world, those who are allowed to live to old age, must find many coming after them younger than themselves, of an active, bustling, and aspiring spirit, seeing places above them which are objects of their ambition; who, if they can discover a good precedent to sustain them in cutting off their elders, will not fail to follow the example. Nor is that all. This spirit once abroad in the church, who will allay its violence? I do not fear that any man will accomplish the destruction of the church: it is, as I believe, founded upon a rock. But who can exorcise that spirit when it is once raised? Nobody. If it begin its domination in injustice, in the prostration of one of those venerable props which support the church, a pillar on which it rests, and which has stood for half a century, no part of the building can ever be secure.

"These are times of restless inquiry, of storm and struggle, and your Honours will see the spirit of the times clearly exemplified in every part of this controversy. What is likely to be the effect of its supremacy? Mark it, and mark it in connexion with the phrases which have fallen from the honourable gentleman on the other side. The only remaining trustee of those appointed in 1799, he who had been respected amid all the changes of party, was the first object of attack. The body that assembled in the First Presbyterian Church, has set us an excellent example, says Mr. Randall; they have appointed no minister of the gospel a trustee. Here is exactly the thing of which I am speaking; that wisdom, that young but confident wisdom, which would exalt itself above all the experience of the past, above all other wisdom. These gentlemen have not only no respect for their predecessors—they may treat them as they please—but they have no respect for the law. That act of the legislature, by which these trustees were incorporated, gives one-third of the number ministers, and this arrangement has been made the pattern in all subsequent times, until the new light has burst upon us, showing all past wisdom to be folly. It seems that there is a concentration of light, in this newly formed body, that the legislature were entirely wrong, and that they are to set every thing to rights; that is, in the first place, they are to set the minority above the majority, and then to exclude all ministers from the Board of Trustees. I do not, however, complain of this at all. It is our business now, merely to show why the verdict of the jury ought not to stand. My colleague has most faithfully discharged his duty I could not have wished for the church, when these most important interests were at stake, a friend of greater learning and ability. Indeed, he has gone into the details of the case so fully and minutely, that all I am astonished at is, that it has not been almost painful to the court to be obliged to listen to them, instructive, and even essential as they are."

For the above extract, see Miller's Church Case. One volume, 8 vo., pages 509 to 514. For the extract following, see page 520.

"For the present, let us confine our attention to the Acts of Assembly, 1837, to see whether they were really unconstitutional and unjust.

"The measures of that body which are here called in question, are, *first*, the Abrogation of the *Plan of Union* of 1801, and *secondly*, what are called the exscinding resolutions, which are consequent upon the former, flowing directly from it, deriving from it their validity, and following it of necessity, in whatever capacity you choose to place it, whether they are considered as judicial or as legislative acts, at least so following it, in the judgment of those who passed them. That the ostensible grounds of those acts were the true grounds on which they were passed, I have meant to assume; and it is important to understand at the outset, whether we are to believe that these men sincerely, honestly, and *bona fide*, meant what they declared, that their measures were really and truly intended for the good of the church. I protest solemnly against the right of any body to question their motives. You cannot, under the constitution, deny my position, that these are to be respected. Presently, I will read a part of the constitution of Pennsylvania, bearing directly, as I think, upon this point, and which it is of infinite importance that we should understand. This case, I believe, was lost before the jury, and if we lose it here, will be lost finally, in a great measure, because, in sincerity, a want of truth, the declaration of motives, not real, has been imputed to my clients. On the trial, and the same thing is very manifest in the argument on this motion, the widest license was taken in commenting upon the character of the Assembly, and contradicting the assumption which I now make. I submit it, therefore, as a clear position, that at every tribunal of the commonwealth of Pennsylvania, a church, with each party in that church, is entitled to the clear concession, that whatever it does within the spirit of its discipline, is done from the motives which are professed. If you do not believe this, you cannot believe it to be a church, only a set of hypocrites, sinners of the worst kind. When, therefore, our opponents quote scripture for purposes to which we think it ought not to be applied, we challenge them to show their authority for casting the first stone at our motives; we do not consent to be put on proof of these, excepting by those to whom we are accountable for them; and we are thus accountable, only to the church, to ourselves. The world does not, and cannot, govern us in matters of faith and conscience. It is, then, of great consequence, that you consider these acts to have been performed honestly, sincerely, and conscientiously, for the good of the church, as my clients believed. We do not claim infallibility for them, more than for any other men. Presently, I shall point your Honours to the strongest evidence of the fact, that the true reasons for their acts were those on their face exhibited. But we are, at all events, entitled to assume it.

"In entering upon the discussion of the acts of 1837, I have first to propound to this court a great question, which must be decided in the outset. To whom does it belong to determine whether the proceedings of my clients were, or were not, for the good of the church? I do not now speak of motives. That they were right, I have assumed; and that this should be believed is secured to us by the fundamental principles of our government. None can call our motives in question, so long as we are careful in our observance of respect for the laws. Assuming this as undeniable, I respectfully demand, who is to decide whether the acts of 1837 were, or were not, for the good of the church? Or supposing a certain end confessedly desirable, who is to decide *how* that end is to be reached? It has been argued, that in order to attain a certain object, we were bound to follow the course of a regular trial; to commence proceedings in an inferior judicatory, unless where the superior had original jurisdiction, and conduct them in regular judicial form. I do not know how this law is to be established. In the first place, we have the question, who is to decide whether the proposed *end* is for the good of the church or not; and then, who is to decide how that end can best be attained? Can the civil tribunal prescribe the course to be pursued by the church? No. Suppose we say, 'We do not make any charge against our brethren, with whom, in time past, we have lived in unity; we do not mean to dismiss them with the mark of heresy, or other criminality upon them. All that we allege is, that they do not live according to the discipline of our church; that disorders may thence arise—that, in our opinion, they have already arisen' And suppose, too, that the act is performed by a competent tribunal, and involves nought but a separation of the parties. The question is, not whether our purpose is the best and wisest, but who is to judge whether it is, or is not so? the church, or a civil tribunal? If the latter can interfere at all in such matters, you had better dissolve the whole system of church government from top to bottom. If we cannot follow our own judgment throughout, we had better not form any judgment. Suppose farther, that we consider not only the *end*, but also the *means* proposed, to be essential; both *method* and *end*, we maintain, are for the consideration of the Assembly alone. Whatever method they adopt, is sure to be protested against by some person or other. But suppose they select a certain method, and are conscientious in their choice, is the judgment of any body to interfere? That selection is as much a matter of conscience, as the final decision itself. The rights of conscience are as clearly invaded by interfering with the one, as the other. I am speaking of the proceedings of the Assembly of 1837. The consideration of them involves the pure question, were they good or bad—constitutional or unconstitutional? This single question is now proposed; I go no farther at present. I maintain that no temporal tribunal can have cognizance of such an issue. I do not mean the question, which are the legal trustees, but the single one in regard to the acts of 1837, and I say, that of it no civil court has cognizance—that it belongs exclusively to the jurisdiction of the church.

"I know that in this part of the argument, I must encounter the denunciations of the opposite side. Why did you not institute regular process? Why did you not give us a trial, and a hearing? Why did you not do this, that, or the other thing? Of course, we expected them to make objection and find fault; we took it for granted, they would think that any thing else would have been more acceptable than just what we did. We disregard this clamor. But, as I am well aware, we here meet a much more formidable obstacle, the opinion of Judge Rogers, made up at the trial and propounded in his charge; which, of course, should be very seriously weighed; we should proceed with extreme caution, step by step, before arriving at a conclusion contrary to his. And I do not know that I have ever bestowed, upon any single subject, more thought than I have upon this, to view it in every aspect, to understand its bearing in every particular, that I might not be led into a false track, to avoid error in judgment, and the more especially because my opinion was contrary to that expressed in the charge. I will state the grounds of my conclusion, acknowledging, at the same time, that I am liable to error; possibly I am in error here. I think I am not. I am happy that Judge Rogers agrees with us in one important point. He says—

"'I have been requested by the respondents' counsel, to instruct you, that the introduction of lay delegates from Congregational establishments into the judicatories of the Presbyterian Church, was a violation of the fundamental principles of Presbyterianism, and in contravention of the act of the legislature of Pennsylvania, incorporating the trustees of the church; that any act permitting such introduction, would therefore have been void, although submitted to the Presbyteries. As an abstract question on this point, I give an affirmative answer, although, gentlemen, I am unable to see the bearing it has on the matter at issue in this cause.' (See Rogers' charge.)

"In another part of the charge, which I have not time to read, his Honour gives the opinion, that the act repealing the Plan of Union of 1801, was not liable to any legal objection, was entirely valid. His opinion, therefore, is in favour of the abrogation. Of this I am very glad, because the subject has been earnestly discussed, and the opposite counsel have pronounced the abrogation unconstitutional and void, and here is the key of the whole matter. From the assumption, that it was unconstitutional and void, the proceedings of the New School, in 1838, derive all their virtue. Now, let us endeavour, soberly, seriously, and quietly, to look at this matter. First, let us look at the *nature of the thing done;* that is to say, let us inquire whether it was a purely spiritual and moral act, or whether it had any touch or admixture of a civil nature. To determine this, I refer to the resolutions themselves, (vide ante, page 37.) I need call your strict attention to the third only, but the whole should be taken in connexion, and should be taken —I cannot too often repeat this—every word spoken should be taken as coming directly from the heart. You must consider these gentlemen to have meant what they have here said; if you do not, we cannot proceed at all.

"'In regard to the relation existing between the Presbyterian and Congregational Churches, the committee recommend the adoption of the following resolutions:'

"That is, in regard to the voluntary association hitherto existing; for I maintain, that whatever constitutes a voluntary association, this was one; and as such, it was treated throughout these acts. In fact, every religious association is voluntary.

"'1. That between these two branches of the American Church, there ought, in the judgment of this Assembly, to be maintained sentiments of mutual respect and esteem, and for that purpose, no reasonable effort should be omitted to preserve a perfectly good understanding between these branches of the Church of Christ.'

"Here is exactly the spirit which I have before described; we wish to abrogate the *Plan of Union,* but we are not going to denounce you as wanting in either doctrine and faith—or form of government and discipline—to assert that you are not a church. By no means. We desire to live in peace with you, and not to quarrel. If you choose to maintain your own form of worship, as before, we shall not, on that account, respect you the less. All that we say is, that Congregationalism and Presbyterianism are immiscible; when associated, one destroys the discipline of the other; the union produces disorder and confusion. You see a specimen of this in Mr. Bissil's case, (vide ante, p. 77,) by which the Assembly was distracted to the length of a protest. He was neither an elder or committee-man, and yet claimed a seat in the Assembly, and was admitted. This was only one occurrence, to be sure, yet it was in itself sufficient to condemn the *Plan of Union*. That is no longer an assembly of Presbyterians or Congregationalists, an assembly in which one man, coming through the channel of no church, claims a seat and all feel bound to admit him.

"'2. That it is expedient to continue the plan of friendly intercourse between this church and the Congregational Churches of New England, as it now exists.

"'3. But as the *Plan of Union* adopted for the New Settlements in 1801, was originally an unconstitutional act on the part of that Assembly, these important standing rules having never been submitted to the Presbyteries, and as they were totally destitute of authority, as proceeding from the General Association of Connecticut, which is invested with no power to legislate in such cases, and especially, to enact laws to regulate churches not within her limits; and as much confusion and irregularity have arisen from this unnatural and unconstitutional system of union, therefore it is resolved, that the act of Assembly of 1801, entitled a *Plan of Union*, be, and the same is hereby abrogated.'

"That plan was entirely voluntary from beginning to end. Now, in the judgment of the Assembly, sufficient grounds for the abrogation existed, and none can say that they did not exist. It is asserted that the plan was originally unconstitutional—they don't say, however, that it was a constitutional regulation, nor what character precisely it bore; but speak only of certain 'important standing rules,' whether constitutional rules or not is left undecided. It was a system of rules, and, as such, not binding, unless sent down to the Presbyteries, and by them approved. Admit that it was unconstitutional, and no doubt the Assembly had a right to abrogate it, and besides being lawful, the abrogation was certainly expedient, if the plan had introduced disorders, and threatened others still more serious. My clients say that it had. This being alleged by the Assembly, it was clearly an adequate ground for their proceeding. What objections are urged against the abrogation of the *Plan of Union?* On the supposition that the Plan was constitutional, it is contended, that it was a compact; as if, in agreements purely spiritual, there can be any consideration, by reason of which the compact can be enforced, though a party is desirous of rescinding it, because it is productive of mischief. When a compact or bargain is made between man and man, it is perfectly well understood that this is cognizable by the law; our constitution recognizes such contracts, and you have a doctrine of consideration applicable to them. You may have a contract, cognizable by the civil law, in which legal obligation mingles with that which is purely moral; but here you have no mixture, nothing whatever that is worldly; if binding at all, this agreement is binding only in conscience. Where you have nothing like a consideration, you can have no contract that can be enforced at law. You cannot keep joined by the sanction of law, elements which have come together on the principle of voluntary association. How, then, is such an agreement to be determined? Evidently by the will of the majority. The majority on either side may resolve that its operation shall cease. The resolution that I have read, then, abrogated the *Plan* of 1801; and it is abrogated—it ceases to have any force.

"Next comes a series of resolutions, resting on the supposition that the *Plan of Union* was unconstitutional and void, which are merely administrative. I do not mean to say whether they are legislative or judicial, because we do not find the government of the Presbyterian Church divided, like our national government, into three distinct and well defined branches, but I call them simply administrative, as they were passed to carry into effect that which was already adopted. I might have referred to the protest against the other, but leave that for the present. Here is the first of the resolutions:

"'That, in consequence of the abrogation, by this Assembly, of the "Plan of Union," of 1801, between it and the General Association of Connecticut, as utterly unconstitutional, and therefore null and void from the beginning, the Synods of Utica, Geneva, and Genesee, which were formed and attached to this body, under and in execution of said *Plan of Union*, be, and are hereby declared to be, out of the ecclesiastical connexion of the Presbyterian Church of the United States of America, and that they are not, in form or in fact, an integral portion of said church.' ante 46.

"On which resolution, the ayes and noes being called, it was carried by a majority of twenty-seven, one not voting. This then, so far as I have gone, declares simply the practical effect of the abrogation. If such was its practical effect, all that the General Assembly did, in passing this resolution, was purely administrative. They made known to their own churches, and gave notice to those associated with them, what the effect of the abrogation was, and then adjudicated accordingly. What is the next resolution?

"Particular attention is requested to the following—the second resolution:

"'That the solicitude of this Assembly on the whole subject and its urgency for the immediate decision of it, are greatly increased by reason of the great disorders which are ascertained to have prevailed in those Synods, (as well as that of the Western Reserve, against which a declarative resolution, similar to the first of these, has been passed during our present session,) *it being made clear to us* that even the *Plan of Union* itself, was never consistently carried into effect by those professing to act under it.' (p. 526, Argument.)

"Consider next, the nature of the body by which the act was done. This is the definition of a church: first, it is a voluntary association; secondly, established for divine worship and godly living, agreeably to the Holy Scriptures; 'and, thirdly, submitting to a certain form of government.' All these are material to its existence, and they are things which, as I understand the *Constitution of Pennsylvania, are by it left, entirely left, to the church itself, and to every man's conscience.* What says the constitution? This part of it has undergone no change in the recent revision; I wish I could say as much of the whole. The third section of the declaration of rights, guarantees certain religious rights, reserved out of those delegated to the government, not granted to the legislature, the judiciary, or the executive.

"'All men have a natural and indefeasible right to worship Almighty God according to the dictates of their own consciences; no man can of right be compelled to attend, erect, or support any place of worship, or to maintain any ministry, against his consent; no human authority can, in any case whatever, control or interfere with the rights of conscience; and no preference shall ever be given by law to any religious establishments or modes of worship.'

"This provision is carefully, studiously, and redundantly written, with a view to fence round conscience, to fence round the church, so that the civil authorities may not even look into them, unless to see that the peace of society is preserved; for all denominations are bound to obey the laws of the land, according to the precept of Christ, who inculcated every civil duty, the payment of every lawful tribute, but the conscience we hold sacred. What right has the civil power to interfere with conscience? If certain forms of government and discipline are part of the belief of a church, conscience has as much to do in the maintenance of these, as in the preservation of sound doctrine, and it is my right of conscience to choose such form of religion as I think best. If I do not like the denomination with which I am connected, at any moment I may depart; if the majority of the sect do not like me, they may turn me out. I don't know of any other rule. I might be turned out of the Presbyterian Church because I did not submit to its government and discipline, but the wide world would be before me, and I at liberty to choose my associates. If I desired to join the Congregationalists, I might do it. If I chose to attend as a hearer in a Presbyterian place of worship, I should not be excluded. It might be supposed, from the argument addressed to the court, that these men were turned out to starve—to starve for lack of spiritual food.

"When a question arises, in regard to any thing, which, in our judgment, interferes with the proper administration of discipline, which produces disorder and confusion, and endangers sound doctrine, how is it to be settled? Here comes into operation, the established principles of our republican constitution; for the government of the Presbyterian Church bears a close affinity to our national government. We may alter that constitution whenever we see fit. How is this to be done? By the vote of the majority. What rule will you establish other than that which prevails in the civil affairs of state—the rule that the majority shall govern? Whenever the majority decide any question, it is finally settled, unless you have recourse to some other principle of government. But the power of the majority is annulled, if their decision may be overborne, if it may be referred to another tribunal for correction. Look at the instance of these resolutions of the Assembly of 1837. How were they decided? By a majority. There can be no doubt of that. They concern discipline, government, and doctrine. Then it was a rightful decision. The majority alone could decide in such matters. And more than this, the decision being according to *conscience*, it is not our right to interfere. If the Assembly is left to itself, there is nothing to be apprehended. Alien interposition must lead to trouble and difficulty. If evil results from their measures, they alone are responsible for it. Now, let us get back to the plain language of the constitution; and where does it give to a civil court, the right of interference in matters of conscience? the right of deciding on spiritual concerns? If the civil power claims authority to prescribe or modify our religious creed, this is manifestly wrong—an usurpation of authority. Yet not more so, than an interference with ecclesiastical government and discipline. Every church has a right to settle these matters for itself; and that any other power should interpose to expound their creed, or to prescribe ecclesiastical laws, is destructive of spiritual liberty. It has become very much the fashion of late, to speak against creeds. If a creed is to be enforced by any measure of compulsion, let it be admitted that our liberties would be in greater danger than if mere civil rights were attacked —our rights of property, our security of life and limb. But if a church establishes a certain creed, what right have I to go in among its members, when I do not receive that creed? And what right to remain among them, when I cease to believe in its doctrines? I may be right and they wrong, but still I am no more at liberty to overturn the fundamental principles of their faith, because it does not agree with mine, than is a man to disturb the peace, because he does not like a republican government. The creed is but the agreed principle of association, the common faith, which is the ground of union. No man is bound to adopt the creed. But no man has a right to insist upon being a member of the society without adopting it, or to remain so, after he has ceased to believe in it.

"Now, in the constitution of the Presbyterian Church, we find the sanction of that authority which the church exercises in all its branches. I read from the 'preliminary principles' to the Form of Government, section eighth. 'Lastly, that if the preceding scriptural and rational principles be steadfastly adhered to, the vigor and strictness of its discipline will contribute to the glory and happiness of any church. Since ecclesiastical discipline must be purely *moral* or *spiritual* in its *object*, and *not attended with any civil effects*, it can derive no force whatever, but from its own justice, the approbation of an impartial public, and the countenance and blessing of the great Head of the church universal.' And again, chap. viii: 'These assemblies ought not to possess any civil jurisdiction, or to inflict any civil penalties. Their power is wholly moral or spiritual, and that only ministerial and declarative. They possess the right of requiring obedience to the laws of Christ, and of excluding the disobedient and disorderly from the privileges of the church.'

"Here, then, is the whole sanction of the jurisdiction exercised by the church—that moral or spiritual power which operates by means exclusively its own, and is not to be interfered with by the civil authority. How is the great frame work of the Presbyterian Church to be maintained in its established order? Here is that frame work. First, the congregation, governed by its own *Session;* then the *Presbytery;* thirdly, the *Synod;* and then a power above all the rest, the last object in the sight of a member of this church, the ultimate tribunal to which he can appeal—beyond it he knows no appeal—the *General Assembly*, which is just as supreme in ecclesiastical matters, as this honourable court is in civil affairs, the highest tribunal in the commonwealth of Pennsylvania. I call upon the court to say, is there any thing within the whole circle of this jurisdiction with which you would deem it right to interfere?

"These bodies we have been speaking of, are a law unto themselves. They owe no submission to any other tribunal. Is it lawful, is it consistent with spiritual liberty, that the church should be carried out of its own sphere, before a tribunal where prevails a law that is not applicable to it? and this, when the constitution forbids the civil authority to interfere in any manner with the rights of conscience? Talk of a violation of the constitution of the church! What greater violation of it, in its essence, its life, its soul, can there be, than dragging it before a tribunal entirely alien, here to compel its members to prove facts and to justify their own judgments upon those facts? Demand of any Presbyterian, that he point out the place where he finds authority for this proceeding. Where does he find the liberty given to refuse to submit to the judicatories of the church, and to refer his dispute to other tribunals? And how does he find that this is to be done? Is his appeal to be entertained *thus*—not by calling upon us to show our minutes, and prove that the question has already been decided by the church, but, without crediting our statements, putting no confidence in our sincerity, by summoning us, as if already convicted of an atrocious crime, to justify ourselves, or else suffer the penalty of being hunted down as we have been? Where in the Presbyterian constitution will you find this? There is no such thing.

"When the four Synods were disconnected, immediately their whole power ceased. Who can complain that four Synods are separated from a voluntary association? Even without any reason, the Assembly had a right to separate them, just as the Synods had a right to secede at pleasure. Whether they shall submit, is not a question to be entertained here. I mean to contend for that doctrine, to its whole extent, that it is not for this tribunal to look into the constitution of the church, and decide whether they have been rightfully excluded; that the question, who is of the church, belongs exclusively to the church to determine, and that when it has decided, the judgment is final.

"I propose now, to examine into the acts of the Assembly of 1837, upon their own footing, as if the court had the power to examine them. For if it can take cognizance of this and all other ecclesiastical bodies, we must submit, though we should like to be more thoroughly persuaded of its right of jurisdiction, and do not feel bound to conform to the verdict of a single jury, or the charge of a single judge, when entitled to the opinion of the entire tribunal. If here, finally, the jurisdiction be established, there can no longer be any question of its constitutionality. The decision of this court is conclusive. I propose, therefore, to examine the proceedings of 1837, and will end this part of the case with that examination, which will be brief. And I begin by asking, by what law will you judge those proceedings? According to whose judgment will you judge them? What will you appeal to as a ground of argument? I say, that the acts of the Assembly of 1837 were good. Why? Because I think they were right. What I think is, however, of no consequence to any one else. We must have some rule. What is it? The Presbyterian Church, by its highest tribunal, regularly constituted, has performed certain acts, deliberative and administrative; these, *prima facie*, are certainly good. But it is argued, that on some ground or other they are wrong. Now, let us look closely at this matter. I do not indeed feel myself competent to form an opinion on spiritual questions, for others. I go for one grand, consistent, constitutional principle, in all such matters, that every man must have exclusive cognizance of his own spiritual concerns. I cannot judge at all in regard to the spirit of another. How, then, am I to argue the question now proposed? Where will I find authority for my doctrines? Let us go to the constitution of the church. The constitution declares, that the power of the church and its jurisdiction, are purely spiritual and moral, and that the civil authority has no spiritual power. Now, how will you test these acts, and determine whether they are right or wrong? Will you appeal to the scriptures? No, that would be a profane use of them. They are not to be brought into court, except where the law requires their use, in the administration of oaths, or there are other cases of like necessity. But, if we do open the sacred volume, I may not understand it, as others do, and they have a perfect right to understand it for themselves. My understanding of it, is a guide for my own conduct only, not a directory for theirs. Yet the scriptures are the rock on which they believe, their peculiar system, their church, to be built. I am not competent to say how they understand their Bibles. But our only security is, on the foundation of the scriptures; from this rock we must endeavour to avoid being shifted or thrown off, each man upon his own individual responsibility."

Mr. Sergeant read Form of Government, chap. XII, sections 4 and 5, pages 335, 336, for the general powers entrusted to the General Assembly.

"To this body then is given entire authority over all the affairs of the church, authority to determine, not only the ends to be attained, but also the mode in which power shall be exercised for their attainment. They are to correct the errors of other judicatories, but are not themselves subject to correction. They have a general superintending jurisdiction. The act here complained of is, that four Synods have been laid down or dissolved, for what the Assembly considered a sufficient cause. (p. 556, argument.)

"The act of abrogation and the exscinding resolutions, while they state that irregularities had occurred, inconsistent with those laws which the Assembly was bound to enforce, do not allege any individual or criminal misconduct, but impute all the fault to the 'Plan of Union,' itself. Instead of laying the blame upon their adversaries alone, the Old School charge both sides with disorders, that were owing to the act of 1801, in which they had mutually concurred. Censure is cast as much upon the General Assembly as upon the General Association of Connecticut, and the Synods formed under that act. Was there any criminal charge made against the other side? Where can you show this, in either the resolution abrogating the 'Plan of Union,' or the resolutions by which the abrogation was carried out, to its legitimate consequences? There was no such censure pronounced upon those connected with the four Synods, as a judicial sentence involves? They were not charged with attachment to the Congregational Form of Government as a crime, and besides, they were immediately afterwards assured that no offence was imputed; that it was not intended to fasten upon them any stigma or reproach, for they were invited to come back, to prove not their innocence, but their Presbyterianism, with the promise, that whenever satisfactory proof upon that point had been given, their connexion with the church should be restored. Nay, still more to facilitate their return, they were told to apply for admission, to the nearest and most convenient Presbyteries. Each individual and church was told, 'we do not charge you with any crime—we do not say that you are unfit to associate with us; we say, on the contrary, that you are fit, if you are Presbyterians. Go to the nearest, most convenient Presbytery, and prove your orthodoxy.' I take it, that this was not a criminal proceeding at all. The exscinding resolutions profess to be, what I suppose those who passed them, understood that they were, the only legitimate and necessary consequences of the resolution, abrogating the 'Plan of Union.'

"In the next place, what was the whole effect of these exscinding resolutions, as they are commonly called? Did they impose a penalty upon any individual or collection of individuals? They merely dissolved the connexion of the four Synods, with the General Assembly, but not for contumacy; not for any crime alleged against them. All that the resolutions proposed was, to abandon them for the good of that church, under the protection of which they had thus far grown and flourished. The investigation had proceeded upon general grounds, without doing any prejudice to personal character. Not a reproachful word was uttered against the members of the four Synods, unless it was a reproach to say, that they were Congregationalists. I do not hold that to be a reproach. If the Assembly had a right to cut them off from the Presbyterian Church, because they preferred another

Form of Government and worship, it had no right to censure them for this preference. If being members of the church, and professing Presbyterianism, their belief and practice had been inconsistent with the doctrines and laws of the church, they might have been brought to trial; but if the Synods were formed, or under the Plan of 1801, and that Plan was so vicious as to render the connexion repugnant and detrimental to the church, this, in the estimation of the Assembly, for I do not myself say anything now about the Plan, or the formation of the four Synods; this might be, and was a good reason for separating them, but certainly was no reason for pronouncing a judicial sentence or imputing crime.

"Now, may it please your Honours, I have stated the nature of the act of exscision, and the Assembly's grounds for that act. Suppose the Assembly entertained the opinion expressed in the second resolution, which from the beginning, I had intended to notice, and now take up, as well for my original reasons, as for the construction upon it by Mr. Randall. Suppose it had been made clear to the Assembly, that disorders and irregularities prevailed in the four Synods, which were a proper subject for the application of the process provided in the constitution, which would have justified a criminal charge, and a citation to the bar of the Assembly for trial. Then there were two grounds of proceeding against the Synods; first, the unavoidable consequences of the *Plan of Union;* and secondly, the actual working of the Plan in those Synods. A proceeding resting on one ground might work their dissolution, without the imputation of any crime; a proceeding on the other ground might have resulted in the same thing, but must have been a criminal proceeding. Either one, independently of the other, might have been sufficient to blot them out of existence. But the first ground being sufficient, it alone is taken. Then the second ground is exhibited, not to support the measure of exscision, but to show the importance of having acted promptly. I would call your attention again to the statements made by the two committees, of the majority and minority. They both concurred in the opinion that a separation was indispensable." (See Minutes of the Assembly, for 1838.)

A few brief extracts from Mr. Sergeant's speech, in reference to the organization and action of the General Assembly, of 1838, will close this argument.

"The Assembly of 1838 met with full powers, excepting that the antecedent Assembly had sent down to it a moderator, whom, up to a certain period of their session, they had no right to remove. That moderator, and the clerks who were to assist him in the organization, were continued in office to perform certain acts, and until those were performed, they were beyond the reach of the New Assembly, or rather, that Assembly had not yet acquired the capacity to touch them.

* * * * * * * * * *

"Then we come to the conduct of the moderator, Dr. Elliott. He too had been appointed by the antecedent body, and sent down to preside in the new organization. The Assembly of 1838 were not accountable for him, nor he to them; I mean, that for a certain time, he was not accountable to them. The language of the rule is, that the last moderator shall preside until a new one is appointed. This rule has been read several times. Being one of great importance, it is laid down in two distinct places in the constitution. (Form of Gov., chap. XIX, sec. 3.) 'The moderator of the Presbytery shall be chosen from year to year, or at every meeting of the Presbytery, as the Presbytery may think best. The moderator of the Synod and of the General Assembly, shall be chosen at each meeting of those judicatories; and the moderator, and in case of his absence, another member appointed for the purpose, shall open the next meeting with a sermon, and shall hold the chair until a new moderator be chosen.' It is obvious that this means, till a new one can be chosen, and when that time arrives, is the next matter for our consideration.

"Here I would submit to your Honours, that when points of form acquire such power, as to be able to overturn a whole church, they must be very closely and strictly examined; they are equivalent in importance and force, to the greatest laws. Now, by the rules of the Assembly, what is the next thing to be done, after the report of the clerks on the roll? The rules provide, that the clerks, as a committee of commissions, shall examine the commissions presented, and report the names of the undoubted members, who shall then take their seats and proceed to business; but they do not stop here. They direct, that the first thing which the house shall do, after being thus ready for business, shall be the appointment of a committee of elections. Well, I suppose that is equivalent to saying, that nothing else shall be done, until a committee of elections has been appointed. I interpret the whole of these provisions together, as ordering that the several things which they direct to be done, shall all be done before the Assembly proceed to the choice of a new moderator. I am not inquiring, at present, into the power of the Assembly to make such rules. I do not ask what was their effect, but simply what they were? There was, in 1826, a change in the form prescribed by the constitution, for examining commissions and enrolling the names. Previously, it had been required that the commissions should be publicly read, but then it was ordered that they should be only examined. After the adoption of this change by the Presbyteries, it was also

"'*Resolved,* That so soon as the alteration proposed in the 7th item, above enumerated, shall appear to have been constitutionally adopted by the Presbyteries, the following rules of the Assembly shall be in force.

"'1. Immediately after each Assembly is constituted with prayer, the moderator shall appoint a *committee of commissions.'*

"This committee report the regular commissioners to the house.

"'5. The first act of the Assembly, when thus ready for business, shall be the appointment of a *committee of elections,* whose duty is to examine all informal and unconstitutional commissions, and report on the same as soon as practicable.' (p. 150.) These are the sum of the provisions made by these standing rules. They are as strong and binding as any articles in the constitution. Now it was clearly not in the power of the house to do any thing, until a committee of *elections* had been appointed. The old moderator was continued there to direct and see that the rules were complied with. If Dr. Patton, Dr. Mason, Mr. Squier, or anybody else, arise and propose some business, differing from that required by the rule, the moderator is bound to tell them, respectfully, that they are all out of order. Now, there could be no appeal from the chair, until the rules of the house were complied with; there was nothing on which an appeal could arise, and no *body* by whom an appeal could be decided. But again, there is a provision beyond this, a provision for the vacancy of the chair. Who shall put a question then? To enable any body not in the chair, to assume the duty of presiding, it is absolutely essential, that the chair should first be vacant. So long as it is occupied *de facto,* as regards the members, it is occupied *de jure,* and nobody else than the actual occupant can propose any business to the house. If the chair is vacant, of course that is an emergency requiring a new rule. Then the next person in the eyes of the members, as they all look towards the chair, the clerk must put any resolution offered, and this until the chair is filled. All these rules are essential to the due transaction of business.

"To return to the Assembly of 1838. I say, that until the committee of elections had been appointed, the body was in the hands of the officers of the preceding year. They were not under its control, or responsible to it, until the organization was complete, and it was clothed with its full and legitimate powers. And I say further, that Dr. Elliott could not entertain a motion or appeal; that he had been placed in the chair merely to keep order, and to perform a specific duty, ending with the organization, which was to be completed by the appointment of a committee of elections. Now, it is clearly in evidence, that Dr. Elliott was keeping very good order, as any body must acknowledge who reads he provision, which has been referred to. But if it were otherwise—if any thing improper had been done by Dr. Elliott, this was not to be visited upon the body which had no control over him, which as I contend, could not remove him. Now, I am attempting to vindicate the majority of the Assembly and Dr. Elliott; to establish the point that it was not consistent with justice, for them to depart in the smallest degree from the rules prescribed, the five rules which were to govern in the organization of the body, and at the same time to vindicate the rules themselves; showing, that when a contest was expected, and a black cloud lowered over them, sufficient to envelope the whole body in storm; when Dr. Elliott knew that the elements of discord and strife were gathering in fury, and unless pent up, would break forth in the midst of those who had collected *in the house* of prayer for *religious worship;* that the Assembly was composed of all descriptions of people, of friends and foes; of those belonging to the household of strangers, and of persons claiming to be of the household, though their title was disputed; this was a sufficient, an imperative reason, why he should not swerve for a single instant from the precise letter of his instructions. From the five rules of the Presbyterian law book, which are to govern the church, it is plain that no questions could be put but such as are incident to the organization, at this stage of progress; none such were put. Dr. Patton's motion not being of this nature, it was disallowed. Judge Rogers says, that in deciding it out of order, the *moderator was right.* Next, Dr. Mason made a motion, it was declared out of order; he appealed—the appeal was not sustained. In these several motions, all acquiesced. Mr. Squier moved, but was out of order, too. Next, Mr. Cleaveland rises and delivers a written speech. That paper has been secreted and suppressed. It is unfortunate for the respondents. Instead of having the very words uttered, we are left to select and interpret the document from the testimony of hearers. Here we put one important question. In such circumstances, in such a crowd and excitement, was it proper, was it possible, to pursue the old business of the Assembly then on hand, correctly and suitably, much less to introduce a new, untried, tumultuous, if not revolutionary item?" (For the details of this transaction, we must refer to Sergeant's argument, p. 574, and in Miller's Church Case.) Mr. Hubbel's remarks on the same side are clear and convincing, and the conclusive observations of Judge Gibson, in his opinion of the court. The several steps by which the New School, pursuing a concerted scheme through Mr. Cleaveland, as their chief organ for the purpose, exhibits a series of gross departures from order and constitutional rule, through all their progress, tending only to demonstrate the extravagance of their designs, and the wildness and folly of their measures.

CHAPTER XXIV.

Introductory Remarks—The Contrast—Including eight principal points in Theology—Old School and New School compared—I. Confession of Faith, &c.—II. Extracts from New School Books.

THAT the spirit and the habit of wild and reckless speculation upon theological subjects, have prevailed to a very great extent within the Presbyterian Church, during the last twenty or thirty years, is perfectly notorious. The question presented here, is, how far heretical and unsound opinions have been published and circulated in the Presbyterian Church, by her ministers and members, in conflict with her Confession of Faith, her catechisms and her church policy, thus offering violence to her constitution, impairing her character and influence, and demanding from her supreme judicatory an appropriate remedy. In all similar cases, the avowed sentiments of prominent leaders constitute the standard of truth, and the evidence of the facts upon which the investigation is to rest, and they form the test by which the party held in default must be tried and estimated, their guilt graduated, and the award proportioned.

To bring the unsound, in the shortest and easiest manner possible, to the constitutional touch-stone, we shall present, in the form of extracts from the writings and speculations of New School men, some of their opinions on the fundamental points of truth revealed in the Sacred Scriptures, and contrast them, item by item, with the doctrines contained in the Confession of Faith and catechisms of the church, as based upon the word of God. This is the only method we can properly pursue in ascertaining the purity and fidelity, or detecting the unsoundness and criminality, of gospel ministers and professing Christians in our ecclesiastical connexion. It is perfectly just to infer, as a general principle, that the followers of those who are recognized as leaders in theological opinions and church policy, agree with their leaders; and they are, therefore, in common with them, responsible for whatever of truth, or of error, they may hold and propagate. Pursuing this course, we shall place on opposite pages or columns, under the several heads, *First*, the doctrines of our Confession and Standards. *Second,* the published opinions of New School theologians belonging to the Presbyterian Church. From the contrast, every reader may easily decide as to the agreement or discrepancy between these different forms of expression.

All we have to do, is to see that the members *of our own church* do not violate *our own system;* that they observe and comply with their sacred obligations to the church, to one another, and to God.

With other denominations, of whatever name or characteristics, we have no quarrel, but stand in a peaceful, friendly alliance. We are not bound to favour their notions, nor they ours. Whatever they or we publish to the world, becomes common property, which may be criticised and controverted before the great public tribunal, which tests and decides every question, and by public sentiment, the great arbiter in human affairs, we and they stand or fall. We claim no exemption from the common amenabilities of the heart and the pen to this decisive tribunal.

In this exhibition, it is of little importance to show, as other writers have attempted to do, what a diversity of tongues have spoken, what a confusion of opinions on religious subjects has been uttered, by other denominations and speculators through the land. Such a review would teach us what kind of company the New School party have kept; who were probably their associates, their guides, and seducers into error, into the very kennels of contamination and guilt, which they had solemnly promised to avoid. For the sake of brevity, we shall restrict our view to a few specimens on each side of the contrast.

OLD SCHOOL, OR CONFESSION OF FAITH.

Federal Headship of Adam.

"The covenant being made with Adam, as a public person, *not for himself only*, but *for his posterity*, *all mankind* descending from him by ordinary generation, *sinned in him, and fell with him*, in that first transgression." Larger Catechism, question 22. "They being *the root* of all mankind, the guilt of this sin was *imputed*, and the death in sin and corrupted nature *conveyed to all their posterity*, descending from them by ordinary generation." Confession of Faith, chap. vi, sec. 3.

"Original sin is conveyed from our first parents unto their posterity, by natural generation, so as all that proceed from them in that way, are conceived and born in sin." Larger Catechism, question 26.

NEW SCHOOL.

Federal Headship of Adam.

"That Adam was not the covenant head or federal representative of his posterity, and sustained no other relation to them, than that which subsists between every parent and his offspring."

"It has been supposed by many, that there was a covenant made with Adam, such as this, that if *he continued to obey* the law for a limited period, all *his posterity* should be confirmed in holiness and happiness forever. What the reason is for this belief, I am unable to ascertain. I am not aware that the doctrine is taught in the Bible. I suppose that mankind were all originally under a covenant of works, and that Adam *was not* so their *head* or *representative*, that his obedience or disobedience, involved them irresistibly in sin and condemnation, irrespective of their own acts." Finney's Lectures.

"Nothing is said of a covenant with him," that is, Adam. "No where in Scripture is the term covenant applied to any transaction with Adam. All that is established here, is the simple fact, that Adam sinned, and that this made it certain that all his posterity would be sinners. Beyond this, the language of the apostle does not go; and all else that has been said of this, is the result of mere philosophical speculation."*

Mr. Barnes again: "A comparison is also instituted between Adam and Christ, 1 Cor. 15, 22, 25. The reason is, *not* that Adam was the *representative* or *federal head* of the human race, about which the apostle says nothing, and which is not even implied, but that *he* was the *first* of the *race*—he was the fountain, the head, the father; and the consequences of that first act, introducing sin into the world, could be seen every where. The words *representative* and *federal* head, are never applied to Adam in the Bible. The reason is, that the word representative implies an idea which could not have existed in the case, *the consent of those who are represented*. Besides, the Bible does not teach that they *acted in him* and *by him*, or that he acted for them. No passage has ever yet been found that stated this doctrine."

* Barnes' Notes on Romans, first edition, p. 128.

Again, Barnes' sermon: "Sinners have no federal relation to Adam, and are not answerable for his guilt."

Old Divinity—Confession of Faith.

Imputation.

"The sinfulness of that estate whereinto man fell, consisteth in *the guilt of Adam's first sin*, the want of that righteousness wherein he was created, and the corruption of his nature, whereby he is utterly indisposed, disabled, and made opposite to all that is spiritually good, and wholly inclined to all evil, and that continually, which is *commonly called original sin*, and *from which* do *proceed all* actual transgressions." Question 25, Larger Catechism.

"They being the root of all mankind, *the guilt of this sin was imputed*, and the *death in sin and corrupted nature conveyed* to all *their posterity*," &c. Confession of Faith, sec. 3.

Dr. Beecher, though generally wrong, sometimes unwittingly testifies against himself and his party:

"The Reformers," says he, "with one accord, taught that the *sin of Adam was imputed to all his posterity*, and that a *corrupt nature descends from him*, to every one of his posterity, in consequence of which infants are unholy, unfit for heaven, and justly exposed to future punishment." "Our puritan fathers," he continues, "adhered to the doctrine of original sin, as consisting in the imputation of

New School.

No Imputation.

Mr. Barnes, in his Sermon on the Way of Salvation, says, "Sinners have no federal relation to Adam. The notion of *imputation* is an invention of modern times."

Mr. Finney, in his Lectures, says, "The truth is, Adam was the *natural head* of the human race—from the *relation* in which he stood as their *natural head*, as a matter of fact, his sin has resulted in the sin and ruin of his posterity."

Barnes, p. 95, Notes on the Romans, says, "I have examined all the passages where the word imputation occurs in the Old Testament, and have come to the conclusion, that there is not one in which the word is used in the sense of *reckoning* or *imputing* to a man that which does not strictly belong to him, or of charging on him that which ought not to be charged on him, as a matter of personal right. The word is never used to denote *imputing* in the sense of *transferring*, or of charging that on one which does not properly belong to him. The same is the case in the New Testament. The word occurs about forty times, and in a similar signification. No doctrine of transferring, or of setting over to a man, what does not properly belong to him, be it sin or holi-

Adam's sin, and in hereditary depravity; and this continued to be the received doctrine of the churches of New England, until after the time of *Edwards.* He adopted the views of the Reformers on the subject of original sin, as consisting in the imputation of Adam's sin, and a depraved nature, transmitted by descent." Spirit of the Pilgrims for 1828.

ness, can be derived, therefore, from this word." Men are "subject to pain, and death, and depravity, as the consequence of his (Adam's) sin, he being the head, fountain, father, or root of the race, and having secured, as a certain result, that all the race will be sinners also, such being the organization of the great society of which he was the head and father. The drunkard," says he, "secures a result, commonly, that his family will be reduced to beggary, want, and woe. A pirate or a traitor will whelm, not himself only, but his family, in ruin. Such is the great law or constitution on which society is now organized; and we are not to be surprised, that the *same principle* occurred in the primary organization of human affairs."

Mr. Barnes, Notes, 7th edition, pp. 121–222, says, "That doctrine, (imputation) is nothing but an effort to explain the manner of an event which the apostle did not think it proper to attempt to explain. That doctrine is, in fact, no explanation. It is introducing an additional difficulty. For, to say that I am blameworthy, or ill-deserving, for a sin in which I had no agency, is no explanation, but is involving me in an additional difficulty, still more perplexing, to ascertain how such a doctrine can possibly be just." "Christianity does not charge on men crimes of which they are not guilty. It does not say, as I suppose, that the sinner is held to be personally answerable for the transgressions of Adam, or of any other man." Way of Salvation.

"It is admitted, that this language does not accord with that used on the same subject in the *Confession of Faith*, and in other standards of doctrine. The main difference is, that it is difficult to affix any clear and definite meaning to the expression, 'we sinned in him, and fell with him.' It is manifest, so far as it is capable of interpretation, that it is intended to convey the idea, not that the sin of Adam is *imputed* to us, or set over to our account, but that there was a personal *identity*, constituted between Adam and his posterity, so that it was really *our act* and *ours only*, after all, that is chargeable on us. This was the idea of Edwards. The notion of *imputing sin*, is an invention of modern times, and it is not, it is believed, the doctrine of the Confession of Faith.

"Christianity affirms the fact, that in connexion with the sin of Adam, or as a result, all moral agents in this world will sin, and sinning will die. Rom. v, 12–19. It does not, however, affirm any thing about the *mode* in which this would be done. There are many ways conceivable in which that sin might secure the result, as there are many ways in which all similar *facts* may be explained. The drunkard commonly secures as a result, the fact that his family will be beggared, illiterate, perhaps profane or intemperate. Both facts are evidently to be explained *on the same principle* as a part of moral government."

"When Paul," says he, "states a simple fact, men often advance a *theory*. A melancholy instance of this we have in the account which the apostle gives, chap. v, about the effect of the sin of Adam. . . They have sought for a theory to account for it. And many suppose they have found it in the doctrine, that the sin of Adam is *imputed*, or set over, by an arbitrary arrangement, to beings otherwise innocent, and that they are held to be responsible for a deed committed by a man thousands of years before they were born. This is the *theory*, and men insensibly forget that it is mere *theory*."

OLD DIVINITY—CONFESSION OF FAITH.

Moral state of Infants.

"They being the root of all mankind, the guilt of this sin was imputed, and the same death in sin and *corrupted nature, conveyed to all their posterity*, descending from them by ordinary *generation*." Confession of Faith, chap. 6, sec. 3.

"Original sin is conveyed from our first parents, *unto their posterity*, by natural generation, so as all that proceed from them in that way, are concieved and born in sin." Larger Catechism, question 26.

NEW SCHOOL.

State of Infants—No Moral Character.

"It is a question alike pertinent and important, whether in the incipient period of infancy and childhood, there can be any *moral character* whatever, possessed. Moral character, is character acquired by acts of a moral nature. Moral acts, are those acts which are contemplated by the law, prescribing the rule of human conduct." "It is obvious, that in infancy and incipient childhood, when none of the actions are deliberate, or the result of motive, operating in connexion with the knowledge of law, and of the great end of all human actions, no moral character can appropriately be predicated." "Properly speaking, therefore, we can predicate of it, neither sin or holiness, personally considered." Duffield on Regeneration, pp., 377—78—79.

Again, p. 389: "There is no manner of necessity, in order to account for the death of infants, to suppose that the sin of Adam became their personal sin, either in respect of its act, or of its *ill desert.*"

Finney says: "Children universally adopt the principle of *selfishness,* because they possess *human nature,* but *not because human nature is itself sinful.*" Sermons.

"Temptation alone is sufficient, under present circumstances." Duffield's Regeneration.

"The infant is placed in a rebellious world, subject to the influence of ignorance, with very limited and imperfect experience, and liable to the strong impulses of appetite and passion. Instinct, animal sensation, constitutional susceptibilities, create an impulse, which not being counteracted by moral considerations or gracious influence, lead the will in a wrong direction, and to wrong objects." Duffield on Regeneration, pp. 310—379—380.

Mr. Finney again says: "Here are two systems, the *one* maintains that infants have no moral character at all, until they have committed actual transgression; that their first moral actions are universally sinful, but that previous to moral action, they are *neither sinful nor holy*; that, as they have no moral character, they deserve neither praise nor blame, *neither life nor death*, at the hand of God. God might annihilate them without injustice, or he may bestow upon them eternal life, as a free and unearned gift. The other system maintains that infants have a sinful nature which they have inherited from Adam." Sermons.

Old Divinity—Confession of Faith—Scripture.

Depravity.

Rom. 5, 12, 21. "As by one man sin entered into the world, and death by sin, so death passed upon all men, for that all have sinned." Larger Catechism—-before recited in full.

Man's nature is *so corrupted by the fall*, "that he is utterly *indisposed*, *disabled*, and *made opposite* unto all that is spiritually good and *wholly inclined to all evil*, and that continually, which is commonly called *original sin*, and from which do proceed all actual transgressions." "And God saw that the wickedness of man was great in the earth, and every imagination of the thoughts of his heart was only evil continually." Genesis, 6, 5. Job 14, 4. "Who can bring a clean thing out an unclean? Not one." Ps. 51, 5. "Behold I was shapen in iniquity, and in sin did my mother concieve me."

Dr. Beecher states the views of the reformers and of the New England churches, on the subject of original sin, as formerly

New School.

Depravity.

"All sin consists *in voluntary acts*, no innate, inherent or derived corruption in human nature.

"In order to admit the *sinfulness* of nature, we must believe sin to consist in the substance of the constitution, instead of *voluntary action*, which is impossible." Sermons, (p. 158) Finney.

"Holiness, or sin, which is its opposite, has a direct and immediate reference to those voluntary *acts* and *exercises*, which the law is designed to secure or prevent." Duffield on Regeneration.

Finney says: "All depravity is *voluntary*, consisting in *voluntary* transgression. It is the sinner's *own act*; something of his *own creation*. That over which he has a perfect *control*, and for which he is entirely responsible." Sermons.

"A depraved nature can no more exist without *voluntary* agency and accountability, than a material nature can exist without solidity and extension." Beecher.

consisting in the imputation of Adam's sin, *and a depraved nature transmitted by descent,* but it is changed, and *now is wholly voluntary, and consists in a transgression of the law.*" Spirit of the Pilgrims, 1828.

"From this original corruption, whereby we are utterly indisposed, disabled, and made opposite to all good, and wholly inclined to all evil, do proceed *all actual transgressions!*" Confession of Faith. "The carnal mind is enmity against God, and is not subject to the law of God, neither indeed can be." Romans. "The natural man discerneth not the things of the spirit of God." Romans. "For I know that in me (that is, in my flesh) dwelleth no good thing." Romans, 7, 18, &c. "And were by nature the children of wrath, even as others." Ephesians, 2, 3.

"Now, if I do that I would not, it is no more I that do it, but *sin that dwelleth in me.*" Romans.

"If therefore," says Dr. Beecher, "man is depraved by nature, it is a voluntary and accountable nature, which is depraved, exercised in disobedience to the law of God. Native depravity, then, is a state of the affections, in a voluntary accountable creature." Sermon on the Native Character of Man.

"When Adam was first created and awoke into being, before he had obeyed or disobeyed his Maker, he could have had no moral character at all; he had exercised no affections, no desires, nor put forth any actions." Sermons, p. 10, 11, Finney.

Dr. Lansing on Regeneration, says: "nothing more is necessary for God to do for you, than to make you willing, and hence your *voluntary* opposition to him is the only *obstacle* to your salvation."

Barnes, with approbation, gives the following as the meaning of the Confession of Faith, and its framers, a very false construction. "They affirm that the *difficulty is in the will.* Nor do they mention any *other difficulty or obstacle* in the way of man's conversion; evidently implying that if *the will were right, there were no other obstacle.*"

"Duffield, after much apparent search, adopts the same theory, "that man's (disability) difficulty, moral defect, 'consists in acts and exercises,' or 'in some deranged and inappropriate exercises.' "

Again: "We are infallibly directed in making our estimate of human depravity, to have *exclusive regard to the acts and exercises* of the human soul." Man's "depravity consists in the misdirection and inappropriate *exercise* of his faculties, not in *wrong faculties inherited.*" Regeneration, p. 310, &c.

Finney teaches, in his sermon on total depravity, "some persons have spoken of depravity, and of the pollution of our nature, as if there were some moral depravity *cleaving to* or *incorporated with,* the very substance of our being. Now this is to talk utter nonsense. If such a depravity were possible, it would not be moral, but physical depravity. It could not be a depravity for which we are blameworthy. It could not be a sinful depravity. It would be a disease and not a crime. Moral depravity is a quality of *voluntary* action. It is not meant that there are appetites or *propensities* that are *constitutional,* which are enmity against God. I do not mean that there is some constitutional depravity which lies back, and is the cause of actual transgression. By total depravity, I do not mean that there is any sin in human beings, or in any other beings, separate from actual transgression."

Dr. Lansing says, "that all sin consists in the voluntary exercises of the sinning agent." Sermon on Inability.

Barnes says, "all sin consists in voluntary action." Sermon on Salvation. In his note upon Romans, chapter viii, 7th verse—"The carnal mind is enmity against God"—he says: "It does not mean the *mind itself*, the intellect or the will; it does not suppose that the mind or soul is physically depraved, or opposed to God, but it means that the minding of the things of the flesh, giving to them supreme attention, is hostility to God."

"The heart is deceitful above all things, and desperately wicked." Jeremiah, xvii, 9.

Old Divinity—Confession and Catechisms.

Man's Inability.

Confession of Faith, chap. ix. sec. 3. "Man, by his fall into a state of sin, *hath wholly lost all ability of will to any spiritual good, accompanying salvation*, so as a natural man, being altogether averse from that which is good, and dead in sin, is not able, *by his own strength*, to convert himself, or to prepare himself, thereunto."

"The sinfulness of that state whereinto man fell, consists . . . . . *in the* corruption of his nature, whereby he is utterly *disabled*, and made opposite to all that is spiritually good." Lar. Cat., question 26.

"Can the Ethiopean change his skin, or the leopard his spots? Then may ye also do good that are accustomed to do evil." Jeremiah xiii, 23.

"No man can come to me, except the Father who hath sent me, draw him." John vi, 44.

"The carnal mind is not sub-

New School.

Man's entire ability, &c.

Dr. Beecher's *Views in Theology*, pp. 30, 31. "That man possesses, since the fall, the powers of agency requisite to obligation, *on the ground of the possibility of obedience*, is a matter of notoriety. Not one of the powers of mind, which constituted ability before the fall, has been obliterated by that event. All that has ever been conceived, or that can now be conceived, as entering into the constitution of a free agent, capable of choosing life or death, or which did exist in Adam, when he could and did obey, yet mutable, survived the fall."

Page 47. "This *doctrine*, of the *natural ability of choice commensurate with obligation*, has been, and is, the received doctrine of the universal orthodox church, from the primitive age down to this day."

Duffield on Regeneration, p. 542. "Not much less deluding are the system and tactics of

ject to the law of God—neither, indeed, can be." "Without me, ye can do nothing." John v, 4, 5.

"The natural man discerneth not the things of the spirit of God, *neither can* he know them, because they are spiritually discerned." 1 Cor. ii, 14.

"The flesh lusteth against the spirit, and the spirit against the flesh; so that ye cannot do the things that ye would."

those, who, fearing to invade the province of the spirit, are careful to remind the sinner, that he is utterly unable, by his own unassisted powers, either to believe or to repent, to the saving of his soul. *It might as truly be said, that he cannot rise and walk,* by his own unassisted powers."

Finney says, Sermons, &c., pp. 18, 37, 38: "As God requires men to make themselves a new heart, on pain of eternal death, it is the strongest possible evidence, that they are able to do it: to say he has commanded them to do it, without telling them they *are able,* is consummate trifling. . . . . If the sinner ever has a new heart, he must obey the command of the text, and make it himself." "Sinner! instead of waiting and praying for God to change your heart, you should at once summon up your powers, put forth the effort, and change the governing preferences of your mind."

Dr. Beecher, p. 67, (Views in Theology,) defines natural ability to be "the plenary powers of a free agent—the intellectual and moral faculties which God has given to man, *commensurate with his requirements.*"

Old Divinity.

Regeneration.

"Except a man be born again, he cannot see the kingdom of God." John iii, 3.

"A new heart will I give you,

New School.

Regeneration.

Mr. Finney says: "A change of heart (regeneration) then, consists in changing the controlling preference of the mind,

and a new spirit will I put within you." Ezekiel xxxvi, 26.

"Create in me a clean heart, O God, and renew a right spirit within me." Psalms li, 10.

"Which were born, not of blood, nor of the will of the flesh, nor of the will of man, but of God." John i, 13.

"He saved us, by the washing of regeneration, and renewing of the Holy Ghost." Titus iii, 5.

"And you hath he quickened, who were dead in trespasses and sins." Ephesians ii, 1.

"For we are his workmanship, created in Christ Jesus. . . . If any man be in Christ, he is a new creature, old things are passed away, and all things are become new." See Confession of Faith, chap. x, sec. 1.

"All those whom God hath predestinated unto life, and those only, he is pleased, in his appointed and accepted time, effectually to call by his word and spirit, out of that state of sin and death, in which they are by nature, to grace and salvation, by Jesus Christ; enlightening their minds, spiritually and savingly, to understand the things of God, taking away their heart of stone and giving unto them a heart of flesh, renewing their wills, and by his almighty power, determining them to that which is good, and effectually drawing them to Jesus Christ, yet so as they come most freely, being made willing by his grace."

"This effectual call is of God's free and special grace alone; not from any thing at all in regard to the end of pursuit. The selfish heart is a preference of self interest to the glory of God, and the interests of his kingdom. A new heart consists in a preference of the glory of God, and the interests of his kingdom to one's own happiness. . . . . It is a change in the choice of a supreme ruler.

Duffield says: "It is going altogether beyond the analogy in the case, to assert that there is in regeneration, the injection, infusion, implantation or creation, of a new principle of spiritual life." "Whenever the spirit of God excites and secures in the mind and heart of man, those acts and emotions which are appropriate to his rational soul, *i. e.*, when they are directed to God, as his supreme good and chief end, he is renewed, regenerated, born again." As to the mode, hear him: "Shall we suppose that God cannot do with sinners, in reference to himself, what one man has done with another? that a physical efficiency is necessary, to make the sinner willing to confide in him, and repent of his rebellion? To suppose this is, in fact, to attribute a moral influence to a man more potent than that which, in such a case, it would be requisite God should exert. It would be in effect, to say, that man can subdue his foe, and by an appropriate moral influence convert him into a friend: but that God cannot convert his enemy and bring him to believe,

foreseen in man, who is altogether passive therein, until, being quickened and renewed by the Holy Spirit, he is thereby enabled to answer this call, and to embrace the grace offered and conveyed in it."

The language of the New Testament, its figures and descriptions, all imply and represent a change of nature, such as being born again, becoming new creatures, rising from the dead, being renewed in the spirit of the mind, dying to sin and living to righteousness, putting off the old man, and putting on the new man, being ingrafted into a new stock, having a divine seed implanted in the heart, being made partakers of the divine nature.

"Who is altogether passive therein"—passive in the work—passive in the act of regeneration.

except he puts forth his physical power, and literally creates him over again." pp., 492, 493. "Motives, moral suasion, produces the change."

Mr. Finney says; "The spirit pours the expostulation home with such power, that the sinner turns." . . "Now, in speaking of this change, it is perfectly proper to say, that the spirit turned him, just as you would say of a man who had persuaded another to change his mind on the subject of politics; that he had converted him and brought him over. Some have doubted this, and supposed that it is equivalent to denying the spirit's agency, altogether, to maintain that he converts sinners by motives." Sermons, pp., 21, 27, 28, 30, &c.

Old School Divinity.

Reconciliation—Redemption—Satisfaction of Christ—Summed up in Atonement.

Romans, v, 19. "For as by one man's disobedience, many were made sinners, so by the obedience of one, shall many be made righteous."

Hebrews, ix, 14. "How much more shall the blood of Christ, who, through the eternal spirit, offered himself without spot to God, purge your conscience from dead works, to serve the living God."

Romans, iii, 25, 26. "Whom God hath set forth, to be a propitiation, through faith in his blood, to declare his righteous-

New School Divinity.

1. *Christ not the legal substiute of sinners.* 2. *Did not endure the penalty of the law in their behalf.* 3. *Did not pay the debt of his people.*

The following extracts from Dr. Beman's Sermons on the Atonement, and from others on kindred topics, will exhibit clearly the false notions of New School men, on this subject.

"The law can have no penal demand, except against the offender. With a substitute, it has no concern; and though a thousand substitutes should die, the law in itself, considered and left to its own natural operation, would have the same demand

ness for the remission of sins, that are past, through the forbearance of God; to declare, I say, at this time, his righteousness; that he might be just, and the justifier of him which believeth in Jesus."

Hebrews, x, 14. "For by one offering, he hath perfected forever them that are sanctified."

1 Peter, iii, 18. "For Christ also hath once suffered for sins, the just for the unjust, that he might bring us to God, being put to death in the flesh, but quickened by the spirit."

See Confession of Faith, chap. viii, sec. 5. "The Lord Jesus Christ, by his perfect obedience, and sacrifice of himself, which he, through the eternal spirit, once offered up unto God, hath fully satisfied the justice of his father, and purchased not only reconciliation, but an everlasting inheritance in the kingdom of heaven, for all those whom the Father hath given unto him." "For he hath made him who knew no sin, to be made sin for us, that we might be made the righteousness of God in him."

We observe here, by way of explanation, that by Christ's enduring the penalty of the law, is not meant that he endured literally the same sufferings, either in kind or in duration, which would have been inflicted upon the sinner, if a saviour had not been provided. In a penalty, some things are essential—others incidental. It was essential to the penalty, that Christ should suffer a violent and ignominious death, but upon the transgressor, which it always had. This claim can never be invalidated; this penal demand can never be extinguished." "Others," he says, "contend that the real penalty of the law was inflicted upon Christ, and at the same time acknowledge, that the sufferings of Christ were not the same, in nature or degree, as those sufferings which were threatened against the transgressor. The words of our text are considered by many, as furnishing unequivocal testimony to the fact, that Christ endured the penalty of the law, in the room of his people. 'Christ hath redeemed us from the curse of the law, being made a curse for us.' The apostle tells us in what sense he was made a curse for us. 'Cursed is every one that hangeth on a tree.' Believers are saved from the curse or penalty of the law, by the consideration that Christ was made a curse for them, in another and very different sense. He was made a curse, inasmuch as he suffered, in order to open the door of hope to man, the pains and ignomy of crucifixion; he hung upon a tree! he died as one accursed."

He adds afterwards, "If it should be said, that the divine veracity was pledged to execute the law, we reply, that the divine veracity can find no support in that kind of infliction of the curse, which is here supposed. A substantial execution of the law, an endurance of the penalty, so far as the nature of

whether he should die by decapitation, or by crucifixion, was incidental. It was essential that he should suffer for our sins, but how long his sufferings should continue, was incidental. If inflicted upon us, they must necessarily be eternal, because sin is an infinite evil, and finite beings cannot endure the punishment which is due to it, except by an eternal duration. But from the infinite dignity of Christ's character, the penal demands of the law could be fully answered by his suffering ever so short a time. The imputation of our sins to Christ, does not involve a transfer of moral character, but only of legal responsibility. In being made sin for us, Christ did not become personally a sinner. What is intended, then, by Christ's suffering the penalty of the law as our substitute is, that in law he assumed our place, whereby he fully satisfied divine justice, being made a curse for us." Wood's Old and New Divinity, pp. 91, 92. In support of these passages, we might refer to an impressive catalogue of wise and holy men, of ages past, holding these views, Bellamy, Bates, Owen, Beza, Witherspoon, Edwards, Davies, Finley, and a long list of like character.

the case admitted or required, an infliction of suffering, not upon the transgressor, but upon a surety, when the law had not made the most distant allusion to a surety, certainly has much more the appearance of an evasion, than execution, of the law. As to imputation, he says, we do deny that the sins of men, or of any part of our race, were so transferred to Christ, that they became his sins, or were so reckoned to him, that he sustained their legal responsibilities." Again, "There is nothing in the character of Christ's sufferings, which can affect or modify the penalty of the law. These sufferings were not legal. They constituted no part of that curse which was threatened against the transgressor." pp. 64, 65. "The penalty of the law, strictly speaking, was not inflicted at all; for this penalty in which was embodied the principles of distributive justice, required the death of the sinner, and did not require the death of Christ."

Dr. Beman says, p. 65: "The law or justice, that is, distributive justice, as expressed in the law, has received no satisfaction at all. The whole legal system has been suspended, at least for the present, in order to make way for the operation of one of a different character. In introducing this system of mercy, which involves a suspension of the penal curse, God has required a satisfaction to the principles of general or public justice; a satisfaction which will effectually secure all the good to the universe, which is intended to be accomplished by the penalty of the law, when inflicted, and at the same time, prevent all that practical mischief which would result from arresting the hand of punitive justice, without the intervention of an atonement." pp. 63, 66. This general or public justice, he says, "has no direct reference to law, but embraces those principles of virtue or benevolence, by which we are bound to govern our conduct, and by which God himself governs the universe. This atonement was required, that God might be just or righteous, that is, that he might do the thing which was fit and proper, and best and most expedient to be done, and at the same time be at perfect liberty to justify him which believeth in Jesus." "The necessity of this atonement," he says, "will farther appear, if we contemplate the relations of this doctrine with the rational universe. We may naturally suppose it was the intention of God, in saving sinners, to make a grand impression on the universe." Observe in Dr. Beman's scheme, particularly, the following expressions: "the provisions of the law are entirely set aside in our world;" atonement "has no direct reference to law," and yet "involves a suspension of its legal curse; "the law has no concern with a substitute." In all that God has done, "it was his intention to make a grand impression upon the universe." . . . . The death of Christ was not a real, vicarious, atoning sacrifice, but a mere exhibition or display of what God might do for some high state purposes; a brilliant masquerade, to excite profound and universal gaze; an empty parade, a splendid sham, deeply to impress the universe, to satisfy public justice.

Old Divinity.

On Justification.

"Those whom God effectually calleth, he also freely justifieth; not by infusing righteousness into them, but by pardoning their sins, and by accounting and accepting their persons as righteous; not for any thing wrought in them, or done by them, but for Christ's sake alone; not by imputing faith itself, the act of believing, or any other evangelical obedience, to them, as their righteousness, but by imputing the obedience and satisfaction of Christ unto them, they receiving and resting on him and his righteousness, by faith, which faith they have not of themselves, it is the gift of God." Confession of Faith, chap. xi, sec. 1.

Section 2. "Faith, thus receiving and resting on Christ and his righteousness, is the alone instrument of justification," &c. Section 3. "Christ, by his obedience and death, did fully discharge the debt of all those that are thus justified, and did make a proper, real, and full satisfaction to his Father's justice, in their behalf; yet inas-

New School.

On Justification.

Mr. Finney says: "Gospel justification is not by the imputed righteousness of Christ. Under the gospel, sinners are not justified by having the obedience of Jesus Christ set down to their account, as if he had obeyed the law for them, or in their stead. It is not an uncommon mistake, to suppose that when sinners are justified under the gospel, they are accounted righteous in the eye of the law, by having the obedience or righteousness of Christ imputed to them. I can only say, that this idea is absurd and impossible, for the reason that Jesus Christ was bound to obey the law for himself, and could no more perform works of supererogation, or obey on our account, than any body else:" "this would have been true, if Christ had been a human, finite, and ordinary being, but being *divine* in his nature, as well as human, and infinite in perfection, the objection here made, and usually urged by Socinians, is of no force." "Abraham's faith was imputed to him for righteous-

much as he was given by the Father for them, and his obedience and satisfaction accepted in their stead, and both freely, not for anything in them, their justification is only of free grace; that both the exact justice and rich grace of God, might be glorified in the justification of sinners."

ness, and because it worked by love, and therefore produced holiness. Justifying faith is holiness, so far as it goes, and produces holiness of heart and life, and is imputed to the believer as holiness, not instead of holiness." Lectures, pp. 215, 216.

Mr. Barnes says, "the phrase righteousness of God, is equivalent to God's plan of justifying man." On this he observes: "It is not that his righteousness becomes ours; this is not true, and there is no intelligible sense in which that can be understood. But it is God's plan for pardoning sin, and for treating us as if we had not committed it." Notes on the Romans, pp. 28, 29. At p. 94: "Abraham believed God, and it was counted unto him for righteousness;" he observes: "the word 'it,' here, evidently refers to the act of believing. It does not refer to the righteousness of another, of God, or of the Messiah; but the discussion is solely of the strong act of Abraham's faith, which in some sense was counted to him for righteousness. In what sense this was, is explained directly after. All that is material to remark here, is, that the act of Abraham, the strong confidence of his mind in the promises of God, his unwavering assurance, that what God promised he would perform, was reckoned for righteousness. The same thing is more fully expressed, verses 18, 22. When, therefore, it is said that the righteousness of Christ is accounted or imputed to us; when it is said that his merits are transferred and reckoned as ours; whatever may be the truth of the doctrine, it cannot be defended by this passage of scripture; faith is always an act of the mind; God promises, the man believes, and this is the whole of it.' . . . . Thus Mr. Barnes teaches that the act of believing is imputed for righteousness; the Confession of Faith says, "not by imputing faith itself, the act of believing, or any other evangelic obedience to them, as their righteousness." The Confession of Faith adds, that we are justified on principles of law and justice, as well as of grace and mercy, all harmoniously meeting in the cross of Christ. Mr. Barnes says, "It does not (Romans, i. 17) touch the question, whether it is by imputed righteousness or not; it does not say that it is on legal principles." p. 28.

We might easily, did our limits permit and the case require it extend this exhibition of false theology or mutilated Scripture, indefinitely, as New School publications are replete with repeated and multiplied statements of this erroneous and enormous character. If what is presented, is not sufficient to establish the charge of heresy against the New School, a larger amount of quotations from their printed works of a like nature, would also fail of this object.

CHAPTER XXV.

Remarks upon the eleventh chapter of Dr. Judd's Volume, p. 214, &c., headed, "Our position—Duty—Prospects"—Substantial renunciation of Presbyterianism.

The avowals and disclosures contained in this chapter, will satisfy any intelligent and candid reader, of two facts:

First, that the reasons alleged by the Old School for the Abrogation, were real and honest in themselves, and sufficient to justify that act.

Second, that the same reasons now exist, in such form and force, as to warrant the permanence of that separation or exclusion.

I. To justify the Abrogation: They say, p. 215, "Our position, in respect to doctrine, is between latitudinarianism and uniformity." They consider themselves, then, half-way men between truth and error, not strictly bound to either. Now, our preceding illustrations show, that there never was a place for such men, in the Presbyterian Church. They go on to say: "We maintain, the Confession of Faith and catechisms, framed and adopted by the Westminster Assembly, as containing the *system of doctrines* taught in the Holy Scriptures." This is, when properly viewed, a rejection of the very *Confession and catechism* which they are professing to receive. Did the Assembly of divines at Westminster, who framed and adopted this Confession and Catechism, perform that act with reserves and modifications? did they adopt and publish it as containing the undefined *system of doctrines* taught in the Holy Scriptures? The term "system," is a latitudinarian, deceptive term, selected and employed as an inlet to error. In this application, it is intended to admit the idea of amplification or restriction, of engrafture or change, of invention or perversion, of multiplication or deduction of items. No such modification, not the slightest shade of such a thought or imagination, was conceived of, by the framers of these standards of truth. And they who do not receive and adopt these documents, these specific, sound words, just as they were written and uttered at first, do not receive them at all. They "maintain" something else, entirely different; some vague and indefinite phase of thought or fancy, which they secretly intend to originate and mature into a shape, more or less, at pleasure, conformed to the *Confession and catechism*, and then call it a system of doctrines taught by the Westminster Assembly, and founded on the Holy Scriptures. But who can tell what that system of doctrines now is, or may become? Here is profound ambiguity and uncertainty. This is no adoption at all. It is impossible to tell what such pretended adopters intended. There is no distinct and positive obligation arising out of it. Such adopters cannot be held to any construction, which is not defined and understood. Hence, Dr. Judd, speaking for the New School mass, proceeds to say: "We believe that perfect uniformity, in reference to a system so comprehensive, is not to be expected, and ought not to be required. It must be so, or there will be almost endless strife and divisions." This is enough to show that these men ought never to have been connected with us.

On the subject of church order and discipline, to strengthen this conviction, we single out but one point, and that in the following terms, p. 217: "As regards the most eligible organizations for evangelizing our nation and the world, our *preferences* are generally in favour of that type of evangelism, which seeks the attainment of its object by *voluntary societies*, composed of members of various denominations." This is clear and candid, but conclusive against themselves; for nothing can be conceived of, more preposterous than such a declaration coming from a sworn Presbyterian minister. "Voluntary societies, composed of members of various denominations!" This is voluntary and perfect confusion. As an exemplification of it, we may state, that in the greatest agitation that almost ever occurred in the Presbyterian Church, and as the chief procuring cause of it, Dr. Judd states this very predilection for voluntary societies. In reference to the memorable Pittsburgh struggle of 1836, p. 101, he says: "The advocates for conducting all the benevolent operations of the church, by *boards* under *ecclesiastical supervision*, increased in number, and their policy became more and more *exclusive* and *intolerant.* Hence those who were, from *principle*, in favour of *voluntary societies*, were laid under the necessity of either abandoning their *conscientious preferences*, or of defending them. A sense of duty constrained them to adopt the latter course." Here they assert that they were conscientious in endeavouring to revolutionize the church.

The reflecting reader will observe, that the term *voluntary*, repudiates all ecclesiastical supervision or control; denies and rejects all responsibility to the church, is a complete substitution for it. A society of this class is a mere secular or political engine, self-constituted and self-governed.

On the contrary, the whole organization of the Presbyterian Church is republican, and in its action, conducted upon representative principles. She has an admirable order of church judicatories, rising gradually in power and importance, from the Church Session to the General Assembly, embracing the intermediate

Presbytery and Synod. All these, are so connected and combined, that under the direction of the Assembly, their united influence and zeal in any work of benevolence, in raising funds or in distributing them, can be drawn to a point or diversified at pleasure, by competent authority.

Here is perfect unity, harmony, concentration of strength and unity of action in the whole church, in the prosecution of any object of benevolence, church extension, diffusion of knowledge, or of missions. And to accomplish these and other great ends, the Presbyterian body have been laboriously engaged for more than fifty years, in organizing and maturing into full vigor, an admirable company of ecclesiastical boards, to act as her organs and instruments in the accomplishment of her great and momentous duties.

Here is then presented a striking and decisive antagonism in church form and church action; voluntaryism against Presbyterial organization; the one a political or secular compact, without any ecclesiastical feature, amenability or appeal; the latter, the creature of the churches, established by them, controlled by them, supplied with the means of operation by them, accountable to them for every measure they adopt, instructed in regard to the objects they are to pursue, furnished by the voice of the people, or their representatives in the Assembly, with boards of missions, of education, of publication, of church extension, as appropriate and consecrated organs, to be employed in building up the church and securing the great object of the Gospel.

Now, we appeal to the world and honestly ask, with what propriety or color of excuse, these New School men could come into our church, assume our common vows, without intending to regard them, and insidiously and pertinaciously attempt to supplant and demolish the whole organic structure of Presbyterianism, by forcing upon us the *voluntary principle* or *system*, and mode of action, diametrically opposed to that already existing there, and then complain of us for maintaining our venerable church inviolate, as arbitrary, ultra, bigoted, intolerant? Their system can no more amalgamate with ours, than oil with water. The abrogation was, therefore, as Dr. Alexander says, absolutely indispensable to the peace and life of the church. And the true Presbyterian orthodox body have reason to thank the committee of the New School Synod, for declaring through their agent, Dr. Judd, that their mind is still the same as before the exscision; "that they are in favor of *voluntary societies!*" We have no doubt of the fact as stated. They are not, therefore, Presbyterians at all; they never had an honest and just standing in the Presbyterian Church, on account of this as well as other reasons; and with their principles unchanged, they never can have it, never ought to. Hence, our second observation is, that since the same obstacles to union exist now as before the abrogation, and will probably continue to operate for ages to come, there is no prospect of a harmonious and happy reunion of these parties. The New School now publish to the world, most positively, their determination to persist in their former corrupt theology, decisive and distracting policy. Barnes and others, are still publishing their "false views, in every variety of form." Our principles, say they, p. 221, "lay us under obligations to do all in our power to give increased efficiency to *voluntary societies*, for the spread of the gospel and the conversion of the world." After all this, they proceed to say: "We had no desire to interfere with their preferences." But, was their opposition to the Assembly's plan, of transferring the Western Foreign Missionary Society, no interference with their preferences? How could they establish, as they laboured for many years with their utmost power to do, their *voluntary* plan of action in our church, without interfering with our ecclesiastical boards? "Especially," they say, on the same page, "should we hold fast and defend that feature of the *voluntary* principle, which unites the labours of Christians, of all denominations." After this, it is amusing to hear Dr. J., pp. 218, 19, speaking of the "brethren of the New Basis, the measures of the New Basis Assembly," &c.

Surely, the New School are well identified by their name, the novelty of their opinions, the youthfulness of their *voluntary* creations. The orthodox, Old School church, which has existed here, just as they are now, in principle and form, about one hundred years, have now become *New Basis men, a New Basis Assembly!*

Can any thing be imagined, more repulsive, than compromise or re-union with the New School body, while they make no renunciation of their false doctrines, and declaring their fixed purpose "to do all in their power to give increased efficiency to *voluntary societies?*" Such a re-union would secure to the Presbyterian Church perpetual, internal strife, and speedily, either violent separation or complete extinction.

Dr. Judd desires to prove that the exscision, as he calls it, was produced by the operation or influence of these voluntary societies. Extending the idea of these societies a little, so as to comprehend the fact, that they were the principal organs or channels through which their corrupt theology was propagated, and their church-distracting operations carried on, and it is true. The orthodox have avowed, hundreds of times, that the Presbyterian Church could not exist, maintain its integrity, and attain the end of its being, if these societies were permitted to continue and operate within our bounds. The reason is perfectly obvious. The voluntary societies act capriciously, without church connexion or authority; are composed of heterogeneous materials, thrown promiscuously together, without regard to any standard or model, qualification or rule. The Presbyterian Church observes a perfectly defined and ascertained law; is founded upon and sustained by the sovereign authority and will of the people. They framed the system in all its detail and symmetry; they speak and act through it by a well digested *pro rata* representation in every measure; they must be appealed to and consulted for their approval and ratification, when any thing new is attempted, or old found defective. Unity, in organization and action, was the cardinal principle or feature, aimed at in the Presbyterian Church; she laboured to get clear and keep clear, of all heterogeneous mixtures; to maintain their own organic system unimpaired, by the intestine or aggressive influence of strangers, who know us not, and whose hearts were far away, set upon systems and objects diametrically opposed to ours.

Why, then, need Dr. Judd, or any body else, say, "hostility to voluntary societies, and a desire to rule the church, were the chief causes of the" abrogating or exscinding acts? If the orthodox were honest and sincere, how could it be otherwise? There was, in reality, previously no union; neither could there be, among elements so discordant. They were, while nominally connected, truly separated. At every public meeting, especially of the Assembly, the line of demarcation was distinctly drawn, as between conflicting armies. These exhibitions had become the scorn and derision of the world. Nothing was needed to break the rope of sand which attached these parties together, but a mere declaration. That declaration was uttered by the Assembly of 1837. It is called by many hard names; but it was a peace measure, intended to terminate strife. The New School had been separating themselves more and more, for many years, from the true church. The Presbyterian body, after waiting, suffering, entreating, all ineffectually, at last resolved to let the New School go, to take a position where they had long been expected to place themselves, aside from the Presbyterian body, with which they possessed no real sympathy, or desire to be amalgamated.

CHAPTER XXVI.

Brief Summary—Conclusion.

The measures adopted by the General Assembly for the purification and safety of the church, were not presented at all as punitive or disciplinary. This will appear from the fact that no charge was tabled, and all thought of criminal process, or citation to answer, was formally abandoned, as the minutes of the Assembly prove. Even Mr. Barnes himself attests, that "not one of their number was accused or tried.* Sermon.

The following questions are proposed and affirmatively answered, especially at the ordination of gospel ministers, viz:

I. "Do you sincerely *receive and adopt the Confession of Faith of this Church*, as containing the system of doctrines taught in the Holy Scriptures?"

II. "Do you approve of the government and discipline of the Presbyterian Church in these United States?"

III. "Do you promise subjection to your brethren in the Lord?"

IV. "Do you promise to be zealous and faithful in maintaining the truths of the gospel, and the purity and peace of the church, whatever persecution or opposition may arise unto you, on that account?"

This solemn contract with, and pledge to, the church, in heaven and upon earth, is publicly made before many witnesses—to receive and adopt the Confession of Faith as it stands, to support the government of the Presbyterian Church as it is, to be *zealous* and *faithful* in maintaining the *truths of the gospel*, the *purity* and *peace* of the church, whatever may oppose, and that under the guidance of the assumed standards and control of the brethren. Now, the simple inquiry is, have the New School men been true and faithful to their promises? On the contrary, have they not habitually warred against every *interest* they covenanted to support? Remonstrances and entreaties, multiplied upon them, to check their violence, have only increased it. The church had a right to expect in them friends and auxiliaries, but she has found them to be inveterate and implacable opposers. All the talents and industry, and art and power, at their disposal, have been employed against her. They bound themselves to maintain the purity and peace of the church, but, through all her bounds, they have created a disgusting scene of strife and confusion. Combinations and conspiracies against our church, schemes of change and subversion, exhibitions of disaffection and hostility to our standards and ecclesiastical order, have been for many years a constant and affecting spectacle throughout the land, causing the ways of Zion to mourn, and her friends to wear sackcloth and weep. While we mourn over all the injuries inflicted upon the church, and feel that we may justly exclaim, in reference to most of the prime truths of the gospel, with Mary Magdalene, to

* Strictly speaking, there had been a few attempts to try unsound ministers, but the state of the church prevented their conviction. Barnes, Duffield, and Beecher, are the men here referred to.

Peter and the other disciple in relation to the body of Jesus, "They have taken away the Lord out of the sepulchre, and we know not where they have laid him," we offer neither crimination nor revenge, but refer them, for the settlement of their accounts, to the just decisions of an indignant world and offended God.

Now, if any man asks the members of the orthodox body, why they declared the four Synods no longer belonging to the Presbyterian Church, and virtually excluded them from our communion, we answer, in a brief recapitulation:

I. Because, as has been proved in the preceding sheets, they came into our body on the Plan of Union of 1801, and so stood upon a foundation which was unconstitutional in its nature, inconsistent and irreconcilable with the elementary principles, real spirit, and true letter of our plan of ecclesiastical organization and government. The Assembly of 1837, did, therefore, after long and solemn consideration, abrogate and expunge that unconstitutional *Plan of Union*, on which these Synods were standing, and, of course, their connexion with the orthodox body ceased.

II. The Assembly of 1837 were induced to pass this act of abrogation, by the fact, which we have most abundantly shown in the preceding pages, that from the *Plan of Union*, multitudes of derangements and confusions, injurious to the peace and prosperity of the church, inundated the new settlements, and gradually spread over the whole land, introducing disorder, and threatening entire dissolution to the church, under circumstances too flagrant to be any longer tolerated. The alternative was then strongly presented, either to abandon the church to her foes, which was seriously contemplated by some of her best members, or to deliver her from her sufferings and apprehensions, by cutting off her intestine destroyers. The most lawful and constitutional, most harmonious and feasible process for accomplishing this object, was reluctantly embraced, as a last resort, to redeem the church, by the discharge of a high and solemn duty to God, to his people and their posterity, in exscinding the offending members.

III. The third great cause of this decision, and ground of its vindication, was the fact, that the New School having formed a plan to revolutionize the church, had passed such acts, formed such combinations, pursued such a system of action, had so far multiplied their numbers and means, had so greatly augmented, ramified, and strengthened their corrupting influences, by virtue of their overgrown and dangerous power, that the friends of Zion clearly saw her imminent peril, and the abrogation as her only remedy. From overt acts committed in her public assemblies, and numerous developments constructive and confirmatory accompanying, it became evident that her members, her resources, her boards, her judicatories, her formularies, her whole character, substance, policy, and destiny, were marked out by the invading foe as objects of their arbitrary control or sweeping rapacity. In such circumstances, presented in full detail, with appropriate evidence, in what precedes, their course of action was distinctly drawn, and a voice from heaven seemed to say to the uncontaminated, though oppressed church of Jesus, "this is the way—walk ye in it!"

IV. The *fourth* and principal ground upon which we vindicate the great *relief measure* of 1837, is the introduction, by the New School, of false doctrines upon almost every cardinal point of Christianity.

For the evidence of this statement, we refer the inquirer to the *contrast* in the pages preceding. The statement is brief, and from it there is no appeal. The adversaries of our church and of God's truth, have unblushingly published their obliquity and their shame, to the whole world. We take their own record, and place it in *contrast* with our Confession of Faith. It there stands, as a perpetual monument of their unsoundness in the faith. This is enough!

It could not rationally be expected, that such a company of men as compose the orthodox body in the Presbyterian Church, realizing their sacred obligations and responsibility, with adequate power in their hands, should or would stand idly by and see the enemy sowing tares, broadcast, in every field, without an effort to expel them, and preserve the soil pure; to receive from their own hands, or those of their successors, the uncorrupted seed of God's word.

The decisive *relief measure*, of the General Assembly of 1837, is written in prominent and inerascable letters, and commences a new era in the history of the Presbyterian Church, in these United States. The substance of this record will be recited by children and youth of coming generations; saints of both sexes and of all ages, will celebrate that act with triumph, as an escape for the church from bondage and oppression, worse than Egyptain; it will be "said and sung" by sacred bards, rehearsed by poets and orators, in strains more thrilling than those which celebrate the emancipation of the mother church in Scotland, and published by history and by fame to an admiring world, till the end of time.

CHAPTER XXVII.

Chief Justice Gibson delivered the following opinion of the court:

To extricate the question from the multifarious mass of irrelevant matter in which it is enclosed, we must, in the first place, ascertain the specific character of the General Assembly, and the relation it bears to the corporation, which is the immediate subject of our cognizance. This Assembly has been called a *quasi* corporation, of which it has not a feature. A quasi corporation has capacity to sue and be sued, as an artificial person, which the Assembly has not. It is also established by law, which the Assembly is not. Neither is the Assembly a particular order, or rank, in the corporation, though the latter was created for its convenience; such, for instance, as the shareholders of a bank, or joint stock company, who are an integrant part of the body. It is a segregated association, which, though it is the reproductive organ of corporate succession, is not itself a member of the body, and in that respect, it is anomalous. Having no corporate quality in itself, it is not a subject of our corrective jurisdiction, or of our scrutiny, farther than to ascertain its organic structure, may bear on the question of its personal identity or individuality. By the charter of the corporation, of which it is the handmaid and nurse, it has a limited capacity to create vacancies in it, and an unlimited power over the power and manner of choice in filling them. It would be sufficient for the civil tribunals, therefore, that the assembled commissioners had constituted an actual body, and that it had made its appointment in its own way, without regard to its fairness, in respect to its members; with this limitation, however, that it had the assent of the constitutional majority, of which the official act of authentication would be, at least, *prima facie* evidence. It would be to the legality of the choice, that the majority had expelled the minority, provided a majority of the whole body concurred in the choice. This may be safely predicated of an undivided Assembly, and it would be an unerring test in the case of a division, could a quorum not be constituted of less than such a majority; but unfortunately, a quorum of the General Assembly may be constituted of a very small minority, so that two, or even more distinct parts, may have all the external organs of legitimate existence. Hence, where, as in this instance, the members have formed themselves into separate bodies, numerically sufficient for corporate capacity and organic action, it becomes necessary to ascertain how far either of them was formed, in obedience to the conventional law of the association, which for that purpose only, is to be treated as a rule of civil obligation. The division which for purposes of designation, it is convenient to call the Old School party, was certainly organized in obedience to the established order; and, to legitimate the separate organization of its rival in contravention, as it certainly was, of every thing like precedent, would require the presentation of a very urgent emergency. At the stated time and place for the opening of the session, the parties assembled without any ostensible division; and when the organization of the whole had proceeded to a certain point, by the instrumentality of the moderator of the preceding session, who, for that purpose, was the constitutional organ, a provisional moderator was suddenly chosen, by a minority of those who could be entitled to vote, including the exscinded commissioners. The question on the motion to elect was put, not by the chair, but by the mover himself; after which the seceding party elected a permanent moderator and immediately withdrew, leaving the other party to finish its process of organization, by the choice of its moderator for the session.

In justification of this apparent irregularity, it is urged that the constitutional moderator had refused an appeal to the commissioners in attendance, from his decision, which had excluded from the roll the names of certain commissioners, who had been unconstitutionally severed, as it is alleged, from the Presbyterian connexion, by a vote of the preceding session. It is conceded by the argument, that if the Synods, with the dependent Presbyteries by which those commissioners were sent, had been constitutionally dissolved, the motion was one which the moderator was not bound to put, or the commissioners to notice; and that whatever implication of assent to the decision which ensued, might otherwise be deduced from the silence of those who refused to speak out, about which, it will be necessary to say something in the sequel, there was no room for any such implication in the particular instance. It would follow also, that there was no pretence for the deposal of the moderator, if indeed such a thing could be legitimated by any circumstances, for refusing an appeal from his exclusion of those who had not color of title, and consequently, that what else might be reform, would be revolution. And this leads to an inquiry into the constitutionality of the act of exscision.

The sentence of exscision, as it has been called, was nothing else than an ordinance of dissolution. It bore, that the Synods in question, having been formed and attached to the body of the Presbyterian Church, under and in execution of the *Plan of Union*, be, and are hereby declared to be, out of the connexion of the Presbyterian Church in the United States of America; and that they are not, in form or in fact, an integral portion of said church. Now, it will not be said, that if the dissolved Synods had no other basis than the Plan of Union, they did not necessarily fall along with it, and it is not pretended that the Assembly was incompetent to repeal the union prospectively, but it is contended that the repeal could not impair rights of membership which had grown up under it. On the other hand, it is contended, that the *Plan of Union* was unconstitutional and void from the beginning, because it was not submitted to the Presbyteries for their sanction; and that no right of membership could spring from it. But, viewed not as a constitutional regulation, which implies permanency of duration, but as a temporary expedient, it acquired the force of a law without the ratification of those bodies. It was evidently not intended to be permanent, and it, consequently, was constitutionally enacted and constitutionally repealed by an ordinary act of legislation; and those Synods which had their root in it, could not be expected to survive it. There never was a design to attempt an amalgamation of ecclesiastical principles, which are as immiscible as water and oil; much less to effect a commixture of them, only at particular geographical points. Such an attempt would have compromised a principle at the very root of Presbyterial government, which requires that the officers of the church be set apart by special ordination for the work. Now, the character of the Plan is palpable, not only in its title and provisions, but in the minute of its introduction into the Assembly. We find in the proceedings of 1801, p. 256, that a committee was raised to "consider and digest a plan of government for the churches in the New Settlements, agreeably to the proposal of the General Association of Connecticut," and that the plan adopted in conformity to its report, is called "A Plan of Union for the New Settlements." The avowed object of it was to prevent alienation, in other words, the affiliation of Presbyterians in other churches, by suffering those who were yet too few and too poor for the maintenance of a minister, temporarily to call to their assistance, the members of a sect who differed from them, in principles, not of faith, but of ecclesiastical government. To that end, Presbyterians were suffered to preach to Congregational Churches, while Presbyterian Churches were suffered to settle Congregational ministers; and mixed congregations were allowed to settle a Presbyterian or Congregational minister, at their election, but under a plan of government and discipline adapted to the circumstances. Surely this was not intended to outlast the inability of the respective sects to provide separately for themselves, or to perpetuate the innovations on Presbyterial government, which it was calculated to produce. It was obviously a missionary arrangement from the first; and those who built up Presbyteries and Synods on the basis of it, had no reason to expect that their structure would survive it, or that Congregationalists might, by force of it, gain a foothold in the Presbyterian

Church, despite of Presbyterial discipline. They embraced it with all its defeasable properties plainly put before them, and the power which constituted it, might fairly repeal it, and dissolve the bodies that had grown out of it, whenever the good of the church should seem to require it.

Could the Synods, however, be dissolved by a legislative act? I know not how they could have been legitimately dissolved by any other. The Assembly is a homogeneous body, uniting in itself, without separation of parts, the legislative, executive, and judicial functions of the government; and its acts are referable to the one or the other of them, according to the capacity in which it sat when they were performed. Now, had the exscinded Synods been cut off by a judicial sentence without hearing or notice, the act would have been contrary to the cardinal principles of natural justice, and consequently void. But though it was at first resolved to proceed judicially, the measure was abandoned, probably because it came to be perceived that the Synods had committed no offence.

A glance at the Plan of Union is enough to convince us that the disorder had come in with the sanction of the Assembly itself. The first article directed *missionaries*, (the word is significant) to the New Settlements, to promote a good understanding betwixt the kindred sects. The second and third permitted a Presbyterian congregation to settle a Congregational minister, or a Presbyterian minister to be settled by a Congregational Church; but these provided for no recognition of the people in charge as a part of the Presbyterian body—at least they gave them no representation in its government. But the fourth allowed a mixed congregation to settle a minister of either denomination, and committed the government of it to a standing committee, but with a right to appeal to the body of male communicants, if the appellant were a Congregationalist, or to the Presbytery, if he were a Presbyterian. Now, it is evident, that the Assembly designed that every such congregation should belong to a Presbytery, as an integrant part of it, for if its minister were a Congregationalist, in no way connected with the Presbyterian Church, it would be impossible to refer the appellate jurisdiction to any Presbytery in particular. This alone would show, that it was designed to place such a congregation in ecclesiastical connexion with the Presbytery of the district; but this is not all. It was expressly provided, in conclusion, that if the said standing committee of any church shall depute one of themselves to attend the Presbytery, he may have the same right "to sit and act in the Presbytery, as a ruling elder in the Presbyterian Church." For what purpose, if the congregation were not in Presbyterial fellowship?

It is said, that this *jus representationis* was predicated of the appeal, precedently mentioned, and that the exercise of it was to be restrained to the trial of it. The words; however, were predicated without restriction, and an implied limitation of their meaning would impute to the Assembly the injustice of allowing a party to sit in his own cause, by introducing into the composition of the appellate court, a part of the subordinate one. That such an implication would be inconsistent with the temper displayed by the Assembly, on other occasions, is proved by the order which it took as early as 1791, in the case of an appeal from the sentence of the Synod of Philadelphia, whose members it prevented from voting on the question, (Assembly Digest, p. 332) as well as by its general provision, "that members of a judicatory may not vote in a superior judicatory, on a question of approving or disapproving their records." Judd, p. 333.

The principle has since become a rule of the constitution, as appears by the book of discipline, chapter vii., sec. 3, paragraph 12. As the representations of those anomalous congregations could not, therefore, sit in judgment on their own controversies, it is pretty clear that it was intended they should be represented generally, else they could not be represented at all in the councils of the church, by those who might be Presbyterians; and that to effect it, the principles of Presbyterial ordination was to be relaxed, as regards both the ministry and eldership; and it is equally clear, that had the Synods been cited to answer for the consequent relaxation, as an offence, they might have triumphantly appeared at the bar of the Assembly, with the *Plan of Union* in their hand. That body, however, resorted to the only constitutional remedy in its power; it fell back, so to speak on its legislative jurisdiction, in the exercise of which the Synods were competently represented and heard by their commissioners.

Now, the apparent injustice of the measure arises from the contemplation of it as a judicial sentence, pronounced against persons who were neither cited nor heard, which it evidently was not. Even as a legislative act, it may have been a hard one, though certainly constitutional and strictly just. It was impossible to eradicate the disorder by any thing less than a dissolution of those bodies, with whose existence its roots were so entwined as to be inseparable from it, leaving their elements to form new and less heterogeneous combinations. Though deprived of Presbyterial organization, the Presbyterial parts were not excluded from the church, provision being made for them, by allowing them to attach themselves to the nearest Presbytery.

It is said, there is not sufficient evidence to establish the fact,

V

that the exscinded Synods had been actually constituted on the *Plan of Union,* in order to have given the Assembly, even legislative jurisdiction. The testimony, however, of the Rev. Mr. Squier shows, that in some of the three which were within the state of New York, congregations were sometimes constituted without elders; and the Synod of the Western Reserve, when charged with delinquency on that head, instead of denying the fact, promptly pointed to the *Plan of Union* for its justification. But what matters it, whether the fact were actually what the Assembly supposed it to be? If that body proceeded in good faith, the validity of its enactment cannot depend on the justness of its conclusion. We have, as already remarked, no authority to rejudge its judgments, on their merits; and this principle was asserted with conclusive force by the presiding judge, who tried the cause. Upon an objection, made to an inquiry into the composition of the Presbytery of Medina, it was ruled that, "with the proceedings of 1837, (the act of exscision) we have nothing to do. We are to determine only what was done, the reasons of those who did it are immaterial. If the acts complained of were within the jurisdiction of the Assembly, their decision must be final, though they decided wrong." This was predicted of judicial jurisdiction. But the principle is necessarily as applicable to jurisdiction for purposes of legislation. I cite the passage, however, to show that after a successful resistance to the introduction of evidence of the fact, it lies not with the relators to allege the want of it. If then, the Synods in question were constitutionally dissolved, the Presbyteries of which they had been composed were at least, for purposes of representation, dissolved along with them, for no Presbytery can be in connexion with the General Assembly, unless it be at the same time subordinate to a Synod, also in connexion with it, because an appeal from its judgment can reach the tribunal of the last resort, only through that channel. It is immaterial that the Presbyteries are the electors; a Synod is a part of the machinery which is essential to the existence of every branch of the church. It appears, therefore, that the commissioners from the exscinded Synods were not entitled to seats in the Assembly, and that their names were properly excluded from the roll.

The inquiry might be rested here, for if there were no color of right in them, there was no color of right in the adversary proceedings, which were founded on their exclusion. But even if their title were clear, the refusal of an appeal from the decision of the moderator, would be no just ground for the degradation of the officer, at the call of a minority, nor could it impose upon the majority an obligation to vote on a question, put unofficially and out of the usual course. To all questions put by the established organ, it is the duty of every member to respond, or be counted with the greater number, because he is supposed to have assented beforehand to the result of the process, pre-established to ascertain the general will; but the rule of implied assent is certainly inapplicable, to a measure which, when justifiable even by extreme necessity, is essentially revolutionary, and based on no pre-established process of ascertaining, whatever.

To apply it to an extreme case of inorganic action, as was done here, might work the degradation of any presiding officer in our legislative halls, by the motion and actual vote of a single member, sustained by the constructive votes of all the rest; and though such an enterprise may never be attempted, it shows the danger of resorting to a conventional rule, when the body is to be resolved into its original elements, and its rules and conventions to be superseded by the very motion. For this reason, the choice of a moderator to supplant the officer in the chair, even if he were removable at the pleasure of the commissioners, would seem to have been unconstitutional.

But he was not removable by them, because he had not derived his office from them; nor was he answerable to them for the use of the power. He was not *their* moderator; he was the mechanical instrument of their organization; and till that was accomplished, they were subject to his rule, not he to theirs. They were chosen by the authority of his mandate, and with the power of self-organization only in the event of his absence, at the opening of the session. Corporally present, but refusing to perform his function, he might be deemed constructively absent, for constitutional purposes, insomuch that the commissioners might proceed to the choice of a substitute without him; but not if he had entered on the performance of that task; and the reason is, that the decision of such questions as were prematurely pressed here, is proper for the decision of the body, when prepared for organization, which it cannot be before it is fully constituted and under the presidency of its own moderator; the moderator of the preceding session being *functus officiis*. There can be no occasion for its action sooner, for though the commissioners are necessarily called upon to vote for their moderator, their action is not organic, but individual. Dr. Mason's motion and appeal, though the clerk had reported the roll, were premature; for though it is declared in the twelfth chapter of the Form of Government, that no commissioner shall deliberate or vote, before his name shall have been enrolled, it follows not that the capacity consummated by enrollment was expected to be exercised during any part of the process of organization, but the choice of a moderator; and moreover, the provision may have been intended for the case of a commissioner appearing for the first time, when the house was constituted.

Many instances may doubtless be found among the minutes, of motions entertained previously; for our public bodies, whether legislative or judicial, secular or ecclesiastical, are too prone to forget the golden precept, "Let all things be done decently and in order." But these are merely instances of irregularity, which have passed *sub selentio*, and which cannot change a rule of positive enactment. It seems, then, that an appeal from the decision of the moderator did not lie, and that he incurred no penalty by the disallowance of it. The title of the exscinded commissioners, could be determined only by the action of the house, which could not be had before its organization were complete; and, in the mean time, he was bound, as the executive instrument of the preceding Assembly, to put its ordinance into execution; for to the actual Assembly, and not to the moderator of the preceding one, it belonged to repeal it.

It would be decisive, that the motion, as it was proposed, purported not to be, in fact, a question of degradation for the disallowance of an appeal, but one of new and independent organization. It was ostensibly, as well as actually, a measure of transcendental power, whose purpose was, to treat the ordinance of the preceding Assembly as a nullity, and its moderator as a nonentity. It had been prepared for the event, avowedly before the meeting. The witnesses concur, that it was propounded as a measure of original organization, transcending the customary order; and not as a recourse to the *ultima ratio*, for a specific violation of it. The ground of the motion, as it was opened by the mover, was not the disallowance of an appeal, which alone could afford a pretext of forfeiture, but the fact of exclusion. To affect silent members with an implication of assent, however, the ground of the motion and the nature of the question must be so explicitly put before them, as to prevent misconception or mistake; and the remarks that heralded the question, in this instance, pointed at, not a removal of the presiding incumbent, but a separate organization, to be accomplished, with the least practicable interruption of the business in hand; and if they indicated any thing else, they were deceptive. The measure was proposed, not as that of the body, but as the measure of a party; and the cause assigned for not having proposed it elsewhere, was, that individuals of the party had been instructed by counsel, that the purpose of it could not be legally accomplished in any other place. No witness speaks of a motion to degrade, and the rapidity of the process by which the choice of a substitute, not a successor, was effected, left no space for reflection or debate. Now, before the passive commissioners could be affected by acquiescence, implied from their silence, it ought to have appeared, that they were apprised of what was going on; but it appears that even an attentive ear-witness was unable to understand what was done. The whole scene was one of unprecedented haste, insomuch that it is still matter of doubt, how the questions were put. Now, though these facts were fairly put to the jury, it is impossible not to see, that the verdict is, in this respect, manifestly against the current of the evidence.

Other corroborative views have been suggested, but it is difficult to compress a division of the leading points in this case, into the old fashioned limits of a judicial opinion. The preceding observations, however, are deemed enough to show the grounds on which we hold, that the Assembly which met in the First Presbyterian Church, was not the legitimate successor of the Assembly of 1837, and that the defendants are not guilty of the usurpation with which they are charged.

Rule for a new trial made absolute.

Judge Rogers: I have nothing at this time to add, except that my opinion remains unchanged, on all the points ruled at the trial.

In all their schemes and movements, harmony, union, amalgamation, carrying out to perfection the great system of Presbyterianism, formed no part of their object; but change in every cardinal feature, perversion, engrafture, substitution, revolution, was visible triumphantly in their earliest plans and efforts, till at last, emboldened by increase of numbers and devices of measures, they here proclaim their devotion to voluntary societies, which is but another avowal of their inveterate hostility to Presbyterianism, in all the glory of her system, her boards, and radical features. As to their wide and deadly apostacy from the standards of the church, and fundamental principles of the gospel, let him that doubts read the contrast.

www.ingramcontent.com/pod-product-compliance
Lightning Source LLC
LaVergne TN
LVHW020217110826
845151LV00003B/743

* 9 7 8 1 4 2 5 5 3 3 3 1 1 *